AN OUTDOOR LIFE BOOK

Complete Guide to GAME ANIMALS

A Field Book of North American Species

---

by Leonard Lee Rue III

**Photographs by the author,
unless otherwise noted**

Introduction by Richard G. Van Gelder

*Curator of Mammals, Department of Mammalogy
American Museum of Natural History*

OUTDOOR LIFE BOOKS

VAN NOSTRAND REINHOLD COMPANY

New York   Cincinnati   Toronto
London   Melbourne

Library of Congress Catalog Card Number: 80-8779
ISBN: 0-442-27796-2

Manufactured in the United States of America

First edition, 1968, twelve printings
Second revised edition, 1981

Second Printing, 1981

Preface to the Second Edition

It was a delight to update and expand this book. The first edition sold over 370,000 copies and was a reliable reference.

Yet, over the years many changes have occurred. For example, there have been changes in animal ranges, populations, trophy records, and game laws. Biologists and ecologists have given us a more detailed body of knowledge on the various species. And I myself have traveled farther, observed more, and continued to devour the ever-increasing amounts of wildlife information. I have also taken literally hundreds of thousands more photos; many of the more telling and dramatic of those photos appear in this edition.

Although this book was originally aimed at sportsmen, its utility is not limited to hunters with guns. It is a solid source book for hunters of every type, including those armed only with camera, binoculars, naked eye, or an armchair with enough light for reading.

Whenever possible, I try to live with the animals I am studying. I want to know what they do at different times of the day, in different seasons, and to learn their reactions to different stimuli. I am eager to know everything about every species and its environment.

In this book, I share with you the knowledge that I have gained over the years. Add to it your own first-hand knowledge, and then test my observations against your own. If the book increases your enjoyment of your trips into the outdoors, I shall have succeeded in my mission.

Acknowledgments

Most of my close friends are also interested in the outdoors, and almost all of them have helped me in some way or another. A special word of thanks goes to Ivan Sanderson, who played a large part in the early planning of this book.

Thanks also to John Sill, editor-publisher of Times Mirror Books, for perseverence and patience while this was being written; to Henry Gross, who edited the first edition, and to Neil Soderstrom, who edited this second edition. Thanks, too, to my friend Dr. Richard Van Gelder of the American Museum of Natural History for reading over the manuscript, offering valuable suggestions, and writing the Introduction.

I am also grateful to William H. Nesbitt for assisting with the updating of the trophy records material and for arranging for permission to reprint the new Boone and Crockett Club scoring charts.

My deep thanks go to Elizabeth Rue, Evelyn Guthrie, Barbara Stoneback, and Carol Lippmann, who typed the manuscript. To my three sons—Len Rue Jr, Tim Lewis Rue, and James Keith Rue—who have worked in the field with me and contributed photos to this edition. And to a special woman, Irene Vandermolen, who shares my life and my love—and who is a fine wildlife photographer.

Leonard Lee Rue III
Blairstown, New Jersey

Contents

Pouched Mammals (*Order Marsupialia*)   **1**

  Opossum   5

Carnivores (*Order Carnivora*)   **17**

  Black Bear   21

  Alaskan Brown Bear   39

  Grizzly Bear   55

  Polar Bear   71

  Raccoon   82

  Gray and Red Wolves   101

  Gray Fox   113

  Red Fox   123

  Arctic Fox   137

  Coyote   151

  Jaguar   163

  Mountain Lion   172

  Lynx   188

  Bobcat   201

Seals and Walrus (*Order Pinnipedia*)   **213**

  Harbor Seal   217

  Walrus   225

Rodents (*Order Rodentia*)   **233**

  Woodchuck   237

  Yellow-Bellied Marmot   251

  Hoary Marmot   259

  Gray Squirrel   267

  Fox Squirrel   283

  Arctic Ground Squirrel   297

Prairie Dog   305

Porcupine   315

Brown Rat   329

Hares and Rabbits (*Order Lagomorpha*)   **337**

Cottontail Rabbit   341

Varying Hare   361

Arctic Hare   375

Jackrabbit   383

European Rabbit   394

Hoofed Mammals (*Order Artiodactyla*)   **401**

Collared Peccary   405

European Wild Hog   415

Elk   426

Whitetail Deer   444

Mule Deer   475

Moose   493

Caribou   509

Pronghorn   528

Bison   541

Bighorn Sheep   555

Dall's and Stone's Sheep   572

Mountain Goat   585

Musk-Ox   599

Selected Bibliography   **611**

Trophy Scoring Charts   **621**

Index   **633**

Introduction

In the world of living things, mammals are relatively few in number and kind. Compared with the millions of protozoans, worms, and insects that inhabit each square mile, the populations of mammals are small. Compared with nearly a million kinds of insects, tens of thousands of kinds of protozoans, more than 20,000 kinds of fishes, and some 8,500 species of birds, mammals are relatively few in kind. Nevertheless, the 4,000 species of mammals are, because of their size, their habits, and their distribution, important creatures in the overall biological picture of the earth.

In the scheme of classification, the mammals are a *class*, one of several such groups of vertebrates—the animals with backbones. The other classes of vertebrates, in addition to the mammals, are the birds, reptiles, amphibians, and several of fishes. All of these have in common a segmented backbone, the vertebral column.

Within the vertebrate group, the mammals are the only class in which the animals produce milk to suckle their young. Mammals are the only vertebrates that have hair as a body covering, and even some seemingly hairless mammals such as whales do have hair during their embryological development. In common with the birds, but unlike the other vertebrates, mammals are warm-blooded—they maintain a rather high, relatively constant body temperature. There are many other anatomical and physiological features that distinguish mammals to the specialist—a single lower jawbone on each side, three middle-ear bones, a muscular diaphragm dividing the chest and abdomen—but the combination of hair, warm-bloodedness, and milk production is sufficient.

The scientific names that appear in this book are part of the general arrangement of animal classification. The Class Mammalia is divided into *orders*, each of which contains animals that have certain characteristics in common. The orders are further divided into *families*. For example, with the Order Carnivora are the bears, the wild dogs, the raccoons, and the cats—each in its own family and all members of each family having more characters in common than they have with any other family. Families are composed of smaller groups called *genera* (the singular is *genus*). In the dog family, Canidae, are the genus *Canis* (with the red wolf, the gray wolf, and coyote), the genus *Urocyon* (the gray foxes), the genus *Vulpes* (the red fox), and the genus *Alopex* (the Arctic fox). A genus is composed of one or more *species* (the word is the same in both the singular and the plural). The scientific name of a species is made up of the generic name plus a species name, and is always written in italics. *Canis lupus* is the gray wolf, *Canis niger* is the red wolf, and *Canis latrans* is the coyote. Each is a member of the genus *Canis*, but a different species.

There are rules for forming these names, and an international commission of zoologists regulates nomenclature. The reason for using scientific names is evident to any traveler—the name is the same no matter which language you speak. A scientist from Afghanistan knows what animal *Felis concolor* is, even though he may not know that in English it may be called puma, cougar, mountain lion, panther, painted devil, or catamount.

Geographic races of mammals are often given a third scientific name, the subspecies name. These names are generally of interest only to the specialist, although a few subspecies are sufficiently distinct so that laymen distinguish them. The key deer, a diminutive whitetail, has the name *Odocoileus virginianus clavium*. The last name is the subspecific one.

The game species discussed in this book comprise about 10 percent of the species of North American mammals. They include South American immigrants (the opossum) and ones that originated in North America (pronghorn and raccoon). There are Eurasian immigrants (moose and bison), and introduced species (brown rats and wild boar).

The European colonists who came to North America were impressed with the abundance of game that was here. In Europe the common man held little land, and hunting was generally reserved for the landed gentry and royalty. Hunting became a way of life for the first colonists, and animals provided them with food and clothing, as well as furs for trade. Much of the early commerce was solely in the form of animal skins. The Americans quickly established the tradition that the animals were public property, that hunting was every man's right. They denied the concept of "royal game," and poaching, a widespread European vocation or avocation, is still an American rarity.

But if the American took a democratic attitude toward the wildlife, he denied the knowledge that was available in Europe. There was no profession of game-keeping, and no one could even conceive of the extermination of animals, so abundant they were. With the destruction of forests, the draining of swamps, heavy hunting, and a rapidly expanding population, the wildlife picture in North America changed drastically and quickly. By the beginning of the 20th century American wildlife was at its most critical stage. Bison had been reduced from an estimated 60 million to fewer than 1,000. The passenger pigeon and the Carolina parakeet were gone from the skies, and their last representatives were to die, in zoos, before 1915. Beaver were gone from most of the country, deer were extirpated in many places, elk were gone from the East, the grizzlies persisted only in mountain strongholds. Several kinds of whales were almost extinct, and the sea otter had only a few years remaining before it, too, was thought to be extinct. Were it not for the devoted efforts of a small group of naturalists at the close of the 19th century, much of the fauna we know today would be gone. Gradually species were protected, refuges established, and national parks passed through legislation. A profession of game management came into being, and scientific studies of wildlife were undertaken. The first half of the present century saw some notable changes in natural philosophy, and some dramatic results in the recovery of American wildlife.

Oddly, a half century of wildlife management still leaves us with critical problems. The sensible management of species has not been extended to all mammals, and while deer, moose, elk, antelope, and mountain sheep have been afforded protection through restricted hunting seasons and "buck only" laws, the predators have been reduced further in number both by hunting and control measures. Grizzlies, which once inhabited most of western North America are, for all practical purposes, gone from the United States and much diminished in Canada. The cougar and the timber wolf, both of which inhabited most of the continent originally, are gone from most of it. The red wolf teeters on the edge of extinction, being regarded as an endangered species and highly worthy of protection.

One of the results of this reduction of predators, and of some recovery of forests, is that other game species have become more abundant. Deer are probably more numerous now in the United States than before the arrival of Europeans. They are, in fact, too numerous, and each winter sees a weakening and dying off of some herds because there is insufficient food. From the biological point of view, man has substituted himself for the wolves and cougars that once kept the numbers of deer in check. But now, even the hunters cannot cope with the numbers of deer, and the emotional refusal to shoot does means that even hunting will not reduce the herds to more practical numbers. The predatory animals hunt for food, and they take does and bucks, adults and fawns alike. Those animals that, for whatever reason, are weaker, less alert, slower, or dumber, are quickly eliminated by a predator. The benefit is to the herd, for it means that those animals that are better adapted to escape their enemies survive, and if these attributes are hereditary, they are passed on to their offspring. But the hunting by man is not for food—each year sees fewer and fewer hunters going into the field for meat—and tradition and emotion, not logic, has it that it is unsporting to shoot females. Many states allow doe hunting, but others refuse to open a season on does in areas where the deer populations are excessive. If the herds are not reduced by hunting, a bad winter will do the job, but only after damage has been done to the herd as well as to the surrounding forest. Man has eliminated many of the natural predators of the larger hoofed animals, and he must substitute for them in his hunting, or, even better, let the predators come back.

Hunting is a huge industry in North America. It not only involves the direct expenditures by hunters on firearms and ammunition, but even greater sums for clothing, transportation, lodging, camping equipment, books, films and cameras, and food. From the economic point of view it would be undesirable to eliminate hunting, and from the biological view, as well, for many species, it would be equally disrupting should hunting be banned.

The professional game managers have been successful in giving hunters adequate material to hunt. The "game crop" philosophy had been workable during the middle 1900s, but I fear its heyday is over and a new philosophy is needed. With the great increase in human population in North America, the amount of land available for wildlife has decreased, and the environment has been generally disrupted. Simultaneously, the habitat available for animals is reduced and there are more people who want to hunt or see the animals. Even attempts to protect blocks of land are not successful. No sanctuary is sacred when it comes to the needs of man. Atom bombs are tested in wildlife refuges, power transmission lines are run across sanctuaries, and airstrips are proposed for wilderness areas. Hunters must take a broader view of the wildlife of the country and take an active part in the conservation movement, for by conserving the environment and by preserving wildlife in general, they will be insuring the future of an American heritage.

Richard G. Van Gelder
The American Museum of Natural History

To my kid brother,
Thomas Arthur Rue
and his family:
Judy, Tommy, and Amy

Complete
Guide to GAME
ANIMALS

POUCHED MAMMALS

Order Marsupialia

The members of this order are characterized by producing relatively underdeveloped young. The babies complete their development attached to the mother's nipples, which are in a pouch in many marsupials. Australia, New Guinea and South America are the main areas of the world where marsupials are found. The opossum is the only representative that occurs north of Mexico.

NEW WORLD OPOSSUMS

Family Didelphiidae

OPOSSUM

With its prehensile tail, the opossum can hang from a limb and carry leaves into its den.

OPOSSUM

Didelphis virginiana

The opossum is the only pouched animal in North America. Most of the marsupials are found in Australia. Though its tiny brain case indicates it is one of the stupidest animals alive, it has managed to survive since that time 70 million years ago when it kept company on this continent with the dinosaurs. Those huge beasts perished because they couldn't adapt to changing conditions, and other animals became specialized and slowly evolved into different forms, but the opossum waddled through the ages unchanged. In many wooded regions of the country, particularly in the South, it is one of our favorite small-game animals and is hunted almost as avidly as the raccoon.

Description: The opossum has a white face, pink nose, black eyes, and black ears that are often white-rimmed. Due to the silver tips on the guard hairs, its fur is a salt-and-pepper gray, but the underfur is a cottony white. The throat of the male is stained yellow-white from the secretion of a gland.

The tail is long, nearly hairless and white. Occasionally all black opossums are found and albinos are not rare. Some litters have both whitish and blackish babies. The opossum is the only mammal in North America that has a prehensile tail that can be used for grasping. The legs and feet are black and the toes are white. There are five toes on each foot. The toes on the forefeet fan out widely. The hind foot looks almost exactly like a human hand. All the toes except the thumb have nails.

The opossum may measure as much as 36 inches long

Handlike hind foot of the opossum has five toes, but only four have claws. The clawless big toe is an opposable thumb that moves at right angles to the others and aids in grasping. All the toes on the animal's forefoot have claws.

of which 12 to 14 inches is tail length. Weights average about 5 to 6 pounds, although the largest males exceed 10 pounds.

The opossum has more teeth than any of our other animals: 18 incisors, 4 canines, 12 premolars and 16 molars, for a total of 50, all of which it shows frequently in a wide grimace.

Distribution: Originally found in only our southern states, the opossum has been expanding its range

Distribution of the opossum.

steadily since the 1890s and has invaded Canada. It inhabits woods and agricultural lands from Ontario to Florida in the east, west as far as eastern Colorado, and it has been introduced on the Pacific Coast where it has spread from California to Canada.

Travel: Essentially a homebody, the opossum prefers to live on a range of about 15 to 40 acres. I have often tracked opossums in the snow and at no time did the tracks lead for a distance of more than two or three fields. Opossums invade new territory as their population increases, those on the edge of the range spilling over into the new region.

The opossum is not a hibernator, but its ears and tail have no protection against the cold. Yet, despite this, the opossum is steadily moving north. Around my home in New Jersey the opossums suffer from frostbite and lose pieces of their ears and tail. This leads to conjecture about the future. Will the opossum's range finally be restricted by the cold? Will it become a hibernator? Will its ears and tail become smaller, with less surface to be affected by the cold, or will they acquire a protective covering of fur?

Habits: The most widely known fact about the opossum is that it "plays 'possum." According to most people, it is supposed to collapse whenever it is attacked or frightened. Some opossums do this. When scared they fall on their sides, their mouths gape open, and they become completely limp. If picked up and shaken, they flap around like a rag doll. Yet of the thousands of opossums that I have encountered and personally handled, not more than fifty reacted in this manner. The majority of opossums dash for safety, dodging down a hole in the earth or scrambling up a nearby tree. Those that cannot escape turn to face their attacker with their large mouths open wide and emitting strings of saliva.

Is playing 'possum an act learned by the animal or is it an involuntary reaction? After considerable study, Dr. Carl Hartman, one of the great authorities on these animals, ventures that the reaction of the opossum is due to a chemical substance that affects the nerve centers of the brain, setting up a short circuit that causes a paralysis of the muscles. He likens it to adrenaline that is pumped into the human nervous system in time of stress. Whereas humans are speeded up by adrenaline, the opossum is slowed down by it. Although much work remains to be done on this theory, it is the best we have at this time, though it is still not clear why all opossums do not react in the same way. Many other creatures besides the opossum display this death-feigning act, the most notable being the common hognose snake.

The opossum is primarily nocturnal, coming out to feed under the cover of darkness. Unable to hibernate, or even become lethargic for long periods, it wanders about on all but the coldest of winter nights. Although it can climb well, the opossum spends most of its time on the ground. For one thing, most of its food is found there, even fallen persimmons, which are one of its favorite meals. Unfortunately, persimmon trees are not too common over much of the opossum's range, and the ripe fruit season is short.

A common misconception is that the opossum is primarily a scavenger. True, the opossum will scavenge, but then so will most of the carnivores. Dr. William Hamilton of Cornell discovered that in New York State insects were the most important item of food for the opossum. Of course, in cold weather when insects were not available, other animal matter became the most important food. Mice, ground-nesting birds, rabbits, shrews and moles are all part of the opossum's diet. During the hunting season the incidence of animal matter increases sharply, and the opossum, as well as other meat-eating mammals, feeds upon dead and crippled game that human hunters can't locate. Green vegetation and fruits are eaten in about equal proportions. Amphibians, reptiles, earthworms and some grain help to round out their menu. Late summer and early fall months are periods of gluttony, for at this time a large food supply is available, and the opossum makes the best of the opportunity to build up a large reserve of body fat.

The opossum is endowed with a great tenacity for life. The animal can stand more physical abuse than any creature that I know of. I have seen people beat opossums with clubs, attempt to drown them and even hang them, and although the opossums certainly didn't enjoy this treatment, they frequently were able to survive.

Senses: The sense of smell is probably the best developed and most important to the opossum. Comparatively slow and clumsy, it needs an acute nose to ferret out food. Its hearing is acute and is important mainly for protection rather than for locating food. Eyesight is not especially good.

Although the opossum may be aware of danger, it seldom seems to react until the danger is very close. For example, the animal will sometimes raid a chicken coop and, after killing one of the noisy fowl, will sit and eat its fill, heedless of the danger of an avenging farmer.

The opossum's taste is probably undeveloped; it will eat an American toad whose poisonous skin secretions would sicken a dog.

Communication: The most commonly heard sound of an angry or frightened opossum is a loud hiss. On several occasions I have heard them growl but most of the time they remain mute. They are also said to make a grunting sound.

Locomotion: The opossum is not built for speed, usually meandering about. The animal presents a ludicrous appearance when it walks at a fast gait. Its body rocks from side to side and its long tail lashes about in a circle trying to maintain balance. The main advantage the opossum has is that, being built low to the ground, it can elude most of its larger pursuers by running through dense underbrush. Although opossums can swim well, they seldom do so, even though they frequent water's edge searching for food.

Breeding: Over most of its range the opossum has two litters of young per year, except in the southern areas where a third litter may be produced. The breeding season starts in January and may last till late September in the south and until June or July in the north. Opossums are polygamous, the male breeding with any receptive female he encounters.

The male opossum has a double-headed penis, and hence the animal's breeding habits have been a source of much folklore. One commonly held notion is that the male breeds the female through the nostrils and that she blows the young into her pouch. Actually, the opossum breeds the same way as most other mammals. The male's penis is shaped to serve the female's double womb. Linnaeus gave the opossum the Greek name *Didelphis*, which means double womb, because of this unusual feature.

Baby opossums are born as tiny, hairless embryos and remain in their mother's pouch after birth, each attached to a nipple, for up to seventy days. These are two weeks old.

Birth and Young: Opossums have the amazingly short gestation period of just thirteen days. The embryos are often called living abortions, although I often refer to this as nature's attempt at painless birth. At the time of birth the baby opossum weighs 2.5 grains or 1/1700 of a pound; twenty would fit into a tablespoon. At birth these tiny mites are naked, their eyes are undeveloped, their hind feet are mere stubs, and their tail looks like a little club. Their forefeet, however, are well developed, including toenails, because the young must pull themselves from the vagina into the pouch. The mother opossum may make the journey easier for the little ones by licking a path through her fur with her tongue.

The pouch serves as an incubator, a place where the little ones will be provided with food, warmth and shelter. The female usually has thirteen teats in her pouch, arranged in the shape of a horseshoe. As she frequently has as many as sixteen to seventeen young (there is one record of twenty-five) it is a case of first come, first served.

As soon as the baby opossum crawls into the pouch it seeks out a teat, which it swallows. The young suck the milk from the nipples with their strong oral muscles; formerly it was thought that the mother pumped the milk into them. The young stay fastened to the teat for

After emerging from mother's pouch, baby opossums often travel about on her back. They still suckle for another month, then go off on their own.

about eight weeks. Any baby that doesn't get a teat at the start perishes and is expelled from the pouch. The mother has special muscles by which she can close the opening of her pouch like a pocketbook.

By the end of two months the young opossums are about the size of mice. They now begin to venture out of the pouch, although they all try to crawl back in if they are frightened. When the young crawl out of the pouch, they ride around clinging to their mother's fur. Occasionally one of the babies will fall off and be left behind. It doesn't really matter because by the time they are three months old they will all leave to go out in the world on their own.

Life Span: The average life span of an opossum is about four years, with some in captivity living as long as seven years.

Sign: The most frequently seen sign of an opossum is its tracks. As mentioned before, its hind foot looks exactly like a human hand. There is no other track in North America that even remotely resembles the track of an opossum's hind foot. The front toes spread out into almost a star shape. Because the opossum spends so much of its time roaming the woodlands, its tracks are seldom seen. They are, however, readily seen in the snow because the opossum seldom dens up for more than three or four days.

Den sites can be identified by the opossum's silvery hair. Good spots to check are culverts, drain pipes, burrows under old buildings and the rough bark of trees that have cavities in them.

The scat of an opossum is about one-half inch in diameter with segments two to four inches long, depending on the diet.

Enemies: The opossum seems to be relatively free from predation. I have never seen a dog, fox or any other animal eat an opossum. I once found the remains of an opossum that had evidently been killed and eaten by a great horned owl. This owl feeds upon almost anything that it can kill, so it can't be considered a fussy eater. In the Everglades I have seen vultures feed upon carcasses of opossums that had been killed on the road, but I have never seen anything kill an opossum and eat it.

Dogs kill a large number of opossums, but just because they like to hunt them. I have also seen dogs that wouldn't even bite an opossum because of its slightly disagreeable odor.

The opossum is seldom bothered by ectoparasites. Furbearers generally carry all kinds of body lice, mites and ticks, but few are found on the opossum.

However, the opossum is infested with endoparasites—flukes, nematodes and trematodes. In some instances these worms must cause the opossum considerable discomfort, as they almost fill the stomach cavity.

Human Relations: Man, of course, is the principal enemy of all wild creatures. Even people who don't hunt, unintentionally kill many opossums with their automobiles. The opossum is rather slow-moving and dim-witted, and on a dark road it is blinded by a car's bright lights. It either stands still or waits until the car is almost upon it before attempting to escape. I have often seen as many as six dead opossums in a 10-mile stretch of road.

Almost everyone who hunts for raccoons also hunts for opossums because a coon dog will apparently tree one as readily as the other. With long-haired fur now in demand, opossum skins bring modest returns. When prices are down, most fur dealers don't bother handling the skins.

During the Depression, in the poor sections of the South, the opossum was hunted as much for its meat as for its fur. During World War II I took many opossums mainly for their fat, which the government needed for making soap and munitions.

Opossums are becoming more numerous, not only because man doesn't hunt them as often but because man has helped them to increase their range. Many opossums taken as pets when young are either released or escape into new areas when full grown. Man has deliberately introduced the opossum into Washington, Oregon, and California. In some areas opossums have become so numerous that they are now nuisance animals. On the whole, though, the opossums neither disrupt nor add to the areas where they are found.

Trophy Records: The greatest weight that I can find recorded for the opossum is 14 pounds.

Table Fare: The opossum is as eagerly eaten by some people as it is shunned by others. In the South " 'possum and sweet taters" are famed in story and song. Many people who have eaten the meat say it is tasty.

CARNIVORES

Order Carnivora

The carnivores are flesh-eating animals that range in size from the diminutive least weasel up to the giant brown bear. There are four families in North America, not including the three families of marine carnivores, Order Pinnipedia, which are considered separately in this book.

There are few distinctive characters of this family, but one of them is the four long canine teeth that are used for seizing prey and for stabbing.

All of the members of this order have strong claws that are used for capturing prey, fighting, digging or climbing. The claws of the members of the cat family are retractible. Some carnivores are plantigrade, walking on the entire foot; others are digitigrade and walk on their toes; almost all have some webbing between the toes, but extremely webbed feet are characteristic of some of the otters and are used for swimming.

The eyes of carnivores are forward on the skull,

giving the animals binocular vision that is useful in finding prey. Some of the carnivores hunt alone, others in packs; some hunt by sight, others by scent; some hunt by stalking and stealth, others resort to an open chase.

Although all carnivores eat meat, most of them will eat vegetation and insects. Bears, skunks and raccoons are largely omnivorous.

Many of the carnivores are hunted for their beautiful coats of fur or hair. Many of them are hunted merely for sport. In many cases carnivores are valuable as predators which keep other species under control. On rare occasions, larger carnivores may attack man.

The young of all carnivores receive a long period of parental care. Although the carnivores are among the more intelligent mammals, and many of their actions are instinctive, they nonetheless must be trained by their parents to become successful hunters and killers.

Most of the carnivores remain active all year, but only a few put aside food for the future. Some become very fat in late autumn and sluggish or dormant during the colder parts of the winter. However, none of the carnivores falls into the deep sleep of true hibernation.

BEARS

Family Ursidae

BLACK BEAR
BROWN BEAR
GRIZZLY BEAR
POLAR BEAR

Straight facial profile and absence of shoulder hump distinguish the black bear from browns and grizzlies.

Black Bear

Ursus americanus

The black bear is the smallest of the North American bears, and the only one that is distinctly American. Our other bears, the brown-grizzly and the polar, also inhabit Asia and Europe. The black did not originate on this continent, however; it came over from Asia on the Bering Land Bridge about 500,000 years ago. Unlike the pugnacious grizzly which is rapidly disappearing, the furtive black bear has learned to adapt to man and has survived in many parts of the country, enhancing the hunting situation by its presence near populated areas. Though known to attack when provoked, the black generally gives humans a wide berth. But going after a bear, even a timid one, provides thrills for thousands of sportsmen nationwide who otherwise would have to travel far for a bruin hunt.

Description: A large male black bear weighs on an average of 300 to 400 pounds (the female considerably less), stands 27 to 36 inches high at the shoulder and is 4 to 5 1/2 feet in length. This bear does not have the prominent shoulder hump which characterizes the brown-grizzly.

The black bear has a straight face when seen in profile. Its eyes are small and the ears are well-rounded. It has 42 teeth: 12 incisors, 4 canines, 16 premolars and 10 molars. The canines are long and well pointed; the premolars are rudimentary or even missing; and the molars have flat crowns.

The bear is plantigrade, walking on the soles of its feet. There are five toes on each foot, each armed with a strong, curved, nonretractible claw. The black bear's front claws are about 1 1/4 inches in length, and it is the only North American bear that often climbs trees as an adult.

The black bear is also unique in that it comes in a wide range of colors. A typical black bear has long, lustrous, jet-black hair over most of the body from its head down to its tiny tail. On its muzzle and around its eyes, the hair is light-colored. Most black bears have a splash of pure white on their chests. This splash may vary from just a few hairs to an area about a foot across. Black bears also come in almost every shade of brown and some are bright blond. One race of the black bear is a smoky-blue and another race is pure white.

Distribution: Black bears inhabit forests, swamps and mountains from Alaska to Labrador as far north as there are forests, and occur southward to northern United States, and south in the mountains to California, Mexico and Georgia. They also occur in northeastern Arkansas and along the Gulf Coast from eastern Texas to Florida.

Travel: Black bears are not migratory, although adult males do wander over large areas. Females with cubs use a more restricted range. An animal's range is usually determined by the availability of food, and no animal usually works any harder than it has to. A range of 5 to 15 square miles is usually sufficient for a bear to satisfy its needs.

A black bear rarely has the driving instinct to return to its home range if it has been moved by certain circumstances. Each year as the Pennsylvania big-game

Distribution of the black bear.

hunting season opens, a few bears swim across the Delaware River to take refuge in a valley in New Jersey. Most of these bears find ample food here and stay on.

In Yellowstone Park, if a bear becomes a nuisance, it is live-trapped, marked and hauled 25 to 30 miles away and released. Occasionally these bears make their way back to their original home. Two bears in Michigan which were live-trapped and used in a transplanting operation returned to their home grounds 96 miles and 64 miles away.

Habits: The black bear is often referred to as the

clown of the woods. Its rolling, flat-footed walk gives it a clumsy, bumble-footed appearance. The antics of bear cubs in the wild, and even those of adults in our national parks, are the antics of court jesters. And it is because of this behavior that many people underestimate the black bear.

This bear is one of the most intelligent of our wild mammals and has been able to survive, yes even to thrive, in the proximity of man. Each year bears are still hunted within 50 miles of New York City, within an area that boasts a total population well in excess of 15 million people. The black bear is able to hide and to stay hidden in woodlands where no one would ever think of looking for a bear. When man, the bear's arch enemy, enters the woods the bear either hides or goes out the other side. Not only has the bear a natural cunning but it also has the ability to learn from experience. This intelligence, coupled with the bear's ability to move swiftly when it must, has allowed it to survive when most of the other large carnivores have passed from the scene. Near civilization the black bear has become strictly nocturnal. It is able to conceal itself and its presence so well that many people are unaware that a bear is in the neighborhood. In wilderness areas and in the national parks, the bears are most active in the daytime, as they can get food as easily in the daytime as at night.

In prehistoric times, the bears' ancestors probably lived on a straight meat diet. As the ages passed, the supply of meat animals dwindled and the bear's diet changed. Although still classed in the Order Carnivoras the bear is omnivorous in its eating habits and, through evolution, its teeth have changed too. Instead of having carnassial shearing teeth like a wolf, the bear's teeth became flattened on the top like those of a cow—and for good reason. The bear, like the cow, consumes volumes of grasses, sedges and other vegetable matter.

The evolution of the bear's teeth is a survival factor almost beyond comprehension. The wolf, which is almost strictly a meat-eater, is far superior to the bear in intelligence, yet its diet forces it to hunt prey animals in order to eat. This brings it into constant conflict with man, and the wolf has been exterminated over most of its range. The bear, although requiring more food than the wolf because it is so much larger, will feed upon almost everything. This single factor has allowed the bear not only to survive where the wolf could not, but also to increase its numbers in some areas.

When the black bear first comes out of its winter dormancy, it fills up on water. It must, in a sense, soak its intestines to allow them to regain their elasticity before cramming them full of food.

Grasses, sedges, buds and the inner bark of evergreen trees, particularly pine, are the first foods available, and the bear eagerly devours them. As the sun becomes warmer and the plants sprout starchy bulbs, the bears tear up the earth and eat their "potatoes."

When the berries ripen, the bears go on an orgy of gluttony, pulling the bushes to their mouths with one paw and consuming not only the berries but the leaves of the plant too. They probably don't want the leaves, but it takes too much time to be selective.

In the fall as the apples ripen, the bears seek out wild apple trees, abandoned orchards or even risk coming into rural backyards. The bear is never content with just picking up apples from the ground. It climbs into the tree to feast. After eating all the apples within reach, the bear uses its paws and claws like hands and pulls the outspreading branches in towards the center of the tree. This invariably breaks most of the branches so that they do not whip back to normal position when released. The tree soon looks like a giant bird had built its giant nest among the uppermost branches. When a bear feeds upon apples or berries, it defecates almost constantly.

In a good acorn year, the ground will be blanketed by nuts. White oak acorns are favored because they are the sweetest, yet the bear stuffs itself with whatever sort is available. Most bears probably accumulate more of their winter's fat supply by feeding on acorns than on any other food. Before the blight wiped out the American chestnut trees, they comprised about 60 percent of the total trees in our eastern forests. At that time the fat chestnuts were the bears' dietetic mainstay. The small three-cornered beechnuts are also a choice food.

The bear is an opportunist that bypasses nothing edible. It overturns rocks and logs to eat the beetles and ants that are hidden under them. Bears have a natural fondness for honey and the sticky nectar often lures them into trouble. When a bear discovers a wild bee tree, it smashes trunk and branches apart and wades right into the hive. The bear eats the honey, wax and even the bees. Although the bees attempt to sting the bear, unless they sting it on the nose or around the eyes, they just get lost in the bear's shaggy hair. An insect's sting apparently does not affect the inside of the bear's mouth. One bear was found to have 2 quarts of yellow jackets in its stomach.

If the bears can't find wild honey, they often raid the cultivated beehives of the rural areas. To many backwoods people, honey is the main source of sweetening, so they can't be blamed for not wanting to share it with the bears.

Bears eagerly eat meat in any form. The eggs and young of ground-nesting birds just serve to whet their appetite. They dig out mice, chipmunks, ground squirrels and marmots. The young of such animals as deer, elk, caribou, mountain sheep and moose will be added to the menu if the bear can locate them and escape the mother's wrath. Adult big game that is weak or sick will be killed by the bears and eaten.

When the salmon runs start, the bears in such areas congregate, sometimes by the hundred, to feed upon the fish. The bears seem to have no idea of their own capacity and gorge themselves until they are almost sick with overeating. Bears also feed on carrion, no matter how rank or rotten.

The black bear's appetite often gets it into trouble with farmers and ranchers. Pork is perhaps a black bear's favorite food, and the bear will raid any pigsty that it can locate. Some bears become confirmed sheep killers, doing a tremendous amount of damage. It must be remembered, though, that the average bear prefers to stay away from farms and ranches and feed upon the plenteous supply of natural food. Most animals try to avoid contact with man.

The main exception to this is the bears of the national parks. Many people claim that the park bears have lost both their intelligence and resourcefulness in accepting handouts from people and from feeding at the dumps.

Others claim that, on the contrary, the bears are continuing to display the intelligence which enabled them to adapt and survive where other animals could not.

As autumn advances, the bears begin to build layers of fat on their bodies. In some cases the fat on a bear's back may be more than 5 inches thick. A bear killed in Wisconsin had a blanket of fat that weighed 212 pounds. Rendered out, this would have produced almost 20 gallons of bear oil. In our country's early days, bear oil was worth about six dollars a gallon and was used for cooking, frying, baking, in the tanning of leather, as medicine, and for many other purposes.

Bears are not true hibernators, for their body temperature drops only a few degrees from normal and their metabolism remains high during their "winter dormancy." Unlike true hibernators, bears can be instantly active if disturbed in their winter den, as some woodsmen have learned to their dismay when they stumbled accidently into a wintering bear's lair. The bear's emergence from the den depends on weather and location. The den may be in almost any kind of shelter. Favorite spots are under the root masses of large trees that have been partially upended. Bear also utilize limestone caves, natural crevasses, abandoned mineshafts, blowdowns or even dense thickets. Some bears go to a lot of trouble to make the dens large enough and carry in leaves and grasses to be used for bedding. The lazier bears accept the conditions just as they find them and make the best of the situation. The bears prefer to den on the north side of mountains.

Before retiring, a bear does not eat for several days and voids all materials in its digestive system. The bear then eats leaves, pine needles and occasionally some of its own hair. This material passes through the digestive system and forms an anal "plug." Plugs have been found that were as long as 12 inches. The plug stays in place all winter and is voided as soon as the bear comes out in the spring. No excrement is ever found in a dormant bear's den. At the start of dormancy, a bear's stomach and intestines shrivel up to a fraction of their former size, and the bear is ready for winter.

Senses: The eyes of a bear always seem to be too small for the animal's size. Sight is not of too great an importance to the bear, and, if anything, it is probably nearsighted.

The bear's sense of smell is its greatest asset. Because the bulk of the bear's diet, about 75 percent, is vegetation, the bear doesn't need keen eyes to locate it. A sharp nose will do the job nicely. Bears can smell carrion many miles away.

The black bear has the largest ears of any of our American bears. By nature, a black bear is shy and retiring, and its large ears help it to hear danger coming for a great distance, thus affording it time to retire into a dense thicket or leave the area.

The sense of taste in a bear is very pronounced. With the exception of the raccoon, the bear probably has the greatest craving for sweets of all our native mammals.

Communication: Bears do not make any vocal sounds unless they are in the company of their own kind. A large boar bear will roar, growl, snarl, snort, cough, grunt and pop its teeth together, according to the situation. The cubs whimper, whine, squeak and bawl, the last sound being reserved for moments when they are really frightened. The sow answers or talks to her cubs with coughs, grunts and low growls. A wounded bear is known to moan and groan with anguish, sounding just like a man.

Locomotion: The black bear's shuffling, flat footed walk seems lazy and indolent—but it is deceptive. When traveling from place to place, the bear averages about 2 to 3 miles per hour. Bears are so inquisitive that it is unlikely one ever walks for an hour without finding at least a half-dozen objects that it must investigate.

Bears don't seem to trot; they just go into a faster walk. When frightened, the bears change to a ground-eating gallop that has been clocked at 30 miles per hour on a road. Grizzly bears are supposed to be able to reach 35 miles per hour when they charge. I have seen grizzlies chase black bears away from a garbage dump, although it may be that the grizzlies weren't really trying because the blacks soon outdistanced their big rivals.

The aspen trees in our western states show evidence of the black bear's ability to climb. Most of the trees have scars in the bark made by a bear's claws. The bears climb into trees to secure food, to escape from danger, to sleep and, apparently some of the time, to amuse themselves. A bear may climb a tree leisurely, utilizing whatever branches are available. If the tree is inclined, the bear climbs up the top side of the curve. When hard pressed it literally gallops up the tree with the back feet working in unison. Bears have also been known to jump 30 to 40 feet out of a tree without suffering any apparent ill effects.

Bears are powerful swimmers and when they set out for a distant point they swim in as straight a line as possible, climbing over any obstacle. Bears have been known to climb right in and over boats and canoes that have gotten in their way.

Breeding: Female black bears do not breed until they are three and a half years old. The bears are monoestrus, with the heat period taking place in June and July. This is the only time of the year that the male consorts with the female, and he probably consorts with more than one female in that period. Apparently the female must be stimulated before copulation and the bears are quite active at "love-making." They caress each other with their tongues, rub against each other and each gently strokes the other with its claws. The pair also engages in light wrestling matches.

Bears are subject to delayed implantation, which means that, although the female's eggs have been fertilized, they develop little and are probably not attached to the uterus wall until late autumn. The gestation period varies from six to eight months, again depending upon many variable conditions. In the final six to eight weeks before parturition, the blastocysts, as the early embryos are called, become implanted in the uterine wall and the embryo develops rapidly.

Birth and Young: The young of the black bear are born in the latter part of January or early February. There are usually twins or triplets. Four cubs at a time are not uncommon, five have been known and, on two occasions, six cubs have been reported from one bear.

The young at birth are covered with a very fine hair, their eyes are sealed shut, and they weigh 8 ounces or less. If the mother weighs an average of 300 pounds, her babies are only 1/600th of her total weight, compared to 1/20th for a human baby. Considering that some black bear males weigh over 500 pounds, and that at birth they were only 1/1000 of their adult size, their growth rate is truly remarkable.

The female has six teats, four located on her chest and two located between her hind legs. Undoubtedly the cubs nurse at the ones between her legs first because they are more convenient.

The cubs open their eyes at about forty days of age. By this time they weigh about 4 pounds. When the cubs weigh about 5 pounds, the female is ready to leave the den two months after they were born.

Life for a bear cub is very secure. The mother is protective and so large that few creatures would dare to molest the young. The cubs, although still nursing, are soon able to pick up extra food by themselves even if the mother does have to catch it for them. With hardly a care in the world, the cubs engage in almost constant wrestling matches or follow their proclivity for getting into trouble. When the mother bear has put up with about all the nonsense she can stand, she gives the cubs a powerful swat. If danger threatens the cubs the mother chases them up the nearest tree. Then she gets ready to fight the intruder. Females with cubs try to avoid the big crotchety males, but if a male is aggressive, the female does not hesitate to fight to protect her young.

The female takes the young into the winter den with her during their first year. The family unit may stay to-

This huge black has accumulated a heavy fat reserve for nourishment and insulation during its winter's sleep.

gether again until fall, or they may split up as soon as they have emerged in spring. A female breeds only every second year.

Life Span: Black bears have a life span of about fifteen years, although many in captivity have lived longer. One black bear in the Frankfort, Germany, zoo was twenty-five years, eleven months and six days old when it was killed in a fight. There is one record of a bear twenty-seven years old. The Delmar, New York, wildlife research laboratory has developed a system of cutting a bear's tooth to study the growth layers of enamel. Their oldest bear specimen was thirty years old.

Signs: The tracks of the black bear, probably the most commonly seen sign, are distinctive and in most of the country cannot be confused with any other mammal's.

Stumps that have been torn apart for ants, evergreen trees that have been chewed on for the inner bark, apple tree branches that have been pulled inward, beehives that have been smashed apart and claw marks on trees are all signs that plainly spell black bear.

The bear's scat is about 1 1/2 inches in diameter and ropelike if it has been feeding on meat. Grasses, apples and berries produce loose scat like a cow flop.

Enemies: Black bears are probably their own worst enemies. The adults fight in the breeding season and over food. An adult may occasionally kill a cub. The grizzly bear can easily kill an adult black bear but has to catch it first.

Black bears seem to enjoy rubbing or scratching themselves against rocks and rough-barked trees. The itching may be caused by fleas, ticks or lice, or simply by old hair coming out.

Internal parasites include trichinae, tapeworms, lungworms and flukes. Black bears have been known to have rabies and tuberculosis. In addition, the bears are subject to accidents from attempting to kill large hoofed game, or perhaps from unfortunate encounters with porcupines.

Tracks of the black bear in mud. The large hind-foot track, which resembles a man's footprint, registers in front of the smaller forefoot print. Claw marks can be seen just ahead of the toes.

Human Relations: National parks often hold the largest concentrations of black bears the public can readily see. Signs throughout the parks warn: DO NOT FEED THE BEARS. Still, almost everyone feeds the bears. These bears have not become pets; they are just following the line of least resistance in accepting handouts. The bears are so cute, cuddly and clownlike that the majority of people forget that these animals can be very dangerous and deadly. Even hunters and many naturalists think of the bear as being cowardly. The truth of the matter is that black bears have attacked and killed more people than have any of our other bears.

The bears may attack out of hunger or fright, in defense of their young or for almost any other reason that only the bears know. In 1963 the black bears in Alaska all seemed to be on a rampage. Reports of attack after attack kept coming in. Most of the attacks were unprovoked. The consensus is that the bears were hungry and on edge because of the shortage of berries. The wilderness cabins in Alaska all have door and window shutters which are studded with hundreds of nails to discourage bears from wrecking the cabins.

Formerly, many states had a bounty on bears because they were plentiful and considered a nuisance animal. Most states have now removed the bounty and have classified the black bear as a game animal.

Trophy Records: The world's-record black bear skull was found in Sanpete County, Utah, in 1975 by Alma Lund and Merrill Daniels. It measured 14 12/16 inches long and 8 14/16 inches wide, scoring 23 10/16 points.

The second place skull is from a bear killed by Rex Peterson and Richard Hardy in 1970 also in Sanpete County, Utah. The skull measured 13 11/16 inches long and 8 11/16 inches wide, for a score of 22 6/16.

The greatest scale weight for a black bear was one killed in 1885, at Stevens Point, Wisconsin, that tallied 802 1/2 pounds. Otto Hedbany's bear weighed 652 pounds after an estimated 97 pounds of entrails and fat were removed, making this a probable 749 pounds. In 1975 Sam Ball of Batavia, New York, shot a black bear that weighed 660 pounds field dressed, for an estimated live weight of 759 pounds. In 1923, Herman Crokyndall killed a bear near Milford, Pennsylvania, that weighed 633 pounds and measured 9 feet from nose tip to tail tip.

In 1957 two New York State biologists live-trapped, tagged, weighed and released a 605-pound black bear at Tupper Lake. One bear that they had trapped in 1956 weighed 332 pounds. When retrapped in 1957, the same bear weighed 562 pounds for a total gain of 230 pounds in one year.

Table Fare: Bear meat, like any other kind of game meat, depends upon proper handling and preparation to make it tasty. Black bear roasts can be very good. The meat is rather coarse and dark.

In June, when the salmon start their spawning runs, brown bears head for the rivers to feast on the abundant fish. The rest of the summer they eat plants, rodents and carrion.

Alaskan Brown Bear

Ursus arctos middendorffi

The Alaskan brown bear is the world's largest, land-based, meat-eating mammal. Once considered a separate and distinct species from the grizzly bear, it has now been included with the grizzly under the scientific name *Ursus arctos*. It has the same dish face and humped shoulder as the grizzly, and men who have spent a lifetime studying these bears cannot tell them apart. Along with the grizzly, the brown is the most dangerous animal in North America. Its huge size and tremendous strength make it a formidable quarry.

Description: A large brown bear stands 4 1/2 feet high to the top of its shoulder and weighs up to 1,500 pounds. It may be 9 to 10 feet in length. Most big males average between 800 and 1,200 pounds, with the females weighing 500 to 800. When a big male stands erect he measures 8 1/2 feet and perhaps even up to 9 feet in height. With the front paws outstretched, an adult male has a spread of 10 to 11 feet. The five huge claws on each of the forefeet are over 4 inches in length. As the bears get older, the claws become longer and lighter in color. Some of the old patriarchs that I saw on the McNeil River had claws that were almost pure white. The claws on the hind feet are much shorter. The bears are plantigrade, waddling along on the soles of their feet.

The hair on a brownie is long and dense and comes in a variety of shadings of brown. A medium-dark brown seems to be the predominant color, but the range runs from almost a blond through a russet to a brown so dark

Grizzly at left makes defensive gestures toward intruder.

Distribution of the brown bear.

as to be almost black. When the bears are wet, they appear darker yet.

The brown bear has 42 teeth: 12 incisors, 4 canines, 16 premolars and 10 molars. The canines are exceptionally long and curved. The premolars are rudimentary and the molars are flat-topped. As the bears are now omnivorous rather than strictly carnivorous, these flat-topped teeth are better adapted for their way of life. Bears grind vegetation more often than they shear meat and their teeth have changed accordingly through evolution.

Distribution: Brown bears live along the coast from the Alaskan Peninsula southeastward to southernmost Alaska, and on some adjacent islands.

Travel: The Alaskan brown bear does not migrate. It only travels from the mountainside where it spends the winter in its den down to the seacoast where it feeds, a distance of from 5 to 25 miles. Some brown bears, however, have followed rivers as far as 100 miles into the interior.

Old boars particularly wander some distances in search of food when the salmon are not running. One young male that I watched on the McNeil River was a study in perpetual motion. When the tide was in, this bear fished at the falls; when the tide was out, he searched the seacoast for miles out on the mud flats. At any time he could be found circling the river's tidal basin. He never stayed long in one place.

Habits: When the brown bear comes out of its winter den in late April or early May, much of the area is still covered with snow, and it carries a lot of dirt on its fur and feet. Against the white blanket of snow these dirt marks are easily visible. Once in a while the bear will do a little more excavating, and the new dirt makes dark smear marks on the snow-covered mountainside.

The bear is hard-pressed for food at this time and must rely on the few new green sprouts and on roots. Perhaps it will find a winter-killed moose or caribou, or a dead seal washed up on the beach. If the carcass contains more meat than the bear can consume at one time, it will jealously guard its cache.

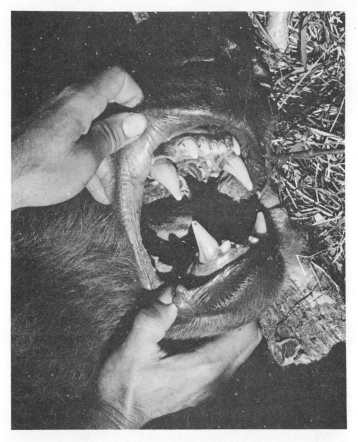

The brown bear has long canine teeth, the mark of a carni-vore, but it is no longer solely a flesh-eater, having become omnivorous by necessity.

With food scarce the bears are scattered far and wide, feeding from the seashore up to the mountaintops. As the various grasses begin to grow, the bears feed more in the lowlands and consume them by the ton. It is odd to see the world's largest land-based carnivore feeding upon grass like a farmer's cow.

Midsummer changes the bear's way of life. Halfway through July the salmon start to run. Countless thousands of these fish return upstream to complete their life cycle, and the bears are there waiting for them. The salmon have two peak periods of activity each day corresponding to the incoming tides. The bears do most of their fishing at falls or in shallow riffles.

Each bear has a slightly different technique of fishing. Some bears sit along the edge of the stream, and when a fish goes by plunge into the water after it. Some bears run about in the riffles trying to catch the fish exposed by shallow water. Some bears run from pool to pool, plunging into the water after the fish. And some bears just sit out in the water and let the fish run into them.

During the time I spent on the McNeil River in Alaska, I took thousands of pictures of brown bears fishing. I saw the bears catch the fish with their mouths or pin them down with their paws, but at no time did I ever see a bear throw a fish up on the bank by using its paws. No one I spoke to had ever seen this happen either, yet artists often depict bears catching fish in this manner. One cannot say that bears *never* do this, but it is rare.

When a bear comes down to fish, it is ravenously hungry. If it can find the head of a fish that has been discarded by another bear, it grabs the fish head and wolfs it down. When the bear starts catching for itself, it eats the entire fish, head and all. After catching and eating several salmon, the bear begins to be choosy and eats just the body, discarding the head and the tail. After the bear has eaten ten or twelve salmon, it becomes glutted but continues fishing. Now it takes only females, allowing males to fall back into the water, tears them open and only eats the roe.

The Alaskan brown bears have a distinct pecking order. The biggest, strongest bear is the boss, and all other bears defer to him. The number-two bear can lord it over the rest of the bears except the boss, and so it goes to the bottom of the hierarchy. Because status in this system depends on each bear's fighting ability and growth, their rank changes constantly. In order to reduce the chaos and the fighting, the bears have adopted the face-saving tactic of avoiding each other as much as possible. Usually when a bear catches its fish, it scampers up the bank to eat it. Then another bear comes down to fish. The bears usually come down one path and go up another. By adhering to this pattern the bears avoid conflict.

If the boss bear is feeding, he does not tolerate any other bear on the river bank. When he has eaten his fill, he retires from the scene to sleep, and then the other bears can fish. When two or more bears come down to fish, they will not look at each other.

After the salmon spawn, they all die. Tens of thousands of their carcasses lie along the river banks or float back down to the ocean. Many creatures scavenge on the dead fish, including the bears. When the spawning run has stopped, the bears go off their fish diet and return to the mountainsides. By this time the berries have begun to ripen and the bears consume them by the ton.

By October snow has covered most of the areas and the bears are fat and resplendent in their thick winter coats. If the bear does not already have a den prepared it will make one. Den sites are usually chosen on the north side of the mountains so that melting snows do not drip into the den. Many of the dens are 1,000 to 2,000 feet in elevation.

The bear picks a spot that it thinks suitable and with its powerful forepaws begins the excavation. Dirt and boulders fly as the hole steadily deepens. When it has dug a small cavelike hollow, it is ready to retire. The records of one den show that is was dug horizontally into a mountainside that had a 60-degree slope, and the entrance was 37 inches wide and 43 inches high. Inside the den was 60 inches wide, 58 inches high and 8 feet deep from the entrance to the rear wall. The floor of the den was littered with willow branches and leaves which were used for bedding. The winter snow seals the entrance shut. Snug inside, the bear sleeps through most of the winter.

In its winter sleep the bear's body metabolism slows down slightly and its digestive track is empty. Although the bears become lethargic, they do not become torpid and are easily aroused. Occasionally brown bears will be found wandering about in the middle of the winter when all the rest of their kind are relaxing. A bear before going into its winter quarters will have gained as much as 400 pounds of fat if the feeding conditions have been right.

Senses: The brown bear's sense of smell is its keenest sense. All bears can smell carrion for many miles, and they depend on their scenting ability to avoid hunters.

Their sense of hearing is also good, but they spend most of their time where external noises such as the sounds of rushing waterfalls or of pounding coastal surf mask all but the closest sounds. The ears of the bear are small and quite round. Its eyesight is poor, and it has difficulty seeing distant stationary objects, though it seems to be able to detect movement quickly.

Communication: An Alaskan brown bear roaring in anger makes a frightening noise. The bears also growl, pop their teeth and make a huffing-snorting sound when alarmed or angered. Bear cubs when hungry or astray whine and cry.

Locomotion: The bear walks with a shuffling gait, an old bear with a ponderous, sedate waddle, a young bear at a fast-moving, sprightly pace.

When disturbed, a bear breaks into an easy, bouncing gallop. When frightened or angered, it can gallop at better than 30 miles per hour for short distances. I have never seen an adult brown bear make a flat all-out charge, but I have seen young bears, surprised by an old one at close range, run at an impressive speed.

Breeding: The breeding season takes place in June through the first part of July. The females only breed every other year or every third year and do not breed until they are four or five years old.

I once watched an old male follow a young female who was about to come into oestrous. She was not quite ready and would not accept his advances. She would look over her shoulder and, seeing the male had shortened the distance between them, would break into a gallop. When she was about 200 feet ahead she would resume a fast walk. The male never hurried his pace but gained on the female. The pursuit lasted for three days, until the female finally submitted to the persistent male. Occasionally two large, evenly matched males will share a receptive female, but they will drive away smaller males.

Birth and Young: The brown bear, like many carnivores, is subject to delayed implantation. The young are born in January or February after a gestation period that varies from six to eight months. The female may give birth to one to four cubs at a time. The birth of the 1-pound cubs produces no strain on the mother. The newborn cubs are covered with short brown hair and their eyes are sealed shut.

On their diet of rich milk the cubs grow rapidly. The mother produces this milk at a time when she is not able to obtain food for herself and must draw upon her body's fat reserves. When she leaves the den in May to search for food, the cubs are large enough to follow her.

All bear mothers take good care of their young. The greatest threat to the young cubs is a large, old boar bear. The adult males would as soon kill a young bear as they would any small animal. The females know this and try to avoid the males. If a male comes near the cubs the female, though she is half the size of the male, bares her teeth, roars her disapproval and charges. The wise male hastily retreats.

While the mother fishes for salmon the little ones sit on the bank. The mother carries her catch ashore and drops it on the ground, where it flops around with such

This female brown bear nurses twins. Female browns have a strong protective instinct toward their cubs and attend them for about fifteen months after birth.

vigor that even the bravest cub approaches it with some trepidation. As the season progresses, the cubs overcome this fear and eagerly await the next catch. Sometimes in their eagerness they get out in the swift water and are swept downstream. At the first bawl of fear, the mother dashes downstream after the cub and, catching it in her teeth, swims to shore with it.

The young cubs learn many things from their mother in the course of the summer. When the air turns nippy and frost whitens the plants, the family goes into the

Brown bears habitually tread in each other's tracks, eventually making deep paths through their areas. These paths are most often seen near salmon streams.

winter den together. The female keeps her cubs with her until they are almost two years old, but sometimes until they are almost three.

Separation time is particularly hard on the young bears because they now meet rebukes and blows on all sides, even from the mother who had always been so protective but who must now care for her new cubs.

Life Span: The Alaskan brown bear has a potential life span of thirty-five years and, unless it is shot or killed in a fight, it is likely to reach fifteen to twenty years of age. The record for an Alaskan brown bear in captivity is thirty-six years, ten months and six days.

Sign: The most obvious sign of these huge bears are their pathways and trails, which are so distinctive that they can be easily seen from the air. Generation after generation of bears use exactly the same paths in walking along the stream banks and over the hills. The paths are about 20 inches wide and sometimes 8 to 10 inches deep. If the bank is steep, the path will be cut up from the bears using their huge claws to get better traction.

The tracks of the brown bear are very large. I saw one hind-foot track in the soft mud along the McNeil River that was 10 inches wide and almost 17 inches long to the tip of the long claws. My wide-brimmed bush hat would not even cover it. Unless the ground is muddy or very soft the long claws do not make much of an impression. The river edges and tidal flats which these bears frequent are usually full of tracks.

The scat of these bears is cow-sized. When they are feeding upon meat or fish the scat is segmented. When their food is grasses and sedges the scat is a soft mass.

Enemies: Under natural conditions the brown bear has no enemies other than large male bears which often pose a threat. The old boars' cannibalistic habits are often a threat to the cubs, but all other animals in the area defer to the bears.

Like all fur-bearers, the bears are host to fleas and body lice externally. Internally there are helminths and nematodes. The bears also have the muscle worm known as trichina that is found most commonly in pork. This worm can be fatal to man, and all bear meat must be thoroughly cooked before it is eaten.

Human Relations: Fortunately, for the bears, they inhabit an area that is not overly populated or accessible to man. Of course, as the human population grows larger and the affluence of Americans results in more leisure, increased pressure will be put on the bears. For this reason the Alaskan Fish and Game Department is carefully studying these bears with a view toward wisely guiding their future. The legal kill of brown-grizzly bears during 1965 was 771. The brown bears are neither as truculent nor as aggressive as the grizzlies, yet they have mauled and killed people and should always be treated with respect. The bears most likely to attack are those wounded by hunters, those just defeated in fights with other bears or those guarding their cubs.

The expansion of economic activity into the bears' range also threatens their existence. Warfare between bears and ranchers on Kodiak Island was inevitable. The bears are meat-eaters; the ranchers are trying to raise cattle. In 1965, forty-one head of cattle were killed and five were wounded by the big brownies. Thirty bears were killed during this period on the land where the cattle were killed. Many commercial fishermen shoot the brown bears because they eat fish, and as the timbering operations expand along the Alaskan coast, more bears will be killed as protection for the loggers.

Trophy Records: The world's-record Alaskan brown bear was killed on Kodiak Island in 1952, by Roy Lindsley. The skull scored 30 12/16 points and measured 17 15/16 inches long and 12 13/16 inches wide.

The Number 2 skull was also taken on Kodiak Island, in 1961, by Erling Hansen. This skull scored 30 11/16 points and measured 18 10/16 inches long and 12 1/16 inches wide. Out of the top twenty-one skulls in the record books, seventeen came from Kodiak Island.

The greatest recorded weight for an Alaskan brown bear is 1,656 pounds. The largest known brown bear is exhibited at the Space Zoological Park near Beemerville, New Jersey. Its live weight is estimated at well over 2,000 pounds.

Table Fare: The brown bear is often eaten by native Alaskans, although seldom by sportsmen.

Grizzlies vary widely in coloration. Above is a specimen with dark-brown fur and light-tipped hairs—a typical silvertip. The Toklat grizzly of Alaska, below, is yellowish-brown.

Grizzly Bear

Ursus arctos horribilis

Although the grizzlies of the Rocky Mountain regions do not grow as large as Alaskan brown bears, they are much more aggressive. The Plains Indians revered this bear and called it "brother," and a brave who killed a grizzly was accorded more honor than one who killed a human enemy. The Indians believed the bear was related to man: it could walk upright, hold objects in its paws, and it resembled a man after it had been skinned. When a bear was killed, its skull was cleaned and placed atop a pole in a place of honor to placate the dead bear's spirit.

In keeping with its reputation for ferocity, the bear was named *Ursus horribilis* by the naturalist Ord in 1815. The common name grizzly was applied because of the grizzled, or silvery, guard hairs in the bear's dark-brown pelage. Recently mammalogists have abandoned the attempt to classify the brown and grizzly bears as different species and have now settled on the Latin name *Ursus arctos* for both.

Description: A powerful, compactly built animal of enormous strength, the grizzly weighs up to 800 pounds, stands 3 1/2 feet high at the humped shoulder and is 6 to 7 1/2 feet in length. Its tail is only 2 to 3 inches long. It has five toes on each foot. The toes on the forefeet have strongly curved claws about 3 3/4 inches long. The claws of the Alaskan brown bear are longer but not as sharply curved. Grizzly bear cubs can climb trees, but the adults can't; their claws are too long. The long claws serve not only as weapons but also as tools. With them the bear can easily tear apart soil as it tries to capture a ground squirrel in its den or hook them under a large rock and lift it aside to search for insects hiding beneath.

The bear's neck tapers only slightly from the shoulder to the head. Its ears are well-rounded and large for a bear. The eyes are small and piglike. In profile the outline of the face is concave between the forehead and the nose. The grizzly has 42 teeth: 12 incisors, 4 canines, 16 pre-molars and 10 molars. Although the canine teeth are sharp for seizing prey, the molars are flattened for grinding vegetation. The jaws are powerful, the tremendous muscles allowing effortless crushing action. The grizzly cannot open its jaws as wide, proportionately, as can the wolf or coyote. There is a fingerlike projection of bone extending from the rear part of the lower jawbone which acts like a door stop against the upper jawbone and limits the jaw's action. The jaws are rather narrow, giving the bear a fairly sharp muzzle.

The grizzly comes in various shadings, the usual color being dark brown with white-tipped guard hairs. Many grizzlies lack this frosting and are black or lighter shades of brown. Most of the Toklat grizzlies of Mt. McKinley National Park are various shades of blond.

The hair is long and dense, providing good protection against the cold. The bears need this protection because, even though they sleep in winter their dens are seldom deep enough or tight enough to be snug. The dense hair prevents body heat loss so that the denned bear does not have an undue drain on its fat reserves.

Distribution: The range of the grizzly bear has been greatly reduced since the coming of the white man. Many types of grizzlies have been wiped out completely. The

Distribution of the grizzly bear.

largest grizzly of all inhabited the Great Plains and fed
upon the bison. Although this bear would eat dead bison,
it could and did kill bison. One record tells of a single
grizzly attacking and killing four adult bison bulls in one
encounter, although it was fatally gored by the last bull.
The Spaniards of California tried several times to match
a grizzly against a bison in an arena. It was never a match;
the grizzly easily smashed the charging bison's head or
broke its neck with one blow.

Grizzlies are now found in Alaska inland of the range
of the brown bear, eastward to northwestern Hudson's
Bay and south in the Rocky Mountains to northern New

Mexico. Formerly they were widespread in western North America.

A well-known study of the grizzly bear population was made by Dr. Victor H. Cahalane, of the New York State Museum in 1964. According to his report, the grizzly bears in Canada are found mainly in British Columbia and the Yukon, and their population is estimated at from 10,000 to 14,000 animals. The Alberta Rockies and the Northwest Territories each have from 500 to 1,000 grizzlies. The Barren Ground grizzly of the Northwest Territories is the only grizzly that is increasing in numbers and actually extending its range.

Most of the United States' grizzly bears are found in Alaska. The estimated population varies between 15,000 and 18,000 animals. The grizzly bear is now classified as threatened in the lower 48 states. The combined grizzly population of Wyoming, Montana, Idaho, Washington, and Colorado is estimated at 200 to 400. The last arid-region grizzlies are found in Mexico's Chihuahua mountains where an estimated 25 bears still survive. Only in the wilderness can this bear survive, and the wilderness is going fast.

Travel: A grizzly bear is not migratory, and if food is comparatively easy to obtain, the bear's home range may be five to ten miles square. If food is scarce, the range has to be larger. Old boars travel about a great deal, and they seem to enjoy climbing to high places where the view is good. Grizzly-bear tracks have been found on the bare tops of some of the smaller mountains, about 5,000 feet high, in Mt. McKinley National Park.

Habits: Over most of its range the grizzly bear is diurnal. Where man has put constant pressure on it, the bear moves about at night. In the northern portion of its range, the bear encounters such a short period of darkness in the summer that all of its activities are governed by its appetite.

The bears come out of their winter den in April or May, according to weather conditions in the area. Ravenously hungry, they eagerly devour the new shoots of grasses and sedges, dig up roots and tubers of various plants and eat them. Much of the grizzly bear's food is found in open country, in swales or on exposed mountainsides.

The grizzly bear is a carnivore by classification and by preference, but it eats vegetation because it is plentiful and easy to obtain. However, the bear much prefers to feed upon meat and will eat it freshly killed or overly ripe as carrion. It will locate by scent dead moose, elk, goat, sheep or deer, and if any of these animals has been weakened by starvation, accident or old age, the grizzly will run it down and kill it. When these animals give birth to their young, the grizzly bear will crisscross meadows and timberlands in the hope of locating such easy prey. All types of marmots and ground squirrels provide food for the grizzly. It is mainly to escape the depredations of the grizzly bear that marmots make their burrows on talus slopes.

In summer and fall, as the salmon runs start, the grizzlies congregate along streams where they gorge themselves upon the succulent fish and gain weight rapidly. During late summer and early fall, the various berries start to ripen and the bears consume them by the bushel.

In addition to the aforementioned foods, the grizzly also eats the eggs and young of ground-nesting birds, mice, snakes and frogs.

When the grizzly finds a large carrion, such as a moose or caribou carcass, it eats its fill and then rakes earth over the remnants. A mountain lion covers its kill with leaves, grass and brush, but the bear just uses earth. Sometimes the bear lies down on top of its cache or, more frequently, retires to the nearest heavy clump of thicket. The bear will attack any animal that attempts to partake of the guarded food, or is thought to be eyeing the food.

Owing to the work of Frank and John Craighead, who have spent a number of years studying grizzly bears in Yellowstone National Park, we now know more about the animals' behavior just prior to winter sleep. The Craigheads trapped the bears, weighed, measured and tagged them, then fitted each with a tiny transistor radio and released them. By the use of powerful receiving sets, they could locate the bears as they moved about in the wilderness. Each bear's radio gave off a distinctive sound to distinguish it from the others.

The Craigheads found that as cold weather approaches in late September or October, the bears separate and head for their denning areas. Most of them have already prepared their dens, but those that have not dig a den beneath the roots of a giant tree on the steep north side of a mountain and carry branches and leaves into the den for bedding. As the weather gets colder and short snowstorms occur, the bears become drowsy but do not enter their dens. This puzzled the researchers. What were the bears waiting for? The answer came when a blinding three-day storm swept the area. This was what

With its powerful claws the grizzly digs in the ground for roots and bulbs, rodents and insects. The bear's tracks are evident throughout this torn-up area.

the bears had been awaiting, a snow heavy enough to obliterate their tracks. On the same day, at almost the same time, all the bears retired for the winter.

Bears are not true hibernators; they can be aroused, and some even come out and walk around a bit in the middle of the winter.

Senses: The grizzly bear has a very keen sense of smell. It can locate carrion with the accuracy of a vulture, following the scent of a potential meal for miles. The bear's hearing is extremely good; it is alert and intelligent enough to pay attention to the slightest sound. Its eyesight can only be classed as between fair and poor.

Communication: A great deal has been written about the marks that grizzly bears claw on trees. Each grizzly is supposed to mark its individual range by reaching up and scratching its claw marks as high as it can on a tree. After that, every bear that passes through the area knows the size of the resident bear. The high-reaching marks of a big resident bear are supposed to strike terror into the hearts of lesser bears. What really happens is that bears rub and claw particular trees because they are handy and in time become "sign" trees, much like a dog's favorite fire hydrant. Also, because the bear's dense fur harbors fleas and mites, and because the winter coat during the shedding process itches, the bear may back up against a convenient tree to scratch itself. In the exuberance generated by a good back-scratching, the bear makes numerous marks on the tree and a "bear tree" is created.

Bears are usually quiet unless they are angered or

afraid. Sometimes, when facing an enemy, they experience both of these emotions at the same time. A bear will growl, whine, snort, bawl, roar and pop its teeth. Bear cubs cry piteously if they become separated from their mother.

Locomotion: Despite its huge size, the grizzly is capable of moving very fast. A big male travels extensively, and when it has its destination in mind it covers a lot of ground.

Bears walk, trot, move at an easy gallop or at an all-out bounding gallop. They have been known to travel at speeds of up to 35 miles per hour when charging or escaping from danger. They are fast enough to actually catch a horse if they can get close enough to start the charge.

Bears are strong swimmers, their broad feet making good paddles and their powerful leg muscles propelling them swiftly through the water.

Breeding: Not too much is known about the grizzly bear's breeding habits in the wild. The size of these bears precludes familiarity, and their temperament is touchy at all times. This temperament seems to develop a hairtrigger during the breeding season when the bears tolerate no one except a bear of the opposite sex.

Bears were thought to be monogamous because they pair up and spend considerable time together. However, the breeding season extends from the latter part of May through the month of June. Not all of the females would be in oestrous at the same time so that a male could spend a couple of weeks with one female and still have time to spend with several more before the season ends.

An observer who witnessed the mating of two grizzlies on the gravel bed of the Toklat River in Alaska reported that the bears rubbed against each other, wrestled a bit and then copulated in the open. As often occurs with dogs, the animals were unable to separate for more than twenty minutes. While the actual mating was going on, a smaller male remained in the vicinity but did not offer to challenge the big male's role.

Birth and Young: Because the grizzly bear is subject to delayed implantation, the gestation table varies from seven to eight months, the young being born in January while the female is in the winter den. The young are covered with short gray hair at birth and their eyes are tightly closed. They are 8 to 9 inches long and weigh 14 to 16 ounces each. Two, three or even four cubs may be born at one time. It had long been claimed that the mother bear is not even awake at the time of birth. But the mother bear is awake. Animal mothers lick and clean off their young as soon as they are born and do whatever they can to help them. Although the mother bear may doze back into dormancy after the cubs are born, she undoubtedly is awake when it happens.

The young grow rapidly and by the time the female leaves the den in late April, the cubs follow along behind her. The mother then sets about finding food for herself and, by example, teaches the cubs what they will accept as food as they grow older.

By June and July, the cubs have started to eat meat in the form of mice and ground squirrels that have been captured by the mother. The cubs continue to nurse until the fall, when they are usually weaned. The female takes the cubs into the winter den with her during their first winter.

Female grizzly bears in zoos will breed every year if the young are taken from them and reared by hand. In the wild, however, the cubs nurse for almost a year and the lactation prevents the female from coming into heat. Some grizzly females do not breed except every third year, which may be caused by the cubs nursing for a much longer period than was previously suspected.

Life Span: The life span based on the female grizzly's first breeding date is between fifteen and twenty years. The record for longevity, achieved by a grizzly bear in the Druid Hill Park Zoo in Baltimore, Maryland, is thirty-three years, eight months and seven days. Old Mose, a male grizzly killed in Colorado in 1904, was known to be 40 years old.

Sign: The trails that the bears create in following the same path year after year are the most conspicuous sign. These trails, made by generations of bears, become rutted highways. Sometimes the paths have two distinct ruts with grass growing between them exactly like miniature car ruts on old dirt roads. The bears have such a broad chest that a man has to walk straddle-legged in order to fit his feet in the ruts. In some instances, the bears place their feet exactly in the paw prints of their predecessors, forming a series of pock marks.

The tracks of a small grizzly bear can be distinguished from those of a large black bear by the position of the claw marks. The grizzly's claws are longer and make

Grizzly tracks reveal the bear's pigeon-toed walk and large (12-inch) hind-foot print. Like all bears, the grizzly leaves a smaller forefoot print, as the heel does not register clearly.

marks farther from the foot. The bear walks on the entire foot, and most of the time all five toes show in the tracks. The heel of the grizzly's forefoot seldom leaves an impression unless the ground is very muddy and soft. The largest toe on the forefoot is not a thumb, as would be expected, but the fifth finger.

Bear trees have already been described. Bears also strip the bark from pine, spruce and fir trees to lap up the sweet resin that collects when the tree "bleeds." In some areas the damage done to new forest growth may be quite extensive.

The scat of a bear is firm and segmented if the bear is feeding upon meat. Grizzly scat is over 2 inches in diameter and is composed of hair, bone or scales. When the bears are feeding upon grass or berries, the scat is a semisolid, shapeless mass.

Where grizzlies have been digging for roots or unearthing ground squirrels, their sign is very evident. No other animal in their area moves so much earth with so little effort.

Enemies: Grizzly bears have no natural enemies. No other animal is big enough or strong enough to challenge a grizzly. Every creature gives way before this bear except a well-armed man.

Human Relations: The huge grizzly bear struck terror into the hearts of all but the bravest of Indian warriors. To hunt one of these big bears armed with only a crude bow required the utmost courage. The brave that wore a necklace of grizzly bear claws was accorded the highest honors and deemed the bravest of the brave. The brave whose arrow failed to find the vital spot was gathered up and buried with ceremony. There were more ceremonies than there were bear-claw necklaces.

Henry Kelsey, of the Hudson's Bay Company, was the

first white man to see and record a grizzly bear. In 1690 Kelsey, starting from York Fort on Hudson Bay, penetrated the heartland of North America as far as the land of the Blackfeet Indians. On August 20, 1690, he wrote, "This plain affords nothing but short round sticky grass and Buffalo, and a great sort of Bear which is bigger than any White Bear and is neither white nor black but silver haired."

The mountain men had many encounters with "Old Ephraim," their nickname for the grizzly bear. Each encounter left them with a greater respect for the silver-haired giant. Kit Carson was treed by two grizzlies and spent hours sitting on his low perch beating off the bears' attack with a club. Joe Meek, Milton Siblette and Jim Bridger all had close calls with grizzlies. Hugh Glass, another mountain man, and his companions wounded a grizzly, which caught him and cruelly raked him with its claws, but Glass stabbed the bear twenty times and killed it. When Glass's companions returned, they assumed that Glass was dead because he was a mass of torn flesh and blood, with cuts so deep that the bones beneath were plainly visible. The men took his guns, knife and even most of his clothing. Glass not only refused to die, he eventually made his way back to a fort and fully recovered. His is one of the most remarkable stories of courage and endurance to come out of the early West.

Indian lore, and advice from men who have been attacked by grizzlies, agree that the best chance of survival for a man attacked by a grizzly or brown bear lies in playing dead and trying to remain face down to protect the vulnerable face and entrails. Bears do not eat people, and if they think a man is dead they leave the carcass.

As the western plains were being wiped clean of the bison, the grizzlies became cattle-killers. This sounded their death knell. The pressure from man became relentless, and today the grizzly is on the verge of extinction in the United States.

Trophy Records: The world's-record grizzly bear skull was picked up by James Shelton in Bella Coola Valley, British Columbia, in 1970. The skull scored 27 2/16 points and measured 7 6/16 inches in length and 9 12/16 inches in width.

The Number 2 skull was collected by Doug Edman from a bear he shot at Alexis Creek, British Columbia, in 1970. The skull scored 27 1/16 points and measured 17 1/16 inches in length and 10 inches in width.

The heaviest grizzly bear on record was one that lived for eighteen years in Union Park Zoo in Chicago. This bear weighed 1,153 pounds. The heaviest wild grizzly was one known as the Okanagan cattle-killer which weighed 1,100 pounds.

Table Fare: The grizzly bear is hunted as a trophy animal by white hunters today. In former days the white trappers and hunters, as well as the Indians, ate the meat.

The polar bear rivals the brown in size, but it has a different body conformation. It is more streamlined than the brown, with a slimmer head and neck. Its long, dense fur remains white throughout the year. (Bottom photo by Len Rue Jr.)

Polar Bear

Ursus maritimus

The polar bear is a land animal that has adapted itself to the water and ice of the polar regions. Living in this harsh and inhospitable clime, the great white bear has been a quarry to tax any hunter's courage and determination. Hunters have shot the bear from boats, but the more intrepid have gone out on the ice with Eskimos and dog teams to stalk the bear in its own domain. At present only native Eskimos, Indians, and Aleuts are allowed to hunt polar bears.

Studies are being conducted to develop more complete knowledge of the bear's life history and ecology, and to more accurately determine and monitor populations. The outcome of these studies could affect the future of hunting.

Description: There is great controversy today over which bear, the polar or the Alaskan brown, is the largest carnivore. According to records of skull sizes, the skull of the brown bear is the larger of the two. However, by actual weight, the polar bear is larger. Weighing such an enormous animal is a difficult chore. Several big polar bears have been killed at sea and hauled aboard with a winch and weighed. There are reports of these giant white bears weighing more than 2,200 pounds.

A large adult male stands about 4 feet high at the shoulder and is about 8 feet in length. An average weight is about 1,000 pounds. The females are smaller.

The polar bear has a rather pear-shaped body. Its neck is long and sinuous and the head small and tapering. This streamlined shape is a great boon to the bear when it is swimming. The legs are long and the feet are big. The soles of the feet are covered with short, stiff hairs that serve the dual purpose of protecting the feet from the cold and providing traction on slippery ice and snow. The claws are not long but they are sharp and are used for gripping the ice when the bear runs. The bear is plantigrade, walking on its entire foot, and has five toes on each foot.

The bear's long hair is yellowish-white. The only parts of a polar bear that are black are the eyes, the nose, the lips and the toenails. Some bears never encounter soil or dirt so that their coat remains light. It may turn yellowish from seal oil or occasionally be reddish from the blood of its latest kill. The white pelage matches the snow and provides a very efficient camouflage for the bear when it is stalking prey in the vast snowy world it inhabits.

The polar bear, being carnivorous, has 42 teeth: 12 incisors, 4 extra-long carnivores, 16 premolars and 10 molars.

Distribution: Polar bears live in arctic coastal regions in North America from the Seward Peninsula of Alaska east to Labrador, and south along the shores of Hudson Bay to James Bay.

Travel: Polar bears, particularly the males, travel almost constantly. They are the most nomadic of all the land carnivores because they do not have a home. They often travel inadvertently, for the big males spend most of their life on the ice fields, which move steadily with the ocean currents, transporting the bears with them. In the months of February, March and April, the ice has

Distribution of the polar bear.

turned so that the bears are carried over to the Alaskan coast, which is why polar bear hunting is concentrated during those months. During the summer months the ice has again turned and the same bears are now found along the northern shores of Siberia. Thus, although the bears travel almost constantly when they are awake, the ice field moves them along even while they are sleeping. They are apt to take exceptionally long journeys when a piece of the ice field breaks up and is carried off by currents outside of the normal pattern. Some bears have floated southward on icebergs down into the Gulf of St. Lawrence. When these bears finally reach shore by the breaking up of the icebergs and floes, they start their trek back north. One bear was killed on Lake St. John, Quebec, which is located a hundred miles from the Gulf up the Saguenay River. Frequently the bears will drift from Hudson Bay into James Bay. At other times the polar bear has been found inland over a hundred miles from any water. In the western portion of their North American range, the bears have gotten as far south as Kodiak Island.

Habits: The polar bear is one of the most solitary of animals because food shortages force it to live alone. A beached whale carcass may provide 100 tons of meat, and polar bears by the dozen have been seen feeding on a carcass for a long time. Under such circumstances the large adult bears get along together, although they undoubtedly establish a hierarchy of dominance. But it does show that the bears can tolerate each other, that they are solitary because of food requirements and shortages. Young bears have to stay clear of the adult males because the big bears will kill them.

Hair seals are the polar bear's main source of food. The Arctic Ocean teems with tiny organisms known as krill. Small fish which feed upon the krill provide food for the larger fish which in turn provide food for the seals. The seals grow fast and fat upon this rich fare. When not actively feeding, the seals spend much of their time dozing along the edge of ice floes. The seals sleep a bit, wake up and look around, perhaps wave a flipper about and then settle down again. Within a few minutes they are awake, rise up to look around for danger and again relax. Thus, the period between feedings, while their digestive system turns raw fish into basic body fuel, is leisurely.

When the bear is hunting for a seal it ambles along the edge of the ice until it spots one. The bear then dives into the water and swims silently towards the seal. In the water the bear is no match for a seal and so the bear uses all of its skill to approach the seal without alarming it. When the bear finally gets close enough to the edge of the ice it quickly pulls itself over the edge and smashes in the seal's head with its powerful paw.

Sometimes a seal will be lying beside its plunge hole in the middle of a huge unbroken expanse of ice. The bear must stalk such a seal with exceptional care because at the slightest sign of danger the seal has only to flop into the hole to be safe. In stalking a seal over ice, a bear has been reported to cover its black nose and mouth with one of its huge paws. Thus the seal is less apt to notice the all-white bear.

If a seal is using a plunge hole a moderate distance from the edge of the ice, the bear will dive beneath the floe and come up in the plunge hole itself. By making the slightest noise, the bear can cause the seal to panic and dive into the hole right into its waiting paws. The plunge hole always represents safety to a seal and, even though it can see the bear below it, the seal cannot change its flight pattern on such short notice.

Seals must have air at least every eight to ten minutes. When everything is frozen over with ice, the seal will maintain a breathing hole (aglos). This is bell-shaped with the widest part being down in the water. Periodically the seal returns to this hole, and its hot breath helps to keep the hole open. The hot breath rising in the frigid air creates a vapor column which is quickly noticed by knowledgeable hunters—both four-footed and two-footed. Both the bear and the Eskimo upon discovering such a hole quickly enlarge it. Then comes a period of waiting. Since the seal has several of these breathing holes, it may not come back to this particular hole for quite some time. When the seal does pop up, the bear tries to hook it out by using its stout claws. When a bear eats a hair seal it gorges itself upon the blubber but does not eat the lean, dark muscle meat. Arctic foxes follow the bears and consider such meat a bonanza.

Polar bears are sometimes able to catch fish, particularly salmon during the spawning runs. Seasonally, birds, eggs, lemmings, mice and even grass are eaten.

Hunger is the clock that determines the polar bear's time of activity. In the summer there is no time of darkness and in the winter there is practically no daylight, so the bear's actions are governed entirely by the dictates of its stomach.

Most polar bears den up for at least the severest part of the winter, but the adult males do so for less time than young bears and pregnant females.

The polar bear also likes to feed upon walrus, but a huge walrus with tusks 12 to 18 inches long is a formidable enemy. Polar bears have been found that have been stabbed to death by the walrus. In a few areas where musk ox can be found, the polar bear does not hesitate to try for one. The massed defensive circle that the musk oxen form is not proof against the attack of a bear, although it is effective against wolves.

Senses: The polar bear has an acute sense of smell and has been known to travel 20 miles tracking down the source of an appetizing odor. This bear is king of all it surveys. Anything it can locate is considered a source of food. Polar bears hunt and stalk human beings not because they are human beings, but because the human looks and smells like something edible. The bear's sight is also very good and any dark object, regardless of size, is almost sure to be investigated. Anything dark represents food, and the polar bear is usually hungry.

The sense of hearing is not too important to the polar bear. Its ears are small and situated below the crown of the head. Most of the prey of the polar bears do not make much noise. The main sound that the bear hears, besides the screaming of wheeling gulls and terns in the summer, is the crashing, grinding thunder of thousands of tons of ice being piled up or split asunder.

Communication: Polar bears are generally quiet but do growl, hiss, roar, and whine. The cubs whimper and whine when hungry or disturbed.

Locomotion: Polar bears have a fast, shuffling walk. All bears can walk very rapidly but the polar bear is the fastest. This is as it should be because the polar bear covers more area than does any other bear. The bear can also trot but is most likely to break into an ambling gallop when hard pressed. It can run at speeds of at least 25 to 30 miles per hour. At swimming it qualifies as an expert. There is no other large four-footed mammal that can swim as far or as fast as the polar bear. Polar bears have been found swimming hundreds of miles out in the open sea. In some of these instances they may have been swimming from unseen ice floes so that the actual distances could not be judged accurately. They have definitely been known to swim 40 to 60 miles without rest.

At times the polar bear swims with just the top of its head sticking out of the water and at other times a large portion of its broad back protrudes. When stalking seals the bear swims as low in the water as possible; when swimming long distances it swims high. How it varies the depth at which it swims is not known.

The best available record shows that a polar bear can swim at 6 miles per hour. But Jacques Cartier, in 1534, wrote about the polar bear as follows: "Our men found one there as great as any cow, and as white as any swan, who in their presence leapt into the sea. And upon Whitsunday following our voyage toward land, we met her by the way, swimming toward land as swiftly as we could sail." He does not record how fast his ship was sailing. A swimming speed of 6 miles per hour for a polar bear must be considered conservative.

Breeding: The breeding season usually occurs from March to May. Not too much is known about the breeding of polar bears. The scanty information available is generally based on observations of bears in captivity. These records are invaluable because, except in rare cases, the bears in captivity will react exactly as would the ones in the wild, particularly in respect to time and frequency of breeding and time of gestation. The young female is at least three or four years old before she breeds.

Birth and Young: The gestation period for the polar bear is about 240 days with most of the young being born in late December and January.

Some polar bears do not den up but pregnant females do. As winter approaches, the bred females seek out areas where pressure has forced the huge slabs of ice into an upended jungle of holes and crevasses. Under these giant-sized building blocks of ice the female finds a den. She retires into the cave and becomes lethargic. Often drifting snow covers the entrance, effectively sealing the cold out. Snug inside, the prospective mother awaits the coming event.

Most polar bears give birth to twins, although triplets and even quadruplets have been known. At birth a baby polar bear weighs between 1 pound, 4 ounces and 1 pound, 12 ounces, a size which produces no great strain on the 600 pound mother. The cubs are about 9 1/2 to 10 1/2 inches long and are covered with a dense coat of fine white hair. The cubs' eyes are sealed shut. The little ones virtually live in their mother's fur so they make little actual contact with the floor of the den.

The young grow fast on their mother's rich milk, which has a butterfat content of about 9 to 10 percent. At six weeks of age their eyes open and their hair has grown long enough to protect them against the cold. When they are four months old they weigh about 24 pounds. Even before this time the female will have opened up the den and started hunting for food, taking the little ones with her. The young stay with the mother for almost two years, until it is time for her to give birth again. By this time they are almost as large as she is and well on their way to maturity.

Life Span: Bears are long-lived mammals and accurate records have been kept on many of them. Polar bears are one of the top attractions at any zoo, so there is a wealth of data on their longevity. The Milwaukee Zoo had a female named Sultana that was captured as a cub in Greenland. This bear lived at the zoo for thirty-four years, eight months and one day. The greatest record is of a polar bear at a Chester, England, zoo that was in captivity for forty-one years, although it was not recorded how old the bear was when obtained. With so few enemies the polar bear in the wild has a good chance of reaching thirty years of age.

Sign: The tracks of the polar bear are about the only sign that anyone is likely to see and these will be recorded only in soft snow and not on the hard ice. The sight of little Arctic foxes on the ice floe is a good sign that polar bears are in the area. These little foxes are dependent on the polar bear during the winter months, for if the foxes are far out on the ice, they feed on the carcasses of seals killed by the bears. The dark scat of the polar bear would be visible against the white snow but such sign is soon drifted over.

Enemies: The only natural enemy of the polar bear is the *Orca*, or killer whale. These huge marine monsters are capable of tearing the largest polar bear to shreds as the bear swims from one floe to another. Bears are sometimes killed by walrus or musk oxen, but these deaths should be classified as accidents.

Human Relations: Currently, polar bears are being managed by the U.S. Fish and Wildlife Service under the aegis of the Marine Mammals Protection Act (MMPA).

Hunting is prohibited except by native Alaskan Eskimos, Indians, and Aleuts. Natives are not subject to seasons or harvest quotas unless the polar bears are "depleted." However, native harvest must be nonwasteful and for subsistence, or for the creation and selling of authentic native handicrafts and clothing. It is unlikely that hunting by nonnatives will be allowed unless the state of Alaska regains management authority. That, in turn, is unlikely without an amendment to the MMPA that would allow the state to regulate native subsistence harvests.

Trophy Records: The world's-record polar bear skull scores 29 15/16 points. The bear was killed by Shelly Longoria in 1963, off Kotzebue, Alaska. The skull is 18 8/16 inches long and 11 7/16 inches wide.

The Number 2 record is held by Louis Mussatto, who killed his bear off Kotzebue, Alaska, in 1965. The skull scored 29 1/16 points, being 18 2/16 inches long and 10 15/16 inches wide.

Table Fare: The polar bear is a prime source of food for the Eskimos. Many white men have also eaten and enjoyed polar bear meat. The liver cannot be eaten since it is so rich in vitamin A as to be poisonous. Some explorers have died from eating polar bear liver.

RACCOONS

Family Procyonidae

RACCOON

As night falls, a raccoon emerges from its den in a hollow
tree to hunt for food. During the day it sleeps curled up in a
ball or stretched out on its back.

Raccoon

Procyon lotor

Perhaps the most common notion about the raccoon is that it washes its food before eating. Actually the animal handles and plays with its food, but it does not necessarily wash it. This misconception led to giving the raccoon the species name *lotor*, which means "washer." It was thought that the animal had to dampen its food because it had insufficient salivary glands, but Dr. Leon F. Whitney, a veterinarian who has made an exhaustive study of raccoons, has proven that the raccoon's salivary glands are sufficient for its needs. Close observation of raccoons that have been kept as pets reveals that they rarely put all of their food in water.

The common name raccoon was probably derived from the Algonquin Indian name for the animal, *arakun*, meaning "he who scratches with his hands." That this name also relates to a manual activity is not surprising; the raccoon has extremely dexterous forepaws.

Description: Raccoons vary in color and size depending on habitat. The two most commonly recognized features are its black mask across the eyes and its ringed tail. The cacomixtle and the coati, which are related to raccoons, are the only other mammals in the United States that have such a tail. The raccoon is up to 36 inches long, stands 9 to 12 inches high at the shoulder and has a 10-inch tail. The average adult raccoon has a chunky body and usually weighs between 15 and 18 pounds, while really large fat males may exceed 25 pounds. Occasionally some giants are taken that weigh over 40 pounds. More large raccoons have been found in Orano, Maine, than in any other part of the country.

The thick underfur on most raccoons is a reddish brown. The guard hairs may be shades of gray, yellow, red or black and are tipped with white. The belly and the insides of the legs are pale yellowish or grayish. The black nose and mask contrast sharply with the white face and ears. The top sides of the feet are light while the soles are jet black.

The raccoon sports an impressive array of sharp teeth. The canines have almost perfect points. In addition to the 4 canines the raccoon has 12 incisors, 16 premolars and 8 molars. Its skull and dentition classifies the raccoon in the order of carnivores, but in habit it is omnivorous and will eat almost anything that it can capture or find.

Raccoons are plantigrade and walk upon the entire foot. They have five toes on each foot, all of which show plainly in their tracks. The forefoot toes are almost as long as the pad. The toes of the hind foot are as long as the front toes, but the pad is much longer.

Distribution: Raccoons are found in almost all of the United States and in extreme southern Canada, northward along the Alberta-Saskatchewan border, and south to the Mexican border.

Travel: Raccoons move no farther than necessary in order to meet the demands of their appetites. During the breeding season, however, males may wander as far as 4 or 5 miles. Female raccoons seldom travel more than a half mile from their den sites.

Distribution of the raccoon.

Habits: If there is one word that describes a raccoon it is adaptable. The animal is flourishing today over most of its range despite the ever-increasing encroachments of civilization. The raccoon has always been primarily a tree-denning animal, and it still prefers a tree den over all others. However, since most of our virgin timber has been cut, and there is a shortage of den sites, the raccoons now utilize woodchuck burrows, caves, mine shafts, deserted buildings, barns, garages and even rain sewers and occupied houses. Actually, raccoons that den underground have a better chance of survival. Those that retire underground when chased by dogs cannot be gotten by hunters, whereas they make easy targets in a tree.

The raccoon in the wild eats frogs, fish, mussels, snakes, eggs, baby birds, baby mice and rabbits, acorns, grapes, apples and berries. Crayfish are a real delicacy and are one of the main reasons that raccoons frequently feed along streams. Sweet corn draws raccoons like a magnet, and they can do great damage to a crop. Always eager to get at the next ear, the raccoon seldom finishes the ear it has started. Consequently, the animal usually destroys much more than it eats. Field corn, too, is an important item of diet. As the suburbs have gradually encroached on the raccoon's territory, it has learned to raid garbage cans, which provide a veritable banquet table. Scavenging along roadsides for animals killed by automobiles provides the raccoon with a good supply of meat. Carrion will be eaten when food is scarce. Along the coastline, the raccoon wreaks havoc among the muskrat dwellings. Some of the raccoons actually live in the plundered houses of muskrats that they have wiped out. Though raccoons rarely can catch adult muskrats, they will visit house after house and tear open the roof and feed upon the babies.

Being nocturnal, raccoons seldom venture from their dens until darkness. Young raccoons are prone to bestir themselves earlier than the adults. Dark, overcast, rainy days often prompt raccoons to feed early. In areas where they are unmolested, they may be seen at almost any time.

In nice weather during late spring, summer and early fall, the raccoons often spend the day stretched out sleeping on large tree limbs. To sleep in the sunshine, they will also clamber onto a squirrel's leaf nest, an abandoned hawk's or crow's nest or a tangle of grapevines.

If curiosity is a measure of intelligence, the raccoon is an intelligent animal. In fact, the raccoon's curiosity is often its undoing. When curiosity gets the better of caution, the raccoon gets into trouble where man is concerned. Anything bright and shiny is attractive to raccoons and this, coupled with their penchant for handling things, means that if the raccoon can get to the shiny object it will handle it. Trappers often take advantage of this trait either by fastening shiny objects on the pans of their traps or by suspending them directly over the traps.

Raccoons, as already noted, have the most nimble forepaws of any North American animal. They can easily open jars and doors, pry into containers and tear loose all but the most sturdy fasteners. As large as a raccoon is, it can squeeze through a hole with a diameter of only 3 1/2 to 4 inches.

Senses: As already noted, the raccoon's sense of touch is its most highly developed one. This is unusual since it is true of very few animals.

Hearing probably ranks second in importance. Although the raccoon's ears are short, the hearing nerves are well developed and the raccoon depends on them to warn of impending danger.

Its eyesight is good, and the raccoon is alert to the slightest movement. Raccoons have been observed watching small objects moving very far away. The eyes are a bright black and give the animal an alert appearance. At night the raccoon's eyes will reflect a green or a reddish color when shined with a strong light. This

An animal of wide tastes, the raccoon finds its food wherever it can. In populated areas it prys open garbage cans with
its dextrous forepaws and has a banquet. Otherwise, it is apt
to raid cornfields or kill rodents.

eyeshine is frequently a detriment because it allows hunters to locate them when they would otherwise be safely hidden in the top of a tall tree. Almost as if they knew better, many raccoons will not look down at a light when treed.

Since raccoons do not pursue their quarry or track it down, the sense of smell is evidently not of great importance. They do locate much of their food by scent, but they don't have to locate it at great distances. And most of their food does not move about but remains where it is until found.

Communication: Raccoons are capable of making a wide variety of sounds. They show deep contentment by a churring sound made far down in the chest. This sound is made by a mother raccoon to her young, by the young when they are well fed, and by adults when they are just talking to one another. The sound seems to be an amplification of a contented house cat's purring. Baby raccoons whimper or whine when they are hungry, tired or frightened. An angered adult will hiss, growl, give a rasping bark or literally scream. A little-known call of an adult raccoon sounds like a screech owl whistling.

Locomotion: The raccoon's most common gait is a shuffling walk. A large, fat raccoon waddles as it walks, the fur rippling in waves. When increased speed is needed, the raccoon trots with the fore and hind feet on opposite sides of the body being used in unison. At full speed, the raccoon bounds along. Like most of the tree climbing animals, the two forefeet come down together side by side and then the two hind feet come down together side by side ahead of the forefeet. Top speed for a raccoon running on the ground is about 15 miles per hour.

The stout, sharp claws of the raccoon allow it to climb with great agility. Baby raccoons begin to clamber about even before they can raise their bodies off the ground to walk. With a spiderlike motion, the baby raccoon drags itself about and can even climb if it has to.

A raccoon climbs up a tree headfirst, but it can climb down either headfirst or tailfirst with equal ease. If it is really in a hurry to get out of a tree, the raccoon doesn't hesitate to launch itself into the air and flop down. To break the fall, the raccoon spreads its legs and tail so that it soars down looking like a miniature bearskin rug. A drop of 35 to 40 feet doesn't seem to phase a raccoon in the least because it gathers itself up and bounds away.

Raccoons are strong swimmers as befits an animal that spends so much of its time in and around water. However, although they swim well, they seem very reluctant to unless it is actually necessary. Their fur is not waterproof, and they take on a lot of weight when soaked. They shake themselves violently to rid themselves of the water as soon as they reach land. A wet raccoon is a very bedraggled animal indeed.

Breeding: The breeding season takes place during January, February or March, depending on the section of the country. Most raccoons are bred in February. The males are polygamous, seeking several mates, while the females usually accept only the advances of a single, preferred male. The females stay in their winter dens while the males travel miles to find them, checking every spot that may contain a receptive female. In a single night during this season, one male was tracked for 8 miles.

A large number of young female raccoons will breed when they are nine to ten months old. Young males are capable of breeding as yearlings, but probably do not breed until they are approaching their second year. For this reason, a baby male raccoon makes a more tractable pet for a longer period of time than does a female.

When a male locates a receptive female, he moves in and may stay with her for a week or more. Copulation may take place many times over a four to five day period. When breeding is completed, the female returns to a lethargic sleep or dormancy to await the coming of spring. The male, meanwhile, continues on his way to seek other mates. If the female does not approve of a male that finds her, she will not accept him. Since the female is almost as large as the male, she is perfectly capable of driving him out if she is thus inclined.

Birth and Young: The raccoons have a gestation period of sixty-three or sixty-four days. The young weigh about 2 1/2 ounces and, although fully furred, their eyes are sealed shut. A litter contains from two to seven young, four being the most common. The female has the complete job of raising the young. The father is never in attendance. In fact, the female would drive the male away if he should show up because the males sometimes kill and eat the babies.

By the tenth day, the markings of the face mask begin to show, and the tail markings show at nineteen days. Although their eyes open at three weeks of age, the young raccoons have great difficulty in focusing on anything.

It doesn't really matter because they are still in the snug confines of a dark den.

The little raccoons sleep in a heap like little pigs. When the top one becomes cold it crawls under the others. When a bottom one feels squashed it climbs to the top of the heap.

By the time the little ones are six to seven weeks old, they weigh about 1 1/2 pounds and are trying to clamber out of the den. They get into as much trouble as kittens do. Most baby animals that climb find it easier to go up than to come down. When the young raccoons climb to the top of the tree they often become frightened and, holding on for dear life, they squall till their mother comes up to rescue them and carry them back to the safety of the den.

By three months of age, the little raccoons, now weighing about 2 pounds, are following the mother on her nightly forays for food. At first, the little ones are more anxious to eat the food than they are to find or to catch it. All young imitate their elders and before long the young start to secure food for themselves.

The young stay with the female until late fall, and the family usually splits up before it is time to retire for the winter. Occasionally, family groups remain together until spring.

Raccoons do not hibernate because they do not experience the drop in body temperature or the decline in body functions that accompany true hibernation. However, raccoons in cold weather will den up and stay there in a drowsy sleep until milder weather sets in. The turning point comes between 26 and 28 degrees. Above that temperature the raccoons move out to feed; below that, they stay holed up. Even though the weather moderates, the raccoons may not venture out of the den if there is deep snow on the ground.

Ordinarily a raccoon will consume between 1/2 and 1 pound of food per day. With the approach of cold weather they become ravenous and will consume up to 5 pounds food a day if they can get it, accumulating layers of fat on their bodies which sustain them over the bleak late winter and early spring months.

Life Span: The normal life span of a raccoon is between seven and ten years. One raccoon, raised in captivity, lived a record twenty-two years.

Raccoon tracks are often seen in the mud of stream banks, where the animal often prowls in search of fish and frogs. Large hind-foot track and smaller forefoot track suggest the raccoon's relation to the bear family.

Sign: The most commonly seen sign of the raccoon is its foot tracks in the mud along river and stream banks. These have already been described and are clearly shown in the accompanying photograph.

The scat, or droppings, is another prominent sign, especially when raccoons are feeding upon fruit and berries, which act as a laxative. The scat of a raccoon is often confused with that of a fox. The easiest way to tell them apart is to examine the diameter of the scat, for the raccoon is a much larger animal.

There is no need to climb a tree to see if a hollow is occupied by raccoons. A careful check of the bark will disclose many stray hairs if the den is being used.

Enemies: Besides man, the raccoon's worst enemy is the dog. The enmity between these two animals seems to be an inborn trait. While there are special breeds of dogs that excel at hunting raccoons, almost all dogs will attack a raccoon if the opportunity presents itself. Fights between the two are ferocious and bloody. The coonhounds usually win in the fights but only because they weigh anywhere from two to four times as much as raccoons. In most of these fights more than one dog participates, making it a very uneven match. In an equal pound for pound fight, a large boar 'coon probably could beat or hold its own against any dog. When a raccoon fights with a dog it will frequently lie on its back so that it can rake its opponent with the claws of all four feet while biting with its teeth. A dog that follows a raccoon into the water is committing suicide. The raccoon will climb on top of the dog's head and, grasping the head tightly in its paws, hold it beneath the surface, while the raccoon will be able to breathe from its elevated perch.

Bobcats could kill an adult raccoon but would probably pass up the opportunity. They would not hesitate, however, to kill a young raccoon. Great horned owls also take an occasional baby raccoon. Fishers, which are rare, are capable of killing raccoons.

Raccoons, like all furbearers, have an assortment of body lice. They are attacked by ticks and pestered by flies and mosquitoes. They are hosts to the internal parasites: roundworms, flatworms, and tapeworms. Raccoons are sometimes carriers of rabies and are particularly susceptible to encephalitis, a disease which affects the brain and eventually causes death. In its first stage, this disease causes the animal to act dopey and to lose all sense of fear. The eyes matter and run. In the course of the disease, the animal becomes weak in the hindquarters as paralysis sets in. Eventually the animal suffers muscular spasms and convulsions and then sinks into a coma which is terminated by death.

Although this disease may be transmitted to other animals, there is no record of it having been transmitted to man. However, man is susceptible to some types of encephalitis so caution is advised if you should discover a raccoon exhibiting these signs. To be safe, put the raccoon out of its misery and burn the carcass.

Human Relations: Hunting raccoons, long a popular sport, is increasing today mainly because the price of fur has skyrocketed. In recent decades raccoon pelts have sold in poor markets for as little as $1.50, but recent high demand has upped the price enormously. Raccoons are hunted primarily for their pelts, rather than their meat, and these pelts make the hunters willing to forsake their warm woodstoves to spend a cold night chasing raccoons.

The biggest thrill in raccoon hunting comes from following a good dog on a hot trail. Some dogs are silent but most hunters prefer an open trailer. The deep bellowing of a bugle-voiced hound coming out of the dark woodland on a frosty night is a thrilling sound. Old raccoons may employ a number of tricks to fool the dog, such as running on the top of fences, swimming down a brook, or climbing up a tree and leaping from the branches in an effort to break its scent trail.

When the raccoon is finally treed, it may be shot or someone may climb up the tree to shake the raccoon out so that the dog can kill it. In fact, Kentucky has a special season during which the only way a hunter can kill a raccoon is to shake it out.

During the 1920s, when everyone *had* to have a raccoon skin coat, raccoons became very scarce. In some areas they were completely wiped out. Laws giving them greater protection were passed and breeding stock was brought in from those states which still had good populations. Today the pendulum has swung too far. In many areas, raccoons have increased to such an extent that they are considered a nuisance animal.

Trophy Records: Although there are no actual trophy records kept on raccoons, some of the trophy weights have been recorded.

Albert Larson of Nelson, Wisconsin, shot a male raccoon on November 4, 1950, that weighed 62 pounds, 6 ounces and measured 55 inches from nose tip to tail tip.

Tolla Brown and Glen King of Sterling, Colorado, shot

a raccoon on November 11, 1960, that weighed 54 pounds on one scale and 56 on another.

Oliver J. Valley of Grant County, Wisconsin, shot a raccoon that weighed 54 pounds.

Table Fare: Raccoons have long been considered a delicacy. The most common way of cooking the animal is to roast it. To produce a really good meal, great care must be taken to remove all of the fat from the body before cooking.

WOLVES AND FOXES

Family Canidae

GRAY AND RED WOLVES
GRAY FOX
ARCTIC FOX
COYOTE

Gray wolf has a massive head and large forefeet. Its fur is long and thick, varying in color from almost white through various shades of gray and brown to black.

Gray and Red Wolves

Canis lupus
Canis niger

These wild members of the canine family have long been regarded as symbols of predatory evil, whereas their domesticated cousins have wagged their way into men's hearts. Our fear of wolves is old and deeply rooted, stemming from tales of European peasants pulled down in their fields, of terror-stricken travelers in open sleighs pursued by howling packs, and of men transformed into fanged beasts when the moon is full. Yet wolves and dogs interbreed, and the offspring have provided men with hearty sled-pullers and, after considerable outbreeding, with loyal hunting companions and pets.

Linnaeus gave the North American gray wolf the same name as the Eurasian wolf, *Canis lupus*, as they are both the same species. Bartram, in 1789, gave the name *niger*, which is Latin for black, to the red wolf because apparently he had seen the black phase, although most red wolves are reddish-brown. The gray wolf is also known as the lobo wolf or timber wolf, but it is also found on the plains and prairies, in the mountains and still commonly on the tundra.

Description: The wolf is a large, doglike animal weighing 100 pounds or more. A wolf's head closely resembles a German shepherd's, but the shepherd has comparatively short hair while the wolf's hair is long and often shaggy.

The color variation in wolves, even among litter mates, is broad and may include every shade between nearly pure white and coal black. The underparts and legs of a wolf are usually lighter than the rest of the body.

Adult male wolves may measure up to 6 feet in length from nose tip to tail tip and stand up to 38 inches high at the shoulder. Females are smaller and of a lighter build.

Wolves have five toes on the forefeet but only four are long enough to register in the tracks. The thumb toe is short, located on the inside of the foot, and is referred to as a dewclaw. There are only four toes on the hind foot.

The wolf has a total of 42 teeth: 12 incisors, 4 canines, 16 premolars and 10 molars. The premolars and molars are carnassial types used for shearing and cutting meat rather than for chewing. Carnivores all have a very powerful digestive system, and the teeth merely have to cut the pieces of meat small enough to be swallowed. The canines are long, curved and strong. Wolves have very powerful jaws, much more so than those of a dog. A wolf has been known to splinter the legbone of a horse by chewing on it.

Wolves have a special scent gland located at the base of the tail above the anus. This gland is used like a calling card and serves to identify its owner to other wolves.

Distribution: The gray wolf (*Canis lupus*) inhabits forests and tundra in most of Canada from the U.S. border north into Alaska and the Arctic, and is found in northern Minnesota, Wisconsin, and Michigan. It also persists in isolated pockets in northeastern Washington; north-western Wyoming; western, northern, and southern sections of Montana; and perhaps Idaho. The red wolf (*Canis niger*) has nearly been exterminated and is now believed

Distribution of the gray wolf (lines) and the red wolf (dots).

to exist only in eastern Texas and western Louisiana. Some red wolves have been transplanted to Bull's Island, South Carolina.

Travel: With the possible exception of the caribou, upon which it feeds, the wolf probably travels more constantly and farther than any other land-based animal. Wolves will often travel 15 to 20 miles a night in their hunting and sometimes that far and back again on a single night. Their hunting range may cover hundreds of square miles. On a big range, the wolves will travel thousands of miles per year as they make periodic circles of their territory. Wolves do not migrate except to shift range to follow game.

During the summer of 1966 a ranger friend of mine in McKinley National Park spent weeks searching for the dens of wolves that were feeding on caribou in the park. When he could not locate the dens, he came to the conclusion that they must be outside the park limits and that the wolves came in to hunt and then returned. This would have necessitated a round trip of anywhere from 40 to 60 miles.

Habits: The name "wolf" is often applied to a lecherous, two-legged predatory male. In reality, wolves establish a most exemplary partnership. Many wolves probably mate for life and both parents are devoted to each other and to their pups.

Wolves have developed one of the highest social orders of any mammals below the primate level. They adhere to strict laws that govern individual actions and status as well as the interactions of members of the group. A wolf that doesn't fit into the pattern or is not accepted by the rest is either driven away or killed.

Occasionally wolves travel in packs that may number as many as twenty to twenty-five animals. In a famous study by Allen and Mech of the wolves on Isle Royale, Michigan, seventeen wolves were recorded as regularly hunting together. Usually these packs are found only in the winter when food is scarce and larger prey must be killed. Such a pack consists of two or three family groups. A pack may stay together for quite some time or it may break up after a single hunt, depending on the whim of the wolves.

In many types of mammalian society, the leader is a female. In the wolves' world, the male is the leader. A family group frequently consists of more than just the parents and their offspring. Unmated adults fit into this group by acting the role of aunts and uncles. As such, they are accepted into the family and do their share by helping to care for and feed the current litter of pups.

Wolves hunt mainly at night and are most active in the late evening. After a kill has been made and the wolves are gorged, they lay up to sleep it off. The hour for retiring is governed by the length of time it takes them to fill their bellies. In Alaska, I saw wolves at all times of the day and night, but the peak period was between nine and eleven in the evening.

When large game such as deer, moose, caribou or mountain sheep are available, the wolves hunt them. To pull down one of these large animals the wolves usually try to hamstring it (cut the tendons in the hind legs). Sometimes the wolves cut the jugular vein by tearing out the throat of the animal, or disembowel it by tearing out a flap of flank skin.

In spring and summer the wolf feeds upon smaller creatures—grouse, ptarmigan, varying hares, marmots, ducks, geese, small birds, eggs and mice. One wolf was seen to have eaten twenty-two mice during one hunting session. The wolf's diet is almost entirely animal matter and depends upon the type available at any particular season. The wolf also eats salmon during the salmon run.

With the coming of cold weather many animals hibernate or shift to winter quarters, but the wolf seldom dens up in even the worst weather. Its dense fur gives it good protection against the cold, allowing the wolf to remain warm while curled up in the midst of a blizzard. Wrapping its bushy tail over its paws and nose, the wolf allows the drifting snow to cover it completely. The soft snow gives the animal added insulation against wind and extreme cold.

Senses: The wolf is one of the most intelligent of all wild creatures. It has the ability to learn from experience. It is being pushed back not because it lacks intelligence, but because it is smart enough to know that all hands are turned against it. Therefore, it strives to keep away from the constant danger that man represents.

The sense of smell is extremely well developed in the wolf. Not only is it used for hunting and for detecting danger, but it is also important in communication. Dogs mark fire hydrants and automobile wheels; wolves mark tufts of grass, rocks and scent posts. A sniff of urine will tell a wolf much about its depositor because the scent is as individualistic as a fingerprint. It tells of sex, emotions, food, time and much more about which we can only conjecture.

Hearing, too, is highly developed in the wolf. Its large, erect ears are constantly turned to catch the slightest sounds of danger or the approach of an unsuspecting prey animal. Members of the canine family can all hear sounds far above the register which the human ear can detect.

Humans and primates have the edge when it comes to sight. We can see color and all of its beauty while the rest of the mammals can only see monochromatic shades of gray. Wolves can detect movement better than most humans can because their lives depend upon it.

The sense of taste is well developed in wolves. In the

past, when poison by the ton was used against them, many wolves could not be decoyed into accepting the poisoned baits. Of course, we don't know if taste played the primary role or if the animal was warned by its nose of the impending danger.

Communication: The deep drawn-out howl of a wolf is a spine-tingling sound. Once heard, it will never be forgotten. In addition to its howl, the wolf whines, cries and growls but seldom barks.

Locomotion: Wolves walk, trot and lope. When they are around the den taking life easy they just walk. When going to and from their hunting grounds they trot at an easy ground-eating pace of 5 to 6 miles per hour. Wolves can keep this up almost indefinitely and have been known to travel 60 miles in a single night.

When they sight their prey and make their charge, wolves swing into a fast-paced lope, attaining speeds up to 40 miles per hour. Two wardens in Minnesota clocked a wolf running on ice at 35 to 40 miles per hour for a distance of 4 miles.

Topography usually influences a wolf's travel route. Most of the herbivores seek out the easiest grades and passageways and the wolves follow suit. In winter, wolves are frequently seen on the ice of lakes. The going is much easier there, where the ice has been swept clean by wind, than it would be in the deep snows of the forest.

Wolves do not hesitate to swim if it is required. They swim well as befits an animal that can run so well. Deer and moose frequently escape from wolves by taking to the water not because the wolves are unable to follow them but because they choose not to.

Breeding: The impending breeding season stirs the wolves into increased activity in February. They howl more frequently. In family groups, usually only the dominant male and his mate breed. Females do not breed until they are almost two years old, but males may breed at two years or not until their third year. Like dogs, wolves come into heat for a four-week period. However, the wolves have only this single period while unbred dogs will come into heat six months later. Dogs, because they are domesticated, may have their heat periods at any time of the year, but wolves must give birth in the spring if their pups are to survive.

Birth and Young: The gestation period for wolves is sixty-three or sixty-four days, the litters being born in early May. Prior to giving birth the female, with assistance from the male, digs a den site. This is usually done in the side of a riverbank or on a slope. Riverbanks are preferred because the soil there is easier to dig. The den may have one or more entrances and extend 30 feet into the earth.

The average wolf litter consists of six pups, since some litters have as few as four and some have as many as eight. There are several records of fourteen pups in one litter and one record of eighteen pups.

The pups at birth are covered with a soft, woolly, brown hair. The eyes are sealed shut. The eyes open in twelve to fifteen days and are blue at first, changing to brown or yellow in two months.

When the pups are newborn the female stays close to them. The male and any unmated wolves attached to the group do the hunting, bringing food to her.

As the pups grow larger and begin to crawl about, the mother has more freedom and hunts for herself close to the den site. If danger threatens, the female tries to counteract it or removes the pups to another den site previously selected for just such an emergency.

Weaning takes place at six to eight weeks of age. Up to this time, the parents gradually feed chunks of meat to the pups. This meat is easily chewed by the pups because it is usually partially digested. The adult wolves cannot carry a large prey back to the den so they eat their fill at the kill and then disgorge the contents of their stomachs for the puppies when they reach the den. From the third week on, the pups usually come out of the den for part of the day, increasing the time spent outside each day as they become older.

Most of the dens are abandoned when the pups are about three months old. The young follow the adults and are taught how to hunt. These lessons are very important as the young of all predators must actually be taught to kill if they are to survive.

The young wolves stay with the adults through the first winter. Some may go out on their own in the spring. The rest will stay until they are two years old and mature enough to raise families of their own, although some do remain with the pack as adults.

Life Span: Wolves have an expected life span of from ten to eighteen years of age. Wolves in captivity have lived to be seventeen years old.

Sign: The most common sign of wolves is their tracks. In the Canadian bush country the wolves follow the lake shore, leaving clear sets of tracks ·in the wet sand and mud. The forefeet tracks are larger than those of the hind feet because the wolf is built much heavier in the shoulders than in the hindquarters. The tracks of a large wolf measure 4 to 5 inches in length and 3 3/4 to 4 3/4 inches in width. On soft mud or snow the tracks naturally show up larger than on a firm surface.

The scat is elongated, usually over an inch in diameter, and consists of a matted mass of fur, hair, feathers and bits of bone, according to what the wolf has been eating. But some of these remnants are always present as the wolf seldom eats anything but animal matter. The remains of prey animals that have been killed by wolves also call out for attention. Most of these kills can be located by noting the concentration of ravens or magpies that quickly come in to clean up the scraps.

Enemies: Grizzly bears, wolverines, lynx and perhaps the golden eagle will kill wolf pups if they get the chance. An adult wolf is either too fast, too smart or too big to be taken by predators.

Wolves suffer occasionally from rabies, mange, tularemia, distemper, and encephalitis. Internal parasites such as tapeworms, roundworms and flukes have been found in wolves. Ticks, flies and mosquitoes, in their season, also make life miserable for wolves.

Human Relations: In times past the wolves of Europe have terrorized whole regions. One wolf from the south of France was known as The Beast of Gevandan. In about four years this wolf killed 123 people. Its depredations against people and livestock became so severe that Louis XV called out an entire army to hunt it down. It took 43,000 men and 2,800 dogs two months to finally kill this wolf.

In America the wolf never became such a menace. There are some authentic records of wolves killing people here, but they are from the early days before the wolf learned respect for guns. In recent years there have been no factual reports of wolves attacking a man.

The first settlers, however, took no chances and killed the wolves at every opportunity. Bounties have been paid on the wolf from the earliest days in an effort to wipe it

Fearsome good looks perhaps partially accounts for the wolf's frequent role in folklore. (Photo by Len Rue Jr.)

out. The wolf has been almost eradicated, not by the bounty hunters but by the encroachments of civilization. The wolf is intelligent enough to avoid man and keeps retreating before him.

When hunters finally succeeded in decimating the bison and opening up the plains to cattle, the wolf began to prey on cattle and horses. Some wolves became famous for the destruction they wreaked. Three Toes, a noted wolf of Harding County, South Dakota, is reputed to have killed more than $50,000 worth of livestock before being killed in 1925. In a single two-night killing spree this wolf killed 66 head of cattle. A Colorado wolf called Old Lefty is known to have killed 384 head of horses, cattle and sheep. The Custer wolf, also of South Dakota, is reputed to have killed more than $25,000 worth of livestock.

It is little wonder then that the wolf has been persecuted at every turn. Guns, traps, snares and dogs have been employed, but strychnine has been the most potent killer. The use of the poison virtually sterilized thousands of square miles of territory as predators of all descriptions, both large and small, fell before this scythe of death.

Today traps and snares account for the greatest toll. In this age of mechanization, wolves are frequently hunted on land by the use of snowmobiles. These machines allow the hunters to travel over packed snow and ice at speeds fast enough to overtake the wolves. Many wolves are also killed by hunters using airplanes. Wolf pelts bring hundreds of dollars apiece.

Trophy Records: A huge male wolf taken in 1939, in east-central Alaska, weighed 175 pounds.

Gray Fox

Urocyon cinereoargenteus

The gray fox possesses one unique ability that distinguishes it from all other members of the dog family: it can climb trees. Many a pack of baying hounds has lost the trail of a gray fox which found safety in a tree—at least temporarily. Once a hunter discovers the fox's arboreal hideout the animal is a sitting duck.

This fox's genus name, *Urocyon*, is a combination of the Greek words *oura* (tail) and *cyon* (dog), and was applied because its tail hairs are short and stiff like a dog's. *Cinereoargenteus*, the species name, means ashy-silvered—an apt description of the fox's color.

Description: This fox is a salt-and-pepper gray on the top of its head and back, but its flanks, as well as its ears and the area directly below, are rusty red, often causing the animal to be confused with the red fox. The throat, chest, belly and the inner sides of its legs are white. The tail is gray with a conspicuous black mane running down the top to the black tip. The pelage is stiff and bristly.

An adult gray fox weighs 8 to 11 pounds, stands about 15 inches high at the shoulder and measures up to 45 inches from nose tip to tail tip. The tail is 12 to 15 inches long. The face, with its upright ears and dark eyes, displays an intelligent alertness.

These members of the wild dog family have a musk gland on the top of their tail which is about 4 1/2 inches long and is important in communication and personal identification. Like other canines, they have 42 teeth: 12 incisors, 4 canines, 16 premolars and 10 molars.

Unlike its cousin the red fox, which prefers open terrain, the gray fox likes to live in areas where there is dense cover. Rather than try to outdistance an enemy, the gray dashes up a tree, as shown here, into brush or a rock den.

This fox has five toes on the front feet, but only four show in the tracks because the inside toe, or dewclaw, is higher on the foot. There are four toes on the hind feet.

Distribution: The gray fox (*Urocyon cinereoargenteus*) lives in brushy country and open forests all across southern United States, northward in the West to Washington and northern Colorado, and to southern Canada in central and eastern North America. A second species, *Urocyon littoralis*, inhabits some of the channel islands off the southern California coast.

Distribution of the gray fox.

Travel: Foxes do not migrate, although their home range is quite large for a small animal. The gray fox may range over 10 square miles, depending on its hunting success. In the breeding season unattached males may travel much greater distances. If one or more foxes are killed in an area, the void is soon filled by other foxes spilling over from an adjoining range.

Habits: The gray fox prefers to live in heavy cover because it doesn't like to run for extended periods of time. If disturbed, it will fade into dense cover and hope that whatever disturbed it will pass by. It will be found in swamplands, in areas of heavy second growth, in mesquite thickets and along rocky ridges.

If pursued by dogs this fox will run a short distance and attempt to elude its enemy by weaving in and out of every available tangle. If hard pressed it finds a den in the earth or rocks or climbs a tree. Its claws, although nonretractable, are short and curved. Ordinarily the fox climbs a sloping tree or one with many branches, scrambles from branch to branch and seeks refuge in the top. On many occasions the gray fox has been seen hiding in an old hawk's nest.

Gray foxes are most active at night, but occasionally they come out on dark, overcast days. Living in heavy cover, they are rarely a nuisance around farms because of their reluctance to expose themselves by raiding poultry yards. Gray foxes take a heavy toll of ruffed grouse and rabbits.

Foxes feed upon the prey animal or food most abundant and most easily obtained in their area. They eat birds, particularly ground-nesting species, and their eggs, rabbits and hares, snakes, insects, fish, rats and mice. They do not often kill squirrels and chipmunks, as these animals are more active during the day. In addition to these animal foods, the fox eats berries, fruits, melons and some grains. During the hunting season, foxes feed on game that has been crippled or killed. Some foxes regularly patrol roads, looking for wildlife killed by automobiles.

Foxes are active year-round. The gray fox, because it generally spends so much of its time in a den, tends to take refuge when the weather turns bitter and snow blankets the countryside. But within a few days, or as soon as the snow packs a bit, hunger forces the gray to resume its hunting.

Comparison of the forefoot of a gray (left) and that of a red fox. The pads on the gray's paw are visible and appear in its tracks. In winter the pads of the red's paw are covered with hair and seldom show in its tracks.

Senses: The sense of smell is important to all canines because they hunt by scent. When hunting, foxes course back and forth across a field, always moving upwind to pick up the scent of prey before the prey is aware of their presence. Foxes seldom track an animal, although they can if the trail is fresh enough.

A fox's hearing is also very keen—it can hear the squeak of a mouse several hundred feet away. The slightest squeak or rustling in the grass or among the leaves is enough to galvanize a fox into action. On hearing such sounds, the fox's body becomes as taut as a set trap. A fox catches most mice by pouncing with both feet on the grass beneath which the mouse is moving, killing it with a quick snap of its jaws. Frequently the fox, in a sense of play, tosses the mouse into the air several times before eating it.

Foxes have good eyesight and locate much of their prey by sight. A fox, like a dog, can recognize a man, even though he stands motionless, something many animals cannot do.

Communication: Foxes growl, bark, whine, squall and hiss. The rasping bark of the gray fox is of a lower pitch than that of the red fox. Gray foxes are heard barking mainly in the February breeding season and in the late summer when the pups are being taught to hunt.

Locomotion: The gray fox has shorter legs than its red cousin and runs at a slower pace. It prefers not to run if it can avoid it, and so it has never developed its running ability. The fox walks, trots and sometimes breaks into a bounding gallop with a rocking-horse motion. Its top speed is about 26 to 28 miles per hour.

Breeding: When breeding season arrives in February the adults seek mates. One can find the tracks of paired gray foxes in the snow during winter. In late February, as the female comes into her heat period, the foxes frequently are heard barking to one another. The male is reluctant to leave the female even to hunt the opposite side of a woodlot and keeps in touch with her by barking. Throughout the daytime, while the female sleeps in the den selected for a maternity ward, the male sleeps on the rocks above.

Birth and Young: The gestation period of the gray fox is about fifty-three days. The pups are usually born between late March and early May. Three to five pups compose the average litter.

When born, the pups weigh about 4 ounces each. Their skin is dark. They are almost hairless, and their eyes are sealed shut. The pups begin to crawl about when they are three or four days old, and their eyes open when they are about ten to twelve days old. At five weeks of age, the young start to come out of the den, and at three months are ready to follow the adults. The parents must teach the young to hunt. Gray foxes are clannish, and even when the young do leave the parents in the late fall, they still associate with each other on a limited basis.

Life Span: The gray fox has a life span of eight to ten years in the wild, although it has a potential of twelve to fourteen years in captivity.

Sign: The most commonly seen fox sign is scat. Foxes have the habit of voiding along the edge of a road or in similar conspicuous spots. Fox scat usually has rabbit hair or bird feathers in it. The scat of the gray fox is usually darker than that of the red fox because the former eats more berries, particularly wild cherries, where they are available. Fox scat is smaller in diameter than raccoon scat and each scat has a sharply tapered end.

Fox tracks show readily in snow and can be confused only with those of a cat, but a cat's claws are retractable and do not show in the track; the fox's claws always do. A fox track is larger than that of a cat, but the claw marks are the clinching sign. The gray fox has larger toe pads than does the red fox. Because a fox has such a narrow chest, it places its feet one in front of the other and the tracks are almost as neat as a dotted line. If the snow is deep, the tail sometimes leaves a drag mark.

At all times of the year, in either dirt or snow, signs of the fox's cached food can be found. The fox uses its feet to dig a hole in which it stores the food, but it always uses its nose to fill in the hole and bury the food. Because the gray fox dens up so frequently, it usually leaves a lot of its hair snagged on rocks and roots at the mouth of the den.

Enemies: The dog is the fox's most persistent foe. Most dogs naturally love to chase foxes even though most can't catch them. Coyotes, bobcats, and wolves will kill foxes. Of the winged predators, the golden eagle is the most deadly while the great horned owl will take a fox pup when it gets the opportunity.

Gray foxes are subject to attack by lice, fleas, mites and ticks. Both roundworms and tapeworms will be found in the intestinal tract. They are susceptible to encephalitis, a paralyzing brain sickness, and also may carry rabies.

Human Relations: Because a gray fox has such a coarse coat of hair, pelts, in the past, seldom brought more than a few-dollar bounty. Bounties were paid on fox with the hope of keeping the population down. But that failed and also led to fraudulent claims. Currently, prices of $50 per pelt make trapping a lucrative proposition.

The most popular method of hunting gray foxes today is by calling them with a predator call. They respond well to the distress squeal of a rabbit, and many hunters are finding great sport hunting them this way.

Many fox hunters run the gray fox with regular fox-hounds and then, when it retreats to its den, drive it out with terriers. These small dogs can enter any hole the gray

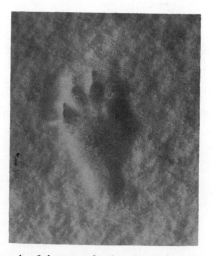

Forefoot track of the gray fox in snow, showing definite prints of the pads. Track is about 1 1/2 inches long.

fox can and worry and torment the fox until it finally flees from the safety of its den.

The gray fox does more damage to wild game but less to poultry than does the red fox.

Trophy Records: The heaviest gray fox on record weighed 19 pounds.

RED FOX

Vulpes vulpes

The sly Reynard of song and story, renowned for his cunning and intelligence, continues to outwit foxhounds and hunters with his clever stratagems. Although the sight of mounted, red-coated hunters galloping after hounds to the cry of "Tally-ho!" is becoming increasingly rare, the red fox is still a favorite quarry of many hunters who stalk the animal afoot with or without hounds.

The red fox of North America was once known as *Vulpes fulva* to distinguish it from *Vulpes vulpes*, the red fox of Europe, but recent studies have shown that the European and American foxes are the same species, for which *Vulpes vulpes* is the correct name. *Vulpes* is Latin for fox.

Description: The red fox is a slightly built animal closely resembling some of our medium-sized domesticated dogs. Deprived of its long, silken fur pelt, the fox discloses a lean, rangy body. It is very hard to convince most people that a fully grown red fox only weighs 8 to 12 pounds. An adult is 36 to 42 inches in length, of which 13 to 15 inches is tail length, and it stands about 16 inches high at the shoulder. It has yellow eyes with elliptical pupils and erect ears that are about 3 1/2 inches long. The tail is very bushy and nearly cylindrical. The scent gland on the upper portion of the tail is small, measuring about 1 inch in length by about a quarter inch in width.

The red fox, like all members of the Canidae family, has forty-two teeth: 12 incisors, 4 canines, 16 premolars and 10 molars. The canines, which are long, thin and curved backwards, are efficient tools for grasping.

A red fox has five toes on each front foot (four main toes and a dewclaw) and four toes on each hind foot. The toe pads are small, and during the winter the hair between the toes grows so long that the pads are almost obscured.

There is a great variation of color among red foxes. They range from a light blond-yellow to a deep russet-red, and these variations are not restricted to any locality. In New Jersey, for example, extensive trapping produced fox pelts which ran the gamut of the color range. The fox has a black nose pad, and the upper part of its face is rusty. Its cheeks and throat are white. Its ear tips are

A red fox will shed his heavy winter coat in spring for a much thinner summer coat. Fur usually ranges from yellow to rust color, with a white-tipped tail and throat. But there are also black, silver, and cross phases.

black on the outside. The back is darkest, with the flanks shading lighter toward the white belly. The feet are black. The tail is generally the same color as the back; the underside is lighter and terminates in a large white tip.

In the colder regions of its range the red fox has several other color variations. There are black foxes with all black hair and silver foxes with black hair tipped with white. The cross fox looks like a regular red fox but has a dark-brown band running down its back from the skull to the haunches with another band crossing the first at the shoulders. A fox bitch giving birth in the far North may produce all the color variations in one litter. A bastard fox is a red fox that has a dark bluish-gray coat. A Samson fox is one that has no guard hairs, just the woolly undercoat. This name comes from Samson's act of routing the Philistines by tying fire brands to foxes and setting the foxes loose in the grain fields. The Biblical foxes' guard hairs were singed off by the fire; hence, the name.

Distribution: The red fox is found from northern Canada and Alaska south to the Gulf of Mexico (except below the fall line of the southeastern states), and southward to the Mexican border in places in the west. It is absent from the high plains from central Alberta to Mexico.

Travel: Foxes do not migrate, but according to records some tagged individuals have traveled as much as 40 miles from their dens during the fall dispersal period. By such records it is easy to see that it would not take many years for the foxes to fill any void left by the death of foxes in any suitable habitat.

Distribution of the red fox.

Ordinarily a fox is content to restrict itself to about a mile-square range. However, changing seasons and the abundance or lack of food will then dictate how far the fox must travel in order to fill its stomach. For a fox to travel 5 miles or more in a night's hunting during the winter is not at all unusual. The red fox will prowl all night till it either catches sufficient food or is forced to retire because of daylight.

Habits: The red fox is an animal that prefers to live

at the edge of open country. Although it is also found in the deep virgin forests of Canada, open country provides it with most necessities of life. Even in virgin country the red fox will visit all of the swales and burned-over areas in its region. The opening up of the forests along the heavily wooded eastern seaboard by the pioneers did much to allow this fox to extend its range. The red fox is well equipped to cope with the more open areas because it is fleet of foot, has good endurance and is intelligent enough to outwit most of its enemies.

Except in the most bitterly cold weather the red fox refuses to den up. Instead it will curl up in the snow, on some elevated surface, wrap its bushy tail around its feet and nose and sleep through the storms. It often is completely buried by drifting snows. Often it is easy to discover red foxes sleeping in the middle of fields because they form the only patches of color in an entire expanse of white.

The intelligence of the red fox is famous, and it has earned respect for its learning capacity. In fox trapping, cleanliness is all important. The traps and all objects connected with the process must be sterilized as if they were to be used in an operating room, to remove all man scent. Still, some foxes will dig up traps and spring them without getting caught. Changing to different types of bait and scent doesn't help. The fox evidently becomes suspicious of the odor of fresh dirt anywhere near the trapper's tracks because it will even locate and dig out hidden blind-set traps.

One observer recounts watching a fox hunt from a nearby hill. The fox was about a field length ahead of the pack of baying hounds, and the hunters on their horses were about a field behind the dogs. The fox ran through a gateway in a high stone fence, then turned and ran along the fence for about 200 feet. Jumping to the top of the fence, the fox made its way, crawling, back to the gateway. When the last dog had run through the gate the fox jumped down the other side of the fence and ran back the way it had come. While the dogs milled about where the fox had jumped to the top of the fence, the fox ran right through the pack of horses and on across a busy highway. By the time the hunters stopped and turned the horses and called back the hounds, the fox had escaped.

The fox is an equivocal animal; it is respected by fox hunters and trappers, hated by poultry farmers, loved by orchardists and feared by small-game hunters. The whole question of the status of a predator revolves around whose interest is being served or hurt.

The meadow mouse is probably the number one food item of the red fox. Mice are easy to catch, plentiful and nutritious. The fox does not stalk mice. If it hears or smells a mouse, it runs over to the area where it thinks the mouse is located and stops a few yards away. The fox knows that the mouse is usually in a runway under the grass, and can't see the fox. When the fox locates the mouse, it pounces on it with its forefeet, pinning it down under the grass, and kills it with a quick bite. If the fox misses the mouse on the first pounce, it will rise up on its hind feet and pirouette with all the grace of a ballerina. From this vantage point it can perhaps spot the mouse's passage through the grass and also be in position to pounce again.

When hunting is good and the food plentiful, a fox

often kills more food than it can immediately consume. It then caches the surplus to be eaten at a later time. If the ground is bare the fox digs a small hole in the earth, drops the food in and covers it up by pushing the dirt back with its nose. If snow blankets the ground, the fox caches its surplus under a light covering of snow. Many times food cached under snow is discovered and eaten by other creatures, particularly crows. Foxes evidently enjoy a full pantry as much as humans do. While out hunting, they often stop at a cache, dig up the animal or bird and then rebury it in the same spot. Evidently they are seeking reassurance that their food is still there.

Rabbits also are high on the red fox's food list, although the gray fox probably takes more rabbits and ruffed grouse than the red fox does. The red fox favors quail and pheasants, but repeated research has proven that its predation does not appreciably affect the population of either species. Woodchucks, hares, squirrels, chipmunks and muskrats are also fox food.

Red foxes often kill prey that they do not eat unless food is extremely scarce. The foxes never pass up a chance to kill weasels, moles, shrews or snakes. These animals are often allowed to lie where they have been killed or are cached and not dug up again.

Red foxes, particularly the young, consume large number of beetles, grasshoppers and crickets. Foxes also eat all types of berries, fruits, melons and corn.

Poultry yards are a temptation to red foxes. Farmers who suffer heavy losses usually do not provide proper care for their chickens. If the area around the poultry yard is fenced in, or if the chickens are at least locked up each night, losses can be kept to a minimum. Many farmers actually invite the foxes into their areas by consistently discarding the carcasses of dead birds in adjoining fields. Foxes never pass up a free meal. Much of the food remains around a fox den are from game and poultry that the fox has scavenged and not killed for itself. In winter every deer carcass will be the hub of radiating fox trails.

A habit typical of dogs, wolves, coyotes and foxes is to rub odorous substances into the ruff at the back of the head and neck. The more rotten the material, the happier these animals are to roll in it, and as yet no one has concluded why they do this.

Senses: The sense of smell is most important to all members of the canid family. Hearing, too, is highly developed and is probably on an equal par with eyesight. As the canids hunt by sight much of the time, their eyes are placed in front of the head, giving them binocular vision, but they are all color blind.

Communication: Red foxes yap, bark, growl, hiss, whine and cry, according to the season and the situation. The female often squalls while the male more often barks.

Locomotion: Although the red fox is not the fastest of animals, it is built for speed and endurance. Often it seems to enjoy running in front of a pack of dogs as though it enjoyed the challenge. When trotting, it moves at a speed of about 6 miles per hour. Loping, it can easily outdistance a man, and it has been clocked running at 45 miles per hour.

The red fox can swim well if it has to but prefers not

to, for its large, bushy tail holds a lot of water and slows it down. When there is a heavy dew on the grass, the red fox will avoid the area to stay dry.

Breeding: Red foxes actively seek out mates and begin to pair up in January. From the last of December on, dual sets of fox tracks are visible in the snow. As the breeding season approaches, the female often emits a whining squall, which the males answer with short, yapping barks. The female comes into heat for about three weeks. In this period repeated matings take place with the single male of her choice.

Shortly thereafter the female selects a den site and begins to renovate it before the arrival of the kits. The den most frequently is an old woodchuck burrow in the middle of a large field, from where it has a clear view in all directions. Sidehills and river banks are also favored sites.

Birth and Young: The gestation period for the red fox is about fifty-three days, with most of the kits being born about the middle of March. As many as ten kits may be in a single litter but most litters fall between six and eight kits.

The kits are a dark-brown color at birth and weigh about 3 1/2 ounces. While their eyes are sealed shut the little ones are quite helpless. Their eyes begin to open when they are eight to nine days old. By the time they are five weeks old, they begin to poke their heads out of the den entrance for a quick look around. The first movement that alarms them sends them tumbling back to the safety of the darkness below.

These fox pups are old enough to venture outside the den, but they still are nursing. At about nine weeks of age they will be weaned, although they'll continue to rely on their parents for food throughout the summer.

Both parents care for the kits. At first the female stays with the kits and nurses them while the male hunts for food and feeds her. As the kits grow, the female resumes hunting nearby. When the kits have reached their eighth week, they play outside the den most of the day and the parents come in only to feed them. The parents bring in whole animals which the kits tear apart for themselves.

At three months of age the kits follow the parents to learn the art of hunting. By the time they are four months old they are ready to go out on their own, and when October arrives the young have scattered and taken up new hunting grounds.

Life Span: Red foxes in the wild may live up to ten years, while some in captivity have lived to be sixteen. One silver fox on record was eighteen years old when it died.

Sign: The most conspicuous sign of the red fox is the den itself. Even a person who has had no experience in reading tracks or sign cannot help noticing the large area of packed dirt around the mouth of the den. Since

A female red fox here delivers a ground squirrel to her two pups at their den entrance.

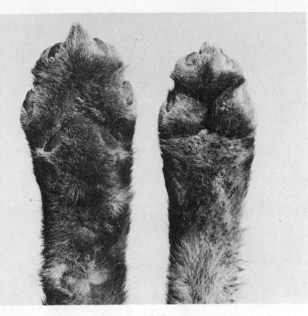

An adult fox's larger front paw (left) may measure 2 1/8 inches wide—the back paw (right), usually 1 3/4 inches wide.

most of these dens are centered in big fields, they are commonly seen and readily identified. The scat of the red fox is deposited along the side of every road it crosses. The scat is sharply tapered on each end and is lighter in color than that of the gray fox and smaller in diameter than that of the raccoon. It contains mostly hair and feathers, while skunk scat, closer in size, is composed primarily of beetle remains.

Enemies: Dogs are the principal enemies of the red

fox. In the wilds, wolves, coyotes and lynx all kill foxes. Golden eagles, and even great horned owls, kill the kits.

Foxes are plagued by fleas, mites, ticks and lice externally and by roundworms and tapeworms internally. They are subject to distemper, rabies and encephalitis.

Human Relations: Foxes are hunted in various fashions in different sections of the country. In the North hunting the fox usually involves shooting it, whereas in the South the hunters would just as soon shoot a hunter who shoots a fox. In the North some hunters still try to walk up on the fox and take it while it is bedded down, or a group of hunters may make a drive similar to that made for deer. The aristocracy of fox hunters follows a pack of hounds astride special horses trained to jump fences and barways. The object in this sport is the chase and not the death of the fox.

Millions of dollars have been paid in bounties in an effort to control the number of foxes and to increase the small game population, but bounties have always been expensive, ineffective, wasteful and subject to abuses. Most states have finally realized that the best way to eliminate fox problems is to employ state trappers who go out on complaints and remove the troublesome foxes. These programs are aimed at control of individuals and not eradication of the species.

Trophy Records: An exceptional weight of 16 3/4 pounds is on record for the red fox. On the average, the gray fox weighs more than the red fox. In a fight the gray fox usually wins. When gray foxes move into an area, the reds tend to move out.

A camouflage coat of white fur renders the Arctic fox almost invisible in winter. When spring arrives, and the snow partially melts, the fox grows a brownish coat to match its new background.

Arctic Fox

Alopex lagopus

Like its northland neighbor the varying hare, the Arctic fox has a dense covering of hair on the soles of its feet for better mobility in the deep snow of its habitat. Hence its species name, *lagopus*, a construct of the Greek words *lagos* (hare) and *pous* (foot). Linnaeus had originally called this fox *Vulpes lagopus*, but the name was changed to *Alopex* (Greek for fox) because the Arctic fox is not a true fox like the red fox, having a differently shaped skull and shorter, rounded ears.

Description: This is a small, short-legged, chunky-bodied fox with long, dense fur and a bushy tail. It weighs from 4 1/2 to 12 pounds, stands from 9 to 12 inches high at the shoulder and is about 36 inches in total length. Its short ears and compact body are adaptations to the sub-zero climate in which it lives. Arctic mammals have shorter extremities and greater body bulk than their southern relatives, for, according to Bergmann's and Allen's laws, heat is lost easily through extremities, and a larger animal has proportionately less surface area than a smaller one.

The Arctic fox has two distinct winter color phases, pure white and blue. The pure white phase is the more common. In the white phase only the eyes, the nose, the claws and a few hairs in the tail are black. In the blue phase the fox is a smoky blue or gray or gray-black color. Both phases turn to a brownish-gray in the summer, although the blue becomes slightly darker than the white phase. The blue phase is dominant only on the Aleutian Islands and along the lower coast of Alaska. Over the rest of its range the blue fox comprises 1 to 2 percent of the total population. The blue phase has a more luxuriant fur which is highly desired by the fur trade, a blue pelt usually bringing three to five times the value of a white pelt.

The Arctic fox has 42 teeth: 12 incisors, 4 canines, 16 premolars and 10 molars. The fourth premolar and the first molar are designated as carnassial or shearing teeth. The third molar in the lower jaw is rudimentary in all of the canids and will probably be completely lost in the continuing process of evolution.

The Arctic fox has five toes on the forefoot and four toes on the hind foot. Only four toes show in each track because the toe corresponding to our thumb on the forefoot is not used for support but has degenerated into a dewclaw. In the winter none of the toes show in the tracks because of the exceedingly dense covering of hair on the pads of the feet.

The Arctic fox has a very small scent gland on the upper part of its tail. This fox is very clean in both its habits and body, but it does have the odor that is usually associated with a red fox.

Distribution: The Arctic fox inhabits the tundra regions of the Arctic from the Alaskan Peninsula to Labrador, south to James Bay.

Travel: The Arctic fox probably travels more than any other North American canid, including the timber wolf. Sometimes it travels deliberately, sometimes it is forced to move, and sometimes it travels inadvertently on moving ice floes.

Distribution of the Arctic fox.

Tabulated records prove the Arctic fox to be on a four-year population cycle which coincides with the lemming cycle and, to a lesser degree, the voles'. The Arctic fox cycle follows the lemming cycle by one year, just as the lynx cycle follows the varying hare cycle by one year. Ernest Thompson Seton in his *Lives of Game Animals* was aware that the Arctic fox made periodic emigrations, but he did not correlate this with the fluctuations in the lemming population. Neither did he have the timetable figured out, but only because the records proving this relationship were not available to him.

The Arctic fox is a territorial animal in the summer,

controlling just enough land on which to secure enough food for its survival. When the lemmings and mice are plentiful the fox needs less territory. When the prey animals are scarce the individual fox needs a larger territory and pressure is put upon the younger, smaller or weaker foxes to move. The emigration of the Arctic fox coincides with that of the snowy owl. Both species move south by the hundreds because the lemmings and mice are in short supply.

The snowy owl often emigrates a thousand miles to the south while the Arctic fox moves up to several hundred miles. In both cases, very few individuals of these two species ever survive the emigration and return to their homeland in the Far North. Death in some form usually catches up with them in the new areas just as surely as it would have if they had remained in the Barrens. Man is usually the death-dealing factor to the emigrants while starvation would have been their lot on the original range.

Records kept by trading posts on the Ungava Peninsula starting from the year 1900 show the four-year cycle of the Arctic fox very plainly. The records are too lengthy to give more than a sampling.

Year	Foxes Taken	Year	Foxes Taken	Year	Foxes Taken
1900	1,494	1907	159	1915	29
1901	4,489	1908	632	1916	344
1902	1,879	1909	3,502	1917	1,607
1903	248	1910	547	1918	768
1904	3,237	1911	78	1919	296
1905	5,019	1912	131	1920	2,397
1906	1,189	1913	704	1921	9,797
		1914	429		

Another interesting fact is that in the year preceding the peak numbers, the foxes were usually taken by hunting and shooting because the lemmings and mice were so plentiful that the foxes were not interested in bait. The peak years saw the prey species disappearing and the foxes becoming very hungry. The hungry foxes often became concentrated in the proximity of man and, being hungry, were taken easily in baited traps, hence the largest catches in the year following the prey population peak.

During the summer the Arctic fox feeds along the coastal areas and stays pretty much in its own back yard. In the winter it moves out on the ice pan to follow the polar bear. Occasionally the pan breaks up or the fox becomes stranded on a moving floe or iceberg and is carried for hundreds of miles before it can reach land again.

Habits: The Arctic fox is neither nocturnal nor diurnal; none of the creatures of the Arctic are. In summer they are exposed to constant daylight and in winter to constant darkness; therefore, hunger is the drum to which they march.

Living in a land of such harsh extremities of either feast or famine, the Arctic fox has become provident. In the summer when the Arctic coasts and shorelines team with birdlife, the fox gorges itself upon the banquet spread before it. Even though glutted, it continues to hunt and begins to store away large amounts of surplus food. With its strong claws it digs through the shallow soil and places the prey on the permanent ice. This natural icebox keeps the food from becoming completely rotten, although it does allow it to ripen. Frequently the foxes fill crevasses or splits in the cliffs with food.

Olaus Murie, the famous naturalist, found one cache under a rock that contained sixty-five crested auklets, thirty-seven least auklets, one whiskered auklet, one parakeet auklet and one pigeon guillemot, and there were additional birds under the rock that he couldn't reach. On Bobrof Island he found 103 petrels, six tufted puffins, four least auklets and one pigeon guillemot in a single cache. On a Semisopochnoi Island around one den Murie discovered 107 least auklets, eighteen crested auklets, three tufted puffins, one horned puffin, one murre and seven fork-tailed petrels. This not only gives an idea of how industrious these foxes are in preparing for the winter, but it also gives a very good accounting of the foods they eat.

Most of these small sea birds nest either along the sides of the cliffs, in burrows in the ground or in rock splits and fissures. The foxes scramble over the cliff faces like veteran mountaineers and have no trouble digging the birds out of their burrows. In addition to eating the adult birds, the foxes wax fat on the eggs and on the flightless young. In fact, in some areas where the foxes have been introduced onto the offshore islands they are decimating the seabird populations. Grouse, ducks, geese and ptarmigan are also taken whenever possible.

Mice, voles and lemmings are not the only mammals on which the foxes feed. They also catch the Arctic hare and feed upon fur seal and sea lion pups. The placentas of these two marine animals are eagerly eaten by the foxes.

When the tide goes out, the foxes swarm along the

mud flats to feed upon whatever sea urchins, mollusks and crustaceans are stranded. Tiny amphipods, known as sea fleas, are a favored food because they can be secured even when the tide is in. These small crustaceans hide under the stranded kelp fronds that festoon northern beaches. Spawning and dead salmon are eaten in season. The fox also feeds upon blueberries, squawberries and huckleberries which grow in such profusion in the Arctic.

In the winter, when sea and shore birds have been driven to the south and snow has buried the countryside, the Arctic foxes forsake their territories and go out to live on the ice. Many of the sea foods that were washed up on the beaches in the summer are often washed up on the ice. Since some beaches never become ice-choked, dead or stranded marine mammals are occasionally washed ashore. A whale carcass will provide food for a multitude of foxes throughout the long winter. The Eskimos have been known to trap over 300 foxes in the vicinity of one whale carcass.

The Arctic fox is the easiest fox to trap because it has no fear of man. Most of these foxes never see a man, and those that do seldom live long enough to become educated. When a man walks through a fox's territory, the fox often follows after him, right at his heels, barking constantly. In times of hunger the foxes have been known to come up and chew on men asleep in their sleeping bags. On a few of the Aleutian Islands the foxes have broken into some of the burial caves and eaten the Aleut mummies. When starving, the foxes often resort to cannibalism.

In the winter many of the Arctic foxes become commensals, following closely behind the giant polar bear and feeding on scraps left from the bear's kill. When a bear kills a seal it seldom eats more than the blubber. Gorged, the bear wanders off to sleep until it is hungry again. If hunting is good the bear may not even attempt to return to its kill. As soon as the bear leaves the kill, the little Arctic foxes swarm upon the carcass to gorge themselves. One to 2 pounds of meat will fill them to the bursting point and is sufficient food for several days.

With its belly distended, the fox burrows into a mound of snow, curls into a ball, wraps its enormous tail around its feet and nose, and sleeps, oblivious to the weather. The deep snow provides excellent insulation against the frigid air temperatures.

Water for drinking is never a problem for an animal that lives most of its life on a limitless expanse of snow.

Senses: The Arctic fox's sense of smell is probably of paramount importance to it. In an area where so much of its food may be covered by drifting snow, scent would be the only way of finding it. These little foxes do not stay in the area of their cached food supplies but continue to hunt for food, coming back to the caches out of dire necessity. With its keen nose the fox is able to locate its hidden treasures, even though they be covered with ice and snow. Feeding upon the caches only in emergencies gives the fox enough strength to continue hunting.

The sense of hearing is also important to the fox, for while the fox is hunting food, some of the larger predators may be hunting it. Even when the Arctic fox is buried beneath the drifting snows, its keen ears keep it ap-

prised of everything that moves in the white wasteland.
Eyesight, although important, is not as significant as the other sense.

Communication: The Arctic fox possesses quite a repertoire of sounds. Its throaty, raspy bark is well known to anyone who frequents the tundra. The bark sounds as if someone were strangling a goose. It also whines, yelps and growls.

Locomotion: Because its legs are shorter, the Arctic fox is much slower than other foxes. Top speed is estimated at 20 to 25 miles per hour. This fox depends more upon camouflage than on speed, not only to outwit its enemies but also to secure food. In the summer, if threatened, it will seek refuge in a burrow or crevice or will run down the face of a cliff. Since many of these foxes live on islands where they head the predation chain, speed is not vital.

This fox can swim, and a number of people have recorded the fact. However, the fox inhabits a region where the water is so cold that it will swim only if forced to. Its fur, not being waterproof, allows cold water to seep right to the skin and its hair is so long that it takes on dangerous weight. The Arctic fox clambers over sea cliffs where one misstep would plunge it into the frothy current below. In traveling over the ice pan or from floe to floe, there is always a chance of the fox being dunked. It will avoid swimming if at all possible, but it can when it must.

Breeding: It is not known if the Arctic fox mates for

life or for just the one year. It is well known that the male is a very good and provident father. Even while mated, the foxes commonly travel apart most of the winter. February sees the pairs reuniting and the young foxes starting their conquests. The young fight noisy, bloody battles for the favors of the female they have selected. As soon as the foxes have paired up, most of them either select a den site or renovate an old one. Breeding usually takes place in March or early April.

Birth and Young: Fifty-two days after copulation the female has come full term and the kits are born. Arctic foxes have large litters, the average being six or seven, although there are instances of as many as 14 kits. At birth the kits, weighing about 2 ounces apiece, are dressed in short, fuzzy, brown hair. The little ones can wiggle about shortly and are able to walk by the time their eyes open nine to ten days later. As if they instinctively knew that their supply of sunshine was rationed, the kits come out of the den by the time they are a month old and spend many hours soaking up the warm, healthful rays of the sun. By July the kits are following their parents, learning to hunt and search for food and to fend for themselves.

By late September the family group splits up and the young are forcefully driven from the area. With the advent of winter, the competition for the diminishing food supply will be too great to allow the young to stay on the home range. The offspring do not have access to the stores of cached food which the parents have laid by. If the lemming population is high, the young have little trouble locating a range of their own. If food is scarce, the great fox emigration gets under way and it is the young foxes that go south, a trip from which few ever return.

Life Span: The life span of the Arctic fox is about fourteen years. There are good records on this species because so many of these animals have been raised commercially on the fox islands off the coast of Alaska. It is highly unlikely that the wild foxes can ever reach their maximum life expectancy.

Sign: Tracks are the most commonly found sign of the Arctic fox. Usually you don't need to look for sign; if there are any foxes in the area they will be looking for you and are probably right behind you barking. Over most of their range there are no other mammals of their size. The red fox and its variations don't inhabit the Arctic coastline. Wolf tracks would be much too large to confuse with the small fox tracks. Wolverines have a plantigrade foot which is much larger. In the snow no pad marks are visible, although the claw marks do show. The scat is usually full of feathers or mouse or lemming fur.

Enemies: Mass starvation is the Arctic fox's chief enemy. Mammal enemies include the great white bear that takes an occasional fox by surprise; the wolf, which is easily able to run down the fox; and the wolverine, which can catch only the kits. During the period of emigration, when the foxes get down into the lynx's bailiwick, some of them are undoubtedly killed by the big cats. The great grey owl and the snowy owl will take an unwary kit but would not be able to manage an adult.

Fleas, lice and mange mites can be a problem. The hordes of blood-sucking mosquitoes can make the beautiful summers a nightmare for the foxes. Internally, it has both roundworms and flatworms. No record of rabies has been discovered.

Human Relations:　The world first learned of the blue phase of Arctic fox in 1741 when Alaska's discoverer, Vitus Bering, was shipwrecked on the island which now bears his name. Many of Bering's men died of scurvy or were dying of it when the shipwreck occurred. When the crew got ashore the island was swarming with blue foxes. A constant watch had to be kept over the dead and dying men to prevent the foxes from eating them. Bering died on the island and was buried there. When Bering's men finally reached Kamchatka eight months later, they had with them some blue fox pelts which created a great interest. The Russians took large numbers of blue foxes during the time they owned Alaska. One ship, in 1754, had a cargo of 7,000 pelts.

The white-pelted Arctic fox is much more common and is found over a much greater range. As such, it is the staple of the fur trade of the Far North, with hundreds of thousands of pelts having been taken. In times of good fur prices, a white fox was worth 15 to 25 dollars while a good blue pelt was worth 50 to 75, although some blue pelts have brought as much as 150 dollars.

Trophy Records:　There are several references made to a record weight of 21 pounds for the Arctic fox, but no further details are available.

Table Fare: The Arctic fox is often eaten by northern hunters who live in such an inhospitable land that nothing of food value is wasted. Many Arctic explorers have also recorded eating this fox for exactly the same reason.

The coyote's face betrays the cunning which has enabled it to outwit its enemies, especially man, and extend its range throughout the country. (Photo by Len Rue Jr.)

Coyote

Canis latrans

The howl of the coyote was once heard only on the western plains, but this hardy and prolific animal has spread across North America despite man's periodic attempts to wipe it out. It is hunted mostly in the West, usually in winter when the pelt is prime and its tracks are visible in the snow.

Description: The coyote is a sharp-faced wild dog with erect ears and a shaggy coat, midway in size between a fox and a wolf. An adult male usually weighs between 25 and 30 pounds, is 44 to 54 inches long, of which 12 to 16 inches is tail length, and stands 23 to 26 inches high at the shoulder. The female is about one-fifth smaller in size and weight.

Like all members of the Canidae family, the coyote has five toes on the forefoot, although the thumb, which is high on the foot, is merely a dewclaw; and four toes on the hind foot. It has 42 teeth: 12 incisors, 4 exceptionally long canines, 16 premolars and 10 molars.

The nose pad of the coyote is black. The upper part of its face, the top of its head and the outside portion of its ears are a sandy reddish-gray interspersed with black hairs. The inside of the ears, around the mouth and the throat are white. The eyes are yellow, with round black pupils unlike the vertical pupil slits of the red fox.

The basic body color of the coyote can be any shade from a dull yellow to gray. The pelage, which is rough-textured, is dark on the back, becoming whiter on the belly. Numerous dark hairs on the back create wavy lines. The tail is the same color as the back but terminates in

151

a dark tip. The tail gland is about 2 inches long and about 1/4 inch wide.

Distribution: The coyote is found in western North America from the Arctic Ocean to Mexico, eastward to James Bay, southern Quebec, Vermont, and to the Mississippi River in the south. The coyote has also been reported in most of the other eastern states, where they have spread both naturally and from introductions.

Travel: The coyote is not a migrating animal, although it may emigrate considerable distances to estab-

Distribution of the coyote.

Forefoot of a coyote resembles that of a dog, but it is longer and narrower.

lish a new range, the young of each litter moving farther into virgin areas. In New York state, the first coyote was taken in 1912, although there were reports of "wolves" as early as 1906. Another coyote was taken in 1925 and another in 1935. From then on the coyotes increased rapidly.

A coyote travels only far enough to fill its stomach. When food is plentiful its home range is only 2 or 3 miles. During the winter the animal may extend its range until, in its search for food, it is patrolling over 100 square miles. Young coyotes, tagged and marked, have been recaptured 100 miles from their birthplace less than a year later.

Habits: The coyote is an intelligent animal which often cooperates not only with other coyotes but with other creatures as well. For example, coyotes frequently team up when hunting, and one of the pair will drive a jackrabbit into the waiting jaws of the other. A lone coyote could not catch an adult antelope yet two or three coyotes sometimes pursue one in relays. The coyotes force the antelope to run in a circle, and as one coyote tires another takes its place until the antelope drops from exhaustion. The coyote often travels with the badger, and when the latter discovers the burrow of a ground squirrel and starts to dig it out, the coyote takes a stand at another exit. If the squirrel panics and tries to escape from the badger, it often is killed by the coyote. The badger doesn't benefit from this arrangement, for the coyote doesn't share its catch, but when two coyotes work together both animals eat the prey. Coyotes have even been observed following elk as they paw the snow to get at the grass below, in the hope of catching a mouse exposed by the elk.

Another measure of an animal's intelligence is its fondness for play. Coyotes frequently have been seen engaging in play with each other as well as with other animals and birds.

The coyote is omnivorous and eats anything it can find. It feeds upon fruits, berries and melons, both wild and domesticated; but favors rabbits, mice, rats and prairie dogs. It eats livestock and poultry when the opportunity presents itself, and coyotes by the tens of thousands are indiscriminately killed annually by farmers and ranchers for these misdeeds. In reality, it is certain individual coyotes that feed heavily upon livestock; the majority prefer wild and natural foods. Many of the animals the coyote eats have been killed by cars or have died of starvation, disease or old age. Consequently the coyote's scat may show signs of predation when it has only been scavenging.

The coyote hunts mainly at night, but like many nocturnal carnivores it frequently ventures out in the daytime. The cool of evening, when the shadows are long and the day's heat is dissipated, is its period of greatest activity. How long the coyote remains active through the night depends only upon how long it takes to fill its stomach. Two to three pounds of food is sufficient to fill a coyote satisfactorily. A coyote knows the location of every spring or stream in its area and will seek them out when it needs water. The coyote seldom dens up except in the breeding season; it just seeks the shelter of a bush or rocky overhang, according to the weather.

In the winter the coyote grows a very dense coat of hair which gives it ample protection against the bitter cold and the biting winds of the open plains where they are most commonly found.

Senses: The sense of smell is the coyote's greatest asset in detecting food and danger. Most of its prey is captured by stalking. When the coyote catches the scent of a jackrabbit, a ground squirrel or a bird, it lowers its body to the ground and crawls forward, taking advantage of every available piece of cover. The coyote must get as close as possible to a hare or a rabbit before launching its attack. Although the coyote may be faster, the smaller animals can turn sharper and try to elude their pursuer in dense cover. Hearing is also a very important sense to the coyote because a noise often gives away its prey's location. Sight is probably on a par with hearing because the coyote lives mainly in open spaces. Mammals living in such an environment usually have good eyesight.

Communication: The yapping, barking howl of the coyote is characteristic of western North America. Almost anything will trigger a coyote into howling. Besides natural sounds, high-pitched sounds such as sirens or whistles will evoke a response. In fact, many people are unaware of the coyote's presence until it howls, and howl it does even within the city limits of Los Angeles. In areas where it is constantly hunted or trapped, the animal suppresses its natural inclination to howl. The coyote also growls, barks, whines and squalls.

Locomotion: In traveling about the coyote, like all canids, prefers to "dog trot." It can sustain this ground-eating gait hour after hour and can cover great distances with little effort. Its trotting speed is between 5 to 6 miles per hour. When it gallops it can average about 25 miles per hour.

There are several records of the coyote running at speeds of better than 35 miles per hour and one of 43 miles per hour. As the coyote prefers to inhabit heavy brushlands, it seldom needs such speed but seeks refuge in the dense cover.

Breeding: The coyote, like the wolf, will mate for life or at least remain with the same mate for several years. Coyotes are sexually mature enough to breed when they are one year old, although some males may not do so until their second year.

Coyotes often breed with domesticated dogs. The cross is referred to as a coy-dog. Usually the results of these crosses are larger, stronger and more intelligent than either of the parents. When coyotes first appeared in New York's Adirondack Mountains, they produced many of these coy-dogs whose size made them feared deer killers. In later years, as the coyotes increased, the coy-dogs steadily diminished because coyote females whelped their pups in early January. Since the male dogs weren't around to help the female feed her pups, as male coyotes do, the coy-dog pups usually starved.

Breeding season occurs in February in the north and somewhat earlier farther south, and those coyotes that are not already paired seek mates. If the pair has been mated previously and its den has not been disturbed, it utilizes the same one year after year. River banks and the sides of gorges are favored spots. The soil must be loose enough so it can readily be removed. As soon as breeding takes place, the female either remodels and cleans the old den or excavates a new one in readiness for her forthcoming litter.

Birth and Young: Coyotes have exceptionally large litters, sometimes as many as nineteen pups at one time. Ordinarily the average litter consists of about five to seven pups. The gestation period is about sixty-three days, the young being born in the latter part of April in the north.

At birth the pups are blind and helpless although covered with short, brown fur. The eyes open in nine to fourteen days, by which time the pups can crawl about fairly well. At three weeks of age the pups venture out of the den to play in the sunshine. By the time the pups are eight to nine weeks old, they have been weaned, the den is abandoned and they follow the parents on hunting trips. The family hunts together, and the pups are taught how to hunt for themselves. By the end of the summer, the pups go off on their own, although some coyote families stay together and hunt together until winter.

Life Span: In the wild, coyotes have been known to live about eight to ten years, although their life expectancy is about fifteen years. One individual in the National Zoological Park in Washington, D.C., lived to be 18 1/2 years old.

Sign: In the forests and brushlands of the coyote's habitat, one seldom finds tracks of this animal. But its tracks are evident in snow or in the dust or sand of desert areas.

Coyotes, like all members of the dog family, leave their sign on posts. Of course, the posts chosen by the coyote are not as conspicuous as the fire hydrants used by the domesticated dog. However, one experienced in coyote ways can usually detect these posts by nearby scratch marks, for wild dogs, like domesticated dogs, frequently scratch the earth with their feet after urinating or defecating.

Scat may often be seen. As wolves are very scarce in the United States, and if there are no dogs in the area, large doglike scat consisting mainly of hair is almost sure to be from a coyote.

Coyote dens can easily be recognized if they can be found, because no other animal in the United States except the wolf makes so large a den.

Enemies: In the North the wolf is still the coyote's enemy. In areas where they have not been wiped out, cougars kill coyotes. A lynx could kill a coyote, but everything would have to be in the lynx's favor before it would attempt it.

The domesticated dog is the coyote's worst enemy, although the average dog has no chance of even catching up to a coyote. Some racing dogs, such as the greyhound and whippet, are large enough and fast enough to kill a coyote, but generally they only kill the male; the female is a potential mate.

Lice, mites and ticks harass the coyote and feed upon its blood. Like the fox, it often suffers severely from mange. The mites that cause this skin disease sometimes infest an animal so heavily that it rubs off almost all its hair in an effort to relieve the itching. Of course, all canids have fleas, and the coyote is no exception. Tapeworms and roundworms usually are present in the coyote's digestive system, and it is subject to tularemia, distemper and rabies.

Human Relations: Few animals have aroused so much controversy as the coyote. Some people favor wiping them out while others believe in giving them complete protection. However, taking an impartial view, in most cases the coyote may be said to be beneficial. True, the coyote feeds primarily on rabbits or hares, but on the western ranges these animals seldom are considered prime game, and in many cases it is necessary to control their numbers. In fact, in many areas ranches are now giving the coyote complete protection because they do control the grass-eating rodents which deplete the food supply for their livestock. On the other hand, an occasional coyote will feed upon livestock, but it is better to trap or kill an individual offender than to condemn the entire species. Millions of dollars have been spent to control the coyote by paying bounties on coyotes killed, but this campaign, after years of payments, has fallen far short of achieving its purported goal. And the use of poison against the coyote is criminal because other species that come into contact with the poison bait are killed. Many Indian tribes will not kill a coyote because the animal is regarded as a lesser deity in their religion.

Today, most coyotes are killed by hunters imitating the distress cry of a rabbit or other rodent. Long-range sniping at the coyote is also done by hunters using varmint rifles. Coyotes are also hunted, though to a lesser extent, by coursing them with dogs or shooting them from airplanes or skimobiles. Coyote pelts are coarse and the pelts bring over $100 apiece.

Trophy Records: There are records of coyotes weighing as much as 75 pounds.

Table Fare: Coyotes were eaten by Indians but are seldom eaten by anyone today.

CATS

Family Felidae

JAGUAR
MOUNTAIN LION
LYNX
BOBCAT

The jaguar's spotted coat gives it excellent camouflage against the yellow light and shifting shadows of its habitat. Like the cougar, it has keen night vision. Here, in the glare of a flashbulb, its eyes shine like lamps.

JAGUAR

Felis onca

The jaguar is the only cat in the Western Hemisphere that may turn into an habitual man-eater. There are two reasons for this. One is the jaguar's large size and superior strength, for the larger the animal, the less fear it has of man. The second reason is that most jaguars live in areas where the natives do not possess firearms. Although the jaguar often has been killed with spears and bows and arrows, it takes an expert hunter to do it. With the opening of the jungle and the introduction of more guns, the big cat is gaining more respect for human beings.

Throughout Spanish-speaking Central and South America, the jaguar is called *el tigre*. The word jaguar is derived from a South American Indian word spelled either *jaguara* or *yaguara*, meaning, "an animal that kills its prey at a single bound."

Description: The jaguar is the largest cat found in the Western Hemisphere. Some specimens have weighed up to 300 pounds and have measured 9 feet in length and 30 inches high at the shoulder. The tail is about 30 inches long, much shorter than a mountain lion's. A compact, heavily muscled animal, the jaguar exudes power when it moves. Almost all mammals increase in size as they get further from the equator, but the opposite is true of the jaguar: the smallest specimens are found in the northern and southern portions of its range.

The jaguar is attractively garbed in a spotted coat. The basic color is yellow shading to tawny, overlaid with small spots on the head, large spots on the legs and combined bands of spots across the chest. The sides and back have large rosettes of black with a yellow middle and a black spot in the center. The rosettes are often rather square in shape. The feet are mainly whitish with small black spots. The head is rounded, the ears short and well rounded. The jaguar's skin is tighter than the mountain lion's, and there is no slackness in the belly area. As the jaguar is primarily a creature of the heavy forest areas, its spotted coat provides excellent camouflage against the sun-dappled shadows. All-black, or melanistic, jaguars are fairly common. Even on the black jaguars, rosettes can still be seen.

The jaguar has five toes on the front feet, four main toes and one dewclaw, and four toes on the hind feet. The claws are retractable.

The 30 teeth of the jaguar are classified as 12 incisors, 4 canines, 10 premolars and 4 molars. The molars and premolars are not flattened for the grinding of food but have sharpened points used for shearing off chunks of meat. None of the felines or the canines chew their food; they cut off pieces of meat that can be swallowed and their internal organs take care of the digestion.

The jaguar's vibrissae, or whiskers, are long, white and very conspicuous. The importance of these whiskers to the felines as a sensing organ is seldom fully appreciated by man. The cats can be sound asleep and yet aware of what is going on around them because of vibrations picked up by the whiskers. When the cats are agitated, the whiskers actively sweep back and forth. The whiskers also act as a guide for gauging the width of spaces. The cat's body can fit through anything that its whiskers can fit through without touching.

Distribution: In the early days of our country's settlement, the jaguar was found in Arizona, New Mexico, Texas, Louisiana and perhaps in California. Today it has become increasingly rare in the United States. Those that have been seen or killed in recent years are thought to be drifters coming up from Mexico.

Distribution of the jaguar.

Travel: Jaguars do not travel great distances. They inhabit tropical and subtropical areas which usually supply ample food of great variety, and no animal travels farther than it has to.

Habits: All cats swim well, but many of them avoid

water because they live in cold regions. The jaguar, which inhabits hot and torrid regions, frequents the water often. Sometimes it goes there to catch sluggish warm-water fish. At other times it will lie in wait for food near a waterhole. Still other times, it will loll about in the water just for relaxation and perhaps as a refuge from stinging insects.

A period of drought makes a hunting bonanza for the jaguars because it concentrates the fish in a few deep pools. These pools also become a magnet for all of the local game species, such as capybaras, agoutis and tapirs. Shunning highlands and open lands, the jaguar prefers dense thickets and underbrush. It probably takes more of its prey by ambushing it than it does by stalking. Lying draped on a tree limb, its spotted coat renders it practically invisible. The jaguar often hunts monkeys and coatis by getting ahead of the troop and allowing the prey to work their way towards where it lies in wait.

Much of the jaguar's hunting is done in the trees, where it tries to catch sleeping monkeys, flocks of parrots and turkeys.

In some sections of its range, peccaries form a large part of the jaguar's diet. Many tales are told about a herd of peccaries turning on a jaguar and driving the cat away. However, the jaguar hunts the peccaries consistently and gives no indication of being afraid of them.

Frequently jaguars will prowl sea beaches in search of huge sea turtles that come out of the ocean to lay their eggs on land. The jaguar not only eats the turtles, it also seeks out their nests and eats the leathery-shelled eggs.

Jaguars will sometimes follow a man more out of curiosity than maliciousness. This is a common habit of the larger, more intelligent cats.

Jaguars seldom have a den, usually curling up to sleep in some dense tangle or blowdown. As they inhabit the warm regions, a den is not needed for protection from cold.

Senses: Animals that stalk or ambush their prey are dependent mainly upon eyesight; thus it is safe to say that the jaguar's eyesight is its most highly developed sense. Hearing ability and the sense of smell are probably about equal in importance to the big cat, though it is difficult to evaluate the senses of some wild mammals. In some, one sense is so outstanding that it is obvious, but just as humans differ in the acuteness of a particular sense, so do other mammals.

Communication: There is some difference of opinion as to whether or not the jaguar can roar like a lion. All agree that the most commonly heard sound made by a jaguar is a series of deep, raspy, coughing grunts—*uh, uh, uh, uh.* The natives sometimes call in jaguars by blowing into earthen jugs to produce a sound similar to the animal's cough.

Jaguars growl, hiss and spit when angered or treed. If a man in the wild is close enough to hear a jaguar spit, he is too close; the jaguar does not remain peacefully treed for long but jumps on the nearest enemy, be it dog or man.

Locomotion: The jaguar is the most arboreal of the larger cats. It climbs easily and well and is only slowed down when it becomes heavy with old age. At those times of the year when its jungle home turns into a huge flooded land, the jaguar takes to the trees and may actually travel long distances hunting for food without descending.

Water holds no fears for the jaguar, and it swims well and fast, frequently crossing very wide rivers. On the ground, jaguars walk, trot, bound and leap. Their speed is great for a short, dashing attack, but the jaguar cannot keep up a fast pace as it quickly tires.

Breeding: The jaguar is unique among the American cats because it is the only one that is monogamous. Jaguars pair up and the male actually helps to raise the young. The chances of the young surviving is much greater when they are cared for by both parents. It is not known for sure if the jaguars mate for life or if only for a single year. Breeding takes place in January or February in the northern part of the jaguar's range but is not confined to any season in the equatorial regions.

Birth: The gestation period for the jaguar averages about 100 days, with the young usually being born in May. Two kittens at a time is the usual litter size, although occasionally there may be three or even four. The young are born fully furred and have brownish coats instead of yellow ones. They are spotted from the start, the rosettes developing later. A baby jaguar measures about 16 inches long and weighs about 2 pounds at birth. The eyes of the kittens are sealed at first but open within seven to thirteen days. By the time six weeks have passed, the young jaguars are about the size of house cats and weigh between 4 to 5 pounds.

The young are taken with the mother to hunt when they have grown large enough to follow her. Their growth is comparatively slow, but they will weigh about 100 pounds or more at one year of age. Even so, the female keeps the young with her for another year of protection and instruction.

Upon the female's breeding in the second year, the young jaguars are then forced on their own. The young female cubs are at this time old enough and large enough to breed and take on the duties of raising their own young.

Life Span: Under ordinary conditions, the life span of a jaguar is considered to be about fifteen to eighteen years. However, in captivity several of them have lived far beyond their allotted time. A jaguar in the Zoological Gardens in Hamburg, Germany, and another in Cologne, each lived to be twenty years old. The longevity record goes to a jaguar that lived to be twenty-two years, four months and twenty-five days old in Rotterdam's zoo.

Sign: In heavy brush country, tracks and sign of the jaguar are hard to locate. Most of the tracks will be found in the mud along rivers and pool edges. The jaguar's tracks may be confused with the smaller track of the cougar. The front-foot tracks are 4 to 4 3/4 inches long and just about equal in width. The hind-foot tracks are slightly smaller. The claw marks do not show.

A jaguar will eat about 7 pounds of meat at a time. If the prey animal is large the jaguar, after eating its fill, will cover the carcass with sticks and vegetation.

The scat of the jaguar is composed mainly of hair and

bone fragment. No other animal except the mountain lion voids scat of the same size and composition.

Enemies: The jaguar in its native habitat does not have any natural enemies. The mountain lion is credited with being able to defeat a jaguar in a fight, but undoubtedly the two big cats avoid each other as much as possible. A young jaguar may be eaten by a large caiman, but adult jaguars regularly hunt full-grown caimans as food. A giant anaconda could kill a young jaguar, but here again adult jaguars eat these giant snakes. The jaguars are not immune to the poison of venomous snakes and some undoubtedly are killed in this manner.

Human Relations: In some areas the jaguar will forsake its dense jungle and move into the pampas highgrass country where it is attracted to livestock. Cattle are a favored food—and readily obtainable. Ranchers often band together and employ full-time hunters to get rid of the cats.

One such hunter, Sasha Siemel of Brazil, hunts jaguars with a spear. Siemel is not only an expert on jaguars, he is an exceptionally brave man. Using a spear about 10 feet long, Siemel tracks down the jaguar with a pack of dogs. The jaguar attacks when it is finally cornered or treed. Advancing until the jaguar leaps, Siemel plants one end of the spear against the ground and allows the jaguar to impale itself upon the sharp point.

Jaguar fur was in demand, and many of the animals were killed to supply the fur market. Seton claimed that as many as 4,000 jaguar pelts a year came out of Central and South America, with Buenos Aires exporting 2,000 skins annually. Today, international treaty forbids the sale of skins of spotted cats.

Trophy Records: Sasha Siemel, who has killed over 250 jaguars, claims that he has killed several that weighed over 350 pounds.

The world's-record jaguar skull was taken by C. J. McElroy in 1965 in Mexico. The skull scored a record 18 7/16 points. It displaced the skull taken by Jack Funk in 1924 in Cibecue, Arizona, which had held the title for over forty years. Funk's jaguar skull scored 18 5/16 points and was 10 14/16 inches long and 7 7/16 inches wide.

The third place is held by Fred Ott, who shot his jaguar in 1926 in Nogales, Arizona. His skull scored 18 3/16 points and measured 10 15/16 inches long and 7 4/16 inches wide.

Mountain Lion

Felis concolor

The mountain lion is known by more names than any other North American mammal. There are forty-two common names in English alone, and the Spanish and local Indian names boosts the number to well over a hundred. Among the most common English names are puma, cougar, painter, catamount, panther and American lion. The animal's Latin name, *Felis* (cat) *concolor* (of one color), was given to it by Linnaeus in 1771.

Mountain lions are hunted in the West, but they are difficult to find. Hunters generally use specially trained dogs to trail the big cat and follow on horseback until the terrain gets too rough; then they dismount and continue the hunt on foot.

Description: The mountain lion is our largest unspotted cat and is second in size only to the jaguar. A full-grown adult is 7 to 9 1/2 feet long, stands 26 to 31 inches at the shoulder and weighs 150 to 175 pounds, although some are much heavier. The female is about two-thirds the size of the male. Its basic body color is uniform but can shade between a russet to almost a gray and may vary seasonally. The fur is about 1 inch in length and uniform over the body. The face is usually marked with dark in the eyes and upper muzzle, and the front of the mouth, lower flanks and belly are an off-white. Melanistic, or all-black, mountain lions are sometimes seen, particularly in Florida. The eyes are usually yellow, the pupils being vertical slits in bright sunlight. The ears are pronounced but well rounded. The whiskers are white and conspicuous. The tail is 26 to 36 inches long

A nocturnal hunter, the mountain lion has eyes that are especially adapted for seeing in dim light, and exceptionally sensitive whiskers that help it to feel its way in dark places. (Photo by Irene Vandermolen)

and has a dark tip. The head is rounded and appears small for the body size of the cat.

The mountain lion has five toes on the forefoot, although the thumb is known as a dewclaw and now serves no useful purpose. There are only four toes on the hind foot. The claws, which are retractable, do not show in the tracks. The mountain lion's 30 teeth are classified as 12 incisors, 4 canines, 10 premolars and 4 molars.

A conspicuous feature of the mountain lion is the slack appearance of the belly, as if it had far too much skin. The belly flap sways from side to side when the mountain lion runs, yet it does not give the cat a flabby appearance.

Distribution: The mountain lion was once the most widely distributed land mammal in the Western Hemisphere. When the white man came to North America, the cat ranged from the Peace River in Canada to Patagonia in South America and from coast to coast. Today it is found mainly in western North America from Alaska to Mexico. Yet, after being nearly extinct in the East, it is making a spotty comeback there.

Travel: The mountain lion does not migrate but as it is a large carnivore with a large appetite for meat, each individual has a large natural range. It frequently travels as much as 10 to 20 miles in a twenty-four hour period

Distribution of the mountain lion.

Forefoot (left) and hind foot of a mountain lion. The furtive, silent cat stalks its prey on soft foot pads. Retractile claws are concealed in their sheaths, but they can be instantly extended when the animal needs them.

and may have an individual range 60 to 70 miles across. Its daily travels, however, are governed by the time of the year and the availability of food. The males, unfettered by young, travel more than the females. The males travel a more or less circular route and thus do not deplete the game in one section; while the females when they have young usually will return to the den site each morning.

Habits: Like most of our native cats, the mountain lion is solitary by nature, only the female being accompanied by her young. Despite its size, this cat is as wary and furtive as the smaller lynx and bobcat. All of our cats do everything within their power to escape detection by man. Their actions may not be deliberate as much as they are instinctive.

Deer, particularly mule deer, are the mountain lion's staff of life. An adult lion will, if possible, kill one to three deer per week. Many times it is not successful in its hunting and must fall back on smaller prey, but deer are its preferred food. Deer are not easy for the mountain lion to catch and to kill. Having been subjected through many generations to hunting pressure by the mountain lion, the deer have become the alert, quick and graceful creatures they are today. The evolution of any prey species is determined to a large extent by its predators. The prey species owes its general health to the predators, for the predators weed out the old or crippled animals, and by killing sick specimens check the disease from further spreading among the prey.

A mountain lion does most of its hunting by stalking, although common lore talks of them pouncing from a rocky ledge. Hunting upwind or quartering against it, the mountain lion is able to detect its prey. When a deer is scented, the lion immediately tries to locate it. Once the lion spots the deer it begins the stalk. Slinking along on its belly, the big cat takes advantage of every bit of concealing vegetation. If the cover is sparse the cat moves so cautiously that it seems almost graven from stone. Fully aware of its own limitations and of the deer's capabilities, the lion knows that it should be within at least 20 to 30 feet before it can launch its attack. If the deer is alarmed beyond this distance the lion's chance of success is greatly reduced.

Closer and closer the cat sneaks; sometimes its only movement is the lashing back and forth of its tail tip. At times it seems almost as if the tail tip moved independently of the cat's wishes—and perhaps it does. The lashing of the tail usually denotes fear, anger or anxiety and is a nervous reaction. Each foot is placed carefully on the ground so as not to make a sound

At last the mountain lion is ready. It is either close enough for the final rush or as close as it dare go without scaring the prey. It draws its feet under its body, extends its claws to get a good grip on the soil and tenses its muscles. Like an uncoiling spring, the lion launches its attack.

Frequently the very momentum of the big cat is strong enough to knock the deer off its feet. The cat takes no chances. Its one set of claws tears into the deer's back while the canine teeth grip down through the top of the neck. The other paw pulls the deer's head sharply backward. The deer may die of a broken neck or a severed spinal column but its death is usually accomplished in a matter of seconds. If the kill is made in the open, the lion will drag its prey to nearby cover.

Many times an obstruction diverts the mountain lion's attack. Or it may not be in the most advantageous position when it starts its attack. The deer may move too fast, for some deer are missed; others are killed. When the attack fails, the mountain lion knows it is futile to attempt to run the deer down so it abandons the chase. It may seek out another deer and start all over again, or it may content itself with some smaller, more easily obtainable game that it chances upon.

When the kill is made, the mountain lion usually tears open the belly first. As an appetizer it may lap up whatever blood is in the body cavity. It pulls out the intestines and may eat them. The liver, heart and lungs are favored choice pieces. It may shear off several of the ribs and clean off the meat. All cats' tongues have a prickly surface that allows them to easily remove the finest meat shreds from the bones. Seven or 8 pounds of meat will satisfy the mountain lion.

The mountain lion possesses enormous strength. One cat had killed a "good sized Indian pony," dragged it across a field and over a high fence. Robert Anderson saw a lioness carry an eight-month-old calf 3 miles up a mountain where no man could climb. M. Musgrave reports a mountain lion dragged a horse weighing 800 to 900 pounds about 30 feet. In moving a heavy carcass, the mountain lion rolls it over on its back so that all four legs stick up in the air, then, biting into the chest or brisket, drags it along.

When the carcass is in a secluded spot, and after feeding, the lion then covers it up with sticks and vegetation and returns to the carcass until the meat starts to spoil.

Occasionally the lion goes on a killing spree and may kill two or three deer in a night, far in excess of its needs. This sometimes occurs when the big cat gets in the habit of killing livestock. Although most mountain lions never raid domestic stock, the few that do bring the wrath of all ranchers down upon every lion.

An adult mountain lion has little trouble killing the biggest horse or steer. Colts are favored food and, in some western regions, ranchers have found it impossible to raise horses. The cat also kills sheep, goats and pigs. Chickens and turkeys do nicely for a meal.

There are many instances of a mountain lion going on a killing orgy. Records exist of a single lion killing twenty to fifty sheep in a single night. The greatest destruction was 192 sheep killed by one lion in one night. Homer Esplin reports seventeen mountain lions in the vicinity of Zion National Park killing 1,250 sheep in a two-month period. Bear in mind that these are outstanding, isolated instances and are not typical of mountain-lion behavior.

After it has eaten, the lion seeks out some sort of shelter. It will get in the shade if the weather is hot or out of the wind if the weather is cold and prefers the higher, more inaccessible spots.

Senses: The mountain lion's eyesight is its most important sense, as befits an animal that secures most of its prey by stalking. The felines, like the dog family, see everything as shades of gray and are not able to distinguish color. They have trouble seeing stationary objects but are extremely alert to the slightest movement. Scent, too, is very important to the mountain lion, although this sense is not as highly developed as it is in the wolf or coyote. None of the cats have the scenting ability of the canids and none of them track down their prey. The internal parts of the mountain lion's ears are well developed, denoting that its hearing is keen.

Communication: Several local names, such as "mountain screamer," pay tribute to this lion's vocal abilities. In reality, the mountain lion is comparatively quiet except during the breeding season. People in some sections of the country have heard the mountain lion scream on many occasions while others have never heard it. Jim De Long of Utah and M. E. Musgrave of Arizona, two of the most famous mountain-lion hunters of all time, report that they have never heard one scream. Although De Long has killed hundreds of mountain lions, he has only seen one that was not being run by his dogs.

Almost everyone agrees that the scream of a mountain lion sounds exactly like the scream of a woman in mortal terror. N. Hollister described it well: "The cry is a long drawn out, shrill trill, weird and startling. It commences low on the scale, gradually ascends, increasing in volume and then lowers at the end." It is claimed that this piercing cry can be heard for at least a mile under favorable conditions.

Young mountain lions make a mewing sound which the mother often answers with a grunt. Mountain lions yowl, growl, hiss, purr and on occasion make a high-pitched, whistling, trilling sound like a bird call.

Locomotion: Mountain lions walk, stalk, trot, gallop, bound and leap. They are amazingly fast for 200 to 300 yards and then become quickly winded. In attacking their prey they usually stalk to less than 100 feet before they launch their whirlwind charge. A mountain lion was seen to run down a deer that had a head start in less than 600 feet. As deer can run about 35 miles per hour in open country, the lion is capable of good speed.

When pursued by dogs, the mountain lion can usually leave the pack behind for a short distance, but eventually the dogs overtake it. However, since the lion is seldom far from heavy cover or broken rock country, that head start is usually enough to allow it to reach the type of terrain that is most favorable to it.

The lion's leaping ability is well known, and it can often leap from one ledge to another, which means that the dogs cannot follow directly but must search for a round-about route. One mountain lion was seen to make a 30-foot leap and clear an 8-foot brush obstruction in the middle of the jump.

Many hunters have recorded seeing a mountain lion jump to a tree limb 12 to 15 feet above the ground. The lion climbs well but often leaps into a tree when pursued. In climbing down from a tree, the lion usually comes down head-first. Musgrave reports seeing a mountain lion leap 50 feet out of a tree, land on its feet and bound away unhurt.

All members of the cat family are famous for their agility and all will twist and turn in the air so that they land on their feet. When dropping from a height, many will spread their legs so that air pressure against their flattened belly surface will help to slow them down. Frequently, when the mountain lion jumps it holds its tail erect over its body. The African leopard is famous for its leaping ability yet people who are familiar with both animals claim that the mountain lion is the better jumper of the two.

Although mountain lions prefer to stay away from water, they do swim well and several have been known to swim across lakes or rivers more than a mile wide.

Breeding: Mountain lions have no set breeding season. Females heavy with young have been killed during every month of the year, but most of the births are in spring. Records show that although there are slightly more males killed, the ratio is very close to 50-50.

The males are polygamous, breeding with any available female. Several males often fight bloody and sometimes fatal battles over a female, and after the victor is sated, the female will mate with the others. A male will stay with the female for about two weeks. During this time she will be in heat for about nine days and will accept the male in copulation many times.

Birth: The gestation period of the mountain lion varies from ninety-one to ninety-six days. Two to four kittens may be born at one time with two or three being most common. Six is the largest number of kittens ever recorded for one birth.

At birth the kittens sport a spotted coat and a ringed tail, weigh from 8 to 16 ounces and their eyes are sealed. The eyes open between ten to fourteen days. When they are a month old, the young start to feed upon bits of meat provided by the mother. This starts a weaning period, although the young may continue to nurse until they are four to six months old.

The den site is usually a cave, a fissure in the rocks or under a wide, rocky overhang. It will be in as inaccessible an area as possible to prevent detection.

At two months of age the kittens weigh about 10 pounds and are able to follow the mother. She will go out, make a kill and, if it is too large to carry back to the den, will return and lead the kittens to the kill. At six months of age the young weigh about 30 to 45 pounds, and they will try to hunt on their own. Often by this age the mountain-lion family will have abandoned the nursery den. The female will take the young on extended hunting trips, and they will stay at each kill until it is consumed.

The young are as playful, and the mother as tolerant,

as domestic cats. The young stalk each other and their mother. As the young grow older and stronger, such play is channeled into actual hunting.

The female keeps the young ones with her for at least a year and sometimes longer. At this age the young are almost full grown, although the young females do not breed until they are two or three years old.

Life Span: One mountain lion in the Space Zoological Park lived for twenty-two years, although the average in zoos is only about seven or eight years. The National Zoological Park in Washington, D.C., acquired one mountain lion when it was six months old which lived seventeen years and eight months. Some mountain lions in the wild that left distinctive tracks because of toe deformities have reached eighteen years of age.

Sign: The scratch signs of the mountain lion are the most commonly seen and most easily recognized marks made by these big cats. With its front feet it scratches a shallow depression 4 to 6 inches deep in the soil, then moves forward and urinates on the loosened mound of dirt. When finished, the cat continues in the direction it was traveling. This habit of continuing in the same direction enables hunters to trail the cat. When other mountain lions come across these scrapes, they add a bit more dirt and a bit more urine. Eventually a small mound develops. Marks on trees where the mountain lion has sharpened its claws are also found.

Occasionally the mountain lion's scat will be found on a hard dirt floor, on a rocky shelf or in a cave. The scat is usually brown in color and almost all deer hair with bits of bone mixed in. The mountain lion may evacuate almost a quart of material at a time.

The mountain lion's tracks are large, about 4 inches long and about 4 1/2 inches wide for the front foot. The hind foot is slightly smaller. Only the four toes show, and in winter long hair grows between the pads so that distinct toe marks seldom are seen. No claw marks are visible. When walking at normal speed, the cat leaves tracks that are about 21 to 23 inches apart.

Enemies: Although man is the mountain lion's greatest enemy, the lion considers man's dog the gravest threat. A lion has no trouble killing a dog, yet even a small terrier can soon tree the big cat because the dog is associated with man and trouble. In the wilds the mountain lion really doesn't have a natural enemy except the male of the species.

Where the range of the mountain lion and the jaguar coincide, battles between the two have been reported. Although the jaguar is heavier and stronger, the mountain lion is faster, and the consensus is that the mountain lion usually emerges the victor.

Mountain lions are relatively free from ectoparasites because they do not continuously use the same den. When the female does use a den, she does not attempt to haul in vegetation for bedding. This denies some kinds of parasites a place to live and helps to eliminate them. Fleas and several species of wood ticks have been found on mountain lions. Internally there are both round and tapeworms. Rabies is the only serious disease that affects the mountain lion, and it is not common.

This mountain lion pauses over a whitetail it killed.

Human Relations: Man's war against the mountain lion has been unrelenting from the earliest days of the first settlements. Bounties, government predator-control men and unlimited hunting combined to push the mountain lion toward extinction. Fortunately this big cat has now been reclassified as a sporting animal, gaining the protection of closed seasons, greatly contributing to the lion's comeback.

There are now 15,000 to 20,000 mountain lions in the United States and Canada. The population in Florida has dropped under 50. Yet there have been recent confirmed sightings in many eastern states formerly barren of lions.

In some instances past persecution has had disastrous results. The most spectacular case of mismanagement occurred on the Kaibab plateau in northern Arizona. This area was set aside as a refuge to protect about 4,000 mule deer. Starting in 1907, government hunters removed 674 mountain lions, eleven wolves, 120 bobcats and 3,000 coyotes in ten years. No hunting by man was permitted and all of the natural predators were eliminated, and by 1917 the deer had increased to 17,000. By 1925 the herd had increased to at least 100,000. The deer destroyed their range. Sickness and starvation set in and 60,000 deer died in the next two winters. What had once been a healthy herd and a healthy range was reduced to a shambles. Predators had kept both in good condition. Today this point is gradually being acknowledged and the mountain lion is finally being given some credit for the job he does in helping to maintain a balance of nature.

How dangerous is a mountain lion to man? Hunters have sometimes found that one of the big cats has been following them—not stalking them, but following them out of curiosity. Will a mountain lion attack a man? Under all but the most unusual circumstances, the answer is NO. However, there have been a number of authenticated instances where mountain lions have attacked, killed and eaten human beings. Some of these attacks were provoked; others were for unknown reasons. Some of the attacks were undoubtedly because the mountain lion mistook the person to be a prey animal. Others were out-and-out attacks. Claude Barnes' book lists twenty-four people who have been killed by mountain lions.

Trophy Records: The heaviest mountain lion on record weighed 276 pounds after being eviscerated. This would have put the live weight at more than 300 pounds.

Most of the length records are probably of skins of pelted animals, and some measure up to 11 feet. Some mountain lions measured before being skinned were over 9 1/2 feet long.

Garth Roberts holds the world's-record mountain-lion skull with a total of 16 points. It was a male killed in Garfield County, Utah, in 1964. The skull is 9 4/16 inches long and 6 12/16 inches wide.

Second place is held by Walter Heller, who killed a large male in Clear Water River, Alberta, in 1973. It rates 15 15/16 points. The skull is 9 1/16 inches long and 6 14/16 wide.

Table Fare: The meat of the mountain lion resembles veal or lamb in flavor, taste and texture but it is a bit dry, having little fat.

Lynx

Lynx lynx

The lynx has a decided advantage over most other animals in its northern habitat. It is equipped with huge, padded feet which enable it to speed across deep snow while its prey becomes helplessly bogged down. Still, the lynx has its problems. The varying hare, its favorite food, also has snowshoe feet which help it in eluding its chief predator. The lynx is also a deer-killer, and in French Canada is known as *loup-cervier* (wolf which attacks deer), although it is a cat.

Description: Besides its foot pads, the most conspicuous feature of the lynx is its long ear tufts. These black tufts of hair stand stiffly erect and are about 2 inches long.

The basic color of the lynx is a soft smoky gray, with many individuals having an intermixed shading of tan. The lynx has an exceptionally large face ruff, and the sharp tips almost meet beneath its chin. The ruff is white with black barring. There is also white around the lynx's muzzle, under its eyes and inside its ears. The insides of the legs are also whitish.

The lynx has a compact body with disproportionately long legs. An adult lynx is between 36 to 40 inches long, stands about 19 to 24 inches high at the shoulders and weighs from 22 to 30 pounds. The lynx's feet are so furry that it is difficult to see the toe pads. There are five toes on the forefeet and four toes on the hind feet. There is some black spotting or barring on the body. The lynx's tail is short, about 4 inches long, bushier than a bobcat's, light in color and has a solid-black tip.

Padding through the Canadian woods on its large furred feet, the lynx is always on the lookout for its favorite quarry, the varying hare. The abundance of varying hares in the area directly affects the lynx population.

Like the bobcat, the lynx has only 28 teeth: 12 incisors, 4 canines, 8 premolars and 4 molars. The premolars and molars have sharp, shearing edges.

The lynx molts only once a year, shedding its long winter hair in the late spring. Its new coat is dark in color, the hair becoming lighter as the prime guard hairs push through in the fall. These hairs are silky and about 3 1/2 inches in length.

Distribution: The lynx is an inhabitant of the northland. In the time of our country's early exploration and settlement, the lynx was found as far south as Virginia and Indiana in the East, and southern Colorado in the West. At that time the forests were undisturbed, the varying hare was commonly found in those regions, the winters were colder.

Today the lynx is found from the Arctic Ocean in Alaska east to Newfoundland, in forested regions, south to northern United States in New England, Minnesota, Wisconsin, and Michigan, and in the Rockies of Utah and

Distribution of the lynx.

Wyoming. In the Pacific Northwest it is found as far south as central Washington and Oregon and in western Montana. The other subspecies, *Lynx subsolanus*, is found only on the island of Newfoundland.

Travel: The lynx's welfare, habitat and behavior are dependent upon its main source of food, the varying hare. When the hares are plentiful the lynx will content itself with a very small area. The evergreen swamps of the taiga country are the favored habitat of the lynx because the varying hares also inhabit them, but also because the dense cover gives the lynx the protection that it prefers. With an abundant supply of hares, the lynx may restrict itself to about a square mile of territory. When hares are scarce some of the lynx are forced to make long journeys in search of food. Some of these trips to the south may be several hundred miles. Other lynx may refuse to move out of their home territory and will die of starvation. Under ordinary conditions the lynx does not travel extensively; when forced to it, some do.

Habits: The lynx prefers to hunt under the cover of darkness, when its huge eyes give it a decided advantage. However, the lynx will travel and hunt in the daytime, particularly in the far north, where darkness is practically nonexistent in the summer. Lynx are frequently seen moving about in the daytime in Alaska, accompanied by the raucous yammering of magpies, which seem to delight in following and tormenting the cat. Birds will follow and annoy members of the cat family much more often than they will the canines, perhaps because the cats are a greater threat and the birds try to drive them from the area.

The lynx may either still-hunt for food, or lie in wait for it along the side of a game path, or attempt to drop down on it from a ledge or tree limb. The scarcer food becomes, the more frequently the lynx will have to actively seek it out. In stalking its prey the lynx slinks along the ground, almost dragging its belly. One thing in the lynx's favor is that the varying hare does not den in holes. This means that the hare is always above ground where its movements or scent are much more likely to pinpoint its presence.

The varying hare of the Far North has about a ten-year cycle in which it goes from a period of peak abundance to almost extinction and again to another peak. When the hares are plentiful, the lynx and all the other meat-eaters of the north are healthy and plentiful. When the hares are scarce, starvation stalks the land. Even the Indians suffer, because the hares are an important item of food and the fur-bearers are a major source of income.

The most accurate records of the fluctuations in the numbers of the varying hares have been made by checking the records of the Hudson's Bay Company. When the hares are plentiful, the fur take of the lynx is high; when the hare's population crashes, the lynx's population also crashes. However, the lynx cycle is always one year behind that of the hares. In checking the records, we see in 1900, 4,473 lynx were purchased by the company. This figure increased steadily until in 1906 61,388 pelts were harvested. In 1906 the rabbit population had reached its peak and started down. In 1907 the number of lynx pelts dropped to 36,201 and many of the lynx were starving and easy to catch or to kill. In 1908 only 9,664 lynx were taken and the decline continued till 1911 when the lynx began to recover along with the rise in the hare population.

In addition to hares, the lynx also feeds upon squirrels, chipmunks, lemmings, voles, mice, an occasional beaver, and both ruffed and spruce grouse. But these foods do not play a large enough role in the lynx's diet to really matter. The lynx is an eater of varying hares, and it is to the varying hare that its entire life is linked.

The fox and the lynx are implacable enemies, with all the advantage belonging to the lynx. The lynx outweighs the fox and, with its needle-sharp claws, is much better equipped for a fight. On bare ground the fox is too swift for the lynx and can easily avoid capture. During periods of deep snow, the cat has all the mobility. In soft snow the fox will often sink in right up to its belly while the lynx, padding along on its oversized feet, only sinks in a few inches. Try as it might, the fox cannot escape the lynx, which soon overtakes and kills it. Many times the lynx will not even bother to eat the fox, being satisfied just to have killed a member of the dog family.

In periods of deep snow and hunger the deer become weakened and the lynx desperate, and at such times the lynx will kill deer. Under such circumstances they have also been known to kill caribou and mountain sheep. And occasionally the lynx will even attempt to kill a porcupine for food. A lynx will have to be starving before it will eat food other than that which it has killed.

Periods of extremely bitter weather and storm may

cause the lynx to restrict its activities for a day or so, but hunger is soon the spur that pushes this big cat out on the hunting trail again.

Senses: Like the bobcat, the lynx's chief sense is sight. And like the bobcat, the lynx's sight, coupled with its great curiosity, is often its undoing. Trappers in the north country often attract a lynx into a trap area by cutting long blazes on all four sides of a small tree. The white inner tree bark stands out glaringly in the dark forest and proves an almost irresistible lure to the curious cat.

Scent is also important to the cat in locating a hidden hare, but the nose just tells the eyes where to look. The lynx will seldom track its prey by scent as the canids do. Of course if the lynx is chasing a hare and loses sight of it in the dark recesses of the swamp, then scent will help to keep the lynx going in the right direction until it sights the hare again.

Communication: The lynx, under normal conditions, is the quietest of the large cats. When caught in a trap or treed, it will growl, hiss and spit. Breeding season, however, is another situation. John Burroughs, the naturalist, described the sound made by the lynx at this time: "It was a cry or scream so loud that I could distinctly hear the echo in the woods about 400 yards away, a cry that tapered off into a long-drawn wail, which for despondency and agony of soul I have never heard equalled. I can find no words suitable to describe its utter hopeless misery and longing. If a lost soul from Hades had been given a few hour's freedom but had to be back on the striking of midnite, it might let off such a heart-breaking moan as I heard. It was a shrill, strident cry, ending in this long-drawn wail, full of the feeling of hopeless despair. The cry was repeated five or six times, then all was still."

Locomotion: Despite its long legs the lynx is not a swift animal. In charging or pouncing on its prey, the lynx moves so fast that it is almost a blur, yet it cannot run an extended race. There are many records of a man outrunning a lynx; it has been estimated that a lynx's top speed is about 10 to 12 miles per hour. In traveling about the lynx walks or trots or, if hurried, bounds. Tracks in the snow indicate that the lynx occasionally makes leaps of 12 to 15 feet for no apparent reason.

The lynx climbs well and spends quite a lot of time in trees. Inhabiting the lake and woods regions of the North, the lynx apparently does not hesitate to take to the water. A powerful swimmer, its broad feet enable it to paddle swiftly.

Breeding: The breeding season begins to manifest itself in late winter with the actual coupling taking place in March. Very little is actually known about the family life of the lynx in the wild, but most of the felines do not form strong familial ties. The male usually seeks out the female, engages in a brief period of courtship and breeding, and then disavows the forthcoming family. In many cases the female may help to foster the latter idea because male cats seldom show any affection for their own young and may even kill them. Cannibalism is known among the lynx.

Birth and Young: After a gestation period of about sixty-two days, the young lynx are born. Three to four young compose the average litter. The kittens at birth are brown in color with black spots and blotches. The eyes remain sealed for the first nine days and are blue when first opened. This color gradually changes to the familiar yellow cat-eyes. The young can crawl about in a matter of just a few hours, although they are unsteady on their feet for the first week.

There are seldom any rocky den sites in most of the area that the lynx inhabits, so it generally makes its den under tree roots, in brushy tangles or in hollow logs. The cat does not do any digging to provide a nest but just tramples down a form among the leaves and sticks that are already found in the nest site.

Although lynx are usually considered solitary animals, there are many cases recorded where the young do not leave the female when the basic hunting and training period is over. Such family groups will hunt together all winter. Unlike the wolf family, which hunts in a single file, the lynx family spreads out and hunts abreast of each other, covering a much larger area. The wolf family hunts by chasing its prey whereas the lynx family depends upon spotting its prey and then carefully stalking it.

The young become sexually mature at one year of age and the family separates at this time.

Life Span: The possible life span is about fifteen years, although the oldest on record was a lynx in the National Zoological Park that lived to be eleven years and four months. Living in the wild, it is exceedingly unlikely that a lynx would ever get to that age, particularly if the low in the rabbit cycle corresponds with its old age.

Sign: Tracks on sandy lake shores and along muddy pond edges are about the only sign of lynx in the summer. The lynx will frequent these open edges only when traveling from one spot to another. When actually hunting, it travels through dense cover where it leaves no tracks.

In the snow, the lynx's large, rounded pads leave readily distinguishable tracks, and as the lynx is active almost every day, it cannot keep its presence hidden.

If the lynx does kill a deer, it cannot possibly eat it all at one time. It will eat its fill, then keep returning until the meat is gone. If the weather is warm, the lynx will only feed until the meat starts to spoil. In either case, in true cat fashion, the lynx will attempt to cover the remainder of the uneaten kill with snow in the winter and vegetation in the warmer weather.

Its scat is seldom seen because the lynx usually attempts to cover it.

Enemies: The lynx is host to such external parasites as ticks, lice, fleas and mites. Occasionally lynx are found suffering from an advanced case of mange. Internal parasites such as roundworms and flatworms are usually present in the digestive tract. Distemper and rabies are comparatively rare yet both occasionally occur among the lynx.

In the early 1960s, there was a rabies scare regarding the wolves and lynx in the Province of Quebec, centered around the upper Ottawa River section. Although control of the situation was being attempted by the Provincial forces, warnings were posted in all public buildings. At that time, I was guiding wilderness canoe trips into the area and had gone to one of the rural trading posts to obtain more supplies where I was notified of the rabies threat. Returning to base camp with my companion, Homer Hicks, in his pick-up truck, we saw a large lynx cross the road and disappear in a ditch alongside the

The lynx eats varying hares mainly. Yet birds such as magpies follow and torment cats more than canines because cats pose a greater threat.

road. Homer stopped his truck and I ran back to get a better look at the lynx. When I neared the spot where the lynx had been, the cat bounded back onto the road and we stood there about 20 feet apart. As the lynx lashed his stubby tail, the thought of rabies flashed through my mind. It was with a sigh of relief that I watched the lynx bound away into the forest.

Human Relations: The lynx has never been a nuisance because its diet is such that it does not compete with man. Nor does it make raids upon livestock. The lynx is subject to pressure by man because man alters its habitat, and the reduction of the range of the varying hare reduces the range of the lynx.

Lynx fur is long and silky, and the pelts bring over $250. The lynx are sometimes hunted, sometimes trapped, but most frequently snared. Snares are preferred because it is easier to keep a snare working in bitter cold, snowy weather than it is a trap. Today snow buggies enable hunters to get farther into lynx areas than they ever could before, and hunting them is becoming more popular.

Trophy Records: The greatest recorded weight of a lynx is 42 pounds.

Table Fare: The flesh of the lynx is frequently eaten by trappers in the Far North. The meat is light in color and reported to have a flavor somewhat like chicken.

Taking advantage of its keen night vision, a bobcat waits on a tree limb for an approaching prey. The cat is most active at night, when the hunting is best and it is less exposed to larger predators and tormenting birds that announce its presence.

Bobcat

Lynx rufus

The bobcat is more adaptable than the lynx and lives comfortably anywhere in North America where there is sufficient forest and brushland to provide food and cover. Once considered a harmful predator, the bobcat had a price on its head, but it has now achieved the status of a game species in most states and is protected except during the open hunting season. As such it is a favorite quarry of many hunters, especially in winter, when using dogs.

The bobcat got its common name from its short, twitching tail. It is also called wildcat or Bay lynx. The species name *rufus* (reddish) was applied by Rafinesque in 1817 but is not entirely accurate as the animal's basic body color varies widely.

Description: The bobcat's most apparent features are its spots, tufted ears, big feet and short tail. It is a medium-sized cat, about 42 inches in length, standing about 22 inches high at the shoulder and weighing between 18 and 25 pounds. The females are slightly smaller and lighter than the males. The northern bobcats are larger than their southern counterparts.

Because of its face ruff, the bobcat appears to have a very broad face. Its ears are erect with short tufts of hair standing up from the tips. The eyes are yellow with black pupils which may narrow to slits in bright light and expanded to full circle in poor light.

The bobcat's legs are long in comparison to its body size. Its paws are large and heavily furred. There are five toes on each of the front feet, although the dewclaws are

Bobcat's ear tufts are small compared to those of the lynx, and its tail is longer.

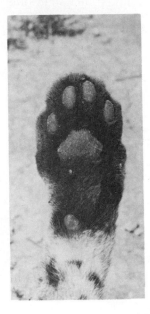

Right front foot of a bobcat is typical feline paw, with toe pads set in semi-circle in front of heel pad, claws concealed within their sheaths.

located high on the inside of the feet and do not show in the tracks.

The bobcat has a total of 28 teeth—fewer than most of the other carnivores. These are divided into 12 incisors, 4 sharp canines, 8 premolars and 4 molars. Evidently this is a sufficient number of teeth because the bobcat does a very good job of catching, killing and cutting up its prey. The Felidae, even more than the Canidae, turn their head sidewise to their food and scissor off chunks of meat with their shearing premolars and molars.

In coloration and pattern, I think the bobcat is the most beautiful of all wild mammals. Its color varies widely; the cats from the northern forested regions are darkest while those of the southwestern desert areas are the palest. Generally the bobcat has a reddish-pink nose. The base color of the face and the back and sides is reddish-brown, yellowish or gray. Both the face and the body have a barring or checkering of black or a darker color than the base color. Around its eyes, under its chin, throat and its belly, the bobcat is white. Its tail, which is from 4 to 7 inches long, is white underneath, barred with black and has a black spot above the tip. The end hairs, however, are white—unlike the lynx, whose tail tip is black. The bobcat's fur, although fairly long and luxurious, is rather brittle. Yet because of its spots and the ban on international sale of fur of spotted cats, demand in domestic markets has greatly increased.

Distribution: The bobcat is found from southern British Columbia eastward across southern Canada to the Maritime Provinces, southward to Mexico and the Gulf of Mexico. It is absent from much of central and

Distribution of the bobcat.

eastern United States except along the Mississippi and Ohio rivers and in the Appalachian Mountains.

Travel: Bobcats do not migrate in the real sense of the word. If they move into a new area because of food abundance, they do not move back to the old area. Bobcats are extending their range into southern Canada at the present time. Because of continued pressure they are being forced out of the Mississippi Valley region.

The bobcat has a home range from 5 miles in diameter to 50 miles. The scarcity of food or the advent of the breeding season will cause fluctuations in the size of the range. Like all predators, the bobcat does not cover the same portion of its range each night but chooses instead to rotate its hunting pattern.

Habits: The bobcat's speciality is stealth. It is neither built nor is it inclined to make long runs. Prowling silently on its large, padded feet, it appears and disappears like a wraith, a wisp of fog. It catches most of its food by stalking, relying more on its eyesight and hearing than on its sense of smell. The bobcat's mottled coat provides it with excellent camouflage, and even in bright daylight, when the animal remains motionless, it is most difficult to see. Taking advantage of this fact, the bobcat often lies in wait for its prey and attacks it as it passes by.

Bobcats are solitary animals and have evolved no social order. Except for a strong mother-young relationship, there is no cooperation between them.

Most of the bobcat's activities take place at night, not only because most of its prey is more active at night, but because it is less exposed to danger at that time.

As the wolf in the north is linked to the caribou, the bobcat is linked to the rabbit and hare. These two animals make up the bulk of the bobcat's diet. However, the bobcat is more varied in its diet than the lynx and although its population is cyclic too, its numbers do not crash as heavily when the hare populations crash. In addition, the bobcat also preys upon mice, rats, squirrels, chipmunks and even porcupines. Birds of all types, particularly the ground-nesting species, provide the bobcat with a small percentage of its food. Of these, ruffed grouse are particularly hard hit in the northeastern section of the bobcat's range because they are the number-one forest bird. In areas where wild turkey are found, the bobcat is more than eager to add them to his diet. When deer are weakened by starvation, in winter, or are caught in deep snow, the bobcat will feed upon them. An adult deer in good health is usually too much for a bobcat to handle, but those that are incapacitated are quickly downed. In the spring the bobcat also feeds upon fawns.

When the bobcat does kill a deer, it seldom eats very much from the carcass because it cannot consume more than 3 to 5 pounds of meat. It then lightly covers the remainder of the carcass with sticks and grasses. So long as the meat remains fresh, the bobcat will return to feed upon it. The Felidae, unlike the Canidae, will not feed upon meat that is spoiled, and some of them will not even eat meat that is not warm or that they did not kill themselves.

The bobcats are strictly meat eaters and only rarely partake of any vegetation. Their rough tongue easily rasps the shreds of meat from the bones of their prey. Grasses and cactus fruits, grapes and pears which have shown up in stomach analysis of bobcats indicate that they will sometimes try other foods.

When hunting is good, the bobcat gorges itself with food and then remains inactive for a day or so till it is compelled by hunger to move on again. The bobcat's habit of preferring to eat only fresh-killed meat often results in its wasting more food than it consumes.

In some instances, the bobcat will feed upon livestock. Although it usually avoids the haunts of man, man has in so many cases invaded the bobcat's home range that the two areas often become one. Poultry that strays into the woodland to roost is fair game. Young pigs provide the bobcat with a change of diet, but an infuriated sow makes a formidable enemy. Lambs, particularly on the western ranges, are probably the most frequently taken livestock. Sheep often graze in the open brush and rim-rock areas where the bobcat lives, and the cat occasionally kills some for food. There is a record of a bobcat killing thirty-eight lambs in a single night. Sheep that are guarded by a good dog are relatively safe, because the bobcat avoids dogs. Bobcats will sometimes kill and eat feral cats and free-ranging house cats that trespass on the bobcat's hunting grounds.

The members of the cat family all appear to be nervous and highstrung. A bobcat that is frightened or disturbed will twitch its stub of a tail from side to side in spasmodic jerks.

Senses: The bobcat's eyesight is its most important sense. It is exceedingly alert to the slightest movement. Trappers take advantage of this fact and attract a bobcat to their traps by suspending a small bird's wing on a string over the trap. The wing flutters in the slightest breeze, proving an irresistible lure to the bobcat.

The sense of hearing ranks second because the bobcat, like all cats, tries to remain hidden at all times. The slightest sound will alert the animal for evasive or offensive action, whichever the circumstances require. Like other felines, the bobcat is attracted to the odor of catnip.

Communication: Even the most confirmed city dweller can attest to the noise made by cats. Whether wild or domesticated, cats meow, squall, growl, hiss and spit. When contented, all cats purr. The larger the cat the more vibrations it creates; some of the larger cats actually seem to tremble when purring.

Breeding season brings out the best, or perhaps the worst, in all cats and they render the nights hideous with their laments of love. During actual copulation the cats start off with a low yowling that increases in intensity as passions increase.

Locomotion: Bobcats usually walk, slowly and carefully. Any animal is at a disadvantage when it is moving, and this is particularly true of an animal that hunts by sight. When stalking, the bobcat places its hind feet in the tracks of its front feet. For once the bobcat has placed its front feet quietly, avoiding twigs or other objects, it can put its hind feet in the same spot without fear of making noise.

When traveling, the bobcat either trots or bounds easily along. When pursued or pursuing game, it bounds as much as 10 feet at a time, attaining a top speed of about 30 miles per hour. The bobcat doesn't like to run, though; it seeks shelter among the rocks or scrambles up a tree. It climbs by alternating its feet or bounds up the tree using its two front feet in unison.

The bobcat keeps its retractable claws, each of which has a separate sheath, as sharp as possible. The wild felines sharpen their claws in the same manner as the domestic cats, by scratching them on wood to remove the dead material at the end of the claws, an operation similar to our clipping our fingernails.

Bobcats swim well, although like most cats they prefer to avoid water.

Breeding: In late winter, as the days begin to lengthen and the sun shines just a little brighter, the male bobcat begins to see the folly of his solitary ways. His desire for food is momentarily shunted aside as more pressing desires come to the fore. In the breeding season the bobcat's yowls and screams rend the night, perhaps to let the female know of his whereabouts or to establish territorial rights against any invading males.

If we judge from the behavior of the domesticated cat, which really is not domesticated but just tolerates man, the bobcat does a lot of "tom-catting" around. He stays with the female only long enough to woo her and breed her, and then goes off on his quest for another mate. Breeding usually takes place in February or March, although males are capable of breeding throughout the year. Females that are not bred come into heat periodically, and some may have a second litter later in the year.

Birth and Young: The gestation period of the bobcat is about 62 days. The average number of kits in a litter is two or three. The little ones come into this world wearing spotted coats, weighing about 8 to 9 ounces, and with their eyes sealed shut.

For a den the female prefers a fissure or split in a rocky wall, a hollow log, a hollow under interlacing tree roots or even an earthen burrow. The most important feature of the den site is that it must be dry and secluded.

In nine to ten days the eyes of the kits open. As with domestic kittens, the eyes are blue at first, gradually turning to yellow over a period of the next two months. The kits are fed small birds and pieces of larger game as soon as they can handle them. By the time they are two months old they are usually weaned and are on a straight meat diet. The mother bobcat often brings in smaller rodents alive so the kits can kill them in training for their lives as hunters.

The kits remain with the mother until fall, at which time they will be better than half grown and will weigh about 10 to 12 pounds. As winter advances, the kits will scatter to start their solitary existence on a hunting range of their own.

Life Span: In the wild, bobcats have a life span of about ten to twelve years, but a bobcat at the Space Zoological Park of Beemerville, New Jersey, lived in captivity to be 34 years old.

Sign: The bobcat's tracks in snow are the most commonly seen sign. Living in forested or rocky areas, this cat seldom leaves any visible tracks in warm weather. As it usually avoids water, its tracks are seldom seen in the mud along river edges. But a new carpet of snow will reveal the presence of any bobcats in the area. The bobcat's tracks are about the size of a small dog's of the cocker spaniel class. However, its claws are retractable and do not show in the tracks.

Scat is seldom seen because the bobcat, like the house cat, covers its scat whenever possible.

Game killed by bobcats but not completely eaten can be identified by the covering of leaves, twigs and brush. Only the cats and the bears try to hide their food in this fashion.

Enemies: The old saying about a man being able to

lick his weight in wildcats was based on a real appreciation of the bobcat's ferocity. The animal is a bundle of spring-steel muscles driving canine teeth and sharp, hooked claws. The cat can move so fast that it is just a blur. Because the bobcat is such a formidable foe, it has relatively few enemies. After man, the woods-running dog is probably its worst enemy, although a single dog would find it almost impossible to catch a bobcat, let alone kill it. When a bobcat fights a dog, it lies on its back. When the dog lunges at the bobcat's throat, the bobcat bites the dog, fastens its forefeet claws into the dog to hold it close and attempts to disembowel it with raking strokes of its hind feet.

Great horned owls and coyotes will kill and eat the bobcat kits if they get the chance, and the latter have been known to attack an adult. Mountain lions have also been reported to kill bobcats.

Bobcats have fleas, lice, mites and ticks. These four kinds of parasites are probably found on every mammal in North America. Internally they have roundworms, tapeworms and flukes. Like the canids, they are subject to distemper and rabies.

Human Relations: Bobcats are a rather negligible factor in their native habitat. They are never abundant enough to be more than a partial control on a prey species. Bobcat pelts are much more valuable than in the past.

Trophy Records: The average bobcat weighs 15 to 20 pounds, although there are numerous records of cats in the 40- to 45-pound class. Frank Webb of New York

Mills, New York, shot a bobcat on January 21, 1962, which weighed 46 pounds, 10 ounces. There is record of a Maine bobcat that weighed 76 pounds, but no details were available, and a more reliable record from Colorado in 1951 of a male weighing 69 pounds.

Table Fare: The bobcat has been eaten quite frequently, and the consensus is that it tastes like veal. However, Stanley P. Young, an authority on bobcats, found the meat tough and "with an extremely nauseating odor while cooking."

SEALS AND WALRUS

Order Pinnipedia

The fin-footed carnivores have often been placed in their own order, Pinnipedia, and they are so segregated in this book. However, recent research on both the living species and new fossil finds seems to indicate that grouping these animals together is incorrect, and that the seals are most closely related to the weasel family and that the sea lions, fur seals and walruses are actually most closely related to the bears.

As most of their time is spent in the water, the pinnipeds have evolved many adaptations to enable them to survive in their environment. Their streamlined bodies reduce friction, and their flippers aid in propulsion and steering. Their insulating layer of blubber beneath the skin serves to protect them from the cold, either on land or in the water, as well as making them more buoyant.

The pinnipeds do not usually breathe rhythmically, but instead take many short breaths and then do not inhale for a while—even on land. They can remain submerged for long periods by automatically shunting their blood flow to the brain, while depriving the muscles and viscera of the oxygen-rich blood. Their muscles are far more tolerant of oxygen debt and high concentration of carbon dioxide than are most other mammals, but the debt must be repaid when the animal surfaces and breathes again.

HAIR SEALS

Family Phocidae

Harbor Seal

A harbor seal cow and her pup sun themselves on a rock as the tide recedes. They'll wait for the tide to come in and float them off.

Harbor Seal

Phoca vitulina

The harbor seal is not strictly a creature of the polar regions but is often found in warmer waters. It frequents bays and harbors on both coasts, works its way into freshwater inlets, and even occasionally becomes landlocked in large lakes. Wherever it goes, it is impelled by a driving curiosity to investigate everything in its immediate surroundings. I have seen these seals bobbing up and down in harbors, staring around intently, frequently approaching a boat and inspecting it on one side, then diving beneath it and reappearing on the other side. This curiosity is tempered with caution in Alaska, where the seals have learned to avoid fishermen, who shoot them at every opportunity for suspected salmon thievery.

This seal was given its scientific name by Linnaeus in 1758. *Phoca*, a Greek word which means to swell up, was chosen because of the plumpness of the animal. *Vitulina* is derived from the Latin word for calf and was applied because the seal was often called a sea-calf.

Description: The harbor seal has a streamlined body for easy passage through the water. A large bull seal weighs up to 300 pounds but 250 pounds is about average, while the female is slightly smaller. It has a doglike face with large, prominent, close-set eyes. The muzzle is blunt and contains numerous long whiskers. There is no external ear structure, the canal being closed by muscular valves when the animal submerges. The neck is short and the head tapers directly from the body.

The arms, hands, legs and feet have been shortened and modified into flippers for the seal's aquatic existence.

On the forefeet the thumb is the longest, while on the hind feet the thumb and the little finger are of equal length. Because of its skeletal structure, a seal cannot bend its rear flippers forward and sit upright on them as a sea lion does.

Harbor seals vary widely in color from a light cream to a dark brown and have dark spots or patches. The hair when wet is very dark. The uniform coat, which is not so dense as that of land mammals, is kept waterproof by numerous oil glands.

Seals are members of the Order Carnivora, although they are often classified in a special order, Pinnipedia, together with the walrus and sea lions. The harbor seal has 34 teeth: 10 incisors, 4 canines, 16 premolars and 4 molars.

Distribution: The harbor seal lives along the Pacific Coast from Mexico to the Arctic; and along the Atlantic Coast from the Carolinas northward. It is also found in Hudson Bay and in some lakes in Ungava.

Travel: Unlike some of the other seals, the harbor seal does not migrate. It is the most terrestrial of the seals and spends about half of its time on land, resting on points, sandbars and exposed rock.

Although the harbor seal can operate under the ice, it usually moves ahead of the large ice packs. This movement might be considered migration but is not done on a regular basis. The seal only moves southward when it is forced to do so.

Habits: Fishermen have waged an all-out war on the

seals because they believe they eat the commercially valuable salmon. In a study of the harbor seals along the coast of Washington, 114 were killed and the contents of their stomachs carefully examined. It was found that the seals were feeding primarily upon the most available fish—flounder, tomcod, Pacific herring, sculpin, cod, blue cod, pollack and shiners. Their diet varied as their food supply changed with the seasons. Octopus were frequently eaten during the summer while squid were taken in the winter.

But out of the 114 seals killed, only four had been eating salmon. Some seals do get into the habit of feeding upon salmon that have been caught in gill nets, but they take these fish merely because it is easier than catching their own.

When the tide is flowing, fish come in to feed in the temporarily flooded shallows and the seals slip into the water to feed on the fish. When the tide goes out, the fish leave the area and the seals haul themselves up on rocks or beaches to rest and sleep.

Often the seals get on rocks that are barely exposed by the receding tide and, as the tide goes out, become stranded 15 feet or so above the water. Unless disturbed, when they will quickly plunge off the rocks, the seals just wait for the tide to come back in and float them off.

During their resting periods the seals cannot sleep too soundly as they are always exposed to danger. They sleep for five to ten minutes, wake up, scan the horizon and doze for another short period. Generally the seals change position each time they wake up. They lie on one side, then the other, then roll over on their back, occasionally waving their flippers in a desultory fashion. Since the seals are usually in company of their own kind, the watchfulness of one is protection for them all. At the first sign of danger, they give a barking call and dive into the safety of the water.

Senses: The seal's eyesight is vital to its safety, as it must rely on this sense to detect the approach of danger. It has a nictitating membrane—a transparent eyelid—that covers the eye while it is submerged.

I have never seen a seal sniff the air for scent. When under water, its nostrils close and cease to function. The mother seal, however, uses her sense of smell to locate her own pup amongst a multitude of babies.

The sense of hearing is important to the seal, for any strange or sudden noise will send it tumbling into the water. The fact that seals bark to one another when they are alarmed proves that they depend on their ears as well as their eyes for detecting danger.

Communication: Bull seals roar during the breeding season. The seal calf emits a blat somewhat like that of a domestic sheep, and all adults bark if alarmed or disturbed.

Locomotion: Because the harbor seal's rear legs are turned backward, they are not of much use in getting about on land. When the seal has to travel on land it moves along in much the same fashion as a caterpillar, that is, by hunching its back and contracting its body. Such movements are of necessity slow, and this seal does not venture very far from the water's edge.

Once in the water, though, the adult seal, with its sleek body, propels itself forward with an undulating motion at a top speed of about 15 miles per hour. Like other seals, the harbor seal spends much of its time under water and has been known to dive as deep as 300 feet. A seal can stay submerged for twenty to thirty minutes, and some species even sleep under water for periods of ten minutes or more. The harbor seal does its sleeping on land. Even on land most seals take twenty to thirty short breaths, expel the air, and do not breathe again for about ten minutes. When a harbor seal submerges, it blows the air out of its lungs and relaxes the muscles of its nostrils, closing them. Voluntary muscular action is required to hold the nostrils open; relaxed, they close.

The lungs of a harbor seal are large and uniform in size. The heart is substantial and angular and capable of pumping the exceedingly large amount of blood in its body. The seal probably has more blood vessels, veins and blood for its size than any other mammal.

A large liver and a high tolerance to carbon dioxide allow this seal to remain submerged without difficulty. When the seal submerges, its heart slows down and vascular contraction keeps blood flowing to the vital areas but not to the limbs.

Breeding: During the breeding season, seals gather in their largest concentrations. They are promiscuous and, when the breeding season reaches its peak in September, each bull breeds with as many females as will accept him. The males rarely fight for the females. The seals mate on land, with the male and female lying on their sides facing each other.

Birth and Young: Pups are born about 280 days after

breeding, most of them in July. Usually a female has only a single pup and is a devoted mother.

Before birthing time arrives, the female seeks out a secluded beach or, in rare instances, an ice floe, and the pup is usually born between low and high tides. At birth the pup has a dense, white, woolly coat, or else it will have shed it in the uterus and be a mottled gray. A pup is about 30 to 34 inches long and weighs 17 to 25 pounds at birth. By the time the tide comes back in the pup can swim.

The young seal grows rapidly on its mother's milk, which has a butterfat content of over 40 percent, as compared to a dairy cow's milk, which has 3 to 4 percent butterfat.

The young seals do not swim much at first but just laze around and eat. As they grow older and stronger, they begin to follow after the females. If, while swimming, the pup becomes tired, it clings to its mother's back and rides back to shore. The pups nurse for about six weeks, by which time they are securing food on their own. Not fast enough to catch fish at first, they feed mainly upon the slower octopus and shellfish.

Life Span: Seals continue to grow for about three years and are then considered mature. The older seals will become heavier with age, but there is no more skeletal growth. They have lived nineteen years in captivity.

Sign: When a seal drags its body across a sandbar it leaves tracks. Claw marks from the flippers and fan marks of the flippers themselves are easily recognized to the side of the drag marks left by the body. These tracks have to be seen at low tide because seals seldom come above the high-water mark.

Enemies: Killer whales, sharks and polar bears are the seals' chief natural predators. Both the whales and the sharks grow large enough to swallow seals whole. One killer whale had the remains of fourteen seals in its stomach when it was killed. Sharks usually tear the seals to shreds before eating them. On ice floes, the polar bear kills seals and eats the blubber but usually leaves the meat.

Human Relations: Alaska at one time had a bounty on seals, but that was imposed more to help the Indians and Eskimos than as a full-scale means of control. The fur of the harbor seal had never had much commercial value because of its stiffness, but the fur suddenly became popular and the price shot up. Today harbor seals are managed by the National Marine Fisheries Service under provisions of the Marine Mammals Protection Act. Only native Eskimos and Indians are allowed to hunt the seals, but may do so only if the animals are fully utilized, such as for food, clothing, and handicrafts.

Table Fare: The coastal Indians and the Eskimos use the seal for food. These are practical people who eat whatever is edible. The meat is very dark and has the chewing qualities of an automobile tire.

WALRUS

Family Odobenidae

WALRUS

Walrus

Odobenus rosmarus

This enormous fin-footed mammal with the conspicuous tusks was given the appropriate genus name *Odobenus*, which is derived from the Greek words *odous* (tooth) and *baino* (I walk), because of the habit of using its long ivories to pull itself up on the ice and to turn around on land. *Rosmarus* is from the Norwegian word *rossmaar*, an old Scandinavian name for the walrus; other names for the animal took note of its prodigious size. The Old English *horschwael*, the Icelandic *hrosshvalr* and the Swedish *hvalross* all mean whale-horse.

Description: Often described as our ugliest mammal, the walrus has a large, compact body encased by a thick skin that seems several sizes too big. Large adult bulls may weigh up to 3,000 pounds, measure 12 feet in length and stand 4 feet high at the shoulder. An adult female may be 10 feet long and weigh a ton.

The walrus's most prominent feature, the long ivory tusks which are its canine teeth, have open internal ends and grow throughout its life. Both male and female have tusks, although the female's are shorter, more slender, and generally curved.

The walrus has a blunt, wide muzzle and strong, stout whiskers. It also has muscular muzzle pads which, along with its whiskers, it uses when feeding (explained later).

The eyes are wide-set, small, almost piglike, and often bloodshot. There are no external ears; the auditory opening is covered by a fold of skin.

The walrus has a total of 18 teeth: 2 incisors, 4 canines,

This walrus bull displays two chief means of transport: his tail and his web-toed flippers.

and 12 premolars. The premolars are large, almost round and flat on top. They are strong teeth used for crushing the shells of clams, oysters and other forms of sea life.

The neck of the walrus is very thick and tapers from the shoulders to the animal's jawbones. Under the skin on the neck are two pharyngeal pouches which extend from the neck to the shoulder blades and can be inflated directly from the lungs. When the pouches are filled with air they act as waterwings and allow a sleeping or wounded walrus to float.

The front feet bend backward and the rear feet can be

bent forward so that the animal can sit upright like a sea lion. No tail is visible, the bones being buried in the flesh out of sight.

The skin of a walrus is more than an inch thick over most of the body and over 2 1/2 inches thick around the neck. The skin becomes thicker as the walrus ages. Beneath the skin is a layer of blubber that averages 2 3/4 inches thick and may yield 900 pounds of oil when rendered.

The adult walrus's skin is almost hairless, although the younger animals are covered with short hairs. Sometimes the animal lies out in the sun for so long that it becomes sunburned and its skin turns a bright pink.

Distribution: The walrus lives along the edge of the ice in Arctic waters, south to Ungava on the Atlantic Coast, to the Bering Sea in Alaska, and to Hudson Bay in Canada.

Travel: The walrus spends a large part of its time on ice floes in the open sea. It migrates hundreds of miles southward in the winter and heads back north to the breeding grounds in the spring. It travels from necessity rather than from choice. The walrus is capable of breaking its way up through 4 inches of ice and can live and work with breathing holes as the seals do. However, it much prefers to be able to rest and to sleep on top of the ice and not in the water so when the ice freezes over the Arctic Ocean the walrus heads south.

Habits: The walrus, a true herd animal, prefers to spend all of its time with others of its kind and some herds number in the hundreds. The animals seem to find reassurance in body contact with each other, and they often sleep in a heap. This herding instinct is a protective measure, as some walrus can stay awake to watch for danger while others are sleeping.

Walrus prefer to stay near shallow water where food is more easily found, and if they are carried out to deep water by the drifting ice, they abandon the floe and head back towards shore.

Clams are the walrus's staple item of diet, although it eats all types of mollusks and shellfish. While feeding, the walrus inverts its body and rakes the ocean floor with its tusks to loosen and uncover food. Its foreflippers are too short to aid in getting food into its mouth, so it relies on its muscular muzzle pads and strong whiskers, which it uses almost like fingers to push the food into its mouth. With its flat-topped teeth it crushes and expels the shells and then swallows the meat. Those shells that are swallowed are ejected by the stomach. A gigantic animal, the walrus has an appetite to match its size. The stomach contents of one Pacific walrus weighed 109 pounds and contained over 550 clams of several types.

The walrus also feeds upon some fish, and occasionally a large bull walrus turns into a seal-eater. It stabs the seal to death with its long tusks and tears apart the body with its muzzle pads and sharp, strong whiskers. Evidently the walrus does not chew any of its food but swallows everything whole or, in the case of fish or seals, in chunks. The teeth are used only for crushing shells.

Most of the walrus's need for water is supplied in the food it eats. Like a seal, the walrus ingests some sea water with its food but its body is tolerant of this salt intake.

Senses: The sense of touch is most important to the walrus. Feeding in deep water, sometimes beneath ice, it locates bivalves and other food with its sensitive whiskers. Although Eskimos always try to approach a walrus herd upwind the animal's sense of smell is actually not highly developed. Hearing and eyesight are probably on a par, and both are used to detect danger.

Communication: Walrus are extremely vocal and the roaring of a herd can be heard for several miles. When angered or frightened, they snort blasts of air through their noses. They also emit a seal-like bark and a bell-like chiming sound.

Locomotion: On land the walrus, because of its bulk, appears to be very awkward. Yet it uses its front legs and hind flippers and can move at a rapid pace. It is a strong swimmer, and is extremely agile in the water.

Breeding: Although the walrus travels in large herds, the males usually keep separate from the females and the young except during the breeding season. During April and May the males start to seek out the company of the females, which usually breed every other year. The bulls do not gather a harem, but they do fight for the favors of an individual female. Using their long tusks for stabbing, two bulls of equal size put on a bloody and vicious fight.

Birth and Young: From mid-April to June of the following year, depending on the locality, a single calf is born to each of the mated cows after a gestation period of 380 days. The nursery is on an ice floe. At birth the calf is about 4 feet long and weighs about 100 pounds. It has a gray skin with soft, light fur. This hair is soon shed, leaving the calf almost hairless until it grows its regular dark, coarse hair.

A baby walrus is well cared for. If danger of any kind presents itself, not only the mother but any nearby walrus is ready to fight till the death to protect it.

The young can swim shortly after birth, although they do not have the strength for protracted swims. If a young walrus tires while swimming, it clasps its front flippers around its mother's neck and rides piggy-back, and when the mother goes down to feed on the ocean bottom, sometimes the little one stays with her.

The lactation period is long, and although the mother's milk is very rich and the young ones grow fast, they are dependent upon nursing for almost two years. At the end of that time their own tusks will be about 4 inches long, long enough to be used to forage for their own food. At three years of age the tusks are about 6 inches long; at five years they are about 9 inches long. Female walrus become mature at four to five years of age, the bulls at five years.

Life Span: The walrus has an expected life span of about twenty-five years, although it is thought that quite a few of them live to be at least thirty years of age.

Signs: Walrus are seldom found by signs. Most of the herds are located by sound, their roaring and bellowing carrying for several miles. When the walrus is feeding and using a breathing hole, it may expel bits of shells on the ice as it comes up for air, and these are one visual sign of its presence.

Enemies: The killer whale is the walrus's most feared enemy. The whale can swallow a young walrus whole and tear an adult to shreds. The whales often travel in schools, and a concentrated attack by these rapacious killers results in carnage. In 1936 a pack of killer whales attacked a herd of walrus off St. Lawrence Island, Alaska. In a panic to escape the whales and get ashore, the walrus stampeded over one another and 200 were killed.

Polar bears sometimes stalk the walrus herds in an attempt to kill a young one. The adults are too big for the bears to handle, and some bears have been killed attacking full-grown walrus.

Human Relations: In former days, the walrus was not accorded any protection and was slaughtered by the thousands for the oil that was rendered from its blubber. Today, laws are enforced protecting the walrus from commercial exploitation.

The walrus is very important to the Eskimos. They use the meat for food for themselves and for their dogs, the oil in lamps and for cooking, the skin for boat coverings and dog harnesses, and the half-digested clams in the walrus's stomach for making clam chowder. The tusks as raw ivory are worth about $6 per ounce, but the Eskimos are excellent craftsmen, and by carving the ivory into figurines and other ornaments, they can raise the value to fifty to a hundred times that amount. In the olden days, the ivory was used for tools and weapons but is now too valuable as carving material to be used for such mundane purposes.

Today the walrus is managed by the U.S. Fish and Wildlife Service under the aegis of the Marine Mammals Protection Act. Only native Eskimos, Indians, and Aleuts, may hunt walrus, provided the entire animal is utilized. Ironically, prior to the ban on hunting except by natives, the game-status protection of walrus had fostered a tremendous increase in their population.

There are about 250,000 Pacific walrus today, an all-time high. Authorities predict at least a 50 percent population decline, resulting from increased clamming operations, oil exploration, and marine traffic.

Trophy Records: Walrus are judged by the size and length of their tusks. The world's-record Pacific walrus was killed by Eskimos off Point Hope, Alaska, in 1957. These tusks are now owned by Jonas Bros. of Seattle, Washington. The right tusk is 32 2/8 inches long and 12 2/8 inches in circumference at the base. The left tusk is 32 1/8 inches long and 13 inches at the base. The tusks scored a total of 145 6/8 points.

The tusks of the world's-record Atlantic walrus scored 118 6/8 points. It is not known who killed this walrus, which was taken in Greenland prior to 1954. These tusks were given to the National Collection, a gift from Roy Vail, but were later stolen. The right tusk is 30 5/8 inches long and 8 3/8 inches in circumference at the base while the left tusk is 30 3/8 inches long and 8 1/2 inches at the base.

RODENTS

Order Rodentia

*Rodents are the most abundant as well as the most
diverse of all orders of mammals. Almost half of the
4,000 species of living mammals are rodents.*

*In North America rodents vary in size from tiny
mice weighing a fraction of an ounce to beavers
weighing 70 pounds or more. They live in a wide variety of habitats, from deserts to arctic tundra, and
have evolved numerous anatomical, physiological
and behavioral adaptations to survive. Some, like
squirrels, spend most of their time in trees; some,
like muskrats, inhabit the water; but the majority live
on or beneath the surface of the earth.*

*A characteristic feature that identifies these crea-
tures as a single group is their four incisor teeth.
The chisel-like edge is maintained by working the upper pair against the lower. As the outer surface is
composed of hard enamel and the inner of softer
dentine, a sharp cutting edge is produced as the animal gnaws. As these incisors are continuously growing, the rodent must chew frequently to keep them*

from growing so long that the mouth is forced open and the grinding molars in the back of the mouth cannot chew food. Rodents do not have canine teeth, and there is a wide space separating the incisors from the grinding teeth.

Some rodents are active throughout the daylight hours, but most are active at night. Some are active throughout the winter, protected by dense fur, while others escape this period of bad weather and short food supply by hibernating. A few rodents pass the summer, in areas of intense heat and little green vegetation, in a summer sleep called "estivation."

Because of their numbers, rodents play an important part in the life of man and other mammals. Man uses some rodents for food, many for their fur. Some are hunted for sport, and many are used in laboratories for scientific and medical research. On the other hand, man is plagued by many rodents that eat or destroy his food, carry diseases that may infect him, and cause damage by their gnawing.

MARMOTS AND SQUIRRELS

Family Sciuridae

WOODCHUCK
YELLOW-BELLIED MARMOT
HOARY MARMOT
GRAY SQUIRREL
FOX SQUIRREL
ARCTIC GROUND SQUIRREL
PRAIRIE DOG

To observe woodchucks, first locate a den, betrayed by fresh dirt at the entrance. (Photo by Irene Vandermolen.)

Woodchuck

Marmota monax

According to legend, the woodchuck, or groundhog, emerges from his burrow on February 2 to appraise the weather. If he sees his shadow, he returns, and winter has still six more weeks to run; if he doesn't, spring is imminent. Needless to say, the weather does not always conform to the legend.

The woodchuck is probably hunted more than any other varmint in the eastern part of the United States. It was to satisfy chuck hunters that gun companies developed high-powered, small-caliber, super-accurate rifles. Today hunters with long-range varmint rifles snipe at woodchucks at ranges up to 400 yards.

Description: As befits a tunneling mammal, the woodchuck has a rounded, barrel-shaped body and short, powerful legs. Large males may be up to 26 inches long of which 5 to 6 inches is tail. They stand between 6 and 7 inches high at the shoulder and have an average weight of about 10 pounds. The females are slightly smaller. Their basic body color is brown but this may shade through red to almost black. The silver-tipped guard hairs give them a grizzled appearance. Many woodchucks are very dark and quite a few are truly melanistic, being a shiny jet black. Albinism occurs but less frequently than does melanism.

The woodchuck's ears are short, rounded and contain inner muscles which allow them to be drawn tightly closed so that no dirt can enter. Its black eyes protrude above its flat skull, giving the animal a type of periscope which enables it to peer out of its den and still keep

A melanistic, or black, woodchuck. This color phase is fairly common, but albinism is comparatively rare.

almost its entire body hidden from view.

The woodchuck has five toes on each foot, although the thumb on the forefoot is so reduced that it does not show in the tracks. The front toes are very flexible and can be used for grasping and holding food. The woodchuck walks on the flat of its entire foot.

The white incisors of the woodchuck, which classify it as a rodent, show conspicuously in the older specimens. It has a total of 22 teeth: 4 incisors, 6 premolars and 12 molars.

The woodchuck, more than any other rodent, suffers from malocclusion or mismatching of the incisors. All rodent incisors grow constantly and must be worn down by chewing and gnawing on wood or other hard substances or by wearing against each other. If by chance the teeth are not uniform and do not meet, such wear is not possible. These incisors will continue to grow into great tusks and soon become almost complete circles.

When the woodchuck's incisors don't meet, and cannot be properly worn down, they continue to grow and often kill the animal by piercing its skull, or by preventing it from eating.

I have seen this condition in a number of living specimens. I have also seen several skulls and numerous photographs portraying it. Most of the time the continued growth of such teeth causes death because the teeth either grow back through the skull or finally prevent the animal from securing food.

The woodchuck has three very prominent anal glands that may readily be seen protruding after the animal has been killed. These glands give off the odor peculiar to the animals and are used as a means of communication between them.

Distribution: It has been estimated that there are about 500 million woodchucks in North America, a round estimate arrived at by biologists who calculated the approximate number of acres of good woodchuck habitat and the amount of space needed to support each woodchuck.

The woodchuck inhabits open forests and clearings from eastern Alaska to Labrador, south in eastern and central United States to Alabama and Arkansas, and in the west south to northern Idaho.

Travel: Woodchucks do not travel. If the food supply

Distribution of the woodchuck.

is ample they are unlikely to be found more than 150 feet from their dens. In spring the males will travel from one den to another looking for a mate, but even this activity usually takes place within four or five acres. Young woodchucks at the late summer dispersal time move only as far as they must in order to find an area with sufficient food. Frequently that entails a move of only 100 feet from the maternal den, although sometimes the move will be as much as 1,000 feet.

Habits: The woodchuck is a diurnal, sun-loving creature. It carries on all of its activities in broad daylight, counting on its alertness to allow time to reach the safety of its den. The periods of peak activity are early morning and late afternoon, although it is active all day long. Some authorities claim that woodchucks have four established feeding periods. My personal observations do not bear this out.

When I was a boy living on a farm, my father used to pay me a ten-cent bounty for each woodchuck that I killed in our alfalfa fields. Since my first weapon was a single-barrel 12-gauge shotgun, I became very good at stalking because I had to get close to make a sure kill. I hunted those woodchucks so hard that I completely changed their life patterns and forced them to feed at night. At first I thought I had eliminated all of the 'chucks because I didn't see them, but their dens still showed signs of fresh dirt. It wasn't until I went by the field on a bright moonlit night that I discovered what had happened.

When a young woodchuck goes out on its own, the first thing it must do is to secure a den. If a vacant burrow is available, the young woodchuck will clean it out and do whatever remodeling is needed. If a new den must be dug, the woodchuck will seek out a sandy loam to make the digging easier. The size and structure of each burrow depends upon the individual woodchuck. Some woodchucks are lazy or prefer to live the Spartan life, while others are ambitious and construct elaborate dwellings.

Basically the dens will be alike. The woodchuck will start from some vantage point and drive the tunnel down to about 4 feet below the surface. The tunnel will then be developed as a horizontal shaft, or it may rise back up a foot or two. A bed chamber and sometimes a toilet chamber will be added. All of the excavated dirt will be piled up at the mouth of the den, making a very conspicuous mound. The added height provides an ideal observation platform and allows the woodchuck to see over the surrounding vegetation. Then another entrance is made to the den, but as this one is opened up from the inside, no dirt sits around it and it remains hidden. From here on the diversity becomes apparent. Some woodchucks content themselves with just the two entrances, although most of them end up with an average of five. Of the five entrances, three are usually conspicuous and two are hidden plunge holes. Every entrance means another tunnel, and some woodchucks create quite a maze. Nine entrances are the most I have ever seen at one den, but one naturalist recorded nineteen.

When digging, the woodchuck loosens the dirt with its front feet and pushes it beneath its body. When a sizable heap has been loosened, the woodchuck turns around and bulldozes the dirt out of the den with its head. Sometimes they push the dirt ahead of them with their forefeet, using the same method to roll loose stones out of the burrow. When the den is completed the woodchuck may or may not carry grass in to use as bedding. This, too, is up to the individual.

Woodchucks are vegetarians but not strict vegetarians, though they seldom get a chance to eat meat. Enough records exist to prove that they will eat meat if the opportunity presents itself. They also occasionally feed on insects. However, vegetation unquestionably makes up 99 percent of their diets.

What a woodchuck eats depends on where it lives. Alfalfa, clover, soy beans, corn, beans, peas and lettuce are only some of the cultivated crops which it avidly consumes. A woodchuck can wreak havoc in a garden in a single day, and it eats all types of fruit and berries. In the spring, before much greenery is out, the woodchuck often feeds upon the bark, twigs and buds of such low-growing bushes as the wild cherry and sumac. In fact, it eats almost every type of vegetation.

An adult woodchuck consumes about 1 pound of vegetation per day, although there is a record of one woodchuck that had 26 ounces of food in its stomach. Without the food, the woodchuck weighed less than 5 pounds, so it had eaten more than one-third its own body weight. A woodchuck seldom drinks, getting most of its fluids from dew and from the succulence of the plants it consumes. With the advent of cold weather the woodchuck feeds at every opportunity and makes its greatest weight gain prior to hibernation.

In most areas, the woodchuck retires underground to hibernate about the last of October. It crawls into a side room in the burrow and digs up enough dirt to seal off

By chance, an earth-moving tractor scraped away part of the den of this hibernating woodchuck without harming the chuck. "Cold as a stone," the chuck didn't waken.

the sleeping chamber. The woodchuck then curls forward into a ball and becomes drowsy. By progressive steps its body processes and functions slow down. From a normal body temperature of 96 degrees the woodchuck's temperature now drops down to a low of about 39 degrees. Its heart rate slows down to four or five strokes per minute. It may take as few as one breath per minute. In this state of suspended animation the woodchuck feels as cold and hard as a stone. It usually stays this way for about four months, unknowingly sleeping right through its day of fame on February 2. Some of the males do wake in mid-February to seek mates.

The fat reserves that the woodchuck has in its body are appreciably depleted during hibernation. What little remains are utilized when the woodchuck first emerges in the early spring before sufficient quantities of food are available.

Senses: The woodchuck's eyesight is very well developed. An alert adult spends one-third to one-fourth of its feeding time sitting upright watching for danger. The slightest movement even several hundred yards away receives the woodchuck's undivided attention. If the object it is watching drops from sight, the woodchuck races for its den. There, from the comparative safety of the entrance, it watches for further developments. Woodchucks also have a good sense of hearing and are instantly alerted by the slightest sound. However, I have noticed that some woodchucks do not pay too much attention to scent. In hunting them I often have approached downwind and, although my scent must have carried, to most of them it apparently meant nothing. Other woodchucks reacted almost instantly. Perhaps the scent triggered them to make greater use of their eyes and ears.

Communication: Another common name for the woodchuck is "whistle pig," derived from the loud, piercing whistle that the animal gives when alarmed or frightened. This whistle carries for a long distance and serves as a warning to every woodchuck in the area. In many cases the other woodchucks will add their own alarm notes.

When angered, woodchucks chatter their teeth like castanets. They also hiss, growl and squeal. The young woodchucks make a pleading note when disturbed.

Locomotion: Ordinarily the woodchuck walks along,

stopping to eat a bite here and a bite there. Then it raises itself upright to look for danger. Satisfied that all is well, it drops back to all fours and ambles on. If it wants to move faster it trots, or breaks into a bounding gallop in which the hind feet are extended beyond the front feet. A large 12-pound male has been timed at 11 miles per hour, but that is exceptional.

Woodchucks are strong swimmers and don't hesitate to take to water if forced. Their swimming speed is about 2 miles per hour.

Many people are surprised to find that woodchucks can climb. Any country boy knows about their climbing ability because the woodchuck frequently resorts to climbing if it is cut off from its burrow by a dog. Most of the time woodchucks clamber into saplings rather than into large trees. However, on two occasions I have found them up in large trees as high as 40 feet above the ground.

Woodchucks frequently sun themselves on the top of old stumps or even on large fence posts. The extra height makes such spots ideal from which to watch for danger.

Breeding: As soon as the male woodchuck comes out of hibernation some time in February, it sets out to seek a mate. It apparently knows exactly where it is going because in the snow its tracks will lead from its burrow directly to the burrow of the female. Woodchucks may be monogamous, and some observation leads one to believe they will seek out the same mate in succeeding years. If the accustomed female has been killed the male will continue his search until he finds another one. Some males, however, may mate with several females. The final selection of the mate is done by the female. If she is not satisfied with the first male, she drives him from her den. If the searching male comes upon a mated pair he continues his journey. When a receptive female has been found, the male moves into the den with her for a short while. Except for rare instances, this is the only time of the year when two adult woodchucks live in a single den.

Birth and Young: The gestation period for the woodchuck is thirty-one to thirty-two days, and most of the young are born in the first three weeks of April. The average litter is composed of four young.

Young woodchucks at birth are blind, naked and dark pink in color. This fades to a flesh color within twelve hours. Their average weight is about 25 to 26 grams. Body hair, starting at the head, becomes visible in about one week's time. The young at this point will have doubled their weight. At three weeks the body will be fully furred with light reddish-brown hair. The fur is short and erect and at this stage resembles seal fur. At this age the young can crawl about quite readily.

Four weeks of age marks a big change in the young woodchucks. Their eyes open and they begin to crawl out of the den. They soon start to sample some of the surrounding vegetation and start a self-weaning program. Young woodchucks are quite playful. One family that I watched for hours almost killed a little cedar tree by climbing on it. This is the woodchuck's most sociable time of life. When grown, woodchucks are not tolerant of each other, each establishing a territory from which it will expel all others. By the first of July the young woodchucks are ready to break off family ties and set up housekeeping on their own.

Life Span: The life span of a woodchuck is about five years. Those kept in captivity may live longer.

Sign: The most conspicuous sign of the woodchuck is the large mound of dirt at the main entrance to its burrow. These mounds can be spotted a half-mile away, particularly when set against a green hillside.

In the dust or fresh dirt around the burrow, the woodchuck's tracks may be seen. It is rare that any scat is found because the woodchuck usually buries its feces. It may use an underground toilet chamber or it may bury the feces in the dirt of the observation mound.

If a burrow is occupied there is always fresh dirt in evidence at the mouth of the den. A woodchuck seems to be constantly remodeling its apartment. Pathways through the grass will radiate from the main entrance, and the grass will be clipped close to the ground around the burrow.

Enemies: A large woodchuck is too scrappy a fighter for most creatures. Its main enemy is the farm dog. Some dogs become so adept at killing woodchucks that they build up local reputations. My neighbor had a collie that was a superb woodchuck hunter. It would stalk down a fencerow and lie there for hours waiting for a woodchuck to move from its burrow. Then, in a flash, it would make the kill.

The red fox probably ranks next on the list. Woodchucks are a mainstay of this fox's diet. Although the fox doesn't weigh much more than the woodchuck, it is amazingly agile and fast.

Hawks will take a small woodchuck from time to time,

and an eagle may even try for an adult.

Woodchucks, like all mammals, play host to various ticks and fleas. Small flies called *Pegomyia* seem to favor the woodchuck. Although they apparently don't do the woodchuck any harm, they constantly crawl over its face and around the eyes. That this fly is very annoying can be seen by the frequency with which the woodchuck brushes them off. Internally, the woodchuck harbors both threadworms and roundworms.

Human Relations: Many farmers consider the woodchuck a nuisance. Its observation mounds make it difficult for the farmer when he is working the field, particularly when making hay. Although there is always the possibility of cattle or horses breaking a leg by stepping in a woodchuck's burrow, I have never heard of such an occurrence. In areas where shooting does not control the numbers of woodchucks, many farmers employ poisoned grains or cyanide cartridges in the burrows

On the other hand, woodchucks do a great deal of good by providing most of the other small mammals with homes. One hears of rabbit holes, yet rabbits do not dig holes; they utilize those of woodchucks. In many areas the cottontail rabbit would be wiped out if it were not for the safety of the woodchuck's burrow. Foxes, opossums, raccoons, skunks and even ring-neck pheasants will either live in or hide in woodchuck burrows.

Although the skins of the woodchuck have never been used for fur, their hides make a tough leather and were commonly used in making rawhide boot laces.

Trophy Records: In 1967 Ken Nemeth of Elyria,

Ohio, shot a female woodchuck that was 36 inches long, had a heart girth of 26 inches and weighed 25 pounds. In 1966, Jack Wade of Enin Valley, Pennsylvania, shot a woodchuck that weighed 30 pounds.

Table Fare: Woodchucks, especially the young of the year, make very good eating. I always take extra care to remove all fat and membrane from the carcass before cooking.

In the days when the Indians controlled eastern North America, the woodchuck was probably the most important meat staple of their diet. Woodchucks were more plentiful and easier to secure than deer. Midden heaps of the old Indian villages reveal a preponderance of woodchuck bones. Yet, the Algonquin Indians near Quebec regularly eat muskrats and beaver but would not think of eating a woodchuck.

Yellow-Bellied Marmot

Marmota flaviventris

The yellow-bellied marmot, or rockchuck, is the western counterpart of the eastern woodchuck. Living on the steep slopes of rocky hills, this marmot is not as easily found as the woodchuck in its gently rolling habitat. Nevertheless it is a favorite quarry of long-range hunting

These yellow-bellied marmots are ready for hibernation. They den among rocks on talus slopes. To eat, they must descend from the talus to the valley floor.

buffs who sometimes roam the country in jeeps hoping to sight a colony.

Description: This medium-sized member of the marmot family weighs 4 to 12 pounds, stands 7 inches high at the shoulder and is up to 28 inches in length. Its back is brown with grizzled hair tips. There are two buff-colored patches extending from below the ear and behind the jowl down over the foreshoulders. There is white around the mouth, behind the eye and in a band between the eyes. The feet are light brown. Its chest and belly are a bright orange-red. Melanism is common among these marmots, but I can find no record of albinism. Although the yellow-bellied marmot is equipped with the stout claws that are the trademarks of this family, it doesn't use them for digging so much as in climbing over rocks.

The habit of whistling a shrill alarm call is even better developed among the yellow-bellied marmot than it is in the woodchuck. The West, where this marmot is found, abounds with predators, so the animal needs a good warning system.

Distribution: The yellow-bellied marmot lives in rocky areas in western North America from central British Columbia to south-central California, east to the Rocky Mountains in Colorado and to the Black Hills of South Dakota.

Travel: The yellow-bellied marmot is not the traveling type and lives the year round in the same den. It does have to travel farther than the woodchuck in search

Distribution of the yellow-bellied marmot.

of food. The woodchuck digs its burrow in the middle of the lush vegetation upon which it feeds, but the yellow-bellied marmot lives among the rocks where there is no soil to support any vegetation. When it wants to eat it has to come down from its rocky fortress to the nearest patch of plant-supporting soil. This marmot is stronger and more muscular than the woodchuck, and it scrambles up and down the rock slides as easily as the woodchuck runs on level ground.

Habits: Although this marmot seems to spend much of its time sunbathing on a rock, in reality it is more active than the woodchuck. Since it is larger than the woodchuck, its body needs are greater and it has to travel farther for food.

Because one often is able to see large numbers of these marmots on a single rock slope, it does not mean that the rockchuck is instinctively a sociable animal. The yellow-bellied marmot colonies are restricted to areas of outcropping rocks or where there are broken, tumbled rock masses. This marmot lives among the rock slides; the holes among the rocks are its haven, its home. When the marmots feed, they go down to the valley floor. There is no need for disputes over territorial rights among the rocks just so long as each marmot respects the other's den. On rare occasions a marmot may forsake this rocky fortress and take up a residency beneath an abandoned building.

Winter storms hold little terror for the yellow-bellied marmot because like all of its clan it passes the winter in hibernation. Even in the summer on cold, windy days the marmot will remain in its den. Living as it does in mountainous regions, this marmot retires for the winter before the woodchuck does on the lower levels. According to the region and the weather conditions, the yellow-bellied marmot may go into hibernation as early as the first of September or as late as the middle of October. Seldom if ever are any of them seen stirring before the first week of March.

In addition to the various grasses and forbs of the alpine meadows, the yellow-bellied marmot also feeds upon blackberry bushes and service berry. If there are farms in the area, this marmot, like the woodchuck, feeds upon alfalfa, beans, carrots, cabbage and other crops.

Senses: Eyesight is the most important and highly developed sense of the yellow-bellied marmot, with hearing coming in a close second.

Communication: The yellow-bellied marmot can whistle louder than the woodchuck, but its whistle is lower in tone. Like the woodchuck, this marmot rattles its teeth when disturbed.

Locomotion: The foot of this marmot does not appear different than the foot of the woodchuck, yet it spends most of its time scrambling up and down rocks while the woodchuck travels on earth. The claws on the forefeet of the yellow-bellied marmot appear to be slightly shorter than those of the woodchuck. In running up tilting rock faces the animal bounds along with as much ease as the woodchuck does on level ground.

Breeding: In spite of the bitter blasts of wintery wind that are still ricochetting off the mountainsides in March, the yellow-bellied marmot awakens and sets forth to seek a mate. The journey is a short one because the terrain has corralled the species. Apparently this marmot is monogamous and sets up housekeeping with a single female.

Birth and Young: The yellow-bellied marmot brings forth larger litters than does the woodchuck, with eight young not being an uncommon number. The gestation period is about one month. A species reproduces itself in accordance to its survival rate, and evidently this marmot is exposed to greater danger than is the woodchuck and must produce larger litters.

The young are born about the last part of April or the first of May. They are naked, blind and helpless. In about four to six weeks their growth is sufficient for them to venture from the den. If pursued at this time the young instinctively head for the shelter of the rocks. They aren't yet familiar with every nook and cranny that would afford them shelter, so they cram themselves into the first crevice they come to. If the crevice is deep enough the young marmot is safe, but if the crevice is shallow their hind end may be exposed. If they survive they soon learn where and how to escape from the many enemies that consider them fair game. By the end of July the young marmots are seeking out a cranny in the rocks that they can use as dens. The family splits up well before hibernation time, each member seeking solitary quarters. In low, hot valleys these animals may go into a summer sleep—aestivation—which tides them over a period when there is no green forage.

Life Span: The potential life span for the yellow-bellied marmot is ten years, although the average span would be six to eight years.

Sign: As this marmot often dens in the rocks, its burrow is inconspicuous. Occasionally it will fill a crevice with grass for a nest, and this can readily be seen. There is actually little chance of seeing its tracks except in the late winter snow. Its scat is usually buried.

Enemies: The yellow-bellied marmot lives mostly in wild, inaccessible areas where a goodly number of natural predators still abound. The golden eagle probably tops the list of enemies. Dropping from the sky like a bolt of lightning, this eagle can easily catch an unwary marmot. Grizzly bears will dig out any marmot's den that is not built in a rocky fortress. Coyotes, bobcats and lynx also feed upon this marmot.

Ticks are a common parasite on the yellow-bellied marmot. Frequently the ticks are the same ones that transmit Rocky Mountain spotted fever to man. It has been found that this marmot is one of the primary hosts to that deadly tick. The marmots also have internal roundworms and pinworms.

Human Relations: Although it requires work to reach the western marmot areas, more hunting can be had there because of the colony nature of the talus-slope dwellings. This marmot is not hunted as heavily as the woodchuck simply because there are fewer hunters in the vast areas of the West. But it is a sporty little game animal that really tries a hunter's patience.

Trophy Records: I can find no records of yellow-bellied marmots of exceptional size. A top weight of 17 pounds is recorded.

Table Fare: I have not eaten this marmot myself nor do I know of anyone who has, but I see no reason for it tasting any different from the woodchuck.

Silver-gray fur over the shoulders gives the hoary marmot its name. (Photo by Irene Vandermolen.)

Hoary Marmot

Marmota caligata

The hoary marmot, largest member of the family, lives farther north than its two close relatives, underlining the fact that mammals of the same type tend to be larger the farther north they are found. In French Canada it is known as *le siffleur*, the whistler, for it has the loudest whistle of all the marmots. Its species name *caligata* (booted) takes note of the animal's conspicuous black feet.

Description: This marmot measures up to 31 inches in length, stands 8 to 9 inches high at the shoulder and weighs up to 20 pounds. Its basic body color is a silvery gray over the shoulders shading to a darker brown over the rump and tail. Its four feet are black. The head is essentially grayish-white with a patch of black covering the forehead, a black stripe through the eye and one going down through and past the ears. Most specimens also have a black band behind the nose. This marmot has a large, bushy tail. The silvery-gray coat provides excellent camouflage when this marmot flattens itself against one of the similarly colored rocks among which it makes its home.

The hoary marmot's coat has a dense, soft underfur. The Indians and Eskimos of Canada and Alaska prize this animal's pelts for making parkas and robes. The leather is lightweight and the fur soft and warm.

Melanism, which is fairly common among all of the marmots, is particularly prevalent among the hoary marmots of the Glacier Bay area of Alaska. The hoary marmots of the Olympic Mountains of Washington and around

Vancouver, British Columbia, are much darker in coloration, with most of the specimens an overall dark-brown
color instead of silvery-gray.

This marmot possesses ten mammary nipples while
the woodchuck and the yellow-bellied marmot have only
eight.

Distribution: The hoary marmot lives in rocky areas
and alpine meadows in western North America from
northern Alaska south to Washington and Idaho. Within
this range two species are sometimes recognized, *Mar-*

Distribution of the hoary marmot.

mota caligata and *Marmota broweri.* The latter inhabits only extreme northern Alaska, and the former the rest of the range.

Travel: The records show that this marmot travels farther from its den than do its two relatives. Some specimens have been seen as many as 4 miles from typical marmot homesteads. These straying individuals may be the explorers of their tribe setting out to colonize more distant, uninhabited slopes, but I have never seen a hoary marmot venture farther from its den than was necessary to secure food, and that was about 100 yards.

Habits: Hoary marmots come out of hibernation in May, sometimes tunneling up through 10 feet of snow to reach the bright world of sunshine. Before the lush grasses of the alpine meadows send forth their new shoots, the marmot is sustained by the fat reserves left in its body from the previous summer. When the grasses appear the marmot eats constantly and incessantly. Often I have seen a feeding marmot start for its den only to pause and cut off a large mouthful of grass which it carries back to its den to eat in safety.

The hoary marmot lives in fairly close proximity to others of its own kind and might be considered sociable. It will however drive other marmots away from choice feeding grounds that it considers to be its own private domain.

Some of the marmots apparently are self-appointed guardians of the entire mountainside. As soon as these sentinels have appeased their appetites, they scramble up on the highest nearby rock spire to watch for danger and at the same time to enjoy a sunbath. At the slightest movement of an unfamiliar object, the sentinel marmots whistle loudly, instantly alerting not only every other marmot but every wild creature within hearing distance. The danger call is relayed from one marmot to another, until all of the marmots learn of the danger and rush into their burrows. If danger is close they plunge through the entrance and disappear. If the danger is still some distance away they sit at the entrance and continue whistling.

These marmots often engage in wrestling matches. A pair will square off and, raising up on their hind feet, place their forefeet together and push against each other. These encounters may have some deeper significance, but it appears to be just play. Marmots engage in this activity frequently enough so that it is readily witnessed.

Hoary marmots eat all types of natural vegetation: wild flowers, berries, roots, shrubs and grasses. Except for a few isolated cabin sites, they seldom have access to a garden.

By September the marmots have filled the slackness under their loose skins. Having eaten every piece of vegetation in reach, they are ready and anxious to retire for the year. By the time the temperature plummets down and the first snow falls, the marmots have fallen into their deep sleep of hibernation.

Senses: The hoary marmot's eyes are far keener than a human's. Their ears, too, are exceedingly good, as befits an animal whose safety often depends on hearing the whistled warning of a colleague.

Communication: In addition to being able to whistle louder than the other marmots, the hoary also seems to have a larger repertoire of sounds. It can grunt, chatter, growl, hiss, squeal and cry, more than enough to allow it to give full expression of its emotions.

Locomotion: The hoary marmot either walks or bounds. Bounding, it has been clocked at 5 miles per hour. This may not seem very fast on level ground, but the hoary marmot is usually scrambling over rocks. It exhibits the peculiar habit of waving its tail up and down a couple of times before setting forth.

Breeding: Hoary marmots breed as soon as they come out of hibernation, each male apparently seeking out a single mate. Their summer season is short and they must take full advantage of it. Gestation is about twenty-eight to thirty days and two to four young comprise the average litter.

Birth and Young: The young are born naked and with their eyes sealed tightly shut. Hair development is well started within one week's time, and the eyes open in three weeks. It often takes as much as two days for the eyes to open wide. As the young can crawl about long before their eyes are open, they start going out of the den as soon as they can see. The young may be eating some grass before they venture out of the den because it seems very likely that they would be tempted to feed upon the grasses that the adults frequently carry into the dens.

By August the young will have left the mother and sought out den sites of their own. The young eat as ravenously as the adults because they instinctively know that it is only the fat marmots that live to see the bright sun of spring.

Life Span: The hoary marmot has a potential life span of about ten years, but it is unlikely that any of the wild adults ever live to that age.

Sign: In the late spring, when the marmots first come out of hibernation, they tunnel up through the snow. Each time they pass out of the den, they track more dirt up on the snow so that the black holes are very conspicuous. This is about the only time that their tracks can be seen.

Enemies: The golden eagle is the hoary marmot's main enemy. The marmots scrutinize every speck in the sky in their effort to thwart this winged predator. Grizzly bears, with their gigantic strength, often attempt and sometimes succeed in digging the marmots out. Wolves, lynx, wolverines, cougars and coyotes also prey upon the marmots. Foxes will take a young marmot but would have too much trouble trying to kill an adult.

In addition to the usual variety of parasitic worms found in the digestive system, the hoary marmot plays host to fleas and ticks and is pestered by flies and mosquitoes.

Human Relations: The large size of the hoary marmot makes it a very worthwhile game animal to the Indians and the Eskimos. This marmot is seldom hunted for sport because there aren't many varmint hunters inhabiting the regions where it lives. The natives value the meat as well as the hide and hunt this marmot whenever the opportunity presents itself. The hoary marmot is too far removed from farming regions to be a nuisance to crops.

Trophy Records: The heaviest weight that I can find given for the hoary marmot is 25 pounds.

Table Fare: I have been assured by people in Alaska that the hoary marmot is very good to eat.

An alert, ambitious little rodent, the gray squirrel rises at dawn and gathers food for future use, storing each piece in a separate place.

Gray Squirrel

Sciurus carolinensis

The gray squirrel is an arboreal rodent that spends a good part of its life in treetops. Although it often feeds on the ground, it never makes its den underground. Leaping from branch to branch in hardwood forests, the gray has challenged the marksmanship of hunters since frontier days.

The first part of the gray's scientific name comes from two Greek words, *skia* and *oura*, and means, "an animal that sits in the shadow of its tail." The second name was chosen because the squirrel was first described from specimens obtained in the Carolinas. The word squirrel comes from the Old French word *esquireul*.

Description: In the northern part of its range, a large adult gray squirrel measures about 20 inches long, and in the southern part about 17 inches. Of that total length, about 8 to 8 1/2 inches is the beautifully plumed tail. The average gray squirrel weighs a little over a pound. Both male and female are about the same size and weight.

The basic color of the average gray squirrel is best described as a salt-and-pepper gray. The underfur on the body is a solid gray while the guard hairs are gray at the base, then buff-brown, then black and finally white-tipped. The white hair tips give this squirrel its silver-gray appearance and its name.

The short hairs on the squirrel's face, muzzle, ears and the upper part of its paws are a yellowish-tan. This rusty coloring often causes this squirrel to be confused with the fox squirrel where the ranges of the two overlap. However, the tips of the guard hairs on the tail of the

267

gray squirrel are always white, while those on the fox squirrel are rusty-red. The hair beneath the gray squirrel's throat, its underparts and the inside of its legs are a bright white.

Among most animal species, some individuals are born which are either albino (pure white) or melanistic (jet black). These mutations are so common among gray squirrels that often entire areas are inhabited by squirrels of these offshoot colorations. In the northern portion of the gray squirrel's range, the black squirrels become dominant and normal grays may compose no more than 5 percent of the population. Occasional black squirrels may be found throughout the gray's entire range. The same is true of the albinos, except that white squirrels frequently become common or dominant only in isolated pockets. Trenton, New Jersey, has quite a few albino squirrels. Greenwood, South Carolina, has a colony that inhabits about 100 acres. The largest concentration of albinos, over 1,000, can be found in Olney, Illinois. This particular strain can be traced back to 1892, coming from a pair that was owned by a saloonkeeper. Evidently the squirrels were of local origin because the town passed a law giving complete protection to albino squirrels. The state has since done likewise.

Squirrels are rodents and, typical of this group, have four large incisors which grow constantly. Except in rare cases of malocclusion, in which the teeth do not meet, squirrels have ample opportunity to keep their teeth worn chisel-sharp by constant chewing. Sometimes the gray squirrel becomes a nuisance by chewing into attics to make a home or chewing the insulation from electric wires.

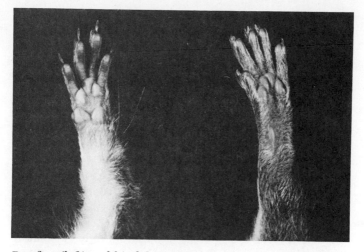

Forefoot (left) and hind foot of gray squirrel have four and five toes respectively, each with a sharp claw. The squirrel bends its claws up when it runs, to keep from dulling them against the ground.

In addition to its incisors, the gray squirrel has 6 premolars and 12 molars. In rare cases, the first premolar on either side in the top of the squirrel's mouth may be absent. All told, the gray squirrel has 22 teeth, none of them canines.

On each front foot the gray squirrel has four, long functional toes and a vestigial thumb. The hind feet have five toes. The claws are not retractable but can be bent up slightly so that they do not become dulled when the squirrel walks on the ground.

The ears of a gray squirrel are slightly pointed. Its whiskers are black, long and pointed.

Distribution: At one time, most of the eastern part of the United States was covered by a dense, mature hardwood forest which extended west to the high grass prairies. Although there were several hundred different types of trees in this area, oaks were the most common, providing an ideal habitat for the proliferation of countless millions of gray squirrels. Ernest Thompson Seton, the famous naturalist, calculated that over 1 billion gray squirrels at one time inhabited 1 million square miles of range.

Today the eastern gray squirrel (*Sciurus carolinensis*)

Distribution of the eastern gray squirrel (vertical lines), western gray squirrel (horizontal), and Arizona gray squirrel (dots).

inhabits hardwood forests from southern Canada to the Gulf of Mexico, and from eastern Texas and eastern Saskatchewan to the Atlantic Coast. The Arizona gray squirrel (*Sciurus arizonensis*) lives in oak and pine forests in central and southeastern Arizona. The western gray squirrel (*Sciurus griseus*) inhabits oak and pine forests from Washington to southern California.

Travel: Under ordinary conditions gray squirrels have been content to stay in a 10-acre area, but under the stress of exploding populations they have emigrated across the country in great waves. Although most of the emigrations were in a westward direction, some were to the east and some ran from north to south. Each exodus left only a nucleus of breeding stock in the area, but with an unlimited amount of food, this breeding stock produced and raised strong litters which soon produced more strong litters. In just five years, the cycle would go from the lowest ebb to a migration peak.

Dr. John Bachman, the naturalist, in 1809 told of great hordes of squirrels coming from the west into New York and Vermont. In 1819 he saw a migration band in Ohio which was 130 miles across. Even in this century some of the smaller emigrations have been recorded—in 1914 in Missouri, 1947 in Arkansas and 1951 in New York. Although gray squirrels ordinarily avoid water, during these eruptions they attempt to swim across rivers and lakes and drown by the thousands.

Habits: Gray squirrels are ambitious, hard-working rodents. They are up at dawn and set to work in the semidarkness feeding or gathering food for future use.

Unlike the red squirrel, which usually stores as much as two bushels of food in one underground hole, the gray squirrel stores each piece of food individually. When food is plentiful, the gray squirrel can bury as many as five nuts in four minutes, selecting burial spots at random, but, strangely enough, always in a different place from where it finds the fallen nut. Its haste is understandable.

In addition to other gray squirrels, there are red, fox and flying squirrels, as well as chipmunks, competing for the same food. And deer, bears, hogs, turkeys and woodchucks all eagerly feed upon acorns and nuts.

John Madson, a biologist, tells of an Indiana farm which had about 180 acres of woodland with white oak predominating. It was estimated that each of the oaks produced between 2,000 and 8,000 acorns. The woods supported a large concentration of gray squirrels, which did such a thorough job of gathering nuts that not a single one could be found by the end of October. Calculations turned up an estimate of 20 million acorns produced in those woods. Although other creatures got some of the acorns, the squirrels buried most of them.

When gray squirrels bury nuts, the method varies according to the individual. Some do the job properly, putting the nut down into an inch or two of earth. Others do a very poor job and just stick the nut in the forest duff and scratch a few leaves over the top. Squirrels excavate the holes with their front feet but use both feet and nose to tamp the earth back on top of the nut.

A squirrel has no way of staking out its caches or preventing other squirrels from digging them up. Undoubtedly, when a squirrel is hungry it digs up the first nut it can locate whether it planted that one or not.

Much of the antagonism between the red and the gray squirrels stems from territorial rights and pilfered stores. Although I have seen many chases between red squirrels and grays, I have never seen a serious fight. I have also seen red and gray squirrels feeding peacefully side by side. Where food is plentiful there is no reason to argue.

Man is a direct beneficiary of the squirrels' nut-planting habit, for every buried nut is a potential tree. While it is true that acorns can lie on top of the ground and sprout, hickory nuts, butternuts and walnuts must be buried so that they stay moist in order to sprout. Even if acorns are left on top of the ground, they undoubtedly will be eaten by other animals. It would be safe to say, then, that almost every hickory, butternut, walnut and oak tree growing today is the product of some squirrel's activity years ago.

A squirrel never cuts into an unsound nut. Any nut found lying on the ground after the squirrels have harvested the crop will be shriveled up inside. When a gray squirrel cuts open a walnut it customarily makes only two cuts, each entering two quarters of the nut. The red squirrel, having smaller teeth and jaws, usually makes four cuts, one in each quarter.

In addition to nuts, gray squirrels feed upon tree blossoms, buds, berries, fruit, fungi and field corn. They go into a frenzy over corn and are capable of doing great damage which cannot be confused with the work of any other animal. Squirrels do not eat the entire corn kernel, just the germ end, allowing the starchy portion to go to waste. Beneath the shredded husk and the bare cob, the golden bits of starch remain to identify the culprit.

All rodents like to eat a little fresh meat now and then,

and gray squirrels are no exception. If these squirrels become numerous they may limit the number of birds in the area, as they eat both eggs and baby birds. At other times, squirrels seem oblivious to nesting birds.

Gray squirrels need water and are seldom found very far from it. They also slake their thirst with maple sap. In early spring, as the sun pulls the first sap to the tops of the trees, both red and gray squirrels gnaw slits in the branches and lick the sap as it flows out. Sometimes the leaking sap freezes during cold nights. Early in the morning, before the sun warms up, the squirrels climb about and eat the sweet icicles.

The gray squirrel's favorite den site is a hollow high in a big tree. Branches that have died and dropped off or that have been torn off in a storm often cause the tree to rot in such places. As soon as the hollow becomes large enough, the squirrels move in. Often the tree proceeds to heal itself and new layers of bark are added each year, in effect closing the cavity. If squirrels are using that particular hollow, they will keep gnawing back the encroaching bark.

Huge dead trees standing among smaller living trees are commonly called "wolf" trees, and are used by woodpeckers for both food and den sites. The cavities that the woodpeckers make are often appropriated by gray squirrels for their own use. They also den in bird houses.

Lacking a hollow for a den site, or perhaps wanting a cooler home for the summer, gray squirrels construct leaf nests for a single night's shelter, for a season's shelter or for a year-round home. The leaf nests do not offer as much protection as a tree hollow. I once found a treetop which had fallen across a leaf nest during a windstorm and crushed the occupant. I have also seen red-tailed hawks plunge into a summer leaf nest and grasp the squirrel inside. And a leaf nest does not protect baby squirrels against a marauding raccoon.

Gray squirrels are active throughout the year. During extremely cold weather they may remain in their dens for several days, but shortly thereafter they are out again. If the snow is too deep and too soft to support the squirrel's weight it will tunnel underneath.

Senses: The squirrel's exceptionally keen sense of smell helps it to locate food and relocate it after burying it. However, I do not believe that a gray squirrel locates its enemies by scent, because I have been seated upwind of squirrels many times and have not been noticed.

A squirrel is quick to notice motion. Usually the slightest movement catches its attention and any further movement sends it scampering away. If the squirrel can reach its den, it pops inside and stays there until it no longer hears any sound of danger outside.

If a squirrel is surprised away from its den, it scampers up the nearest tree and disappears around the other side. As you circle the tree, the squirrel moves to the opposite side. I have often fooled a squirrel into disclosing itself by rolling a stone across the ground on the side where it is hiding, or by tying a long piece of string to a bush on the squirrel's side of the tree and shaking the bush. If it is a tall tree, the squirrel will scoot to the top and stretch out on a limb. Its gray coloration blends with the gray branches, rendering it almost invisible. Usually it can't be seen, although occasionally a breeze blows its tail tip just enough to give away its presence.

Communication: The most commonly heard sound of the gray squirrel is its barking "quack." Usually this sound is accompanied by sharp, vigorous shakes of its tail. The tone varies and is used to denote anger, fear or defiance. This squirrel also makes a buzzing and a purring sound. It expresses extreme anger by rapidly chattering its teeth.

Locomotion: In most of its activities, the squirrel utilizes its bushy tail, which might be considered its most valuable asset. The tail serves as an umbrella when the squirrel feeds in the rain, as a blanket in cold weather when the animal curls it around its body and covers its nose and feet. When the squirrel walks along narrow branches or along power lines, the tail acts as a balance. When it is pursued on the ground by a dog, the tail, acting as a counterbalance, allows the squirrel to make high-speed, right-angle turns. When the squirrel jumps through the treetops, its flat tail acts like a glider's wing, giving it lift through the air. If the squirrel misses its footing and plummets toward the earth, the tail acts like a parachute and slows the speed of descent. The squirrel feints with its tail when pursued by a predator. The predator may strike at the tail instead of the squirrel and end up with nothing but hair or at most a piece of the tail tip. When the squirrel stands erect, the tail acts as a counterbalance; and when it swims, the tail acts as a rudder.

While walking on the ground, the squirrel carries its tail in a gentle arch. When it bounds along, the tail undulates in graceful ripples, balancing the body beautifully. A gray squirrel can run along the ground at better than 12 miles per hour and can run up or down a tree almost as fast.

Breeding: Many hunters believe that because no testicles are visible on the gray squirrels during fall that the red emasculates the gray when they fight. The truth of the matter is that, except during the breeding season, the testicles of the gray squirrel are shrunken and carried inside the body. The testicles begin to enlarge after December 1 as hormone changes occur in the squirrel's body. At this time the males begin to take an interest in the females, and about January 1 the females come into oestrous. Usually the males start chasing after a female before she is physically ready to accept them. Overanxious suitors are rebuked with sharp cries and sharper bites. The males fight for dominance, and the biggest, strongest male is the one chosen by the female. After a few days of frequent copulation, the female's ardor wanes and so does the male's interest in her. He soon drifts away seeking new conquests.

The gray squirrel usually has two litters per year, especially in the South. The first breeding season occurs in January and the second one in May. If food has been scarce that year, the breeding season may be curtailed, or in periods of great hardship it may be skipped entirely.

Birth and Young: The gestation period of gray squirrels is about forty-four days. Most of the young of the first litter are born during the first half of March and those of the second litter come during the last half of July. The average litter contains three young with the number varying from two to five.

At birth baby squirrels are hairless, although their whiskers have broken through the skin. They weigh about a half ounce and measure about 4 1/2 inches in length. Their eyes and ears are sealed shut and no teeth have erupted through the gums.

In one week's time, they have doubled their weights and have grown about three-fourths of an inch. During their second week, hair starts to push through the skin on their backs. At one month of age, their ears are open and their lower incisors have pricked through the gums. By this time the young squirrels are almost completely furred. During the fifth week their eyes open and the upper incisors are visible. The young squirrels now measure about 9 inches in length and weigh 3 to 4 ounces.

As soon as the young squirrels' eyes have opened they begin to climb out of the den and to take an interest in the outside world and in solid food. Although weaning begins during the seventh week, nursing continues until the young are about three months old. By this time, if

Comparison of nuts chewed by gray and red squirrels. Nut at left has been cut by gray, which has larger teeth and makes only two cuts. Two nuts at right, with four cuts, are the work of the smaller red.

The gray squirrel's tracks may be confused with the cotton-tail's as the individual prints are similar. The pattern of the tracks is different, however. The gray's four tracks form a distinct square, as shown here, whereas the cottontail's fore-foot tracks are staggered.

the female is going to have a second litter she will be bred. Prior to this event the mother leaves the first litter and moves to another nest.

Life Span: The gray squirrel has a potential life span of about six years. In captivity some of these squirrels have lived to be over twenty years old.

Sign: Tracks are conspicuous but often confused by the tyro with those of a rabbit. Both tracks are similar although the rabbit's are longer. A squirrel's hind feet are placed side by side ahead of the front feet and the tracks look like exclamation marks!!. A rabbit's hind feet land together but the forefeet do not; one forefoot will be placed 4 to 8 inches ahead of the other, depending on how fast the rabbit is bounding. If the tracks end at a tree, that is conclusive proof that they belong to a squirrel.

Chewed nuts, chewed corn, chewed den entrances and leaf nests all give away the squirrel's whereabouts.

Enemies: During the time that I worked as a camp ranger, five huge maple trees on the lawn were a haven for gray squirrels. The trees had lots of hollows in them and were close to corn fields and nut trees. Squirrels abounded in those trees and their antics were a delight to see, but slowly their population diminished. Eventually I noticed that a large, black rat snake had taken up residence in one of the trees and had killed or driven away every squirrel. Tree-climbing snakes are always the squirrel's most deadly enemies.

Hawks rank next. About twelve years ago, I discovered a redtailed hawk's nest on a high-tension tower. This was the first time I had ever found this type of hawk using a man-made structure for its nest. When I was photographing the young, I discovered that gray squirrels were the basic item of diet for this particular family of hawks. Bits of gray squirrel were present every time I checked the nest. Although the parent hawks were constantly catching gray squirrels, they were acting as a control factor and were not eliminating the squirrels. While I sat up in the tower, I often saw gray squirrels feeding and running about in the forest below. In addition, the red-shouldered, broad-winged, marsh and Cooper's hawks and the goshawks are enemies of the gray squirrel. So, too, are the great horned owl, barred owl and long-eared owl.

Red and gray foxes, bobcats, weasels, raccoons and house cats and dogs all prey on the squirrels.

Scabies, or mange, caused by the scabies mite is often fatal. In the winter the squirrels scratch themselves until their bodies are bloody and hairless, thus becoming weakened and susceptible to predation.

During the summer, in the southern portion of the squirrel's range, the botfly ranks as the most serious pest. The egg of the botfly is believed to be laid on wood. The larva that hatches transfers to the first gray squirrel that happens by. Burrowing under the skin, the tiny larva becomes a large grub. In order to breathe, this grub keeps a hole open in the squirrel's skin. The large bump of the grub and the bloody breathing exit hole are not only very annoying to the animal, but they are also offensive to the hunter. Thousands of squirrels shot early in the fall are wasted because of the presence of these warbles, even though they do not affect the meat.

Ticks, fleas and lice, as well as pinworms, roundworms and tapeworms, live off the squirrel but are seldom more than a nuisance.

Human Relations: The American frontiersman developed his shooting skill hunting squirrels. The squirrels were good to eat, and there were too many of them. In 1749 Pennsylvania placed a threepence bounty on squirrels in an effort to control their depredations against the crops on wilderness farms. After one year, the law was repealed because the treasury had paid out more than 8,000 pounds sterling and the state was nearly bankrupt. In 1834 two teams of fifty men each participated in a three-day shoot for Indiana squirrels. It is not recorded just how many squirrels were killed, but the two top hunters shot 900 and 783 squirrels apiece.

Those days are gone forever, and so are the trees that supported such numbers. Still, the gray squirrel is a very common game animal, but most hunters don't bother to hunt them any more. Squirrel hunting doesn't produce as much meat as, for instance, deer hunting, but it is good for memories. It's mighty peaceful sitting in the quiet woods on a crisp fall morning waiting for a bannertail to show itself.

The gray squirrel has been transported to England where it has now become a nuisance and is driving the red squirrels out of the forest.

Trophy Records: Vernon Bailey, the naturalist, recorded two female gray squirrels weighing 1 pound, 7 ounces and 1 pound, 8 ounces.

Table Fare: So many millions of gray squirrels have been eaten that the numbers alone furnish proof of the quality and flavor of the meat. Many modern hunters don't hunt squirrels because they don't want the trouble of skinning them.

Fox Squirrel

Sciurus niger

The fox squirrel, our largest tree squirrel, was so named because in color it sometimes resembles the red fox. This squirrel actually occurs in three different color phases, one of them black. Each color phase is dominant in a particular section of the country, but all three colors may be found in any part of the range. Linnaeus, who gave the squirrel its Latin name, *niger* (black), probably encountered only the black phase.

Description: In the northeastern part of its range the fox squirrel is usually gray and looks like an oversized gray squirrel with rusty markings along its flanks. In the western portions the squirrel is a bright rust color. In the South black is the dominant color, but some black squirrels may have white faces and white tail tips. The tips of the hairs in the fox squirrel's tail are usually orange, in the gray squirrel's tail they are white.

The fox squirrel weighs from 1 1/2 to 3 pounds. The females often weigh a little more than the males. This squirrel may reach 28 inches in total length and stand 3 1/2 to 4 inches high at the shoulder. Of its total length, up to 12 or 13 inches may be the beautifully plumed tail.

The fox squirrel has four toes and an abbreviated thumb on each forefoot and five toes on each of the hind feet. In the summer the soles of the feet of all fox squirrels are bare. In the winter the northern fox squirrels' soles may be lightly furred over for protection.

Looking at a fox squirrel in profile, one can see that the plane from the nose to the ear is straighter than that of the gray squirrel. The ears of a fox squirrel are large

Largest of the tree squirrels, the fox squirrel lacks the climbing agility of the gray. It spends most of its time on the ground, sunning itself in the open woodlands.

and rounded. Its whiskers are long and prominent.

The chewing armament of the fox squirrel numbers 20: 4 incisors, 4 premolars and 12 molars. The incisors are chisel-shaped and grow constantly, while the premolars and molars are flat-topped for grinding the squirrel's food into a mash.

Often, positive identification of the gray from the fox squirrel is difficult. One difference is that the gray squirrel has two more premolars in the top of its mouth. Positive identification can also be made by checking the bones of the dead animals; they are different in color. The bones of the gray squirrel are white, those of the fox squirrel are pinkish. I tell them apart by recalling that the fox squirrel, which has reddish hair, has the reddish bones. The gray squirrel has white-tipped hair and white bones.

Distribution: The fox squirrel is no longer found as extensively in the Northeast as it was when the white men arrived, although it is spreading in the Midwest. Originally it was found as far east as Rhode Island, but today the northeastern extremity of its range is Pennsylvania. Although conditions are more favorable for this squirrel today in my own state of New Jersey, it disappeared from the scene around 1850. Several attempts to reestablish it have failed.

The eastern fox squirrel *(Sciurus niger)* lives in open woods, hardwoods in the north and conifers in the south, from eastern Colorado to the Atlantic Coast, and from the Canadian border to the Gulf of Mexico. It is absent from New England. The Apache fox squirrel *(Sciurus apache)* lives only in the Chiricahua Mountains of southeastern Arizona, and in Mexico.

Distribution of the eastern fox squirrel.

Travel: If sufficient food can be found in the vicinity of a favorite den tree, these squirrels may travel no farther than 500 or 600 feet. Ten acres is enough for a fox squirrel, and only when driven by the sexual urge does the male squirrel exceed this. Females have an even more restricted range.

Habits: Whereas the gray squirrel is up and about with the day's first light, the fox squirrel is driven by no such compulsion. Gray squirrels are active later in the day, but the fox squirrel is often active at noon.

Both squirrels like to lie out in the sun, but for the fox

squirrel this is almost a way of life. The gray squirrel is a creature of the dense, mature forests, while the fox squirrel is a denizen of more open woodlands. The fox squirrel has to have trees in which to den and escape and from which to obtain nut crops, but these can be small groups of trees or even isolated trees, if they aren't too far apart. The isolated trees, being out in the open, receive more sunlight and water and are able to produce much larger nut crops. The fox squirrel needs only a couple of such trees to be content.

The fox squirrel spends more of its time on the ground and is heavier than the gray—hence it is not as good a climber. If the gray is frightened, it usually seeks shelter in a tree and, if it has the chance, goes back to its den by climbing from one treetop to another without descending to the ground. The fox squirrel, if surprised on the ground, will do its best to reach the safety of its den by running along the ground directly to its tree. In areas where the fox squirrel does inhabit large forests, it prefers to stay upon the ridges and leave the more dense bottomlands to the gray.

A mature white oak makes one of the best den trees for this squirrel. Where a lower limb has dropped off, a hollow soon starts to rot. The main tree lives on and has the strength to withstand wind and storms. But when a dead tree is selected, the squirrel may have to face the hazard of being uprooted. The blight that wiped out the American chestnut tree removed a tremendous food potential for the squirrels, but it did create an almost unlimited number of den trees.

When a suitable den tree cannot be found or when the squirrel builds a second home in the summer, it will make a leaf nest. Those used just for the summer are loosely constructed of branches that still have leaves on them. These leaf nests are often used in the summer because they are cooler and because the den tree may be infested with lice or mites.

Winter nests are usually much more sturdily constructed, with the material more compacted. When these are sufficiently thick, they are as warm as a den tree would be although they do not offer as much protection.

Generally the leaf nest is about 40 feet above the ground, but some may be built as low as 10 feet. A squirrel, by working hard, can complete a good nest in a day. The nests are usually lined with whatever material is available, be it grass, roots or corn husks. Where it is available the shredded bark of the red cedar tree is regularly used.

In the winter when the squirrel goes into a nest, it makes a plug of material and seals up the entrance. In a very short time its body heat has considerably raised the inside temperature. Another advantage of such a nest is that it can be built near a food supply. By using such a nest the squirrel can spend more of its time gathering and burying nuts instead of having to carry them away to be cached. When the nuts have ripened and fallen, time is short and the competition is keen. The squirrel that buries a good store of nuts is the one that is going to survive.

Fox squirrels are active at all times of the year, in the bitterest weather. Even if the nuts are buried under a foot of snow, the squirrels have no trouble finding them. In the fall the squirrel usually buries them just beneath the leaf mold. The leaf mold and the snow prevent the ground from freezing so that the squirrels have little trouble digging up the nuts.

Acorns are the most important food items, the white oak, black oak and red oak heading the list. Nuts of the hickory, beech and hazel are also taken. Black walnuts, butternuts and pecans are important. In the winter the squirrels dig up Osage oranges and eat them. In the spring they eat the blossoms and the fruit of maples and, in season, domesticated and wild fruits and berries, as well as some fungi.

Fox squirrels have a penchant for field corn. From the time the kernels begin to swell with milk until they become flint-hard, these squirrels are after them. Many times raccoons have been blamed for damage done to corn that was in reality the work of fox squirrels. The 'coons do enough damage on their own, without being blamed for someone else's work. One sure sign of a fox squirrel's work is the litter of husks and bare cobs below its den tree. Under one tree in Michigan, Durwood Allen, the biologist, found 136 stripped corn cobs.

In the winter the fox squirrel sometimes does considerable damage to maple trees by stripping off the outer bark to feed upon the cambium layer. Trees that are girdled in this manner die.

The water requirements for the fox squirrel are not high. It evidently gets most of its moisture from the foods that it eats.

Senses: It is extremely difficult to state whether the fox squirrel's eyesight or its hearing is the keenest sense. Both of them stand the squirrel in good stead, and it is a rare hunter who can slip up on the squirrel. Most hunters find that they are most successful when they sit quietly and just wait for the squirrels to come out. This method nullifies the squirrel's keen hearing, but the slightest movement means danger and it is quick to notice motion.

Its sense of smell is also keen. Any animal that can locate a nut beneath 2 inches of dirt and leaf mold and 12 inches of snow has a pretty good nose. When the snow is more than a foot deep, the squirrel digs tunnels to locate food.

Communication: Fox squirrels make quite a bit of noise. The most commonly heard sound is similar to the clucking noise we make with our tongues. I have found that imitating this sound always interests the squirrels, sometimes enough to stay their wild dash away. Their repertoire contains coughs, grunts and churring sounds. They also chatter their teeth at one another as a warning.

Locomotion: Even the tree squirrels spend enough time on the ground so that walking comes to them naturally, or they may hop even if they aren't in a hurry. When going somewhere in a rush, they bound along with their hind feet landing about 4 inches ahead of their front feet. It has been estimated that a fox squirrel's top speed on the ground is between 10 and 12 miles per hour.

In climbing through the treetops, the fox squirrel is not as agile as the lighter gray squirrel. This doesn't daunt the fox squirrel, however; it climbs well enough to fulfill its requirements. If it does slip and fall, it spreads its body and tail and has been known to fall 40 feet with no ill effects.

Although fox squirrels normally are not found too near water, preferring open country or ridges, they can swim well.

Breeding: In December the testicles of the male fox squirrels begin to enlarge and descend. The shrunken testicles have been carried inside the body since the end of the last breeding season. The squirrels' testicles and their fervor grow apace.

The females begin to come into heat about the first of January. Fox squirrels tend to pair up for the breeding season, although there may be competition among the males.

Courtship usually starts off with some wild chases. Since the male is in the mood before the female, he may be intent upon mating; she is just not ready to receive his advances. But as the female comes into oestrous she stops running, and mating occurs over a period of several days.

In most areas the adult fox squirrels bring forth two litters of young per year, and the second breeding season takes place in May. Yearling females usually have only one litter.

Birth and Young: The gestation period for the fox squirrel is about forty-five days. The average litter consists of three young. Baby fox squirrels at birth have a pink tinge on purplish skin and are hairless. They are about 5 inches long and weigh about two-thirds of an ounce. Both their eyes and their ears are sealed.

When the little squirrels are about two weeks old they begin to sprout fur; at three weeks their ears open; and at five weeks they can see. By this time they are fully furred and have been clambering about inside the den. When their eyes open they start to climb out of the den or nest.

A mother squirrel is particularly devoted and solicitous about the young ones' welfare. She spends as much of her time as she can with her babies. If danger should threaten she will attempt to drive it off, if possible. If the danger can not be driven off, the mother will transport the young to another den which has been previously prepared for just such an emergency. In moving her babies, the mother squirrel grasps the loose skin of the baby's belly in her mouth, and the young one curls its body around the mother's head.

At two months of age, the young fox squirrel begins to eat solid food and starts the weaning process. Shortly thereafter, the young are ready to leave the maternal den to seek out homes of their own.

While the female is rearing the young, the male keeps to itself in bachelor quarters. The female doesn't want the male around when she has her little ones. The males are often a threat to the young, and it is only the mother's determination that keeps the male from killing its own offspring.

When a female has borne young, her eight nipples are very much in evidence. Frequently the nipples protrude beyond the length of the hair on the squirrel's belly. After having young, a female's nipples turn dark; a virgin's nipples are pink.

The greatest movement that the fox squirrels make occurs in dispersal of the young. The longest distance that has been recorded for an ear-tagged fox squirrel is 40 miles.

Life Span: In the wilds a fox squirrel has a potential life span of six to eight years. Few of them ever get a chance to live that long, beset by dangers as they are. The longevity record is held by a squirrel in captivity that lived to be ten years old.

Sign: In the winter the tracks of the fox squirrel in the snow are the most obvious sign. The spots where it has stopped to dig up a nut will show a hole, leaf debris from the forest floor and usually particles of the nut shell. Stripped corn cobs and discarded nut hulls beneath a tree in autumn point out the squirrel's favorite feeding spot.

Leaf nests may be overlooked in the summer but stand out when the trees are bare. Small hollows in trees with the bark gnawed off mark the entrances to dens.

The scat of the squirrels are small dark pellets about a half-inch long.

Enemies: Tree-climbing snakes are probably the squirrels' most deadly enemies. They can climb anywhere a squirrel can climb and fit into any hole that a squirrel can fit into. I doubt if a large snake can kill a large squirrel; the squirrel is too good a fighter. Baby squirrels and young squirrels, though, are easy picking.

Hawks, particularly the goshawks and the Cooper's hawk, take a tremendous toll of squirrels. Even the large members of *Buteo*, such as the redtailed, red-shouldered and broadwing hawks catch and eat squirrels. Both the great horned owl and the barred owl are about late enough in the morning and early enough in the evening to catch a few stray squirrels.

On the ground the fox, coyote and bobcat, as well as dogs and cats, stalk squirrels. Raccoons can often take young squirrels directly from the nest if the opening is large enough to afford passage.

Failure of the nut crop is also disastrous. Without proper food, the squirrel does not build up a supply of body fat for winter and it must be abroad in even bitter weather. These excursions, often fruitless, place further demands on its body. Weakened by hunger, the squirrel falls prey to predators and parasites.

External parasites such as ticks, fleas and lice are annoying, but the scabies mite is often fatal. A squirrel suffering an infestation of these mites will scratch itself bare until bleeding and pus-filled sores will cover its body. Without fur, the heat loss is too great for the squirrel to survive. Internal parasites include tapeworms and roundworms.

Human Relations: As with almost all other forms of wildlife, man plays the most important role in the life of the fox squirrel. How man eradicated the fox squirrel in the northeastern states is not known. How man fostered the spread of the fox squirrel's range throughout the Midwest is known. The axe and the plow turned out to be the fox squirrel's best friends. As man cut down the virgin forests and plowed up the fields to plant crops he created the open areas which the fox squirrel needs, as well as unintentionally providing sustenance.

Although the interest in squirrel hunting has waned, it is still a very popular sport that provides many pleasurable hours and tons of meat for the table. Millions of fox squirrels are taken by hunters each year. Hunters in

Michigan annually take over 500,000 fox squirrels.

Man also slaughters squirrel by the hundreds of thousands with his automobiles. Although the squirrels are very alert and active, their periods of peak activity coincide with the peaks of daily automobile travel.

Trophy Records: In an extensive study of fox squirrels' weights undertaken in Michigan in the late 1930s, the heaviest among 4,000 specimens weighed 2 pounds, 11 1/2 ounces. There are records of 3-pound fox squirrels, but these would be exceptional.

Table Fare: That fox squirrels by the millions are eaten each year is proof of their palatability. I have never eaten one myself, but suspect that it would not differ from the gray squirrel, which is very good.

This scolding Arctic ground squirrel will retire into its burrow in September and hibernate through the winter. During the rest of the year it must hustle for food round the clock.

Arctic Ground Squirrel

Spermophilus undulatus

These ground squirrels live in northern regions where they seldom see a human being and are thus quite tame. In the summer of 1966, my son Len and I spent fifteen days on the McNeil River photographing Alaskan brown bears. We slept in a cave which abounded with ground squirrels. When we first moved into the cave we only saw a couple of squirrels and put out food scraps to attract them. That was my big mistake. Not only did they partake of my hospitality, they quickly spread word of the hand-out, and squirrels were soon all over the place. The climax came one morning when I was awakened at about four o'clock by a squirrel sitting on top of my head, obviously waiting for the daily ration.

Description: The Arctic ground squirrel is one of the largest, if not the largest, ground squirrel in North America. It is 14 to 17 inches long and weighs up to 18 ounces or more. Its tail is well furred and is about 3 to 6 inches long.

The body of this squirrel is grayish on the underparts and a brownish-gray over the back. Its face, legs and feet are brown. The squirrel's summer coat is more reddish, while its winter coat has more gray in it. Running from the head to the tail are wavy lines of small white spots. The ears are short and well-rounded.

The ground squirrels have 22 teeth which are classified as 4 incisors, 6 premolars and 12 molars. Being rodents, their incisors grow continuously and must be kept worn down by constant gnawing. They have internal cheek pouches which enable them to carry large stores of seeds to their underground caches.

The ground squirrels have four toes on each of the front feet and five toes on each of the hind feet. The hind foot is about 2 to 2 1/2 inches long. The toenails of the front feet are long, sharp and only slightly curved.

Distribution: The Arctic ground squirrel lives in tundra and brushy areas from Alaska to northern British Columbia, east to northern Hudson Bay.

Travel: The Arctic ground squirrels, like the rest of

Distribution of the Arctic ground squirrel.

their kin, do not travel much. Their legs are short, enabling them to fit through small tunnels, but are not designed for top-speed running. Their safety depends on their being able to reach their tunnels and burrows when danger is imminent, hence they seldom venture more than 400 feet from their burrows.

Habits: Being a social animal, the Arctic ground squirrel lives in colonies of hundreds of individuals which cover large areas. The sites of these colonies are generally on a slight slope or high plateau where good drainage is assured. The squirrels particularly like living on the face of a ridge or in a cutbank, which protects them from predators sneaking up from more than one direction.

It is important for these squirrels to be able to feed throughout the entire day. They hibernate during the winter, and the growing season is so short that they have to make the most of the opportunity that they do have. I have seen these squirrels active throughout the entire twenty-four-hour period.

During September, as the weather turns cold and the first snows start to fall, the squirrels retire to their burrows. Most of their burrows do not go any deeper than 3 to 4 feet because of the permafrost found below that depth. In their burrows the squirrels have a sleeping chamber lined with soft, dry grass which they have brought in for bedding. Curling into a ball, the squirrel becomes drowsy, then drops into a light sleep. This soon deepens until the squirrel is in a torpor and its metabolism drops considerably. Body functions slow down to a point where there is practically no drain on the body reserves. Occasionally, during a very mild winter, a few ground squirrels may awake, bestir themselves, and walk around a bit on the snow outside before they return to the nest chamber and sink back into slumber. During the last part of April, most of the squirrels awake and soon become quite active. Usually there is still snow on the ground at this time, and their muddy tracks radiate from their burrows like the spokes of a wheel.

These squirrels feed mainly upon the grasses of the area but also eat the leaves and stems of some of the bushes. They eat some insects and are not above eating a piece of meat if they can find it as carrion. They can pack a great deal of food into their cheek pouches, and when they dash off to store food in their underground caches they look as if they're suffering from the mumps.

Senses: Eyesight is the ground squirrels' most valuable sense. While feeding, they continually pause to survey the terrain for possible danger. Their hearing is also good, but their sense of smell may be used more for discovering food than for detecting danger. These squirrels are often in the company of hoary marmots, and the marmots seem to have much more highly developed senses than the ground squirrels. Invariably the marmots are the first to sense danger.

Communication: Arctic ground squirrels have a wide repertoire of sounds—from a high, whistling bird-like chirp to a harsh, scolding sound like that made by the red squirrel. They most commonly make a *sic-sic* noise, and the tonal variations have different meanings. When ground squirrels spot danger or think they spot danger, they give the alarm note, and every other squirrel in the area passes it on until it becomes lost in the distance. Not only the ground squirrels but all other creatures heed their alarms, which often call attention to the movements of larger predators. When I was studying the red fox in McKinley Park, the chirping of the ground squirrels would often announce the presence of a fox before I was aware of it.

Locomotion: Most of the time the ground squirrel walks away from its den at a leisurely pace, feeding as it goes. Returning to the den, the squirrel usually bounds along at a gallop because it has discovered something that it considers dangerous.

Although the squirrels do not regularly take to water, they are strong swimmers. In the spring many of the flats that they inhabit contain pools of melted snow water. The squirrels jump right in, splash across and dash on about their business.

Breeding: Because of the short warm-weather period where these squirrels live, they have only one litter per year. By late April the males are awake and, driven by the hormones secreted by their enlarged testicles, are out seeking the females. The squirrels are promiscuous in their mating habits, and by May the females may be seen carrying mouthfuls of dead grass into their burrows to make a new nest. Ordinarily the squirrels are not pugnacious and get along together very well, but during the breeding season the males sometimes fight.

Birth and Young: After a gestation period of about

twenty-five days, the young are born in May. As there is only one litter per year, it is a big one—between five and ten with an average of about seven young.

At birth the young are blind, hairless and weigh about one-third of an ounce. They sprout fur in a week, and in two weeks their eyes open. By July they are one-third grown and are running about outside the den feeding. They are soon weaned, although they continue to live in the same den with the female all summer. In some cases, it is thought that the young may hibernate with the mother, leaving her early in the spring.

Life Span: The Arctic ground squirrel has a potential life span of five years.

Sign: Areas that are inhabited by ground squirrels are honeycombed with tunnels. Unlike the blacktailed prairie dog, the ground squirrel does not build a dike at the entrance nor does it mound up the dirt conspicuously. Some of the main entrances have excavated dirt in front of them and some do not. When there is no dirt in front of a hole, it is because the squirrel either carried it away or dug the hole from the opposite end. The squirrels also wear pathways throughout the grass and leave their tracks in the dust.

Enemies: The ground squirrels are preyed upon by all the meat-eating animals of the Arctic, including the wolf, weasel, wolverine and lynx. Dr. Adolph Murie considered them one of the most important ecological factors in McKinley Park and asserted that these squirrels made up 90 percent of the diet of the golden eagle. Gyrfalcons also prey upon the ground squirrels, and I have found squirrel remains on a ledge where these birds had their nests. Other winged predators include the Arctic owl from the north and the great horned owl from the south.

While I was studying the red foxes in McKinley Park, the foxes at one den were catching two or three ground squirrels every day to feed their pups. The foxes are alert to the calls of the squirrels, and after hearing one get down on their bellies to stalk them.

Because the squirrels cannot dig deep burrows, grizzly bears, with time and effort, can dig them out with their long claws and broad feet. The bears have lots of time and energy, and in an area inhabited by both bears and squirrels, the ground is usually pitted with holes resembling small bomb craters.

Lice, mites and ticks infest the squirrels, and flies and mosquitoes apply for their rations. Internally there are parasitic roundworms and flatworms. Although these are colony animals, I can find no record of disease epidemics.

Human Relations: In the North country this squirrel is known as a parka squirrel, as both the Indians and the Eskimos value this little creature's fur for making lightweight parkas. The natives of the North hunt and trap the ground squirrels at every opportunity. Usually the squirrels are quite rare in the vicinity of Eskimo villages because of this hunting pressure.

Trophy Records: The greatest weight record that I can find for the Arctic ground squirrel is 1 pound, 14 ounces.

Table Fare: The natives of the Far North eat the meat of this squirrel.

Keeping close to its burrow, a prairie dog nibbles on a shoot it managed to find in the rocky terrain. The rodents cut any vegetation near their burrow which might obscure their view of an approaching predator.

Prairie Dog

Cynomys ludovicianus

Prairie dogs are not members of the dog or carnivore family but are rodents. They were called dogs because of their shrill, yapping bark. The first part of their scientific name comes from the Greek words *kuon* (dog) and *mys* (mouse); the second is Latin for Louisiana, which was once used to designate the unsettled land west of the Mississippi River where the prairie dog was found.

Description: An adult prairie dog is about 15 inches in length, stands 5 inches high at the shoulder and weighs between 1 1/2 to 3 pounds. Its short legs terminate in four toes on the front foot and five toes on the hind foot. The claws on all of the toes are long, curved and strong, for this is a burrowing rodent.

The prairie dog has a rather flattened head, conspicuous whiskers, black eyes circled with white and short, rounded ears. Like all rodents, it has 4 large incisors, as well as 4 premolars and 12 molars. Its hair is short, the basic color varying from light gray through a dark reddish-brown. The underparts are light. The tail is slim and about 3 1/2 inches long. In the blacktailed species the terminal tip is black; in the whitetailed species the tail is shorter and tipped with white.

Distribution: The blacktailed prairie dog *(Cynomys ludovicianus)* used to be found over the high plains from southern Alberta and Saskatchewan to the Mexican border, and from the eastern edge of the Rocky Mountains to eastern Kansas and Nebraska. Because of intensive poisoning, they are now extinct over much of this region,

Distribution of the blacktail prairie dog (vertical lines) and the whitetail prairie dog (horizontal).

but some are preserved in national parks and monuments. The whitetailed prairie dogs *(Cynomys gunnisoni, C. leucurus,* and *C. parvidens)* inhabit mountain valleys from southern Montana to central Arizona and New Mexico.

Travel: Prairie dogs do not travel or migrate. Most of them seldom go more than 150 feet from their burrows. Young ones may travel slightly farther to search for a burrow of their own, but they are not travelers.

Habits: Prairie dogs are among the most gregarious of all mammals, living in large "towns" which in former times might extend for 100 miles and contain millions of animals. Within these towns there is a strict social hierarchy enforced by the dominant males. A family group, known as a coterie, consists of a dominant male, two to four females and all the young of the past two years. The male must be strong enough to defend his area and his females against all interlopers. Any prairie dog that wanders into his neighbor's backyard is quickly driven out.

The prairie dog's burrow is the heart of its existence. In Alma, Nebraska, N. H. Osgood dug out a burrow very carefully and made exact measurements from which the following figures are derived.

Usually there is only one entrance to the burrow. The most conspicuous feature of the blacktailed prairie dog's burrow is a cone or dike built around this entrance. The cone is about 24 inches across and 6 to 8 inches high, making the entrance to every burrow look like a miniature volcano. The prairie dog builds this cone of the earth it excavates from the burrow and pounds it into shape by patting it with its forefeet or butting it with the top of its nose and head. Without the dike, the water from heavy rains would pour into the burrow and either drive out or drown the occupant. Only the blacktailed prairie dog builds these dikes. The whitetailed prairie dog lives on sidehills in mountainous areas where floods do not occur.

The burrow angles down at 45 degrees for a distance of 15 feet, providing an escape hatch for the prairie dog when pursued. About 3 to 5 feet from the top of the

Two blacktailed prairie dogs repair the dike at the entrance to their burrow. The animals build the dike of excavated earth to prevent heavy rain from flooding the burrow.

burrow is a short, lateral tunnel which the animal uses as a listening post and for turning around. If disturbed but not actually threatened, it dashes into the burrow but stops at the lateral tunnel where it listens for sounds of danger. If it hears nothing it climbs back to the mouth of the burrow and cautiously peeks outside, revealing no more than a half inch of its head and eyes.

At the bottom of the shaft is a main horizontal tunnel that leads to other short horizontal tunnels and chambers. There may be several nesting or bed chambers and one that is used as a toilet. After voiding, the prairie dog covers its scat with dirt so that as the old toilet fills up it has a new room already dug, the dirt from the one having been used to fill up the other. The nesting or bed chamber, which is lined with dry grass, is usually built above the level of the main tunnel and, in the case of a disastrous flood, acts as an air pocket, providing some chance of survival.

Prairie dogs, the burrowing owls and the rattlesnakes all live together in a prairie dog town, but there is nothing peaceful about the arrangement. The burrowing owl lives in an abandoned burrow only so that it does not have to dig one itself. The rattlesnake lives there because it feeds on prairie dogs. The prairie dog cannot kill a rattlesnake, nor can it do much about an invasion. Occasionally, the prairie dogs will kill an owl. It is just a case of each species making the best of a given situation.

Usually the prairie dog eats all vegetation around its burrow because it is the most easily obtained. If it can't eat all the vegetation, it will cut down anything that grows higher than 6 inches—a protective measure to reduce cover that could be utilized by advancing predators.

Prairie dogs feed upon the vegetation most prevalent in their area. The blacktailed prairie dog's favored foods are wheatgrass, Russian thistle, brome grass, fescue grass, bluegrass and gramagrass. The whitetailed prairie dog likes saltbush, Russian thistle, wheatgrass, sagebrush and wild onion. *Gunnisoni* prairie dogs enjoy dandelion, Russian thistle, wheatgrass and nightshade. All three species occasionally eat insects, particularly grasshoppers. On rare occasions, they eat meat, such as ground nesting birds, or practice cannibalism if one of their members dies. Prairie dogs have little need for water because their body requirements are met through the water content of their food.

In hot weather, prairie dogs are most active early in the morning and late in the afternoon, though some can be seen at any time of the day. Most of them sleep during the midday heat. On cool, lightly overcast days, they are active all day. Stormy days keep them inside until the sun shines again. During the winter months, the white-tailed prairie dogs go into hibernation but the blacktailed dogs do not. Cold, snowy weather may cause them to hole up for extended periods of time but they do not hibernate and are out and active again as soon as the weather moderates.

Senses: A prairie dog feeds for 30 to 40 seconds, then stops to look around, sitting upright while it chews so that it can scan the sky and the horizon for danger. With its keen eyesight it intently watches the slightest speck in the sky as a possible threat. If danger materializes, the prairie dog gives a sharp, nervous "bark" which other prairie dogs can hear at a great distance, proving that their hearing is also very good. Scent is not of too great importance, but they are probably sensitive to ground vibrations.

Communication: The prairie dog sounds very much like a small, noisy dog when it barks. It also chirps, chatters its teeth and sometimes makes a whistling noise. Its alarm call is more strident than its all-clear note.

Locomotion: Prairie dogs are sprightly little fellows, exceedingly fast in their movements. While feeding, they walk from one piece of forage to another. At the first sign of danger they gallop toward the safety of their dens, bouncing along like a rubber ball with their tails held high in the air.

Breeding: Signs of the approaching breeding season become evident from February to March. The males be-

A mother blacktailed prairie dog and her young cluster near their burrow entrance. She will teach them to watch for danger, to heed the warning bark of other prairie dogs and seek shelter below ground.

come very active and are seen entering all the dens in their area.

Birth and Young: The gestation period of the prairie dog is between twenty-eight and thirty-two days. The young are usually born in late April or May. There is only one breeding season per year.

The litter size varies from two to ten young, although four to six is average. At birth the young are blind and hairless. They grow rapidly; by twenty-six days they have a coat of short hair; by thirty-three days their eyes open.

When the young are about seven weeks old, they are able to negotiate the steep vertical shaft of the burrow and climb to the top. The mother must teach them the meaning of danger and to respond to alarm calls. When she hears the danger signal, she herds her little ones before her into the burrow.

As soon as the young come out of the den, they begin to feed upon vegetation and thus start to wean themselves. At three months of age, they are completely weaned. At this time the mother leaves the den to the little ones and goes off to either dig a new den or to renovate one that has been abandoned. As the young do not have to go out at once to dig a burrow of their own but can stay in familiar surroundings, they are better able to avoid danger. But within another month the family begins to separate as the bigger and more aggressive young seek dens of their own.

Life Span: Under ideal conditions, a prairie dog should live to be seven or eight years old. In zoos many have attained this age. One captive prairie dog holds the record at ten years.

Sign: A prairie-dog town with its innumerable mound-topped burrows is the unmistakable sign of these animals. Their long-nailed tracks are often seen in the dust.

Enemies: Golden eagles, hawks and falcons prey on prairie dogs from the air. Through the grass slithers the rattlesnake, the bull, coachwhip and other constricting snakes—all of them enemies. The black-footed ferret, a large member of the weasel family, used to be the most deadly predator, entering burrows with ease and dining continuously on the helpless prairie dogs. Ferrets are exceedingly rare today because man has exterminated most of the prairie dogs. Deprived of its food supply, the ferret population has decreased and is now on the endangered list. Coyotes, bobcats, foxes and dogs all feed upon prairie dogs. But of all animals the badger is today the arch foe of the little rodents. A low-slung, powerful tunneler in its own right, the badger with its powerful forefeet and long claws swiftly slashes through the earth and captures the prairie dog in its burrow.

Flies, fleas, lice and mites all fatten themselves on the prairie dog, and it is infested by roundworms. However, for an animal that lives in such large numbers, in such a close proximity to one another, it is remarkably free of communicable diseases.

Human Relations: The prairie-dog population was once estimated at between 400 million and 600 million— and then the slaughter began. Ranchers used poison grain and poison gas to wipe out the animal over most of its range. Today, except for isolated pockets in government parks and preserves, the wild prairie dog is very rare.

Table Fare: The prairie dog is a clean little rodent and was often eaten by the Indians. It has never been popular with westerners who do not like the "earthy" flavor of the meat.

PORCUPINES

Family Erethizontidae

PORCUPINE

Porcupine

Erethizon dorsatum

One of the most enduring animal myths is that the porcupine shoots its quills at an enemy. The porcupine can inflict damage with its quills, but it does not shoot them. When the animal is attacked, it lowers its head, bristles its quills and lashes out with its tail. If the enemy is within range, the barbed quills will be embedded in its hide. If the enemy tries to circle the porcupine before

An alarmed porcupine erects its quills in defense against possible attack. When a predator shows itself, the porcupine will turn its back to the enemy and lash out with its thickly quilled tail.

launching its attack, the latter swivels with little hops of its hind feet, using its tail to protect its barbless belly. The predator that gets close enough to bite the porcupine will receive a face full of quills that may be fatal.

Description: The porcupine is exceeded in size among the rodents of North America only by the beaver. It stands about 12 inches high at the shoulder and is about 35 inches in length. It weighs 8 to 15 pounds, although some old ones may reach 35 pounds. It has a chunky body with a high-arching back. Its legs are stout, bowed and equipped with strong, sharp, curved claws. There are four toes on the front feet and five toes on the hind. The tail is 6 to 12 inches long.

The quill of a porcupine is a modified hair and, like a hair, drops out and is replaced when full-grown. Most of the shaft is hollow; the tip and the base are solid. Full-grown quills vary in length from a half inch to about 4 inches, according to their location. There are no quills on the underside of the porcupine's body from its chin to its tail tip. The shortest quills are on the cheeks of the face. Those on the sides and tail are about 2 1/2 to 3 inches long, while those on the back reach the maximum length. A porcupine has about 30,000 quills on its body.

The base of the quill is tapered sharply and is very thin where it emerges from the skin. Beneath the exterior skin is a sheet of muscles to which the quills are loosely fastened and over which the animal has full and conscious control. When the porcupine is relaxed, the muscles are relaxed and the quills lay flat. When it is disturbed, it contracts its muscles and erects the quills.

Every quill is needle-sharp and finely barbed at the tip.

These barbs cannot be seen readily with the naked eye, although they can be felt with a fingernail. A microscope reveals that the barbs overlap like shingles. When a quill enters the flesh of an animal, heat and body moisture cause it to expand. Every movement of the muscles works against the quill's barbs, pulling the quill deeper. A quill firmly imbedded in the hide of a dog, for example, cannot be pulled out with the fingers. One must use pliers to get a good grip on the quill. Cutting the end off the quill releases the air pressure and allows the quills to be withdrawn a bit more easily.

Wild animals do not have recourse to human aid and must suffer the consequences of attacking a porcupine. Many animals die as a result of the quills striking a vital internal organ. Often the quills lodge in an animal's mouth, so it cannot eat and dies of starvation.

In the winter the porcupine has a dense coat of soft wool between the quills. Since the animal may sit up in a tree feeding for a week or two at a time in even the most bitter weather, it needs the warmth such an undercoat provides. In the summer this wool falls out and the porcupine's bare, pinkish skin can be seen between the quills. When not feeding, the porcupine may seek a den.

Longer than both the underfur and the quills are the stiff guard hairs. In the eastern forms of the porcupine, these guard hairs are black or brown, tipped with white. The western porcupines have yellow guard hairs. Albino porcupines occur often enough so that they are not considered a great rarity.

The guard hairs are so long the quills may not be seen when the porcupine's quills are relaxed. This fools some people into mistaking the guard hairs for the quills. The Indians used to use the guard hairs and the quills for decoration. They decorated baskets with the quills, which were flattened and sometimes dyed.

A member of the rodent order, the porcupine has the four large incisors in the front of its mouth that are typical of this group. The porcupine's incisors are bright orange. Like those of all rodents, these incisors grow constantly, but the porcupine keeps them worn down by constant chewing. The porcupine's 20 teeth are classified as 4 incisors, 4 premolars and 12 molars. The molars and premolars are flat-topped for grinding bark and vegetation.

Distribution of the porcupine.

Distribution: The porcupine generally inhabits forests, but is occasionally found in brush and even in desert areas. It ranges from the limit of the trees in Alaska and Canada, south to the Mexican border in the West, and to the northern states in the East, south in the mountains to Virginia.

Travel: The porcupine has no desire and little need for travel. If it could find enough food and a suitable den in an acre tract, it would be content to spend its life there. However, the young move out of their mother's home area and seek one of their own, often pushing into areas that may not have been inhabited by porcupines before and thus increasing their range.

Habits: The porcupine's diet varies according to its geographical location and the time of the year. In the winter it eats bark primarily, feeding high in the trees near the tender branch tips. Bark of the maple, ash, beech, elm, cottonwood, willow, pine, spruce and fir are all favored foods. It also eats pine needles in great quantities. In the spring, when the sap starts to flow, the porcupine often cuts off the rough outer pine bark in order to feed upon the sweet inner cambium layer. At this time it also eats the bark from the trunk, often chewing all the way around the base and destroying the tree. As other types of vegetation start to sprout, the porcupine forsakes bark and turns its attention to the more succulent greenery. In the summer it wades into shallow water to feed upon water plants such as lilies and sedge. Nor does it bypass cultivated fields and garden patches, consuming apples, alfalfa, clover, melons and lettuce, especially favoring carrots and potatoes. It has a great appetite for salt and likes to chew on anything that has been touched by a man's sweaty hands or by urine. Axe handles, canoe paddles, gun butts, gloves, saddles, shoes and outdoor toilets are sure to be ruined if the porcupine gets at them.

Rocky ledges provide the porcupine with its favorite type of den site. Lacking these, it uses hollow trees, hollow logs or even underground burrows. It is not a sociable animal, but it tolerates other porcupines which may be concentrated into a small area because of the scarcity of ideal den sites. During bitter winter weather, and particulary when the snow is deep, the porcupine prefers to stay snug in a rock den or ledge hole. Sometimes all the porcupines in an area will take refuge in one available winter den.

Senses: The porcupine's eyesight is extremely weak, and it does not seem to comprehend what it does see. Its hearing is good, and it depends on this sense for detecting approaching danger. Its sense of smell is well-developed and is used to locate food.

Communication: Throughout most of the year the porcupine is silent. With approach of the breeding season both male and female become vociferous, usually emitting a whining sound that varies in pitch and volume according to the individual animal. Young ones whimper and cry, and the female answers with a crooning note or sometimes with a coughing sound.

Locomotion: The porcupine is a plantigrade animal,

that is, it walks on the soles of its feet. It places each foot firmly on the ground before it attempts to lift any of the other three. Because its legs are so widely spread, its body rocks from side to side in a lurching walk. When forced to hurry, which it rarely does, the porcupine is capable of what, with generosity, we could call a gallop.

Although it is not as agile as a squirrel, the porcupine is a strong climber and is at home in the treetops. With its strong, hooked claws it can get a good hold on the bark, but it places each foot carefully and tests the footing before taking the next step. Yet the porcupine's claws are so strong that it can easily hang by one foot with no effort. It uses its tail as a brace against the tree trunk in exactly the same manner as the woodpeckers.

Water is no barrier to a porcupine. Its hollow quills give it a built-in life preserver and it swims high in the water at a moderate speed.

Breeding: Because of its armory of quills, the porcupine's breeding habits have long been a subject of jest and speculation. In reality, a porcupine breeds in the same fashion as do the rest of the mammals—in the dorso-ventral position. The breeding season varies according to geographical location but centers about the middle of October. Males may be in competition for a female but they do not fight over her. The males may raise their quills, shake their bodies to make the quills rattle, chatter their teeth and even growl a bit, but they do not fight. Actually the female is the aggressor in the mating game. When the male and female meet they may rub noses and the male may stroke the female's cheeks with his long claws. He usually sprays urine over her in an effort to stimulate her. When she is aroused she re-laxes her quills, raises her tail over her back and offers herself to the male. Although the males of other species may force a female to mate, the porcupine does not. When she is ready, they mate; when she isn't ready, he waits.

Birth and Young: The gestation period of the por-cupine is 209 days. This is an exceedingly long period for a small mammal—four to five days longer than a whitetail deer's—so the porcupine is very well developed at the time of its birth. One youngster at a time is the general rule.

When a baby porcupine is born, in April or May, it is about 10 inches long and weighs from 3/4 to 1 1/4 pounds. Its guard hair is very dark and its quills are already formed. The quills do not constitute a danger to the mother because the baby is born in a placental sac and the quills are short and soft.

Within a half hour after birth, the young one's quills harden and it already knows how to slap its tail at any-thing that would be dangerous. Within hours, it is nurs-ing and can climb. The baby nurses for a period of two weeks to a month and then it is strictly on its own. The porcupine becomes sexually mature and breeds for the first time when it is seventeen to eighteen months old.

Life Span: The average life span for a porcupine is seven to eight years. Dr. Albert Shadle, at the University of Buffalo, kept one in captivity that was still alive at ten years of age.

Sign: Bright marks on tree trunks are the most con-spicuous sign of porcupines. These are made by the an-

The girdled lower portion of this tree is a sign that porcupines have been in the neighborhood. The animals feed on the bark, killing many trees in a forest.

imals when they feed on bark. The inner bark is usually a bright yellow that stands out among the dark tree trunks like a beacon. In one forest in Colorado, 85 percent of the trees had been chewed or killed by porcupines.

The destruction done to any salt- or fat-impregnated object is also a conspicuous sign. In an effort to obtain calcium and phosphorous, porcupines gnaw upon old bones and shed antlers. Since they are larger than other

Porcupine's hind-foot track is a long oval, with a rough texture from the pebbly surface of the foot pad. The claws usually show in the tracks.

rodents, their teeth are larger and so are the marks they make with them.

The porcupine's dens are always easy to identify by the quantity of scat present. No other animal leaves scat that could be confused with the porcupine's except the beaver, and it always voids in the water. The scat of both species contains undigested pieces of bark.

The pad of the porcupine's hind foot is a long oval with a pebbly surface. The rough texture usually shows in the tracks as do the long claws.

Enemies: The porcupine's quills are an excellent protection against most enemies, but they do not give it complete protection. The fisher, a large member of the weasel family, regularly feeds upon the porcupine, and some lynx, bobcats, mountain lions and coyotes have learned how to deal with it. Rigid laws were passed protecting the fisher in the Adirondack Mountains of New York, and in Vermont and New Hampshire. With protection, the fisher has gained in numbers and serves to act as a check upon the porcupine, which is destroying valuable stands of timber.

The fisher, which is exceedingly agile, dashes around the porcupine, trying to penetrate its guard and get a paw under its unprotected stomach in order to flip it on its back. If the porcupine is in a tree, the fisher can reach under a branch or around the tree trunk to get at its stomach. Fishers have been known to eat some of the porcupine's skin, quills and all; their scat is often full of quills.

Seeking safety and nourishment high up, the porcupine may in winter feed for a week or two on bark and branch tips before descending. (Photo by Len Rue Jr.)

Black flies, gnats, mosquitos, ticks and lice harass the porcupine. Internally, the animal undoubtedly has roundworms and tapeworms.

Human Relations: In its relationship with man, the porcupine has always come out the loser. When man is more numerous, he levels the forests and the porcupine loses its habitat and is exterminated. If the porcupine becomes too numerous, it may do excessive damage to trees and is then exterminated by man.

For many years Maine had a law protecting the porcupine because it was so easily killed—a sharp rap on the nose with a stick would do it—that a man lost in the woods could rely on it for food. Now many states offer a fifty-cent bounty in an effort to keep the number of porcupines and their devastation to a minimum.

Trophy Records: A male porcupine at Prineville, Oregon, weighed 28 pounds, and weights up to 35 pounds have been reported.

Table Fare: Although the porcupine can be eaten, I never have tasted one. The only person I have spoken to who has eaten one claimed that the meat had a flavor suggestive of turpentine.

RATS

Family Muridae

BROWN RAT

Brown rats like to sneak into corn cribs and feast on the succulent grain.

Brown Rat

Rattus norvegicus

The brown rat, also called the Norwegian rat, sewer rat and water rat, originated in central Asia, spread westward to the area around the Caspian Sea, and entered Europe about 1727, when they were seen scurrying about in Russia. From there they spread rapidly across Europe, aided by increased commerce, and by 1728 some had reached England.

In 1776 Hessian troops, hired by King George to fight for the British against the Colonists, arrived in America with huge horse-drawn baggage wagons. To feed the horses, they brought over large boxes of grain, and in the boxes they inadvertently brought brown rats. Where man has gone, the rat has followed. By sailing ship, ox cart, prairie schooner, railroad, truck and by foot, it has penetrated every one of the United States and the Canadian provinces.

Description: The brown rat is about the size of a squirrel. An adult male usually weighs 8 to 24 ounces, stands 3 1/2 inches high at the shoulder and is 12 1/2 to 19 inches long, of which 5 to 8 1/2 inches is tail length. The rat has a pointed face, bright beady eyes, prominent whiskers and naked ears. It varies in colors from a pale to a dark brown with lighter underparts. The white laboratory rat is an albino form of the brown rat. The rat has four toes on the front foot and five on the hind foot. The feet are light colored, sometimes pink, in even the dark wild specimens.

Like all rodents, the brown rat has two large incisor teeth in the top and bottom of its mouth which grow continuously throughout its life. A rodent must keep its teeth worn down by constant gnawing lest it be killed by the overgrown teeth. It has been calculated that, if the rat did not wear down its teeth, they would grow to a length of 29 1/2 inches during its maximum three-year life span. These teeth are very strong, and the rat is able to gnaw through a half inch of solid aluminum in six nights, through 2 inches of foamglass in eight nights. It can even gnaw through concrete, although steel and glass are beyond its capability.

Travel: Rats are the world's greatest emigrants. They are constantly sending out advance scouts to find new areas. In the cities, however, most of the rats tend to stay in one section. Rats that establish themselves in new areas are usually young ones that are forced out by population pressure. Rats that have been live-trapped, tagged, released and retrapped have proven that almost 90 percent of the population stays in its original quarters.

In rural areas there is usually a seasonal migration. In the spring many of the rats abandon dwellings for fields where they can be close to growing grain. As cold weather approaches and the crops are gathered and stored in the barn and adjacent buildings, the rats move back into their winter quarters.

Habits: The brown rat is a burrowing rodent, preferring to live underground where it digs a network of interconnecting passageways. Although these excavations are not laid out as communal projects, they soon take on the aspect of such as the various rats tie in their own tunnels to what soon becomes a trunk line. Whenever possible the rats dig their tunnels under piles of debris, heaps of garbage or buildings. These obstacles protect the tunnels from being excavated by predators.

Sometimes the excavations become so extensive and the ground so hollowed out that they cause buildings to settle and sag. I was raised on a farm where rats were always a nuisance. The most effective way of stopping rats from chewing through the old concrete foundation was to cram the holes full of broken glass and pour new cement in on top.

Rats eat everything that we eat and many things that we cannot. They eat paint, soap, leather, paste, garbage and sewage—anything that contains animal or vegetable matter. And they even eat the dead of their own kind.

Rats that live in crowded, filthy conditions become filthy themselves. When I was a boy, the rats in the town dump had large, festering sores on their bodies, and it was a wonder that they didn't present a serious health problem to the community. Many of us would go to the dump at night with flashlights and .22 rifles and shoot up a carton of ammunition. It was wonderful target practice, and we did a service for the community.

On the other hand, rats in cleaner, uncrowded areas can be very clean. A friend of mine has rats that she feeds on her wildlife preserve. Under such conditions, the rats are as neat and clean as the squirrels which also abound there.

Rats are among the most intelligent of wild creatures. They are quick to learn by experience and are able to retain the knowledge that they gain. They soon learn how to cope with most situations.

Senses: A rat's hearing ability is very keen. As it is preyed on by so many predators, its hearing stands it in good stead by warning it of impending danger.

The rat uses its sense of smell mainly for locating food. It does not appear to try to locate its enemies by scent. Scent is much more important to creatures that live out in the open. As the rat is more at home under the ground, it doesn't have to depend on its sense of smell. Like many other nocturnal mammals, the brown rat's whiskers are sensitive detectors and the animal uses them to maintain contact with its runway walls. A rat quickly notices movement, yet it seems incapable of recognizing stationary objects.

Communication: Almost everyone has probably heard the high-pitched squeal of a rat. The squeal varies in tone and pitch to denote anger, fear, surprise—a whole gamut of emotions.

The rat often deposits feces and urine which serve as sign posts in the same way as a dog uses a fire hydrant. But rats also can communicate in other ways. How a rat knows there is poison in a piece of bait, or how it lets other rats know about the poison, is a mystery, but it has been proven that it can communicate danger.

Locomotion: The rat usually walks when going from one place to another, as it is better able to detect danger at that gait than if it were running. When in a hurry, it bounces along in a gallop, its hind feet landing in front of its front feet. If startled, a rat may jump a foot in the air and turn around before it lands. It can broadjump up to 5 feet.

Rats are strong swimmers; in fact some are even completely aquatic. I first became aware of this fact when I was trapping muskrats in a small brook that ran through a chicken farm. Both the chickens and the feed lured rats into the area. The banks along the edge of the brook were riddled with what appeared to be muskrat burrows. Every rock, log or piece of driftwood in the brook was covered with droppings. But when I looked at my traps I found that I had caught many more brown rats than muskrats. Later when I worked on ships down around New York harbor, I used to watch rats by the hundreds swimming under the wharfs and between the pilings.

Breeding: Rats are extremely prolific. A female rat is capable of bearing four litters of young every three months or fifteen to sixteen litters per year. Luckily, climatic and food conditions prevent them from realizing their full potential. Rats living in the South produce more litters than do those in the North. Overall, there are three to seven litters per year. One female was found to be carrying twenty-two embryos, but the average litter size is eight.

Birth and Young: The gestation period of the brown rat is twenty-one or twenty-two days. Often the female will breed again within a few hours after giving birth, or she may wait up to a week.

The youngsters at birth are pink, hairless, blind and helpless. They grow very rapidly, and their eyes open in two weeks. By the time they are three weeks old, they are fully furred, weaned and ready to go out on their own. Normally young females do not breed until they are three months old, but if food is plentiful many of them start even earlier. After a male rat has passed its second year its reproductive powers decline, and females that reach this age have stopped breeding.

Life Span: Rats have a potential life span of about three years, although not too many of them reach this age. Most of the females have worn themselves out by constant breeding. A rat that reaches the age of three is comparable to a man who reaches the age of ninety.

Sign: There is never any lack of sign when rats are about. They gnaw holes through woodwork, screening and soft concrete, and they pull out insulation. They dig holes in the ground. Their droppings are copious and widely scattered. They chew holes in bags of flour or other commodities that are much larger than those made by mice.

Enemies: In rural areas owls are the most important enemies of rats—the barn owl primarily, followed by the great horned owl and the barred owl. I once discovered a hollow oak tree near a town dump that was used by barn owls as a nesting site. One night I watched the owls feed their young and saw them bring in eleven rats before I left at about 3 a.m.

Hawks also prey on rats, but not to the same extent as owls, for rats are more active at night. Snakes, particularly rat snakes, bull snakes and king snakes, are good ratters and have the advantage of being able to pursue the rats underground and catch them in their lairs. Foxes, coons, skunks, opossums, bobcats—in fact all meat eaters from weasels to bears—will kill rats if they get a chance. Farm dogs, especially terriers, are a constant foe of rats. Some cats make good ratters, and some are afraid of rats. A rat is a plucky beast and will fight desperately when it has to.

Rats are hosts to all sorts of fleas, ticks and lice, as well as internal parasites.

Human Relations: Rats are man's most deadly enemy. Some of the fleas and lice that live on rats will also use man as a host and thus can pass on deadly diseases. The three most deadly diseases that rats spread are Murine typhus fever, bubonic plague and salmonellosis. It was the black rat that spread the plague called the Black Death throughout Europe that killed about 34 million people, or one out of every four on the European continent. Since that time the brown rat has done its share of damage. In 1898 the plague killed over 5 million people in India and another 1,200,000 in 1907.

Dr. Hans Zinsser, in his book *Rats, Lice and History*, states that rats have had more effect on the course of history than have famous men. Dr. Zinsser also claims that rats, by spreading disease, have been responsible for the deaths of more people than all the wars and revolutions of mankind put together. In addition to spreading fatal diseases, rats are tremendously destructive. It is estimated that the damage done by rats amounts to over 200 million dollars a year in the United States alone and into the billions of dollars on a world-wide scale.

Trophy Records: John Jarvis, a rat catcher in England, killed a rat that attacked him in the Old Gaiety Theater which weighed 1 pound, 9 ounces.

Tooth features distinguish rodents from hares and rabbits. Above, are the matched pairs of incisors of a beaver, characteristic of rodents including woodchucks, marmots, squirrels, prairie dogs, porcupines, mice and rats. Below, the skull of a rabbit shows the four upper incisors characteristic of all rabbits, hares and pikas.

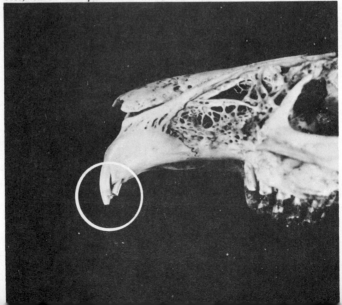

HARES AND RABBITS

Order Lagomorpha

The rabbits, hares and pikas which compose this or-
der were once classified as rodents, but because they
have four incisors in their upper jaws, instead of the
two of rodents, and because they are now known to
have had a long and distinct evolution apart from
the rodents, they are currently classified in their own
order, Lagomorpha.

Hares generally have long legs and usually live in
more open country where they depend upon their
speed to escape enemies. Their young are born fully
furred and with their eyes open—and they are ready
to run and feed shortly after their birth. The Ameri-
can jackrabbits are actually hares.

Rabbits usually have shorter legs and live in or
near dense underbrush, where they readily can hide
from enemies. Their young are born naked and
blind, in a nest that is usually lined with fur plucked
from the chest of the doe, and they require several
weeks of maternal care before they are ready to fend
for themselves.

HARES AND RABBITS

Family Leporidae

COTTONTAIL
VARYING HARE
ARCTIC HARE
JACKRABBIT
EUROPEAN RABBIT

Displaying the long legs characteristic of hares, this hare is popularly called an antelope jackrabbit.

The mountain cottontail rabbit ranges in the West and prefers habitat with good cover.

The cottontail's fluffy white tail is its trademark. Its delicate ears constantly flick back and forth, trying to pick up every sound in the vicinity.

Cottontail Rabbit

Sylvilagus

Hunters spend more time and money, and acquire more meat, gunning for cottontails than for any other species of North American game. The little rabbit is widely distributed across the continent and reproduces so rapidly that it is rarely in short supply. The shotgunner's favorite target, it dashes in and out of cover with lightning speed, requiring fast gun handling to bring it down. There's no better practice for upland bird shooting than hunting cottontails.

The name *Sylvilagus*, given to this genus by Gray in 1867, derived from the Latin word *Silva* (forest) and the Greek word *lagos* (hare). The names hare and rabbit are often used interchangeably, although in proper usage a rabbit is an animal whose young are born naked and blind while a hare's young are born fully furred and with their eyes wide open.

Description: The cottontail is a small animal, having an overall length of about 14 to 19 inches and standing 6 to 7 inches at the shoulder. The females are slightly larger than the males. The weights vary from 2 1/2 to 3 1/2 pounds.

The basic body coloration of the cottontail is a brown that may have a buff or a reddish cast, with black-tipped guard hairs scattered throughout. The belly, chin and insides of its legs are white. The underside of its tail is also white, hence its popular name, cottontail. When the rabbit bounces off to seek cover its little white tail looks exactly like a cotton ball or a powder puff.

Most cottontail rabbits have a white spot on the fore-

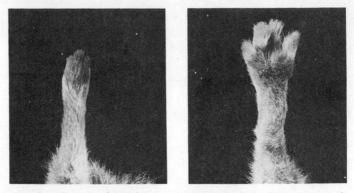

Forefoot (left) and hind foot of a cottontail. Both are covered with dense hair which conceals the toe pads. Unlike rodents, the rabbit cannot turn its forefeet inward and use them for grasping food.

head between the eyes, except the New England cottontail, which has a black spot on its head. The cottontails shed their hair twice a year but do not change color with the seasons. I have found no record of a black, or melanistic, cottontail and only four cases of albinism. There have also been two records of "blue" cottontails. These mutations not only had blue-colored fur, but the fur itself was long and silky like that of the domestic Angora rabbit. Like all lagomorphs, the cottontail has a cleft upper lip. Its whiskers are long but light-colored and not readily noticed. Its ears are about 2 1/2 to 3 inches in length, lightly furred on the outside and almost bare on the inside.

The cottontail has five toes on each of its front feet and four toes on each of its hind. The bottoms of its feet are densely covered with hair so that none of the toe pads are visible, just the toenails. The hind legs are about 12

Distribution of the eastern cottontail (horizontal lines) and the mountain, or Nuttall's, cottontail (vertical).

inches long and powerfully muscled. The leg bones are thin but strong enough to withstand the pressure applied to them when the rabbit leaps. The bones of the forefeet are placed so that the feet cannot be turned inward for grasping as is common with most rodents. The feet are not used for holding food.

The cottontail has a total of 28 teeth: 6 incisors, 10 premolars and 12 molars. Typical of both rodents and lagomorphs is the large gap in the row of teeth between the incisors and the premolars.

Distribution: There are four species of rabbits called

Distribution of the marsh rabbit (horizontal lines) and the desert cottontail (vertical).

cottontails, and several others that are in the same group. Some of them can be distinguished only by the specialist. The eastern cottontail *(Sylvilagus floridanus)* is found in areas with good cover—brush, forest edge and weed fields—from Canada east of the Rockies to the Gulf of Mexico (except northern New England) and west in the southern mountains through Arizona. The mountain cottontail *(Sylvilagus nuttalli)* also prefers good cover and is found throughout the southern Rocky Mountain area from Saskatchewan to New Mexico and Arizona, west to the eastern mountains of the Pacific Coast states. The

Distribution of the New England cottontail (horizontal lines) and the brush rabbit (vertical).

desert cottontail (*Sylvilagus auduboni*) lives in open country from western Texas to the Pacific, north to central North Dakota and Montana and to northern California in the west. The New England cottontail (*Sylvilagus transitionalis*) prefers forested and brushy areas in the mountains of the New England states through the Appalachians to northeastern Alabama. The pigmy rabbit (*Sylvilagus idahoensis*)is the smallest of our rabbits and does not have a conspicuous white tail. It is found in the sagebrush country from southeastern Washington to east-central California, east to central Utah and southwestern Mon-

Distribution of the swamp rabbit (horizontal lines) and the pygmy rabbit (vertical).

tana. The brush rabbit (*Sylvilagus bachmani*) lives in the chaparral from northern Oregon to Baja California. The marsh rabbit (*Sylvilagus palustris*) and the swamp rabbit (*Sylvilagus aquaticus*) are two species that are always found near water in marshes, swamps and moist bottomlands. The former is found east of the fall line from southeastern Virginia to Mississippi and throughout Florida. The swamp rabbit is found from eastern Texas to northwestern South Carolina, north to the lowlands of the Ohio River drainage in southern Illinois and Indiana.

Travel: Survival, to a cottontail, depends upon its knowing intimately every path, rock, bush and burrow in its area. A couple of acres is enough for a female cottontail, while a male has a larger range.

It is because the rabbit is so familiar with its home territory that it runs in a large circle within that territory if pursued by a slow dog. A fast dog will force the rabbit to seek shelter as soon as it can. When the rabbit is flushed from its form it bounds away in a zig-zag pattern, but as soon as it finds one of its well-used paths it follows it. Periodically the rabbit goes over all of these paths and with its teeth snips off any branches, bushes or grass that may prove to be obstacles.

In the winter deep snow and cold weather may force the rabbit to shift to another area to find food or protection against the elements. One tagged rabbit in Massachusetts traveled 45 miles from the point of release.

Habits: Although the cottontail has strong claws on its feet and could dig burrows, it doesn't. The burrows used by a rabbit in the wintertime or during times of danger are usually those of the woodchuck. Rabbits don't like to use burrows because they can become trapped in dead-end passageways. In the winter the rabbit goes into a burrow but usually sits about 6 feet from the entrance. This allows it to keep warm while listening for approaching danger. If there are any weasels in the area, which can go underground even more easily than the rabbit, a cottontail will not enter a burrow.

A cottontail much prefers to sit out in a form. This is a spot usually well hidden beneath a clump of grass or in a thicket. A well-used form is bare on the bottom where the vegetation has been worn down by the rabbit's feet. The grasses around the form sometimes meet overhead, providing a roof. In such a form the rabbit can hear and smell danger but can't be seen. If danger comes near, the rabbit is out of the form like a flash and onto one of its paths.

In all weather short of a cloudburst the rabbit stays in its form, but a torrential rain forces it to seek better shelter because its hair is not waterproof and quickly soaks through. In the winter it makes its forms on the sunny southern faces of hills or at least on the south side of clumps of grass and thickets. It spends most of the daylight hours in the form.

The cottontail is active in the dawn or twilight hours. Activity in the evening starts about 5 p.m. and slows down about dark. In the morning the rabbits are very active from about 4:30 a.m. on, with most of their activity ceasing near 7 a.m.

The cottontail is blessed with an almost unlimited summer food supply. I suppose there are some types of vegetation that the cottontail will not eat, but I don't know what they are. Ordinarily if a plant is able to grow, a cottontail is able to eat it.

A few years ago, biologists studying the contents of rabbit stomachs at the experimental station at Beltsville, Maryland, began coming down with a rash which manifested itself in itchy, red, watery blisters. As this was in the middle of the winter, the biologists could hardly believe the diagnosis—poison ivy. It turned out that the rabbits had been feeding on the bark and berries of poison ivy, which they relish, and the biologists were getting the rash from handling the chewed material in the rabbits' stomachs.

The cottontail eats bluegrass, crabgrass and other grasses; broadleaved plants like plantain; all types of berries and fruits; cultivated crops of wheat, soybeans, alfalfa, clover, lettuce, cabbage and beans; weeds such as goldenrod and yarrow; wild shrubs, sheep shorrel and wild cherry; and, in the winter, the bark of most trees.

Of all the winter foods, perhaps sumac is the rabbit's favorite. The bark of this shrub is very rich and has a high fat content, aiding production of body heat which the rabbit sorely needs for withstanding the cold. Actually, the more sumac the rabbit eats, the more the roots produce. When the rabbit girdles the stems of sumac shoots, they die and this in effect prunes the bush. Since the rabbits don't eat sumac during the summer, new shoots develop and put strength back into the roots. Thus the roots grow very large and strong and develop shoots at an incredible rate.

When rabbits girdle young fruit trees the trees die, provoking an unending war between the rabbits and the orchardists. Much of the rabbit damage in orchards could be alleviated if the orchardists would leave the branches they prune from the trees each winter on the ground till spring. The rabbits would much prefer feeding upon the tender tips and twigs of the pruned branches than upon the rough, heavy bark of the tree's trunk.

The cottontail is often blamed for the damage inflicted upon the trees by the meadow mouse. This small rodent also girdles trees. Damage done by the mouse can be ascertained by a close examination of the cutting. The mouse, which is smaller than the rabbit, has smaller teeth set closer together. The size of the tooth marks are easily seen and the culprit identified by any who take the time to look.

The rabbit does not dig down into the earth to get food, not even to get a carrot, but it will dig through snow to uncover a frozen apple.

By licking off the drops of dew on vegetation, and eating plants with a high water content, the rabbit fulfills its water requirements. In the winter it feeds upon dry bark but satisfies its thirst by eating snow.

Senses: The cottontail's sense of hearing is vital to its survival. Its ears constantly flick forward and backward to catch the faintest sound. The cartilage of the ears is so thin that the blood flowing through the veins is clearly visible, and when the sun is behind the ears they appear to be pink.

Sight is also important to the cottontail. Its eyes are large and protrude from the sides of its head. Each has nearly a 180-degree range of vision. However, the rabbit does seem to have a blind spot directly to the front, an area which it can only see by turning its head slightly.

The cottontail may rely more on its sense of smell to locate food than to detect danger, although it is constantly wriggling its nose in an effort to catch the scent of its enemies.

Communication: When disturbed or alarmed, the cottontail thumps the ground with its hind feet, sending out vibrations that are recognized as a danger signal by other rabbits.

Ordinarily the cottontail does not do much vocalizing.

A mother cottontail may grunt softly to her young while nursing them. It occasionally makes a purring sound. The males during the breeding season sometimes make a chirping sound or growl.

The best-known sound of the cottontail is the piercing scream of terror it emits when caught by a predator. This sound carries far and will alert and congregate every predator in the area.

Locomotion: When a rabbit bursts from its form and starts to run, its speed is very deceptive. Because it bounds along through dense cover it appears to be going very fast. In reality, a rabbit's top speed is about 18 to 20 miles per hour.

If just feeding, a rabbit may walk or progress in short hops, leading off with its front feet and bringing its hind feet up behind them. When bounding at high speed, the rabbit's front feet come down first, one foot ahead of the other, and then the hind feet come down side by side ahead of the front feet. It then compresses its body and drives off into the next bound, its back coiling and bending back with a reflex like the action of a released flat spring. In bounding along at top speed, the rabbit often covers as much as 15 feet at a jump. Occasionally the cottontail makes an extra-high observation leap so it can see what is going on behind it.

Breeding: The breeding season for the cottontail starts in January or February, according to its geographic location, and continues into August. In some parts of its range, the cottontail produces five or six litters, although three or four a year is about average. Some rabbits rush the season, and the young are born while there is still snow on the ground. Needless to say, such litters have almost no chance of surviving.

May is the month of peak cottontail reproduction. In April the hard rains may drown the nestlings or cause them to be chilled and die. In July and August the weather is often very hot and the vegetation is starting to dry up. May is ideal from the standpoint of temperature and food production.

Around the end of December, the testicles of the male cottontail begin to swell and to descend into the scrotum. As this occurs, fights between the males become more common. There is usually a dominant male in each area that services most of the females, but periodically the males fight in an effort to rearrange the hierarchy.

When cottontails fight, they usually advance on each other and then stop to rake the grass with their claws. Then they warily circle each other looking for an opportunity to bite. Sometimes they both rise up on their hind feet and box with their forefeet. As the battle develops, each of the males tries to leap over his opponent so that he can deliver a powerful blow with his hind feet. In a short time the lesser rabbit dashes off, if he is still able. The victor is not interested in pursuit and just chases after his rival for a short distance.

As if vanquishing his rivals were not enough, the male also must win over the female. Usually she charges at him, attempting to bite and kick. The male reacts by leaping high in the air so that the female passes beneath. Then the male dashes at the female, perhaps even hitting her. Or he may jump over her and squirt her with drops of urine. When finally the female is sufficiently impressed, she turns and offers herself to the male, and copulation takes place in about five seconds. The male may copulate several times and is then driven off by the female. She may accept several mates during the breeding period.

Birth and Young: The cottontail has a gestation period of twenty-eight days. Prior to this time, the female digs a saucerlike depression in the earth about 3 to 4 inches deep and 6 to 7 inches across. This is usually the only digging that the cottontail does. When the hole is completed, the female pulls the fur from her belly to expose the nipples. She then mixes the plucked hair with dead grass to line the hole and to make a "blanket" which she can pull over the top for warmth and camouflage.

The young rabbits are born practically naked and with their eyes sealed tightly shut. The babies are about 4 inches long and weigh about 1 ounce apiece. Their ears are a half-inch long and folded tightly against the head, and their tails are about a quarter-inch long.

As soon as the young have been born, the female covers them with the blanket and goes forth to be bred again. Within an hour or so after giving birth to one family, the sperm for the next family has been implanted. After breeding, the female chases the male out of the area because she doesn't trust him any more than she trusts her other enemies. Male cottontails have been known to behead the male babies.

The female does not stay in the area where the nest is located. She usually sits 25 to 30 feet away in a spot from which she can watch the nest. Although rabbits are timid, females in defense of their young have been known

Three-day-old cottontails are barely 4 inches long. Rabbits are born naked, with their eyes sealed shut. Hares are born with fur and with their eyes open.

to attack and to drive off dogs, cats, snakes and even human beings.

When it becomes dark, the female goes to the nest to let the little ones nurse. She carefully rolls the blanket back and stretches out over the hole. When the young have finished, she puts the blanket back into place and goes off to feed.

The little ones are nursed three to four times a night. The female's milk is rich, having a butterfat content of

After giving birth to her young in the nest, the mother covers them with a blanket of grass, and hair pulled from her chest. Here the blanket has been rolled back for a better view of the babies in the nest.

about 13 percent. The young grow rapidly, and at the end of the first week their eyes are open and they can wriggle their ears. By this time they are fully furred and moving about in the nest.

By the age of two weeks, the young weigh about 3 1/2 ounces and begin to leave the nest for short periods. Between the second and third weeks the young ones are weaned, leave the nest and are entirely on their own. The female must now get ready for her next family.

Life Span: A great deal of study and research has been devoted to the longevity of the rabbit. Cottontails in captivity have lived to be ten years old, but it is an exceedingly rare cottontail that ever gets to be three or four years old in the wild. The research shows that 85 percent of all rabbits die or are killed each year, whether they are hunted or not.

Sign: During the summer, sign of the cottontail is very scarce but at that time the rabbits are plentiful. In the winter, the rabbits become scarcer but the sign becomes more plentiful, especially on snow.

In one night a rabbit leaves plentiful sign in an area—brown droppings that stand out against the snow, trees and shrubs with their bark peeled off that gleam in the sun. The tracks may lead to and from a brush heap, a woodchuck's burrow or a dense thicket. The pleasure of tracking animals on fresh snow is like opening a new book; there is a world of information written there for those who can read.

Enemies: It often seems as though everything in the

world is against the rabbit. Rainstorms chill and kill the young. Snowstorms imprison the adults at a time when they desperately need to move around to secure feed. Fire sweeps across a field and in a few moments destroys their nests. Early litters are plowed under. Every meat-eating animal feeds upon the cottontails—weasels, mink, skunk, raccoons, cats, dogs, foxes, bobcats, coyotes. Hawks hunt the rabbits by day and the owls by night. All of the constrictor types of snakes, as well as the rattle-snakes, feed upon the cottontail. If a rabbit falls into the water, the big fish try to eat it. And in addition to these hazards, the cottontail must dodge shotgun pellets and rifle bullets.

As if it didn't have enough troubles, flies, mosquitoes, lice, ticks and mites plague the rabbit externally while roundworms, pinworms and tapeworms infest it internally.

Tracks of a cottontail bounding at high speed in snow. The forefeet come down first, one in front of the other, followed by the hind feet, which come down side by side in front of the forefeet. Compare with photo of gray squirrel's tracks.

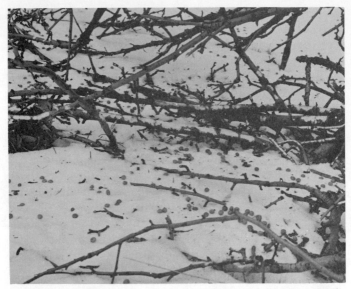

Sign of cottontail in winter—branches stripped of their bark, and a profusion of droppings on the snow.

Many hunters expose their dogs to tapeworms by feeding them the liver of a fresh-killed rabbit. *Never* feed any of the internal organs of a rabbit to a dog.

Cottontails are also plagued by botflies which lay their eggs deep in the rabbit's fur. When the larvae hatch, they burrow beneath the rabbit's skin and live there, developing into large bumps called warbles. Cold weather usually kills the warbles that have not already emerged from the rabbit. These warbles do not affect the meat, but many hunters will throw away a rabbit if warbles are present.

The most dreaded disease of the cottontail affects both

the rabbit and man. It is caused by a parasite that affects the rabbit's lymph glands, liver and spleen, and is known as tularemia. This disease was first noticed in Tulare County, California, hence its name. Rabbits that are afflicted with the disease are lethargic and unable to run when disturbed. Any rabbit that does not act in a normal fashion is suspect and should be dispatched and buried or burned, and never handled with bare hands.

Even rabbits that appear healthy may be coming down with the disease. The liver of such a rabbit will have many pinhead white spots on its liver. To avoid the disease, a hunter should wear rubber gloves when he cleans rabbits or else wash his hands immediately upon completion of the job. The parasite has to enter the body through a cut in the skin so that it can enter the blood stream.

Today's mycin-type drugs can cure the disease in humans, and the death rate has dropped to about four out of every hundred people afflicted. Fortunately, outbreaks of tularemia are comparatively rare.

Human Relations: Cottontail populations are cyclic, but at any time they usually offer good hunting. Most of the hunting seasons for the cottontail open in November when the weather is enjoyably cool and the warbles have been killed. For the best harvest of rabbits, the season should be opened in August when the young born in May are almost full-grown. From that time on, the rabbit population declines rapidly.

Studies made by the Pennsylvania Game Commission show that that state alone loses an estimated 5 million cottontails to predation, highway kill, accidents and some poaching between September 1 and November 1.

That's 5 million rabbits that the legal gunner never gets a shot at. Is it any wonder that the hunter can't imagine what happened to all the rabbits he saw in the summer? And this is happening throughout the cottontail's entire range. By the time the season opens, 60 percent of the year's cottontail population is already gone.

Still, hunters do well. In 1958, Missouri, which has the largest rabbit population of any state, tallied 6,018,914 cottontails killed by hunters. The state figured that over 10 million rabbits were still left for breeding stock. Ohio came in second with 3,500,000 rabbits killed. The total hunting harvest for the United States that year was estimated to be over 25 million.

Missouri biologists did some further calculations and came up with some extraordinary figures. Rabbits that year were bringing fifty cents a pound on the market, and the average rabbit dresses out to 1 1/2 pounds of usable meat. The biologists applied these figures to the national total and came up with 37,500,000 pounds of rabbit worth $18,750,000.

In some areas there have been many attempts at restocking rabbits to raise the population. If the rabbits have been wiped out of an area through starvation or disease, then restocking pays. Otherwise it does not. Unless the habitat is improved by increasing food and shelter, the population cannot be increased by stocking.

Trophy Records: The top weight for a cottontail rabbit is about 3 1/2 pounds.

Table Fare: The meat of the cottontail is light in color, fine in texture and delicious in flavor, and there are hundreds of ways of preparing the rabbit for the table.

Varying Hare

Lepus americanus

The varying hare, also called the snowshoe rabbit, is well endowed to cope with two- and four-legged forest predators. The hare is always camouflaged to suit the season, annually shedding its brown summer coat for a white winter garb. Besides this excellent protective coloration, the animal is equipped with huge, hairy feet that enable it to run across deep snow that bogs down most other animals. Unlike the cottontail, the hare does not run underground when alarmed but depends on speed to outdistance its enemies. It leaves a trail too difficult for a man to unravel and is best hunted with beagles or foxhounds.

Description: Smaller than the jackrabbit and larger than the cottontail, the varying hare may reach 21 inches in length, stand 8 to 9 inches at the shoulder and weigh between 3 and 4 1/2 pounds.

In the summer the hare is basically brown, although some individuals are grayish. It has a dark line down the middle of its back terminating in a dark rump and tail top. The throat is reddish-brown. The chin, belly and the undersides of the tail are white.

It was long thought that the cold or the snow caused the varying hare to change color, but it is actually caused by the effect of the diminishing length of daylight in autumn. In the fall, as the days grow shorter, the hare is exposed to less light and the glandular influence for hair color alters, so that the new hairs are white-tipped (but dark at the base). Starting in December the days grow longer, and the influence of the glands again

The varying hare, true to its name, changes from a white winter coat to a brown summer coat. The hare is thus camouflaged in both seasons.

changes. As the winter coat is shed the new hair grows in brown. Biologists have kept varying hares in complete darkness in the summer and their hair has turned white. They have also exposed them to constant artificial light in early winter and their hair has turned brown. Melanism, or all black coloration, occurs in the varying hare about one in every 100,000, and the hares remain black

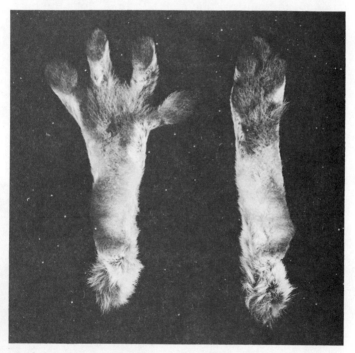

Hind foot (left) and forefoot of a varying hare. The hind foot is spread to show the large surface of the hare's "snowshoe," which enables it to run in deep snow.

all winter. Albinos are very rare. The varying hares of the Cascade and Sierra Nevada Mountains do not turn white at any time.

The varying hare has 28 teeth: 6 incisors, 10 premolars and 12 molars. Malocclusion occurs occasionally, and some growths achieve tusklike proportions. The lower jaws of the hare are much narrower than the upper jaws, forcing it to chew on one side at a time. Both the hare and the deer eat the same type of foods, but the deer is able to rechew its cud so that all of the essential food value and nutrients can be extracted. The hare does not chew its cud but ingests part of its own scat, rechews it and passes it through its system a second time. The dark scat has been through the body twice, the greenish scat only once. Eating scat is called coprophagy.

The varying hare has five toes on its forefeet and four toes on its hind feet. Long hairs grow out on the hare's feet in the winter, but even in the summer the hair is so dense that the toe pads cannot be seen. Besides supporting the hare in deep snow, the long hair also provides insulation that prevents loss of body heat, gives the hare a good grip on ice, prevents snow from sticking to the feet and reduces the amount of body scent in the tracks.

Distribution: The varying hare is found from the limit of the trees in Alaska and Canada south through New England and, in the Appalachians, to Tennessee in the east, and in the Rocky Mountains to northern New Mexico, and to central California in the Sierras.

Travel: Like all hares, the varying hare prefers to stay close to its home area and seldom travels more than

Distribution of the varying hare.

1,000 feet in any direction from its home base. About one mile would be its longest journey. Within its home area it knows every physical feature of the landscape, such knowledge being vital to its survival. As it usually lives in areas of very dense cover it can seldom be driven out of its home territory by predators. Occasionally, during a high peak in the population, hares may emigrate to an area that has more food.

Habits: The varying hare's population cycle cannot be considered a habit, as it is not the result of voluntary behavior, but it is the most unique aspect of the animal and deserves full examination. These cycles occur about every ten years. The peaks of these cycles now occur in years ending in 3, 2 and 1. In the 1800s the cycle was at a high in years ending 7, 6 and 5. The change occurred about 1915, but no one can explain why. Some biologists have tried to tie these cycles to sun spots because celestial control over storms and weather in general is well-known, and weather certainly has a great deal to do with all types of life. But it seems that many factors determine these cycles, and it is difficult to single out one as the principal cause.

In periods of peak populations the varying hares become numerous almost beyond calculation. Ernest Thompson Seton, one of our great naturalists, wrote that, "... hares were very scarce when there was but one to the square mile of woods, and abundant when there was 1,000. I have, nevertheless, seen as many as 10,000 to the square mile." Seton made this observation in 1886 in Carberry, Manitoba. The highest all-time peak in the hare population appears to have occurred that year. Seton stood in one spot and counted eleven hares within a radius of 90 feet. Intervening brush and natural camouflage must have hidden some from view, so that he figured twenty to the acre as being a fair estimate. Assuming that many areas would not have as many hares, Seton halved that figure, even though some areas would probably have held more. Estimating that there were 4 million square miles of good varying hare range and figuring ten hares to the acre he calculated the total number at 20 billion.

When spring came the population crash started, and Seton reported that, "The country from Whitemouth to

Whitesand, 250 miles long by 150 miles wide, was flecked with the bodies of the white-furred hares."

The causes of this sudden decline in population are mixed. The scarcity of food in an overpopulated area undoubtedly has some bearing on the population crash. Thousands of rabbits to an acre certainly must deplete the food supply, destroying the forests to the point where it takes years for them to recover. But recent evidence shows that stress and tension in an overcrowded area also affect the rabbits. Research shows that animals reproduce less when they live under crowded conditions. Stress leads to an enlargement of the adrenal glands, which in turn cuts down the fertility of the species. Observations reveal that when the varying hare population is crashing, not only is the size of the litter reduced but the number of litters per season as well.

The more immediate reaction of the varying hare to overcrowding is known as "shock disease," which affects the hare's liver. Ordinarily the liver produces glycogen from glucose and proteins and stores it to be released to the muscles as energy when needed. Hares affected by shock disease have an abnormally low amount of bloodsugar. Without this bloodsugar, the hares are not active, do not feed and cannot withstand cold. Any excitement causes convulsions, paralysis and death.

This hare seldom, if ever, dens up, much preferring to sit out in a form. If possible, it makes its form on a slight knoll which affords drainage. Although well hidden, the form is not made in cover as dense as that chosen by the cottontail rabbit, because the varying hare depends more for protection on its camouflage coat than on cover and concealment. In addition to using several favorite forms, the hare also has a network of trails that it depends on for traveling about in its area. In the winter these trails become well-packed highways.

The varying hare feeds mainly at night, although it is also active on dark, overcast days. The animal eats about 3/4 of a pound of food per day, selecting from almost any vegetation within its habitat—although it does have certain preferences.

In the summer the hare prefers the succulent grasses and the tender tips of woody plants. Such food is not available in the winter and the hare must then feed upon dead grasses, buds and bark. It first eats the tender bark on the smaller branches before girdling the trunks of shrubs and small trees. White cedar is a favored food. Some hares eat the needles of balsam fir while others ignore them completely. If a hare feeds upon balsam needles they impart a flavor to the meat which renders it almost unpalatable for human consumption. As the snow deepens in the forest new food supplies become available. The hare is now able to walk on top of the snow, and it can reach higher on the bushes with each succeeding storm. At this time it eats snow to alleviate its thirst, but in the summer its water needs are met by the vegetation it consumes.

In the summer the varying hare often resorts to taking dust baths to get relief from the myriad insects that pester it. Both the ruffed grouse and the varying hare may use the same dusting spots.

Senses: Hearing is the sense that is most important to the varying hare; its ears constantly twitch back and forth to pick up the faintest sound. Scent and eyesight.

seem to be about on a par. Of course, when a breeze is blowing downwind from a predator, the hare will smell the danger long before it can see it. Likewise, it will observe the slightest movement of an enemy coming upwind long before it picks up any odor.

Communication: At breeding time or when alarmed the hare thumps the ground with its hind feet, sometimes making an audible hollow sound but always sending vibrations through the ground that are noticed by other hares in the area. A mother hare may grunt to its young, and males make a growling sound when fighting. A common sound in the wilderness is the piercing scream of a dying hare.

Locomotion: The hind feet of the varying hare are about 5 1/2 inches long and appear too big in relation to its body. Nevertheless, the animal can run about 30 miles per hour or about 44 feet per second. When the hare is running hard, the front feet come down one after the other, while the hind feet come down together ahead of the front feet. It can jump 10 feet from a standing position, 15 feet when running.

An adult hare has a large stock of tricks that it can call upon to elude a trailing enemy. Not only can it run across snow in which other animals would flounder, it also can turn its body at almost right angles in the middle of a jump. When pursued by a predator, the hare may follow one of its runways, then leap out sideways and take off on a new tack. It often runs in ever smaller circles; then, streaking out of its circular path in a straight dash, makes a beeline for the other side of its territory, generally leaving its pursuer behind.

Although the hare would rather not get wet, it is a strong swimmer.

Breeding: In December the testes of the varying hare start to enlarge and descend into the scrotum. This hare is fond of socializing with the others of its kind on moonlit nights, scampering over the snow and engaging in a hare's version of tag and leap frog, but at the beginning of March these games become strained and antagonism develops between the males. Soon the breeding battles begin. The hares bite one another, rear up on their hind legs like miniature stallions and strike each other with their front feet, or kick each other with their hind feet. The sharp claws on these strong hind feet make lethal weapons. The hare's hide is thin and easily torn. I saw one vanquished male after a "love battle" which had had most of his hide torn off.

The male then has to pursue the female, who leads him on a merry chase, ultimately submitting to his advances, and after several copulations the marital ties are severed. Varying hares are promiscuous, but a dominant male breeds more frequently than others.

Birth and Young: The young varying hares are born about thirty-six days after the mother has mated. Occasionally the period may extend to forty days. A female usually has two litters per year, sometimes three. While the number of young per litter can vary from two to ten, the average is three.

The female gives birth to her young in one of her more secluded forms. The young are born fully furred and with their eyes wide open. During birth, the female helps in the delivery by tearing open and eating the natal membrane.

At birth the little ones weigh 2 to 3 ounces and are about 4 1/2 inches long. Within minutes they are nursing at the mother's breast; within hours they are hopping about; and within a week they are feeding upon vegetation and starting the weaning process, although they may nurse for almost a month.

Life Span: Although some captive hares and a few wild ones have reached the age of eight, these are rare exceptions. Ordinarily about 70 percent of all the adult hares die annually, and during the crash period the mortality of both adults and juveniles increases. Only about 2 percent of the population reaches the age of five.

Sign: The droppings of the varying hare are about one-third larger than those of the cottontail rabbit. These droppings may be seen scattered throughout the hare's habitat, along its runways, winter or summer.

In the summer the hares' runways *may* be seen winding through the vegetation, but in the winter these runways can't be missed. Sometimes the runways are beaten down so that they are a foot lower than the soft, fluffy snow on either side. The tracks of the varying hare are also very conspicuous because of the wide snowshoe form of the hind foot.

Girdling done by the hares can easily be noticed in the dark forest. Because the hares have opposing incisors and deer do not, the twigs that the hares cut are clipped clean while those clipped by the deer are roughly cut and show stringy fibers.

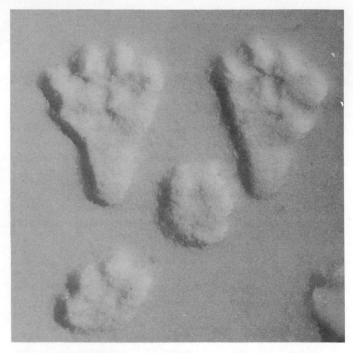

Tracks of the varying hare in snow can easily be identified by the large hind-foot track, which registers in front of the forefoot when the animal is bounding.

Enemies: The big-footed lynx is the varying hare's main enemy. Living in the same area, designed to feed upon the hares, the lynx is also equipped with large snowshoes. Where the varying hare can go, so can the lynx—as far as being able to stay on top of the snow—but the varying hare can duck and weave through brush too dense for the lynx to penetrate.

The weasel, mink, fisher, wolverine, fox, bobcat and coyote are all inclined to feed on tasty hare. Some of these predators do much better in the summer when they are not impeded by deep snow, but for some the snow doesn't matter too much—they wait till the hare comes to their ambush.

Winged predators threaten the hare in winter and summer. The great horned owl probably takes the greatest toll, with the snowy owl, the great gray owl, the barred owl, the gyrfalcon, goshawk and Cooper's hawk all taking their quotas.

Rabbit ticks place a tremendous drain upon the varying hare's system. Sometimes hundreds of ticks may be on one hare. Once while canoeing down the Ottawa River, near its headwaters in the Province of Quebec, I maneuvered close to a hare on shore and took some photographs. The infestation of ticks that encircled the hare's eyes and face amazed me. Dozens of them were busily engorging blood. Lice, flies and mosquitoes add to the hare's annoyances. In addition it sometimes is afflicted by coccidiosis, a disease that affects the liver and upsets the flow of bile, causing nutritional disturbances, as well as a mild form of tularemia.

In areas where their ranges overlap, the whitetail deer is a competitor for almost every mouthful of food that the hare eats. And the deer is able to feed as low as the hare, as well as being able to feed much higher.

My own state of New Jersey has tried some experimental releases of imported hares in an effort to re-establish them here. In my own particular area, I believe the program is doomed to failure from the start because of an overabundance of deer. The deer have all but destroyed their range on the top of the Kittatinny Mountains, where the hares were released. The competition for food almost guarantees the failure of the project.

Human Relations: The varying hare is of inestimable value to people living in the North country. In the United States many people hunt the hare for sport, but in the Far North the livelihood, if not the lives, of the people depends on the hare. When the hares are plentiful, they provide food for the natives and the furbearers, the trapping is good, and a cash income is assured. When the hares are scarce, starvation is the lot of both predators and humans. With the exception of the caribou, no other animal plays as an important role in human lives on this continent as does the varying hare.

Trophy Records: The heaviest varying hare, recorded by C. M. Oves of Pennsylvania, weighed 5 pounds, 4 ounces.

Table Fare: There is seldom any fat on the varying hare, so the meat tends to be dry. In the far North this lack of fat is a serious drawback, for the people living there need the fat so that their own bodies can withstand the intense cold. Still, countless varying hares are used for food.

Arctic Hare

Lepus arcticus
Lepus othus

There are two species of Arctic hares inhabiting the far northern regions of North America, but they are so similar that we shall treat them as one. These hares are rarely encountered by the average hunter, though they are important game species to the Indians and Eskimos of the northlands. Their most unique characteristic is their bounding gait. When traveling at full speed, the hare covers the ground in leaps of 10 feet or more, hitting the earth with all four feet at once and springing away, its body motionless in the air and its feet tucked to the side at an angle.

Description: This is the largest hare in North America. It may reach 28 inches in length, stand 11 inches high at the shoulder and weigh from 6 to 12 pounds or more.

In the winter the hare is pure white except for the black tips of its ears. The fur is white from base to tip, unlike that of the varying hare which is dark at the base. The hare turns brown in the summer, except in certain areas where the summer season is too short for the brown change to be completed. The transition from the white coat to the brown coat generally matches the area's transition from snow to bare ground. At the time that the hare has mixed patches of both brown and white hair, the brown earth is still covered with patches of snow.

This hare has 30 teeth that are classified as 6 incisors, 12 premolars and 12 molars.

It has five toes on each forefoot and four toes on each

hind foot. The feet are densely furred and only the nails are visible.

Distribution: The Arctic hare (*Lepus arcticus*) inhabits the tundra of northern Canada from the Mackenzie River to Newfoundland, northward as far as there is land. A similar species, the Alaskan hare (*Lepus othus*), is found in similar habitat west of the Mackenzie Delta along coastal Alaska to the Alaskan Peninsula.

Travel: The Arctic hare does not move any farther

Distribution of the Arctic hare (vertical lines) and the Alaskan hare (horizontal).

than it must to secure food. The bitterest of weather does not seem to affect it. Whereas ordinarily it would be content to spend its life in a territory 1 or 2 miles wide, deep snow buries its food and often causes it to move to windswept hills or protected valleys.

Habits: This hare is highly tolerant of others of its kind. It cannot really be called gregarious, for it congregates near available food and not strictly for social contact. Often fifty to a hundred or more hares can be found in one small region. Some of the early explorers in the Arctic complained that in some areas these hares were so numerous that it was almost impossible for drivers to control their dog teams. With hares hopping to the left and right of them, the teams were constantly dashing off to chase them despite the efforts of the drivers.

Because there is so little light in the arctic winter, hunger rather than sunlight activates these hares. Even the weather has little effect upon them. The dwarf willow is the hare's basic food and it eats every part of the plant: the buds, catkins, leaves, bark and, in the summer when it can dig them up, even the roots. It also feeds upon the grasses, mosses, herbs and berries that grow so profusely in the short arctic summer.

In the winter the hare eats anything palatable, even meat. Attracted by the meat bait, the hares often become caught in traps set for the Arctic fox. Snow provides whatever additional moisture they need beyond what they obtain from plants. Even in summer they have been known to seek out banks of snow to quench their thirst.

The teeth of the Arctic hare are much less curved than those of any other hare or rabbit. They protrude frontward in an almost straight line, giving this hare a very buck-toothed appearance. These straight teeth are designed to be used as tweezers and allow the hare to extract the smallest plant growing in rock crevasses. In winter the hare uses its teeth to break through the crust of snow to obtain food. Along the coast it avidly consumes long strings of kelp.

This hare prefers to live in areas that are strewn with rocks. When the bitter arctic storms pour down countless tons of snow, the hare huddles on the leeward side of the rock and lets the wind blow. Often the hare is snowed under, but the snow only provides extra insulation and does it no harm. Sometimes the hare tunnels beneath the snow for protection.

If the hare is sitting in the open, it will turn so that it is facing into the prevailing wind, which flows *over* the fur. Wind blowing from behind would turn the hair and allow the air trapped beneath the fur to escape, thus destroying its insulating effect.

Even in the summer the hare prefers open, rocky places. The form, if we can call it that, is just a spot alongside a favorite boulder. As the sun moves around the horizon, the hare moves around the boulder to follow it.

When winter comes the situation changes as the hare's coat changes. Its confidence in this camouflage is so great that the hare will sit still until it can almost be caught by hand.

The hare has a habit of going around or under an object instead of over it, and whenever possible it follows a trail where it can run faster than it could over rough ground. The natives of the region take advantage of this trait by putting up a small row of rocks across a path, leaving a small hole and hanging a snare on a piece of driftwood over the opening.

Senses: The sense of smell is probably the hare's greatest asset. It has been known to dig through more than a foot of snow to uncover a willow twig. It also depends on this sense to detect an enemy's scent upon the wind. The hare's sight is not very good, but its hearing is keen.

If suspicious of something, the hare stands on its hind feet, as if to get a better view, but most of the time it is in the open and there are no obstacles to see over. If the hare is feeding on a hillside, it faces uphill to watch for danger. An animal trying to stalk the hare will use the hill for cover and take advantage of the downhill slope when it charges.

Communication: The Arctic hare is not very vociferous. The only sound it makes is a high-pitched squeal when caught by a predator.

Locomotion: No one has determined the Arctic hare's exact running speed. As it is often pursued by a fox or a wolf, and is able to escape, it must be able to run at least 35 miles per hour. When pursued by airborne enemies the hare dodges among boulders or tries to hide in a willow thicket.

The hare usually hops when it travels about in search of food, bounds if in a hurry. Its hind feet are large, over 7 inches long, and heavily furred, and it can run over the top of soft snow that would bog down most of its enemies. When it bounds, its hind feet come down well ahead of its front feet.

In the regions that the hare inhabits, melting snow turns many a level piece of land into a shallow lake. It is a good swimmer, although it prefers to stay out of the water. This hare is noted for hopping on its hind legs without touching the forelegs to the ground.

Breeding: Most hares have three to four litters a year, but the Arctic hare has one. This is because in the North the warm weather lasts for only a brief period, limiting the time when the hare can give birth in a climate favorable for the survival of the young.

The breeding season arrives about the first of April and lasts about two weeks. At this time the males become fiercely competitive, with frequent fights breaking out. In fighting, these hares use their forefeet lethally compared to the jackrabbits, which do most of their damage with their hind feet. Living in a region where the snow often becomes crusted over, they have exceptionally well-developed claws on the center toes of the front feet. Ordinarily these claws are used to pound and claw through the crusted snow, but during the breeding season the males use them to cut and slash each other to ribbons. After the dominant males have asserted their superiority, the hares mate promiscuously.

Birth and Young: The gestation period of the Arctic hare is about six weeks, and the young ones are born fully furred with their eyes wide open. A litter may contain as many as eight young, but the average is five. Because food is not so abundant as it is farther south, the

Arctic hares take care of their young for a longer period than do other hares.

The mother usually attends and nurses the young for about two weeks. After that time the little ones can scamper about, although they usually "freeze" at the first sound of danger. At two weeks of age, the young are weaned and begin sampling vegetation on their own.

Life Span: The Arctic hare has a potential life span of five to six years, although it is unlikely that many reach this age.

Enemies: The Arctic fox ranks as the Arctic hare's main enemy. The wolf, the polar bear and the grizzly bear will feed upon the hare, but the bears are too slow for a chase, and the wolf is usually interested in bigger game. The wolf is built for the long run to pull down a caribou in the open. The fox, however, just the right size and agile enough, easily chases the hare through cover. Luckily for the baby hares, the foxes are usually gorging themselves on birds' eggs and young birds at the time the young hares are most vulnerable.

Other enemies of the hare are the wolverine, mink and weasel, the Arctic owl and the gyrfalcon. The skuas and jaegers will attack the young.

Like all mammals, the hares are host to lice. Flies, and especially clouds of mosquitoes, make life miserable for them during the brief span of summer. Internally, the hare has tapeworms.

Human Relations: The Arctic hare is an important food item to both the Eskimos and the Indians that inhabit its territory, and the fluctuations in its population seriously affect their lives. The hares provide food for the foxes, and when the hares are scarce, the foxes are scarce—and the trappers' income is drastically reduced.

The Eskimos and Indians also use the skin of the Arctic hare for making blankets. They cut the skin from the carcass in a circular fashion, producing a long, inch-wide strip which is then rolled into a rope. Many of these ropes are then loosely woven into a robe. The weave is so loose that a finger can be poked through it at any point, but the robe is very light and warm, although it loses hair continuously because the hides have not been tanned.

The natives often make socks from the skins by merely sewing one end of the hide together. If the hide is turned with the fur inside and worn while it is still green (not dried), the sock takes the contour of the foot and ankle.

Table Fare: The meat of the Arctic hare is highly regarded by all who have eaten it.

Jackrabbit

Lepus

The jackrabbits of the western plains are the rifleman's favorite small game. Walking them up and hitting them on the run, or taking them at long range when they habitually pause in their escape for a look back, hunters get plenty of practice on these desert speedsters when big game is out of season. Named with the jackass in mind because of its long ears, the jack is actually a hare and not a rabbit, for its young are born fully furred and with their eyes wide open.

Description: The whitetailed jackrabbit is the larger of the two species, measuring between 22 and 26 inches in length and weighing between 6 and 9 1/2 pounds. Its ears are 5 to 6 inches long, and its tail is white on top and bottom. In the summer this jackrabbit is a light brownish-gray over the back and sides, lighter on the belly. The tips of the ears are black. During the winter, in the northern part of its range, it turns white all over and is often mistaken for an Arctic hare, but, because of its long ears and extra-long legs, it cannot be mistaken for a varying hare. Not all whitetailed jacks turn completely white in winter. At lower elevations some of them turn a buff-white. Even those that do turn all white have a buff base to the white hairs, although the hair must be separated to see this.

The blacktailed jackrabbit has a black rump, and the hair on the top of its tail is black. This jack is between 18 and 24 inches in length and weighs between 4 and 7 1/2 pounds. Its ears are longer than those of the whitetails and measure up to 7 inches. The pelage of the black-

Long ears and legs endow the jackrabbits with keen hearing and high speed, valuable assets on the open plains of their habitat. This is a blacktailed jack.

tailed jack is a brownish-gray, with indistinct black lines. The underfur is an off-white. The belly and underside of the tail are white. The ears are brown inside, whitish on the outside and black tipped. The blacktailed jack sheds twice a year, too, but does not change color markedly.

The eyes of all jackrabbits are bright yellow with a black pupil and protrude from the side of the skull. The hind legs of the jacks are long and powerful. The hind feet of the whitetailed jack are over 6 inches long, while those of the blacktailed jack are just over 5 inches long. There are five toes on each of the forefeet and four toes on each of the hind feet. The pads of the feet are densely furred in both species; the toe nails are sharp and protruding.

The jackrabbits have 28 teeth: 6 incisors, 10 premolars and 12 molars. The molars are flat-crowned for chewing vegetation. They have two pairs of incisors in the top jaw, a feature that distinguishes the lagomorphs (hares, rabbits and pikas) from all other rodents. One pair of incisors is rudimentary and serves no purpose.

Distribution: The blacktailed jackrabbit (*Lepus californicus*) inhabits open grasslands and deserts of western United States from central Arkansas to the Pacific Coast, north as far as southeastern Washington in the west and to central South Dakota in the east. The whitetailed jack-

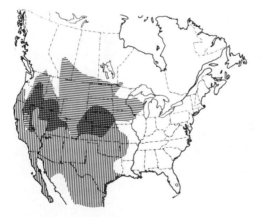

Distribution of the blacktailed jackrabbit (vertical) and the whitetailed jackrabbit (horizontal).

rabbit (*Lepus townsendii*) lives in grasslands and sage-brush country from southern Alberta south to northern New Mexico, and from the Sierras east to Lake Michigan.

Travel: Although the jackrabbits are very fleet-footed, they do not leave their home areas. Only in their own areas are they familiar with the terrain, a knowledge which is vital to their survival. Under ordinary conditions, a jackrabbit is content to spend its entire lifetime in an area of 4 square miles.

The only time that the jacks leave their home areas is when a drought scorches all the vegetation and food is no longer available. At such times the jacks have been known to travel as much as twenty miles seeking food and water. It is during such periods that the jacks are particularly destructive to irrigated farm crops. However, as soon as rainfall has infused the devastated areas with new life, the jacks return to their natural haunts.

Habits: Although a young blacktailed jack may enter a burrow, the adults almost never do. Jackrabbits do not dig burrows, and if a jack should enter a burrow, it would be one made by some other animal. Most jacks have three or four forms, slight hollows scraped out in the earth, which they frequent. Usually a form is under a low bush or against a clump of grass which will provide conceal-ment and shade from the hot sun. Jackrabbit forms are not in such dense cover as are those of the cottontail rabbit.

The jack's basic coloration matches its background well enough to provide excellent camouflage. When threatened by a predator, the jack sits absolutely motionless, and most of the time the enemy passes by and never detects it. Often it outwaits danger by huddling as close to the earth as it can and holding its long ears flat against its back.

Jackrabbits seldom have to drink water unless there is a drought. Under ordinary conditions the jacks can obtain all the moisture they need from the vegetation they eat. Drops of dew provide moisture, too. In the desert areas the jacks eat the pulpy cactus plants which are veritable storehouses of water.

Jackrabbits eat almost any type of vegetation they encounter. Grasses, weedy plants and shrubs make up the bulk of their diet. Among their main food items are snakeweed, rabbit brush, mesquite, grama grass, sagebrush, greasewood, saltbrush, filaree, prickly pear, spiderling and eriogonum. Wherever minerals, salts and trace elements occur, jackrabbits ingest the soil for its nutritional value. They also feed on alfalfa and truck-farm produce, a habit that does not endear them to farmers.

Jackrabbits pose a serious problem when they compete with sheep and cattle for available grasses. Biologists have calculated that twelve jackrabbits can eat as much forage as one sheep, and that sixty jacks can consume enough grass to support one cow. The irony of this is that much of the western and southwestern rangeland is badly overgrazed to start with. Overgrazing by livestock as well as jackrabbits causes erosion and a change in plant life. Since the more desirable vegetation is eaten first, the less palatable types are allowed to become dominant, thus constantly lessening the range's carrying capacity for any form of life.

A great deal of the grass that a jackrabbit cuts down

is wasted. It often cuts down a tall stalk and eats perhaps a quarter or a third of it, then drops it and moves on to cut another. The discarded stalk lies on the ground and is not utilized by either the jacks or the livestock.

Living their life in open areas, the jacks are safer feeding at night. They begin to stir late in the afternoon. When they start to feed they do so for hours, with little pause except to look out for danger, and continue feeding through the night. Jackrabbits eat a large amount of food, about three-quarters of a pound daily, which they digest rapidly. In the early morning the jacks return to their forms, and by 8 a.m. conclude their activities. During the day the jacks doze, sunbathe, take dust baths or try to remove thorns and cactus spines from their feet and bodies. They spend most of the time just relaxing. Except for their personal forms, jacks do not seem to exercise territorial rights.

Senses: The jackrabbit's exceptionally long ears indicate the importance of its sense of hearing. The huge ears are admirably designed for funneling the slightest sound. Since it lives in open areas, hearing is its primary means of detecting danger before it comes too close.

The sense of smell is also very important to the jack and its nose is constantly working and wrinkling, sniffing each breeze for a tell-tale hint of danger. Often a jack stands on its hind legs to get a better sniff. In arid regions where the thermals are strong, scent rises quickly and an odor may be caught 2 feet above the ground that would be missed at a lower level.

The jack detects motion easily but is likely to overlook stationary objects. Its eyes protrude so far from the skull that each eye probably has better than 180-degree vision.

Rabbits and hares show a strong response to ground vibrations, indicating that their sense of touch is well developed. These animals may signal to one another by stamping their feet.

Communication: The jackrabbit is generally silent, but during the breeding season when two males fight or chase one another they sometimes growl or make a "chucking" sound deep in their throats. When captured, injured or badly frightened, the jack emits a high-pitched, piercing shriek that can be heard for about a mile. If the animal is captured it often continues screaming until it is killed.

In some areas jackrabbits defecate in favorite spots which probably serve some communicative function.

When a jack runs it raises its tail like a whitetail deer, and the flash of white alerts every jack that sees it. The antelope jack, like its namesake the pronghorn antelope, has long white hairs that can be muscularly controlled. When this jack runs, the muscles in the skin tighten first on one side and then on the other, heliographing a danger signal that is visible for miles.

Locomotion: Jackrabbits seldom walk; to move even a few feet they hop. The blacktailed jack is inclined to move off while danger is still distant, but the whitetailed jack often waits until the last minute before escaping.

The jackrabbit usually runs with its ears erect, bounding at a speed of about 20 to 25 miles per hour. If pressed by an enemy, its ears come down and it speeds up to about 30 to 35 miles per hour. When in real danger, the jack can attain 40 to 45 miles per hour. Sometimes when the vegetation is high, the whitetailed jackrabbit starts its flight by hopping upright on just its hind legs so that it can look around to locate its enemy.

When running at moderate speed, the jack often makes every fourth or fifth jump a high one so that it can observe its pursuer. At high speeds it eliminates these "lookout" jumps and concentrates on speed.

Although a jack seldom jumps more than 4 feet high, it can broadjump great distances. The blacktailed jack covers 15 feet at a bound, the whitetail 20. One record leap by a whitetailed jack was 22 feet, 4 inches.

Although water is scarce in most of the jack's territory, it can swim well when it must, using all four feet in a dog paddle.

Breeding: There is still much to be learned about the breeding seasons and habits of jackrabbits. No one is quite sure just how long the breeding season lasts. In Arizona, pregnant females have been found ten months of the year, while in the northern sections the season is much shorter. The peak period for most jacks, however, is from January through September.

In late December the testicles of the males enlarge and living sperm is found in the seminal fluid. They engage in vigorous battles, each male "boxing" with the other by striking out with the front feet, occasionally delivering a powerful kick with a hind foot, and biting each other when they can. Many jacks have pieces torn out of their ears, but they inflict most of the damage with the sharp claws of their hind feet. Sometimes one of the combatants is killed, but usually the loser dashes away, followed for a short distance by the victor. When mating begins, the jacks do not pair off. Their promiscuity works both ways, males and females breeding indiscriminantly. In the south the females generally have four litters per year, while two seems to be the rule farther north.

Birth and Young: The gestation period for jackrabbits is about six weeks. The female may or may not dig a shallow nest. Although the female may have one to six young at a time, three or four seems to be the average litter size.

The young jacks are born fully furred with their eyes wide open. They vary in weight from 2 to 6 ounces. There is often a tremendous difference in size among baby jackrabbits, even between litter mates. Some babies will weigh three times as much as others, a phenomenon that biologists are at a loss to explain.

At birth the jacks' ears are short but they grow very rapidly. Within a few minutes after being born, the little ones can nurse. Already their lower incisor teeth are well developed, and the upper ones push through the gums in a few days.

Either at birth or shortly thereafter, the female scatters the young. This is a critical survival factor for this species because it lessens a predator's chance of wiping out an entire family. The female stays away from the young throughout the day and nurses them only at night. Within a period of about one week the young jacks are able to eat vegetation, are weaned and on their own.

Life Span: The life span of a jackrabbit is approximately five to six years. Most of the females do not breed in their first year, and most mammals have a life span of five times their first reproductive date. It is unlikely that many ever die of old age.

Sign: Tracks of the jackrabbit are common in the dust and sand of its arid habitat, and they are abundant in the winter when snow is on the ground. Occasional patches of fur hanging on strands of barbed wire will show where the jacks have passed under. Their dark-brown, round pellets of scat are easily noticed and are sometimes concentrated in a small area. Scars on cacti, or the exposed pulp, are evidence that a jack has been feeding upon them.

Ordinarily one does not need to look for signs of jackrabbits; if they are in the area, they are usually flushed easily from cover.

Enemies: The coyote ranks first among the jack's multitude of enemies. Stomach and scat analyses of the coyote show that jacks provide better than 50 percent of its diet. In areas where sheep are raised, the jackrabbit provides a good buffer between the sheep and the coyote. A coyote that has just eaten a jackrabbit is not likely to bother a lamb. In areas where cattle are raised, the coyote forms a good buffer between the jackrabbits and the forage. Every jackrabbit taken by a coyote leaves more grass for the cattle.

Today, after years of misunderstanding, enlightened ranchers are recognizing the role that wildlife plays in relation to the land. There are fewer attempts to eliminate a species and more efforts made toward control tailored to fit the actual need of a specific area.

Bobcats, badgers, foxes, bears, mountain lions, dogs, cats, hawks, eagles, owls and snakes all find the jackrabbit a tasty meal when they can catch one. Only the winged predators and the coyote, however, can consistently capture this long-eared speedster.

Human Relations: Before the coming of the white man, the Indians used to hold rabbit drives to secure these animals for food. Drives have been popular with the white man, too, but he has held them in order to reduce the number of jacks eating the grass. Many drives have produced upwards of 5,000 jackrabbits at one time. One of the largest took place near Fresno, California, on March 21, 1896. About 8,000 people took part in the hunt, stringing out in a line 18 miles long. The wings of the corral, or tips, were 4 miles long. By the time the hunt was concluded, between 20,000 and 25,000 jackrabbits were slaughtered.

Several million dollars' worth of jackrabbit skins are used annually, chiefly for making felt for the manufacturing of hats.

Trophy Records: The heaviest jackrabbit that I could find on record was a 13-pound whitetail.

Table Fare: After the big drives, many rabbit carcasses would be sold on the open market, given to the poor or used for animal feed at fur farms and chicken ranches. I have never eaten jackrabbit, but people who have don't speak very highly of the flesh of the blacktailed jack, much preferring that of the whitetail. In either case, the younger jacks would be more palatable than the adults.

European Rabbit

Oryctolagus cuniculus

Often called the San Juan rabbit after the islands off the coast of Washington where it was first introduced, this animal is more often found in captivity than in the wild. It is kept as a pet, for food, and for its hair and skin. It still exists in the wild on the San Juan Islands, and has been introduced—with little success—as a game species in various parts of the country.

Description: The European rabbit is similar in color to the cottontail. Most of the hair is light brown, interspersed with black. The nape of the neck is buff-colored whereas our cottontail's is reddish. The tail is white, also the belly and the insides of the legs. The tips of the ears are black.

This rabbit is much larger than the cottontail; it may reach 22 inches in length and weigh up to 5 pounds. The ears are about 3 1/2 inches long. The domesticated strains grow much larger, with some going over 7 pounds.

This rabbit has 28 teeth: 6 incisors, 10 premolars and 12 molars.

There are five toes on each of the front feet and four toes on each of the hind feet. The soles of the feet are covered with dense hairs that conceal the pads, but the nails are visible.

Travel: Whereas our native cottontails and hares do not dig burrows, the European rabbit does. It travels only far enough from its burrow to secure food, then it returns underground.

Habits: The European rabbit digs elaborate tunnels that become so extensive that such areas become known as warrens. As many as 150 rabbits can live in a half-acre area. In Russia these rabbits sometimes live in talus slopes or cracks in the rocks. Their burrows may be 4 to 8 feet underground, the entrance tunnel going deeper, then bending back up to the nest site. Many of the tunnels extend up to 50 feet or more in length, and when the rabbit population is dense, many of the tunnels interconnect. These rabbits do not hibernate but remain active all winter.

Because of the rabbit's tremendous reproductive capacity, many hunters in the United States feel that it would make an important game animal. What they do not realize is that this rabbit is almost strictly nocturnal and seldom comes out before 11 p.m. Our native rabbits and hares feed in the early morning or late in the afternoon, and most of them sit out during the daytime. The European rabbit does not. It comes out under the cover of darkness, feeds and then retires underground with the coming of dawn.

Many years ago, European rabbits were released in the San Juan Islands in Puget Sound. The lighthouse keeper who lived on this island thought they would be a cheap source of food. The results were nearly disastrous; the keeper couldn't keep up with the rabbits. The rabbits, running unchecked by predators, took over the island and riddled it with holes. Within a short time these tunnels had so undermined the island that the lighthouse was in danger of collapsing. Thousands of the animals had to be poisoned to save the structure, and, as a result of this incident, the breed became known in this country as the San Juan rabbit. A few of the rabbits swam to a nearby island that had an area of approximately 58 acres and proceeded to dig their tunnels. Eventually the land along the edges of the island began to collapse and drop into the sea, slowly shrinking the island's surface area. Finally an extensive poisoning program had to be carried out to control the rabbits and to save the island.

Grasses and herbs are the favored food of the European rabbit, yet it readily eats rougher, coarser vegetation when other food is scarce. When feeding upon heavy roughage, the rabbit has a hard time digesting it and practices coprophagy—eating its own dung. Not being able to chew its food twice as the ruminants do, the rabbit ingests the same food material twice. Dung that is to be rechewed and reswallowed is green in color and is taken directly from the anus. Dung composed of material which has passed through the body twice is black and very compacted. By reprocessing the dung, the rabbit's body is thus able to extract all of the vitamins and nutrients in every bit of food, an efficient method of saving on food consumption. The rabbit usually feeds upon its own dung while resting in its burrow. The European rabbit is not alone in this habit: it is common to all hares and rabbits.

Senses: Hearing is a rabbit's most developed sense and the one it relies on most frequently. The rabbit has big ears, and the larger the ear, the more sound is funneled into the auditory nerves.

Anyone watching a rabbit will notice how it keeps wrinkling its nose as it sniffs the air for scent. Not only is the sense of smell important for detecting danger but also for locating food.

A rabbit's eyesight is keen enough to spot moving objects, but it does not notice anything that is immobile.

The sense of touch is also important because rabbits frequently signal to one another to warn of impending danger by thumping the ground with their hind feet. The vibrations can be felt by other rabbits at a considerable distance.

Communication: With the exception of the thumping just described, I know of only one other sound made by this rabbit—a scream of terror or fright. Predators recognize this scream, and most of the predator calls used by hunters imitate the sound.

Locomotion: A rabbit generally hops from place to place, its front feet coming down ahead of the hind ones when it is moving slowly. When it gathers speed its hind feet land well ahead of the front feet. Not a fast runner, it does not try to outdistance a pursuer but dashes down its tunnel and hides underground. If a foe follows it underground, the rabbit attempts to lose it in the maze. Rabbits can swim well, although they prefer not to swim at all.

Breeding: The main breeding season for this rabbit in its native haunts is the period from January to July. Some of the females may have a longer span.

During the breeding season the male rabbits become pugnacious and fights are common. Although the males do the fighting, it is the female that selects the mate. These animals are polygamous, the males breeding with more than one female.

Birth and Young: The gestation period is from twenty-eight to thirty-two days. The litters vary in size from four to twelve. It has been figured that one pair of rabbits and their offspring could produce a total of 1,-274,840 rabbits in four years. The young when born are naked, helpless and blind, They are born underground in a grass-lined den and are well cared for by the mother. She has to be particularly careful not to let the male near the young, because he frequently kills the young males.

The female usually breeds again within twelve hours after giving birth. Four to six litters per year are common, although the female may be bred more frequently than this. Weather and other conditions often limit the number of litters, and the embryos may be resorbed instead of completing their development.

By the tenth day the young rabbits can walk, by the eleventh day their eyes open and by the twelfth day their ears are functional. They are feeding on vegetation outside of the den by the third week, and by the end of the month are completely weaned and on their own.

By this time the female is about ready to give birth to her next litter. Although the previous litter is now weaned, the young may not leave the warren. Some do, some don't. Those that stay either take over unoccupied tunnels or else start to dig ones of their own.

The young females are capable of breeding when they are 5 1/2 months old if they were born in the fall, and in 8 1/2 months if they were born in the spring.

Life Span: In the wild, the European rabbit has a potential life span of six to seven years, although it is unlikely that many ever reach that age. Some domesticated rabbits, derived from this stock, have lived to be thirteen years old.

Sign: The lack of vegetation and the innumerable holes make the identification of a rabbit warren an easy matter. Round, dark scat will be found scattered throughout the entire area. Tracks in dust or mud are easy to identify: no other animal in this rabbit's area has such a long hind-foot track in which no pad marks are visible. During the winter, when these animals are forced to feed upon the bark of shrubs, their teeth marks are evident in the wood.

Enemies: In Europe the stoat, or ferret, is probably this rabbit's principal foe. This large, blood-thirsty weasel can easily follow the rabbit underground and pursues it relentlessly until it has made its kill. Often the ferret just curls up in its victim's nest and sleeps until it is hungry again. A warren supplies it with several lifetimes of food.

Hawks, owls, badgers, foxes, dogs, snakes—in fact, all of the European predators—feed upon this rabbit. In areas where predators are lacking, the rabbit population explodes.

Human Relations: In Europe many of the poorer people either cannot afford a gun or are not allowed to own one. Poaching for all types of game is very common and the rabbit is the chief target. Since the rabbit is nocturnal, most of the poachers hunt with a ferret. They place nets over the holes of the burrow and release the ferret down another one. In a short time the rabbits start popping out of holes and into the nets. If the poacher doesn't have a ferret, he can set snares in the paths going through the high grass or hedgerows. To these Europeans the rabbit is very important as a food item. When the virus myxomatosis was introduced in France, the death of the rabbits caused real hardships by depriving the people of food. The hair of the rabbit is used to make felt.

Trophy Records: The largest wild rabbit on record weighed 5 pounds.

Table Fare: These rabbits are eaten frequently. The meat is light in color and very tasty.

HOOFED MAMMALS

Order Artiodactyla

This order is among the most important to the hunter because it contains many of the animals generally classified as big game. The name *Artiodactyla* means "even-toed," and most of the members of this order have either two or four toes on each foot. In North America there are four families of this order: Cervidae (deer, moose, elk, caribou); Bovidae (bison, sheep, goats); Antilocapridae (pronghorn); and Tayasuiidae (peccaries).

The hooves on which these animals walk correspond to our fingernails, the two main hooves representing the third and fourth digits, with those that would represent our little and index fingers being reduced in size. They are generally called "dewclaws" and only touch the ground when the animal is walking in snow or mud. The peccary has four toes on each of the forefeet, but only three on the hind feet.

Except for the peccary, all the native North American representatives of this order have a four-chambered stomach and are ruminants—they chew their cud. Again, with the exception of the peccary, our native artiodactyls have a gristly pad, rather than teeth, at the front end of the upper jaw.

Adornments on the head are characteristic of several families of artiodactyls. The males of the Cervidae have antlers which grow each spring, are fully developed by fall and are shed in winter. The caribou is unusual in that the female, too, has antlers. The wild cattle, Family Bovidae, have horns present in both males and females, and these are permanent structures that grow throughout the life of the animal. The horns of the males, however, are generally much larger than those of the females.

The pronghorn antelope, the only living member of its family, Antilocapridae, is unique in being the only mammal in the world that has true horns, but which sheds the outside layer each year.

PECCARIES

Family Tayassuidae

COLLARED PECCARY

The collared peccary is found in the Southwest, where it travels in herds and lives in thick cover or caves.

Collared Peccary

Dicotyles tajacu

The peccary is descended from a gigantic wild pig that lived during the Lower Miocene period 25 million years ago. Judging from remains of this animal's jaws and teeth found in the Agate Springs Quarry in Nebraska, its skull was about 3 feet long. Compared to its ancient ancestor, the peccary is a midget, yet it has gotten a reputation for fierceness that it does not deserve. Though when cornered it can inflict damage with its sharp tusks, the little pig is more apt to run than charge. Tales of ferocious peccaries were probably spread by people who confused the animals with wild hogs.

In the Southwest where the peccary is found, it is generally known as the javelina, a Spanish name that refers to the animal's javeline-like tusks. The name peccary is derived from a Brazilian Indian word, *pecari*, which means, "animal that makes paths through the woods."

Description: The peccary is a small, pig-like animal that stands 22 inches high at the shoulder, measures 30 to 37 inches in length and weighs, on the average, 40 to 65 pounds. It has a long snout, tipped by a tough disc used for rooting in the earth. The eyes are small and the lids have long eyelashes. The ears are small, pointed and erect. The neck is so short and blunt as to appear non-existant. The back is slightly arched. The legs are stout but rather short. There are four toes on each of the front feet, two hooves and two dewclaws; but only three toes on each of the hind feet, two hooves and one dewclaw.

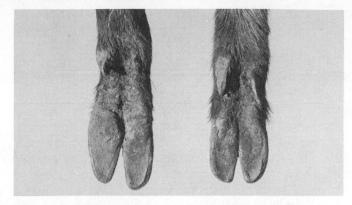

The peccary differs from other hoofed animals in having only one dewclaw, or vestigial toe, on the hind foot (left) and two on the forefoot.

The tail is short. The body is covered with bristly hair that is about 2 inches long and of a salt-and-pepper gray. The hair on the neck can be erected into a mane. A narrow, white band extends from under the throat and meets on the back; hence the name collared peccary. In the center of the peccary's back, 8 inches above the tail, is a large, open musk gland.

The peccary has 38 teeth: 10 incisors, 4 canines, 12 premolars and 12 molars. The canine teeth are enlarged to form tusks. Unlike the wild boar's upper tusks, which curve upwards, the peccary's upper tusks point straight down. These tusks are over 2 inches long and are very sharp.

Distribution: The collared peccary inhabits dry, brushy country, and scrub oak forests along the U.S.-Mexico border from Arizona to eastern Texas.

Distribution of the collared peccary.

Travel: Peccaries do not migrate, but the aridity of their habitat often forces them to travel considerable distances for water and food.

Habits: Peccaries travel in herds of from six to thirty because they are gregarious and because the herd offers protection. When the peccaries are surprised or alarmed the entire herd makes a wild dash for safety, exploding out of a thicket and running in all directions. Anyone nearby could easily imagine that he was being attacked, but the ferocity of these animals is vastly overrated. However, if a peccary is wounded or cornered it will fight. It is a plucky little beast and is equipped to fight if it has to. Once I was about to climb into a pen containing a peccary when it rushed me and made a pass at my leg with its tusk. I didn't give it the opportunity to make another. But this was a penned peccary; it couldn't run away.

Peccaries are most active in the early morning hours and again late in the afternoon when the heat has lessened as well as at night. During the middle of the day, they root holes in shaded earth and lie in them to cool off. When they can locate a cave, peccaries will take possession. A cave keeps them dry during the infrequent storms, warm in the winter and cool in the summer. Although most of the peccaries live in the mesquite tangles or thickets, or the marshy areas along watercourses, some of them may live on a mountainside as high as 6,000 feet.

With a modicum of protection the peccaries are more than able to hold their own because they are omnivorous. Vegetation is their mainstay and prickly pears their favorite. They eat the fruit, spines and all. Although the insides of their stomachs are often full of these spines, they seem to suffer no ill effects. They dig into the earth after roots and tubers and also for the nests of mice and rats. They eat all sorts of berries, fruits, nuts and acorns but very little grass. They eat insects and the eggs and young of ground-nesting birds, also reptiles and amphibians. Snakes are an especially choice item, and a herd of peccaries will almost make an area snake-free.

When a peccary kills a rattlesnake it uses its feet in the same way as a deer. It approaches the snake quietly and at the right moment jumps into the air and comes down on it with all four, sharp hooves, and continues jumping until the snake is dead.

Senses: The peccary's sense of smell is especially keen. The nostrils are in the center of the nose disk, and they are richly supplied with olfactory nerves. The peccary has no trouble locating food buried under 6 inches of earth. It must dig up so much of its food that a good sense of smell is vital. Hearing is also an important sense, and the peccary continually turns its head from left to right to monitor every sound it can pick up. Its eyesight is poor, but in its habitat the brush is so thick that it couldn't see anything if it wanted to, and most creatures are not likely to see the peccary.

Communication: Peccaries emit a soft, muted grunt, a constant sound that serves to keep the herd together. At the first sight of danger, they give an almost barklike coughing sound. When frightened or injured, they squeal loudly.

The musk gland on a peccary's back is also used for communication. As the little pigs pass through an area, they rub some of this musk on branches and bushes. The odor, which smells like a skunk's, can easily be detected by humans. When the animal is angered or frightened, the hair along its back rises and this gland is uncovered, automatically discharging scent. By means of this scent, a peccary can warn other members of the herd downwind without making a sound.

Locomotion: Peccaries are agile animals. They can turn end for end in a twinkling and can broadjump 6 feet from a standstill. They gallop with a stiff-legged gait and can achieve speeds of 25 miles per hour. Built low to the ground and well-tapered, they can dash away through the underbrush leaving nothing but dust and a touch of scent. Water is no obstacle; peccaries take rivers and streams in their stride.

Breeding: As peccaries are animals of the tropics, where food may be readily available all year round, breeding may take place at any time of the year. Being herd animals, they are undoubtedly polygamous, and the males are in constant attendance at all times. Prior to giving birth, the female seeks out some sort of den site. A cave is ideal, a hollow log acceptable, and just a thick clump of brush, if it is roofed over, will serve.

Birth and Young: The babies are born four months after breeding. Twins are the rule, and at birth are about the size of young rabbits. They are clothed in a deep reddish-brown pelage and have a single black stripe running down the center of their backs. They are active just a few hours after birth, and the mother usually takes them to rejoin the main herd within three or four days.

A female peccary becomes sexually mature and can breed in her second year. Males have to wait till they are older, because the older males do not allow them to usurp their rights

Life Span: In the wild, a peccary would have a life span of fifteen to twenty years. Zoo records exceed this considerably. The New York Zoological Park recorded one female that lived to be twenty-one years, five months and one day old. A male collared peccary in that same park lived twenty-four years, eight months and eight days.

Sign: Since there are no European wild boars in the southwestern states, and few if any domesticated hogs, any area in that region which has been rooted up indicates the presence of peccaries. The various cactus plants on which the peccaries feed will show teeth marks 18 to 24 inches above the ground. Tracks are common, and the only ones that could be confused with them are sheep tracks. Sheep scat is usually in small, single pellets, and the peccary's scat is in much larger segments. Caves frequented by peccaries will have traces of the vile, skunk-like odor of their musk.

Enemies: The jaguar is the peccary's traditional enemy. Both animals inhabit the same range, and the peccary has been a mainstay of the jaguar's diet from time immemorial. These cats are so strong that they have nothing to fear from the peccary, although there are records of herds of peccaries driving jaguars away. The ocelot will feed on young peccaries, but is no match for an adult. Coyotes and fox also take young peccaries but they, too, would not stand up to the full-grown animal.

As a protection against flies, lice and ticks, peccaries often take dust baths. Internally, they have roundworms, tapeworms and trichinosis.

Human Relations: At one time, peccaries were found as far north as Arkansas, but indiscriminate shooting has reduced their range to its present size. It is estimated that there are now more than 70,000 in the United States.

Occasionally they may do some damage to crops, but they do not constitute a serious threat to agriculture because the majority of them live in ranch areas. Consequently, peccaries are now receiving protection in the form of closed seasons, whereas once they were legal game year-round.

Peccary hides make a soft, strong leather but only bring 50 to 75 cents apiece on the market.

Trophy Records: Peccaries are not recognized as trophy animals by the Boone and Crockett Club. The head does make a nice mount, if a somewhat ferocious one, because it is usually mounted with the mouth wide open and the tusks prominently displayed. The heaviest weight that I can find on record is 65 pounds.

Table Fare: Some people like the meat of the peccary; others claim that it is not very tasty. The meat is light in color and dry in texture.

HOGS

Family Suidae

EUROPEAN WILD HOG

The wild hog is a dangerous game animal. Agile, strong and vicious, it attacks at the slightest provocation, using its tusks to slash an enemy. (Photo by Irene Vandermolen.)

European Wild Hog

Sus scrofa

The wild hog is native to Europe and Asia. It was first introduced in the United States in 1893 by Austin Corbin to stock his private game preserve in the Blue Mountains of New Hampshire. Fifty of the animals were imported from the Black Forest of Germany. In 1900 fifteen to twenty wild hogs were imported from Germany and released in New York's Adirondack Mountains. They were able to reproduce themselves until about 1920, when the last of them were killed. Another importation occurred in 1910. George Moore, an Englishman, released several wild hogs on a private game preserve that he maintained in the Great Smoky Mountains of Tennessee. Again, in 1912, fourteen wild hogs were brought in, this time from Russia, and released on a private preserve in the western mountains of North Carolina known as Hooper's Bald. They were kept in a fenced-in area of about 600 acres, and no hunting was allowed for eight years. A European-style hunt was held in 1920, with the hunters using horses and spears. In the ensuing melee, many of the wild boars escaped through the fence and scattered in the Great Smoky Mountains. Since these main importations, there have been a few others recently, one on Santa Cruz Island off the California coast. Nowhere are the animals extremely numerous, and the ones that are hunted are found near the areas of the first importations and releases.

Description: The wild hog does not become fat and complacent like its domesticated relative. Having to rely on its wits and speed, it stays thin and muscular. An adult boar stands about 30 inches high at the shoulders and is from 4 to 5 feet in length. The North American wild boars do not grow as large or as heavy as do wild boars in their native European haunts. This may be due to the fact that they don't get sufficient food; our native animals such as the deer and squirrels compete too heavily for acorns. The average weight for a big boar in this country is 300 to 350 pounds, while some of the European boars have weighed up to 600 pounds.

Wild hogs make formidable foes because of their tusks, which may reach 9 inches in length. The hog is agile and quick to anger, and slashes with its tusks at the slightest provocation. All told, the hog has 42 teeth: 12 incisors, 4 canines, 14 premolars and 12 molars. The upper canines usually curve upward.

The hog's long, saucer-shaped snout, a heavy piece of cartilaginous tissue, is useful in grubbing for food. The eyes are small and often seem to be obscured by bristles. The ears are about 5 inches long and are always carried erect. They never flop down like the ears of most domestic hogs.

The wild hog's legs are long, and the animal is almost as fast as a deer. There are four toes on each foot. The second and third toes form the hooves while the first and fourth are the dewclaws. The dewclaws are long, extending to within a half inch of the ground, and when the ground is soft help to support the animal's weight. The wild hog's tail is long, with a heavy tuft of hair on its tip.

Most wild hogs are almost jet black, but occasionally the guard hairs have a light frosting of white on the tips.

These guard hairs are very stiff and bristly. Usually the descendants of wild hogs imported from Russia are the darkest, while those stemming from German imports are a little lighter. The hair on the neck and shoulders sometimes grows long enough to be considered a mane. Beneath the long guard hairs are short, dense hairs that give the hog protection against the cold.

Travel: The wild hog moves about only as much as it must to find sufficient food. When the crop is good it stays in its home area, which is perhaps 10 miles square. When there is a food shortage, these animals have been known to travel 50 to 60 miles. One year when the acorn crop failed in Tennessee, several hundred wild hogs crossed over the mountains to feed on the North Carolina side.

Habits: Wild hogs are gregarious and travel in herds that may number from five to fifty. Except during the breeding season, the boars stay in a separate group, or they may become solitary.

Most of the hog's activities take place during the daylight hours, although they do feed very early in the morning. Late afternoon is also a peak period. In the spring and summer wild hogs feed upon a wide variety of vegetation. They favor roots and tubers and turn up large areas of dirt looking for them. They also eat many types of grasses, fruits and berries. Whenever possible the hogs add meat to their diet, gobbling up the eggs and young of ground-nesting birds, as well as mice, baby rabbits and fawns. Even frogs, salamanders and snakes become part of their menu. Hogs seem to be immune to the poison of rattlesnakes and eat them regularly. In the fall acorns are their mainstay, along with beechnuts, hickory nuts and pecans. In the coldest part of the winter months, after the forest has been stripped bare of fallen nuts, the wild hogs retire to marsh and swamp areas where they can still root in the earth. At that time, roots are the primary food. Wild hogs are omnivorous and opportunistic. They will eat almost anything they can discover or overcome.

Swine are often thought to be dirty creatures, but this is not so. If domesticated pigs live in dirty conditions, it is because they are kept in them. This is just as true of wild hogs. Though wild hogs like to wallow in mud, they do this for comfort and relief from heat and insects. When they can't find or create a wallow, they root into the earth and then lie on the moist soil. Sometimes the hogs cut grass and pile it into a heap and crawl under it. In cold weather they frequently scoop out beds for themselves in protected areas and pile up mounds of branches and grasses for warmth. For even greater warmth, they sleep in a heap, each helping to warm the others.

Senses: The hog's sense of smell is highly developed, for the tip of its nostril is packed with olfactory nerves. It locates most of its food, even that which is underground, by scent. It may detect danger by scent but more likely depends on hearing. Its large, upright ears serve as good funnels to the auditory nerves. The hog's eyes are small, indicating that it does not depend on them to a great extent.

Communication: The noises made by a wild hog are similar to those made by a domesticated hog. When angered or frightened, the hog emits a loud, shrill squeal which can be heard far away. It also grunts, although this is usually a sound of contentment and is used to hold the herd together. A sow gives a soft grunting sound to her piglets, and she also has a special grunting sound for calling the little ones when she has uncovered some choice tidbit for them to eat.

Locomotion: The wild hog, like the domesticated hog, does not like to hurry unless it must. Ordinarily it walks from place to place, trots when it has to. When frightened or when it attacks, the hog can gallop at a speed of 30 miles per hour. Not only is the wild hog fast, but it can maneuver at high speed in extremely dense thickets which a man would find almost impenetrable. It is a strong swimmer and has been known to swim over a mile.

Breeding: The breeding season usually occurs in December, the sow coming into heat for a period of two to three days. If she is not bred in this period, she will again be in heat twenty-one days later. Since a sow may miss two or even three periods, the young may be born at different times of the year. Only those that are born in the spring or summer have much chance of surviving.

Birth and Young: The gestation period for the wild hogs is 112 to 115 days, and the number of young varies from three to twelve. At birth the piglets have nine or ten white stripes running the length of their bodies. They are 6 to 8 inches in length. For the first week the piglets do not leave their nest.

Prior to giving birth, the female cuts off branches of trees, shrubs and grass and places them in a pile—if possible under a protecting bush or tree. Then the female crawls in and makes a hollow which she lines with grass. In this oversized nest the young are born.

After a week's time the little ones accompany the mother when she rejoins the herd. Here again the herd affords the piglets a greater measure of protection. Wild sows are devoted mothers, and all of the herd will rally to defend the young. The young females become sexually mature and breed when they are eighteen months old.

Life Span: The expected life span of the wild hog is between fifteen and twenty years. One wild sow in the London Zoological Gardens lived to be nineteen years, six months and six days old. The record for longevity is twenty-seven years.

Sign: When hogs of any type have been rooting in the forest for acorns or roots, it looks as though the place had been attacked by a mad plowman. In the soft earth exposed by the digging many tracks will be visible. The walls of the hoof are set very close together on the rear part of the foot, and the dewclaws usually leave marks. The scat of the wild hog looks like a segmented sausage and is about the same diameter.

Enemies: Only a brave animal will attack a wild hog. The black bear is the only animal in the eastern part of the United States large enough to take this chance. Even the bear would prefer taking a young pig to attacking a fullgrown boar. Bobcats and perhaps foxes may try for a very young pig. Wild dogs also are a threat to the young pigs.

Human Relations: In Europe wild boar hunting was considered a sport for only the bravest men. Dogs were used and the hunters were either on horseback or afoot. A spear was their only weapon. When a boar was brought to bay by dogs, it usually attacked the first man in sight. With its sharp tusks, a boar could disembowel a dog or tear open a man with only a few slashing cuts.

Today boars are hunted in the United States mainly with rifles or shotguns, although bows and arrows are becoming increasingly popular. Dogs are still used to bring the quarry to bay.

Wild boars have not made any noticeable increase in numbers. They appear to be holding their own, and it is likely that they will continue to do only that and hunting will always be on a limited scale.

In Europe wild boars frequently cause crop damage, but in the United States they are found only in mountainous regions where farming is at a minimum.

Trophy Records: Wild boars are not accorded trophy status by the Boone and Crockett Club. The heaviest specimen on record was about 600 pounds.

Table Fare: Wild hogs have been used for food for centuries. Most of the older males were hunted for sport and as trophies. Young wild hogs should be as tender and succulent as our domesticated pigs. I have never eaten wild hog, but I did try a wild domesticated boar and found the meat to be tough.

DEER

Family Cervidae

ELK
WHITETAIL DEER
MULE DEER
MOOSE
CARIBOU

In the left-hand photo, a bull elk sports an extraordinarily large and many-pointed set of antlers. In the right-hand photo, the whitetail buck has eight points (eastern count). Note that the points grow from one main beam, in contrast to those of the mule-deer buck below. (Whitetail photo by Irene Vandermolen.)

This mule deer buck displays a characteristic bifurcated (branched) antler on each side that distinguishes it from a whitetail antler, on which the points extend upward from one main beam. (Photo by Len Rue Jr.)

In the rutting season, this
bull moose displays broad
palmate antlers that on
some bulls may measure
six feet across and weigh
90 pounds. (Photo by Len
Rue Jr.)

Here, a barren ground caribou shows bifurcated, palmated,
and many-tined antlers that large bulls develop, as well as a
palmated "shovel" extending over his face. (Photo by Tim
Lewis Rue.)

ELK

Cervus elaphus

Some of North America's most impressive antlers belong
to bull elk. When the rut is under way the bull's rack is
full grown, the points polished and sharp, and hunters
climb into the high country to take this regal game animal
at his prime. Often they use artificial calls to mimic the
bugling cry the bulls give as they challenge one another
in competition for the cows. The answering bugle of a
bull to a call signals the start of a thrilling stalk for a
prized trophy.

The elk is also called the wapiti, a Shawnee Indian
name which has never gained wide acceptance. In Europe the animal we call the moose is referred to as the
elk, or elch, and the animal most similar to North American elk is the red deer. Elk probably originated in Asia,
spread west to Europe and east to North America across
the Bering Land Bridge at about the same time as the
ancestors of the moose and deer.

Description: After the moose, the elk is the largest
antlered mammal in North America. Ordinarily a large
bull elk will weigh in the vicinity of 600 to 800 pounds,
with the cow being about 25 percent lighter. Occasionally
the elk rivals the moose in weight. Three elk killed in
Washington and Oregon weighed 737, 758 and 857
pounds field dressed. The estimated live weights were
between 1,000 and 1,200 pounds. Three elk killed on Af-
ognak Island, Alaska, where they were introduced in the
1920s, each weighed over 1,000 pounds field dressed and
were estimated to weigh up to 1,500 pounds on the hoof.

In spring this bull elk with antlers in velvet sheds its warm, grayish winter coat for a lighter summer coat of reddish hue. The winter coat will begin to grow again in late summer.

A large bull will stand 5 feet high at the shoulder and be 8 to 10 feet in length. Elk have one of the blockiest body builds of any of our big game. A good bull will have antlers measuring 5 feet across from tip to tip and over 5 feet long following the outside curve of one beam.

The elk's basic body color is a brownish-gray. The head and neck is covered with long hair of rich chestnut-brown. The short tail and the large rump patch are a whitish-yellow. The belly is almost black and the legs are very dark. Females are lighter in color than males.

By spring the elk's winter hair has become much lighter, and it molts into a summer coat, often somewhat reddish. This summer pelage has no dense undercoat, and the fine muscling of the elk is apparent. The molt to a more grayish winter coat starts in August, and beneath is a very dense, woolly undercoat, for warmth.

The elk's canine teeth were a highly sought after trophy. Alone among our native deer, most elk have two rudimentary canines in the upper jaw. As these teeth meet with no other teeth, their function is not known. Thousands of elk have been killed for just these miniature tusks. They were highly valued by the Indians before they became a symbol of the Benevolent and Protective Order of Elks. Because of these two extra teeth, most elk have a total of 34 teeth instead of the usual 32 of deer and moose. The teeth are classified as 8 incisors, 2 canines, 12 premolars and 12 molars. (The last incisor on each side may, in truth, be an incisor-like lower canine.)

The elk have four toes on each foot, the center toes forming the main hooves, with the two outside toes having degenerated into dewclaws.

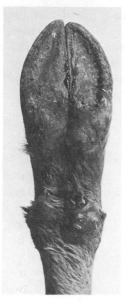

Right forefoot of an elk, showing the two large toes forming the hoof, and the two vestigial toes, or dewclaws, typical of all members of the deer family.

Elk have well-developed lachrymal glands on the inside corner of each eye. Here a bull with spike antlers in velvet rubs its gland against a tree to advertise its presence.

Elk have well-developed lachrymal glands, or tear ducts, on the inside corner of the eye. They also have a small metatarsal gland on the outside of the hind legs. There is also a gland under the skin surrounding the tail vertebrae which gives the tail its slightly swollen appearance.

Distribution: Formerly widespread throughout North America, elk *(Cervus e. nelsoni)* are now restricted to the Rocky Mountain area from British Columbia to northern Arizona and New Mexico. Roosevelt elk *(c.e. roosevelti)* range along the Pacific Coast from Vancouver

Distribution of the elk.

to San Francisco Bay. Manitoba elk *(c.e. manitobensis)* occur in isolated pockets in Manitoba and Saskatchewan. In Kern County, California, are Tule elk, considered a distinct species *(Cervus e. nannodes)* by some specialists. Merriam's elk *(Cervus merriami)* was still another species that inhabited Arizona, but it is now extinct and *C. e. nelsoni* has been introduced into its range. There are also small herds of imported elk in Virginia, Pennsylvania, New York, New Hampshire, Texas, Arkansas, Michigan, and South Dakota.

Travel: In the summer the elk climb to the highest alpine meadows where they find ample food and relief from the hordes of stinging, biting insects which frequent the lowlands. The constant breezes keep the insects under cover.

In late summer or early fall, when the snows begin, the elk start to move down to the sheltered valleys. Breeding usually takes place here, and each big bull drives his harem before him. From the high country the elk travel mainly down the ridges until they reach a valley. Most of the migration occurs at night. As the snow drifts higher, the elk move farther down the valleys where the drifts are lower.

Elk may not migrate as far today as formerly. They may be stopped by all sorts of man-made obstructions or be able to obtain food from haystacks. Some elk still migrate more than 100 miles, but most travel much less. In the spring a reverse migration takes place, but it is not as concentrated as the fall trip. The elk, singly and in small bands, start up the mountain slopes with the females leading the way.

Habits: A large bull elk with wide-spreading, high-branching antlers is truly a regal animal. When he stands alert with head held high he appears to be king of all he surveys. When he runs, he carries his nose high in the air, a habit that has been learned by countless generations of bull elks which have had to lay their antlers back along their bodies so as not to entangle them in branches when running through dense cover. Even the cows, which do not have antlers, carry their heads in this position.

Elk are herd animals and feed mainly upon grass. Large areas of grass are found only in open country, and feeding in open country exposes the animals to more danger from all sides. Animals that travel in herds can better cope with these dangers because some of the animals are always on the alert while others may be resting or feeding. Herding definitely increases their chances of survival. As is true of most herd animals, the herd is usually led by an old female and not by one of the majestic bulls. In fact, during the warm weather the bulls keep separate from the cows and calves.

In the spring the elk are widely scattered. This break-up occurs as soon as new green shoots start to appear. The cows start to band up after calving; by the time the high summer pastures are reached, some herds may number into the hundreds. Such a herd will be composed of the cow and her new calf, yearling calves and young bulls. These herds will stay together until the breeding season.

Where elk are undisturbed by man, they prefer to feed in the daytime. The periods of greatest activity are just before the dawn and again in late afternoon. Midday is occupied mainly with cud chewing and resting, although the elk rarely sleep in the daytime. Elk will feed on moon-lit nights or if they are hunted during the day. At such times they will spend the daylight hours hidden in heavy brush. When possible, elk seek out knolls or other ele-vated spots on which to rest, and from where they can sniff the rising thermals for the scent of an enemy below.

In hot weather the elk seek shade, and as the heat periods grow longer in the summer their midday periods of inactivity grow correspondingly longer. Elk also take cover under trees during a rainstorm. They seem to have an aversion to getting wet by rain, but in hot weather they find a stream and wade and wallow about for relief. They also look for salt or mineral springs in an area where they can drink the water and eat the enriched soil.

Grasses form the bulk of an elk's diet, although it also feeds on browse. Just about anything that will appeal to a horse or a cow will satisfy an elk. Some of the important grasses are bluegrass, bromegrass, wheatgrass, pinegrass, junegrass, bluebunch grass and sweet vernal grass. Elk eat almost all types of conifers as browse and the decid-uous aspen and willows. They also eat serviceberry, ma-ple, alder, blackberry and, on occasion, ferns, berries and some fungi.

Elk are ruminants. They eat enough to fill their paunch, then retire to regurgitate their food in small lumps as a cud, which is rechewed and then reswallowed and passed along to be digested.

Senses: Elk have a very keen sense of smell, and this undoubtedly is of the greatest importance to them. Ed-dying winds may spoil good scenting conditions and predators may stalk the elk upwind, but if conditions are favorable the elk can detect danger quicker, with greater certainty and at longer distances by scent than by the use of any other sense.

The sense of hearing ranks second in importance. Because the elk also depend on hearing danger approaching, they become nervous on windy days when the crashing and thrashing of tree limbs and branches mask any sounds that an enemy might make.

During the breeding season, bull elk challenge their competitors with a high-pitched bugling call that can be heard for miles. Hunters often mimic the bugling of elk on artificial calls to lure them into range.

Elk are quick to note the slightest movement of any kind, but tend to overlook stationary objects.

Communication: Elk are famous for the high-pitched bugling which the bulls sound during the breeding season. John Madson describes the sound as *A-a-a-ae-e-eeeee-eough! E-uh! E-uh!* The bugling is a scream, a warning, a spine-tingling expression of challenge. After the breeding season is over, the bull seldom utters a sound for the rest of the year. Occasionally a cow elk will also bugle, although she makes a softer sound. The cow squeals when angered or alarmed at being separated from her calf. She also has a coughing grunt or a bark. The calves make a bleating sound and at times an almost calflike sound.

Locomotion: An elk can run for short distances at speeds of 30 to 35 miles per hour. For longer distances, it can maintain a trotting gait at about 18 miles per hour. Elk walk, trot and gallop. They are very strong swimmers, and even calves have been seen to swim distances of a mile with no trouble.

Jumping is the elk's forte, for it lives in areas where blowdowns and fallen trees are common. Elk have no trouble clearing an 8-foot fence; they have been seen to do this on many occasions. Observers have also witnessed jumps of 10 feet in height. An elk never jumps any higher than it has to and always seems to hit the top of the obstruction with its feet. Barbed wire fences are rarely obstacles for an elk; when excited, it will run right through the wire, breaking the strands like straws.

Breeding: The antlers of the elk develop earlier and faster than do those of other species of North American cervids. The pedicels start to swell as early as the first of March, and before the month is over the antlers begin to branch. By late April or early May, the four forward-projecting tines, often called "dog-catcher tines," have achieved full growth—from 12 to 18 inches. By late July the antlers have achieved maximum growth, and in August the velvet starts to dry up as the antlers harden beneath it. The bulls strip the velvet by rubbing their antlers against trees and rocks. In September the necks of the bulls become engorged with blood, a condition similar to an erection in man, and remain enlarged and swollen for about two months.

The frosty mornings now resound with the bugled challenges of the huge bulls. Bulls that have traveled together peacefully for many months separate and seek out the herds of cows they have neglected for so long. They pause just long enough to slash at saplings and resilient bushes with their antlers. They dig shallow holes in the turf with their forefeet and urinate in the hole and on themselves. Then they wallow in the mud they have just created, plastering gobs of it all over their bodies.

Elk are the most polygynous of all the North American deer. Each huge bull will gather unto himself all the cows that he can locate and that he can keep away from other bulls. Some bulls will have cows and young in their harems. The competition is keen. On a few occasions a bull elk has been known to take over a herd of dairy cows as his harem, even chasing the farmer away. Lesser bulls continually lurk around the fringe of the herd master's harem. These outrider bulls are usually not large enough,

The most polygynous of all males of the deer family, bull elk gather a harem of as many cows as they can find. Here a bull herds his cows and calves. (Photo by Irene Vandermolen.)

strong enough or foolish enough to engage the herd master in actual combat. They may try to entice a stray cow from the herd or try to mingle with the herd and mount a cow. The herd master does not attempt to engage these lesser bulls in battle, for while fighting with one bull the others could divide his harem between them. So most of the herd bull's time is spent posturing, bugling and making a few fast and furious charges at the outrider bulls. He also drives all the cows before him, freely using his antlers on any reluctant cow. In the midst of this fury, he services those cows in heat.

Occasionally two big bulls do meet, and the matter must be settled by combat. The challenges are bugled and accepted, and the bulls trot into position about 30 feet apart. Then with heads lowered, and all the power they can muster, they ram together with the impact of bulldozers. After the initial charge, the fight becomes a contest of brute strength, each bull trying to throw the other and gore him.

This frenzied period usually lasts four to six weeks, during which time the bulls get little rest or food. The handsome specimens that entered the lists in September are now reduced to gaunt, hollow-eyed, tired animals that must eat heartily to regain weight before the worst of winter sets in. Many of these largest bulls die during a hard winter.

Birth and Young: Elk carry their young for eight to eight and a half months, giving birth in the latter part of May or the first part of June. The cow will separate from the herd and seek out dense cover for her nursery. One calf at a time is the rule, though on rare occasions twins may be born. An elk calf will weigh between 25 to 30 pounds at birth. It is clothed in a dark russet coat having a liberal splashing of white spots along its back and sides.

Within hours the calf is strong enough to move, and the cow leads it from the birthing spot to a safer hiding place. During the first week of its life, the calf will flatten itself on the ground at the first sign of danger. By the time it is a week old the calf can run moderately fast, and the cow takes it to join other cows with their calves.

These groups give the calves very good protection, as danger to one calf puts all the cows on the defense, and a group of enraged cows is not to be trifled with. Sometimes older, barren cows act as babysitters for the calves while the mothers feed.

Before the calf is a month old, it starts to feed upon grasses, though it still continues to nurse as often as the cow allows it to. By late August most of the calves are weaned, but occasionally some pampered calf nurses up to November and December. Even yearlings have been seen nursing, but this sometimes occurs among domestic cows, too.

By September the calves have shed their juvenile spotted coats and begin to look like small editions of the adults. Young females do not breed until they are about twenty-eight months old. The young bulls are capable of breeding at that time, but they seldom get a chance to try until they are bigger, stronger and more competitive.

Life Span: Judging from the female's sexual maturity an elk has a potential life span of about fifteen years, though a number of elk have reached twenty years of age or more. The record is held by an elk killed in 1937 by a hunter in Arizona. This elk had been tagged when it was one year old by the Biological Survey and was twenty-five years old when shot.

Sign: The most commonly found sign of elk is their large cowlike hoof tracks, which can easily be confused with the tracks of cattle that are sharing the same range.

Scat of elk varies with the season and the food they are eating. In summer, when the elk feeds on grass, the scat is a loose mass. When the elk feeds on browse, in both summer and winter, the scat is composed of pellets.

In late summer, as the breeding season approaches, gashes on saplings show where the big bulls were

Elk tracks can be identified by their large size and round outline. They may be confused with tracks of domesticated cattle, but never with those of deer. Deer tracks are smaller, and the hoofs taper to a point.

shadowboxing. Elk also gnaw marks into the bark of such trees as aspen with their canine teeth, as well as strip the bark for winter food. During the breeding season, the wallows are always signs of big bulls in the area.

Enemies: Starvation is the elk's principal enemy. Man should take priority as the cause, as he does with all creatures, because it is man's tampering with the balance of nature that has set the stage for the elk's starvation. Today the elk are restricted to certain areas because of man, and the largest concentrations of elk are where they are protected by man. These two situations are not compatible and the elk overpopulate their ranges, destroy their habitat and eventually starve.

The timber wolf used to be one of the elk's main natural predators. It is unlikely that a single wolf could kill an elk, but with a concentrated pack effort wolves could easily overcome the largest elk. Today, the wolf is found only in Canada in numbers large enough to have an effect on the elk populations.

The mountain lion, too, has been so reduced in population that it is no longer a threat to the elk herds. It has been so reduced in some areas that it can't even help the herds by eliminating the unfit animals.

Black bears, grizzly bears, coyotes and bobcats feed upon elk calves. Although bears are large enough to kill the adults, they are seldom fast enough to catch them.

Elk scat varies according to the animal's diet. At left, segmented scat indicates elk has been feeding on grass. Pellet scat, right, mean browse has been the principal food. This is true of all the deer family.

Elk are relatively free from disease, but they do suffer from necrotic stomatitis, an ailment caused by a bacterium. It is most common when the elk are crowded and eat coarse roughage to subsist. The sharp points and splinters of the rough forage pierce the lining of the elk's mouth and throat, and the infection sets in and spreads to other parts of the body. The toxin produced by the bacteria causes a form of blood poisoning.

Ticks are commonly found on elk and are the most serious external parasites. In the summer, flies, mosquitoes, mites and deer flies pester the elk and drive them into high country. Tapeworms and lungworms occur too.

Human Relations: At the time of the coming of the white man, there were perhaps 10 million elk in North America. Elk withstood the slaughter of hunters a little better than did the bison because they inhabited rougher terrain. The western Indians hunted elk for food, but the bison was their staff of life.

Most of the eastern elk were wiped out between 1850 and 1870. In the prairie states, most of the elk were killed between 1870 and 1880. By 1897 the Merriam's elk of New Mexico, Oklahoma and Arizona was extinct. The creation of Yellowstone Park saved the elk. It became a reservoir from which breeding stock was shipped to help repopulate the country. By the 1940s the elk had increased and were being hunted in eleven states; by the 1950s elk were found in twenty-five states. But the pendulum has swung too far, too fast in the other direction. In many areas the elk have increased to such numbers that they are destroying their range. From a small band of 400 in 1881, the elk in the Yellowstone area increased to 25,000 in ten years. Although 5,000 elk died of starvation in 1892 and 1899, the herds increased to more than 35,000 by 1914. In the winter of 1919-1920, more than 14,000 elk died of starvation. The herd has never recovered nor should it be allowed to. The huge herd did so much damage to the range that only 5,000 elk can now be supported there. This is the number that the park officials try to maintain.

One of the fundamentals of wildlife management is that just so many units of wildlife can be supported on a given number of acres. Then either the carrying capacity of the range must be increased to support the increase in wildlife, or surplus animals must be eliminated to maintain a balance. To prosper, our elk herds must be harvested systematically according to the particular requirements of each area.

Trophy Records: The world's-record elk head was taken in 1915 by John Plute, in Dark Canyon, Anthracite County, Colorado, and totaled 442 3/8 points. The length of the right beam is 55 5/8 inches and has 8 points. The left beam is 59 5/8 inches long and has 7 points. The inside spread measures 45 1/2 inches.

It is not known who shot the elk holding the Number 2 spot. This elk was taken in the Big Horn Mountains, Wyoming, in 1890 and totals 441 6/8 points. The right beam is 61 6/8 inches long and has 8 points while the left beam is 61 2/8 inches long and has 7 points.

Table Fare: Elk meat is very good to eat, and hundreds of tons reach the tables of sportsmen every year. The meat is dark and is similar to beef in taste and texture.

Whitetail Deer

Odocoileus virginianus

The whitetail deer is the most plentiful big-game animal in North America. It has adapted to man's continual encroachments of its habitat and has survived vigorous hunting pressure while other species that were once as widely distributed have steadily declined. With its superb senses and its ability to live near man, the whitetail is at once an available and infinitely challenging quarry. When a hunter goes after a whitetail deer, he is matching wits with one of the smartest game animals in the country.

Unlike many members of the Cervidae family, the deer are native to North America, having developed in the Miocene and Pliocene periods, 20 million to 10 million years ago, and evolved into the form we see today about a million years ago during the Pleistocene period. When the Isthmus of Panama bridged the gap between North and South America, the deer spread southward.

The deer genus was given the name *Odocoileus* by Rafinesque in 1832. The naturalist had found a deer tooth as a fossil in a Virginia cave, and it is thought that he was naming the animal "hollow tooth," which should have produced the name *Odontocoelus*, but his Greek was poor and *Odocoileus* it became.

Description: The whitetail differs from the mule or blacktail deer mainly in the shape of its antlers. The whitetail's antlers consist of two main beams that grow out and backward from their bases and then sweep forward. Single tines, or points, grow upward off these main beams, and there is a small tine above the brow. The

*A whitetail buck pauses in a meadow, alert to the slightest
sound or scent of danger. The deer's superb senses have enabled it to survive near man. (Photo by Irene Vandermolen.)*

mule and blacktail deer have antlers that branch into forks, with each fork branching again into two tines. There is also a brow tine near the base of each antler, but it is smaller than the whitetail's.

The most common misconception about the whitetail is its size. Almost everyone, including experienced hunters who should know better, usually holds his hand shoulder-high when indicating the size of this deer. He would do better to hold his hand a little above his belt, for the average whitetail stands between 36 and 40 inches high at the top of the shoulder. Especially big bucks may be 42 inches high. They have a total length of between 60 to 75 inches and an average weight of about 150 pounds. The Florida Key deer seldom weigh more than 80 pounds, while the largest whitetail deer on record is 511 pounds.

As previously mentioned, deer vary in color shadings from area to area. They also vary with the season. All whitetails shed twice a year. In the spring they get a new coat that is a bright reddish-brown, the hair solid and thin. As cold weather approaches in the fall this hair is replaced by the winter coat, which shades from bluish to a grayish-brown. The winter hair is long, kinky and filled with air pockets providing excellent insulation. I have often seen deer whose bodies lost so little heat that snow and sleet did not melt on their backs but remained encrusted on the hair.

Despite regional differences, deer are colored basically alike. They have a jet-black nose with two white bands behind it. The face is brown, the eyes circled with white. The insides of the ears, beneath the chin and the large throat patch are pure white. The body is darkest down the middle of the back, shading lighter till it abruptly reaches the white stomach. The upper portion of the legs on the outside are brown and the insides are white. The top side of the tail is brown with some having various amounts of black at the tip. The underside of the tail and rear portion of the deer is a sparkling white. Like the pronghorn antelope, the whitetail can erect and flare its rump hairs when alarmed. However, bucks do not flaunt their tails as commonly as do the does. It is thought that does do this to guide their young as they flee from danger through the dark night or deep forest. When the deer clasps its tail down tightly and keeps the rump hairs bent inwardly, it is almost impossible to see any of the telltale white.

Albinism, which appears in most forms of life, is a genetic change that prevents pigments from forming in the body. Without pigment, the hair is white, the eyes are pink (due to visible blood vessels) and the hooves are gray. While some true albinos occur in deer, most of the so-called "white" deer are only partial albinos and have patches of white hair on a normally brown coat. It has been observed that these "white" deer usually have a hearing deficiency and that the normal deer avoid them.

The ancestors of the deer originally had five toes on each of their feet. Through evolution the first toe corresponding to our thumb disappeared entirely. The second and fifth toes diminished in size and moved to the rear where they now function as dewclaws. The third and fourth toes became enlarged and form the main hooves as we know them today. Actually the deer walks on its toenails instead of its toes. This type of foot is very efficient for fast movement over well-packed earth.

Deer's metatarsal gland, halfway between the toes and the heel of the foot, on the outside of the hind leg, gives off musk, but its purpose is not well understood.

Between the center hooves is the interdigital gland, which gives off a yellow, waxy substance that marks the ground as the deer walks. This enables the animals to track one another, particularly the doe to follow a straying fawn. Of course, it also enables predators to track the deer.

Halfway between the toes and the heel of the foot on the outside of the hind leg, the deer has a metatarsal gland. Of the three deer found in the United States, the whitetail has the smallest metatarsal gland. The size of this gland is often used as a means of identification if only the legs are available. Supposedly this gland also gives off a musk; its purpose is not well understood. At the deer's hock on the inside of the leg is the tarsal gland. This gland plays a very important sexual role. In addition to giving off a strong musk, which is attractive to other deer, both bucks and does bend their legs together and curve their bodies so that they urinate on the hair tufts covering the glands.

Many hunters advise cutting off the tarsal glands as soon as you kill a buck, before they taint the meat. These glands do not taint the meat while the deer is alive and cannot do so when the deer is dead. If a hunter is sloppy and handles the glands and then handles the meat, he can transfer the odor. One method is to leave the glands intact until you are ready to skin and butcher the deer, then cut off the entire leg about 2 inches above the gland.

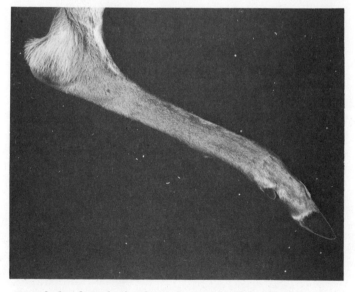

Tarsal gland, at the hock on the inside of the hind leg, gives off musk which attracts opposite sex during breeding time.

In front of the deer's eye is the lachrymal or preorbital gland. It is used to mark bushes.

Members of the deer family, unlike most mammals, do not have any teeth in the front of the upper jawbone. Replacing the teeth is a resilient pad that makes contact with the lower incisors. Deer have 32 teeth: 8 incisors, 12 premolars and 12 molars. They usually do not have any canine teeth.

The most common way of determining a deer's age is to check the amount of wear on the premolars and the molars. At birth the fawn has eight incisors. Four premolars develop in about a week and the last pair is in place in a month. At three months of age the first set of molars erupt, the second set of molars at six month's, and in nine months the third set of molars completes the dentition. At seventeen months of age the three cusped cap of the rear premolar drops off and is replaced by the permanent two cusped cap. From this time on, the age of the deer can only be estimated by wear on the teeth. Many factors affect this wear, but it is still the best field method of telling a deer's age. A more accurate method, counting annual rings inside a deer's tooth, requires laboratory equipment.

The members of the deer family are ruminants, having a four-compartmented stomach, which allows the deer to feed very rapidly, chewing its food just enough to swallow it. This partially chewed food goes into the storage section of the stomach known as the rumen. A feeding deer is at a disadvantage because while feeding it cannot be alert to danger. Not having to masticate its food thoroughly, the deer can fill its paunch rapidly and then retire to a safe place to do the job properly. When the deer is ready, it regurgitates a ball of partially chewed food about the size of an orange and rechews it. It then reswallows the food, which now enters the second section of the stomach, the reticulum. From there it goes into the omasum, then through the abomasum into the intestines where digestion is completed.

Deer do not have a gall bladder on their livers. This allows them to eat vegetation that would kill domestic animals.

Distribution: Whitetail deer generally inhabit forest, forest edge and brushy areas from the southern edge of

Distribution of the whitetail deer.

the coniferous forest in Canada to the southern border of the United States. They are absent from the drier regions of the West where, if present, they tend to inhabit stream bottoms.

According to the latest figures compiled by the Bureau of Sport Fisheries and Wildlife for 1964, our total whitetail population is estimated in the vicinity of 13 million. Texas leads with 3,100,000, followed by Alabama's 1,000,000, Michigan's 1,000,000 and Wisconsin's 725,000.

Travel: When lots of good food is available, the white tail deer restricts its movements to about 1 square mile. If food is scarce or the winter weather bitter, the deer forsake their usual haunts and retire to coulees, canebrakes, thickets and draws. These deer do not have even a limited migration. They prefer to stay near the spot where they were born and raised and where they know the countryside intimately. This reluctance to move is often their undoing. They die of starvation because they refuse to leave their home range for another where food may be plentiful.

At one time there was a seasonal migration of whitetail deer in Michigan's Upper Peninsula. By 1870 lumbermen had invaded the area and the forests began to fall. With the clearing of those forests with no underbrush, huge tracts of brushland came into being, providing excellent deer food. This is the only authenticated record of whitetail migration known.

During the rutting season, the bucks forsake their usual haunts and travel far and wide in search of receptive does. This, however, is not a migration but merely a seasonal expansion of range.

Habits: Deer live in a matriarchal society. The bucks live separately from the does and their offspring except during the breeding season and part of the winter. Even when the bucks are with the herd, they do not take over the lead but are led by an old doe.

Deer are creatures of habit. If unmolested, they follow the same routine, the same trails, day after day, shifting the pattern only because of weather conditions and the availability of food.

Originally deer were more active during daylight hours. Pressure from hunters forced them to move under the protective cover of darkness. By preference deer start to feed about 4:30 each afternoon. If food is plentiful, they can fill their paunches in less than an hour. However, if food *is* plentiful the deer are more fussy and select only the choicest tidbits. They walk along slowly and nibble at this shoot or that herb, pausing here and there to taste a few leaves.

Deer need 10 to 12 pounds of food per day to satisfy their needs. The list of foods they eat covers most types of vegetation. The diet changes with the season as well as the section of the country the deer inhabit. High on the list of deer food are red maple, white cedar, white acorns, apples, dogwood, sweetfern, oak, witchhazel, sumac, hemlock, willow, wintergreen, fir, arborvitae, snowberry, greenbriar, bearberry, oregon-grape and pine. Of the cultivated crops, corn, alfalfa, clover, cabbage, rape, soybeans, rye, lespedeza and trefoil are all eagerly sought and eaten.

Within a couple of hours the deer has appeased its hunger; it then seeks out a place of safety to chew its cud. As darkness has usually fallen by this time, the deer frequently lie down in fields or brushland. About dawn they become active again and feed till about 6:30 or 7 a.m., when they retire for the day. Now they look for heavier cover and, if possible, take to the ridges. As the sun warms the earth, the thermals rise to the top of the ridges, carrying the scent of everything below up to the deer. Thus the deer are usually warned well in advance of an enemy's presence.

Deer need 10 to 12 pounds of food per day, and consume most types of vegetation to fulfill their needs. This buck, with its antlers in summer velvet, is feeding on sumac.

When a deer is startled, it leaps from its bed and dashes off as if it had an appointment in the next county. Actually the deer only runs as far as the nearest cover, then stops and watches its back trail to see if it is being followed. If it is being followed, it attempts to circle around its pursuer and get back to its original location. If the deer is not pursued, it generally lies down again in the first patch of protective cover.

In warm weather deer seek ponds and lakes, not only to drink but also to feed upon aquatic vegetation. Wading in deep water also gives them protection against stinging insects.

Senses: The deer's keen sense of smell is perhaps its greatest asset. Deer can smell an enemy long before it is in sight or can be heard. Deer also have a good sense of hearing and constantly flick their ears back and forth, straining for the slighest sound of danger. A windy, stormy day makes deer very skittish and nervous because the crashing and banging of branches and brush and the swirling eddies of wind rob them of the reliable use of their nose and ears. Deer seem to hear sounds in the higher register better than low-pitched ones.

Deer are color blind and see everything in monochromatic shades of gray. This is the reason hunters can wear bright, phosphorescent clothing without being noticed by deer. The deer's eyes are very sharp and quick to take in the slightest movement but will pass right over a stationary object. Many hunters, standing absolutely still, have had deer walk up to within a few feet and never see them.

Their sense of taste is well developed because deer show decided preferences in the food they eat. Of course succulence may be a more deciding factor than taste. However, deer prefer to feed upon vegetation on previously fertilized ground because it contains some of the trace minerals that they desire and need.

Communication: Deer possess quite a repertoire of sounds. A young fawn will bleat like a lamb, while an older deer will sound quite a bit like a hoarse, raspy sheep. They whistle and snort through their noses and communicate by stamping their feet, particularly when nervous. This stamping sets up a vibration felt by other deer quite a distance away and never fails to alert all the deer in the area. Like the pronghorn, the deer can signal danger by flashing the white hair on its rump.

Locomotion: Everyone has the impression that a deer is a swift animal. Actually its top speed is between 35 to 40 miles per hour, which means there are many animals that can run faster, but it is fast enough for the type of terrain it inhabits. The deer's ability to jump over high windfalls and fallen tree trunks while dashing off at this speed enables it to lose most of its pursuers. A deer can clear an 8-foot hurdle from a standing position. Although 15 feet is a good broad jump for a deer, some deer have been known to jump 29 feet.

A deer customarily walks from place to place while feeding. The faster it moves, the more it is at a disadvantage in seeing an enemy before it is seen. When anxious to get to a spot more quickly, a deer trots, picking up the left front foot and the right hind foot at the same time.

At full speed it bounds along with all the grace attributed to this species. When the deer is bounding the front and hind feet work in unison. The two front feet touch down and then the hind feet come down ahead of the front feet. As the front feet come down the body is bunched together, and when the deer pushes off with its hind feet the action is like the uncoiling of a flat spring.

When a deer cannot outrun an enemy, it frequently takes to water to escape. Deer swim well and at a good pace. They have been clocked at speeds up to 13 miles per hour and have been seen five miles out from the nearest point of land. Many does often swim out to an island before giving birth so that the fawns have the protection of the water barrier.

Deer are at a disadvantage on ice. Their hard hooves with receding centers are insecure, and if they lose their footing the deer may become exhausted and be unable to rise. When deer slip on ice they often dislocate their legs.

Breeding: Buck deer have antlers for the main purpose of fighting other bucks during the breeding season. Recent research shows that the antlers may also be an erotic stimulant. Most bucks lose their antlers during the months of December or January. They have nothing but the antler bases, called pedicels, on their heads until April. During this month these bases start to swell with the growth of new cells. Horns that are not shed, such as those on mountain sheep, have a center core filled with blood cells which foster growth. Antlers of the deer are solid and nourished externally by a network of blood vessels called "velvet."

The deer's hard hoofs are ill suited for walking on ice, and many slip, dislocate their legs, and are unable to rise.

Antlers grow at a rapid rate, and the buck is very careful of them. During this growth period the antlers are soft, tender and easily damaged, and the bucks live a retiring life.

By September the antlers reach full size and the blood vessels dry up, split and start to peel off. To hasten the process the buck rubs his antlers against small, resilient saplings and brush. The buck shadowboxes at the same time, thrusting and turning his antlers at the bush as if he were fighting a rival. These mock battles also serve to strengthen the buck's neck, which has already begun to swell with increased blood engorgement. The testicles drop down and are easily visible.

Sometimes the bucks paw shallow, circular depressions in the earth. These scrapes are usually under overhanging bushes that the bucks chew and hook with their

Between January and April, after the antlers of the previous year have fallen off, a buck has only pedicels on his head, the bases on which the new antlers will grow.

antlers and revisit often. A buck in rut fears little, and this is the only time of the year that he may be dangerous to man.

The doe's oestrous period usually starts in November, though varying according to the section of the country.

During the summer, the antlers grow rapidly. Encased in "velvet," which contains a network of blood vessels to nourish growth, the antlers are soft and delicate, and bucks lead a quiet life.

Each doe is in heat for about thirty hours. If she is not bred in that time she comes back in heat twenty-eight days later. Although all does are bred in their first or second heat period, occasionally some may be missed until their third or fourth. This explains why some fawns are born so late that they still have their spots during the hunting season.

By September the antlers have achieved full growth. The velvet begins to peel off, the buck hastening the process by rubbing his antlers against saplings and branches. Now he is ready for the battles of the rutting season.

As the does start to come into their heat periods, the bucks track and follow them. Occasionally a doe accepts the favors of several bucks, but more often the bucks do not share the doe.

A large buck has no trouble driving away a smaller rival, but the challenge of another large buck results in a fight. Deer do not meet with repeated head-on clashes

A whitetail buck following a doe during breeding season.

but charge each other only once. The fight is then one of brute strength as each buck tries to shove the other backwards or to upset him. They are quick to take advantage of the slightest opportunity to drive their antlers into their rival's body. Barring this chance, the fight goes on until one deer weakens, breaks off and runs away. This battling is beneficial to the species because it allows the superior buck to breed the doe and to pass on his desirable genes to the next generation. Occasionally when the bucks battle, the force of the impact causes their antlers to spring apart and to become enmeshed with each other. Thus securely locked, the two bucks are doomed to the slow death of starvation. Many skeletons bear mute testimony to the frequency of this occurrence. Often someone tries to save such bucks by sawing off

In battling for the favors of a doe, two bucks charge once, then try to throw each other to the ground or inflict wounds with their sharp antlers. Occasionally bucks lock antlers and cannot separate, eventually dying of starvation.

one of the deer's antlers. In most instances his kindness is repaid by one of the bucks trying to gore him. As the breeding season wanes, the bucks lose their antlers and their belligerency and again become shy and furtive.

Birth and Young: A deer's gestation period is 200 to 205 days, most of the fawns being born in the latter part of May or the first part of June. A doe giving birth for her first time will have a single fawn, thereafter she will have twins. In areas of good food, triplets are common as well as occasional quadruplets. There are even three records of quintuplets.

At birth a baby doe weighs about 4 1/2 pounds while a buck weighs 5 1/2 pounds. At the time of birth, the doe may return to a preselected spot or she may give birth wherever she happens to be. The fawns are born over a period of time that may extend from ten minutes up to two hours.

As soon as the fawn is born, the doe licks it dry with her tongue. Even before it can walk, the fawn in a matter of minutes seeks out the doe's udder and starts to nurse. The doe remains lying down so that the wobbly young can reach her nipples.

By the time the fawns are twenty minutes old, they can walk slowly on very shaky legs. The doe, as soon as possible, will lead her fawns away from the place of birth where her body fluids have soaked into the earth and may attract predators.

When a suitable place of concealment is reached, the doe leaves her fawns and moves off perhaps 100 yards away. The fawns in their spotted coats are almost im-

Immediately after giving birth to her fawn a doe licks it clean with her tongue. As soon as it can walk—in about twenty minutes—she will lead it to a secluded place in the forest and conceal it from predators.

In its spotted coat, a four-day-old fawn tries its gangly legs before returning to cover. (Photo by Irene Vandermolen.)

possible to see and are almost odorless. The doe comes back five to eight times a day to nurse the young and then leaves again. She always remains somewhere in the area where she can see if danger approaches or can hear the little ones if they call to her.

After two to three weeks' time, the little ones are strong enough to follow the doe when she feeds. They then begin a process of self-weaning. Imitating their mother, the fawns taste various types of vegetation. As they increase this type of food intake, their demand for milk lessens and soon they are completely weaned. Before it is a week old, a fawn can easily outrun a man.

The young does may stay with the female throughout the winter but the bucks may leave in the first fall. About 40 percent of the young does may breed in their first autumn so that they give birth when they are one year old.

Life Span: Although most bucks are killed before they even reach their prime at five years of age, many does live to be much older. Deer have a usual life span of eight to eleven years. There is one authenticated record of a deer kept in captivity that lived to be nineteen years old. Does begin to decrease in fertility after they are nine years old, although most does bear at least one fawn a year till they die.

Pennsylvania's Game Research Division has found from records of antlered deer killed that the age of bucks breaks down as follows:

> 67 percent are 1 1/2 years old.
> 20 percent are 2 1/2 years old.
> 9 percent are 3 1/2 years old.
> 2 percent are 4 1/2 years old.
> 2 percent are 5 1/2 years old.

The sex composition of any deer herd is influenced strongly by the hunting procedures allowed. Slightly more bucks than does are born but it is close to a 50-50 ratio. However, many states do not allow does to be hunted, and the mature does soon exceed the number of bucks. Where well fed, deer will reproduce to the point where the newborn fawns comprise 30 to 40 percent of the total herd.

Sign: Although deer are plentiful enough to be seen frequently, the signs of their having been in an area are a hundredfold more common. Tracks and hoof marks are most commonly seen and recognized. In fact, most of the other sign of deer may not even be identified as such by the average hunter.

One of the most popular misconceptions is that it is easy to tell a buck's tracks from those of a doe. Nothing could be further from the truth. While it is true that mature bucks are larger than mature does, most bucks never reach their full size before being shot. Thus an old eight- or nine-year-old doe will be larger and heavier than a one- or two-year-old buck. Her hoofs are broader, blunter, and more widely spread than the buck's simply because she is larger and weighs more. Once a buck is mature, at 3 1/2 to 5 years old, he has obtained full growth and of course has larger feet. But there aren't many of these bucks around.

Many hunters claim they can tell a buck's track because the dewclaws show. On soft earth the dewclaws of either sex will show if the animals are heavy, and on hard earth the dewclaws do not register at all.

If there is less than three-quarters of an inch of snow, one can tell a buck's tracks because of the drag marks of the toes. A doe walks more gracefully and raises her feet clear of the ground, but once there is over three-quarters of an inch of snow all deer tracks show drag marks.

Deer may frequent the same area day after day, but they make a new bed mark each time. In dry leaves or grass the bed is just packed down by the body weight and shows body size. In shallow snow the deer scrape the snow away, revealing dry leaves in the bottom of the bed.

Since a deer has no teeth in the front of its mouth on the top jaw, every bite that it makes is ragged. This is also an easy sign to recognize on browse.

In very light snow, the tracks of a whitetail buck can be distinguished from those of a doe by the presence of drag marks (above). A doe lifts her feet higher when she walks and leaves no drag marks (below).

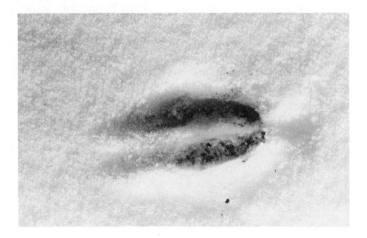

Droppings are also readily seen. In the winter when deer are feeding upon brush, the pellets are hard, brown and about three-quarters of an inch long. In the summer when deer are feeding upon soft vegetation, the scat is often segmented and tube-shaped. They void thirteen times a day.

"Buck rubs" are evident signs that the bucks in the area are preparing for the battles of the coming breeding season by rubbing the bark off saplings and bushes with their antlers. These bright scars against the dark bark can be seen from far away.

Enemies: The mountain lion and the wolf were originally the deer's greatest control. Eliminating these predators helped the deer to expand both its range and numbers. Today the deer's chief enemy is man the hunter, although in many areas man as the spoiler of habitat may soon be the prime foe. Men driving automobiles kill numerous deer, too. Dogs are the worst of the deer's four-footed enemies; the friendly family pooch may be a slavering deer killer at night. In areas where they are found, the mountain lion, wolf and bear still kill deer. Lynx, bobcats and coyotes are a lesser threat because of their smaller size.

The elements also take their toll. High winds and biting cold force the deer to seek protected swamps and ravines. If the snow is deep, the deer tramp a network of trails throughout their yard leading to all available food. If the cold period is of an extended duration, or if the snow is deep, the deer soon consume their food supply and may be too weak to search further. At such times the deer yards become death traps and deer by the tens of thousands die of starvation each winter.

Less frequently seen but also a threat to the deer's health are the various parasites. All creatures have some types of body lice—flies, mosquitoes and wood ticks feed upon all warm-blooded hosts. Botflies crawl up a deer's nostrils and lay their eggs on the deer's nasal membranes. When the larvae hatch out, they move further back into the nasal passageway. They stay there until the following spring when they drop out to complete their life cycle. Deer also have lungworms, footworms, liver flukes and tapeworms.

Disease is the most insidious enemy. The whitetail deer has been known to have Bang's disease, fibrous tumors and the epizootic hemorrhagic disease.

Human Relations: The whitetail deer has always been the most important big-game animal on this continent. Its range was much greater than the bison's, and it provided food for more Indians than did the bison. The first white settlers eagerly switched from their staple diet of mutton to venison. Both the hides and the meat were early items of barter. The citizens of the short-lived state of Franklin even paid their officials salaries in deer skins.

Our deer population is probably at its all-time high at the present time. The deer is a fringe animal and not an inhabitant of the deep climax forests. As the white man moved into the various sections of the country, he reduced the predators with his gun and felled the forests with his axe—and the deer boom began. The deer increased in population until the middle 1800s when constant hunting by settlers and professionals began to make serious inroads into the deer population. The 1890s saw the deer at their lowest numbers. As the deer herds were reduced, conservationists struggled to alert the populace to the fact that this splendid animal was almost on the brink of extinction in many areas. The northeastern states were the hardest hit. Rhode Island and Connecticut had no deer at all. New Jersey was down to less than 200; and in Massachusetts, New Hampshire and Vermont, deer were so scarce that the sighting of one made headlines in the local papers.

Through more rigid laws, better enforcement and importation from other states, the pendulum started to swing again in the deer's favor. Today we often have the problem of too many deer in some areas. A deer is its own worst enemy and will rapidly destroy its own range by overpopulating it. The same rigid laws that brought the deer back often work against the deer today by destroying them. Deer must be managed and harvested for their own good. The enlightened states now allow does to be taken when the herd has reached such proportions that it must be reduced to keep it in line with the available food. The main factor influencing the population of any species is the availability of food and shelter, but in spite of overwhelming evidence that deer cannot be stockpiled, there are still some states that refuse to harvest their does and lose many deer each year by starvation. Although our deer herd is currently at a peak, it has to decline. Our exploding human population is gobbling up land at such a rate that the deer's range will be seriously curtailed in the future.

Deer hunting is big business worth millions of dollars. Many communities derive a large portion of their income catering to deer hunters. In addition to the money spent on licenses, guides and lodging, there are the added costs of transportation, food, firearms, ammunition and clothing.

The esthetic value of deer cannot be measured. There are fully as many, if not more, people who just enjoy watching deer or photographing them as there are hunters. Both groups are sure that the world is a better place because of the deer.

Trophy Records: The head of a typical whitetail buck makes a very handsome trophy, particularly if the beams and points are symmetrical. The present world's record was shot in Danbury, Wisconsin, by James Jordan in 1914. This head has a score of 206 5/8 points. The right and left main beams are 30 inches long. There are five points on each beam and the rack measures 20 1/8 inches at the widest spread. The second place buck scored 205 points and was taken by Larry Gibson in Randolph County, Missouri, in 1971. The right beam is 26 6/8 inches long and the left beam is 25 4/8 inches long. There are six points on the right beam and six on the left. The widest spread of the rack is 24 2/8 inches.

In 1964 Dwight Green shot a buck in Warren County, Iowa, that scored 187 2/8 points. This head has an inside spread of 30 3/8 inches between the main beams, the widest on record.

Table Fare: Many people talk about the "wild" taste of venison. In preparing the meat for the table they soak it, saute it, cover it with vinegar, brandy, wine and otherwise attempt to camouflage it. Venison should be treated like good beef. Proper and prompt field dressing and butchering of the deer is important. Thereafter the meat can be prepared in any fashion you like, depending on the particular cut.

Today we don't use as many parts of the deer as the Indians did. They used the hoofs for rattles, the sinew for thread, the bones for awls and needles, the hide for leather, the hair for stuffing pillows and socks and, of course, the meat for food. Even today deer hides are an important item of trade and many garments are made from them. The United States Armed Forces use thousands of hides each year for special clothing, gloves and other equipment for servicemen.

With tail flagged in alarm, this whitetail buck explodes away, his sudden action alarming the bucks behind him. (Photo by Irene Vandermolen.)

Mule deer bucks have bifurcated antlers (with two distinct Ys on each side) as above. Note also the white rump patch and black tip of the tail. Below, this mule deer buck is in velvet, his antlers soon to become much larger and harder. (Top photo by Len Rue Jr.)

Mule Deer

Odocoileus hemionus

The mule deer inhabits the deserts, prairies and mountains of our western states. It is a deer of the open spaces, less furtive perhaps than the brush-loving whitetail, but a fine game animal in its own right. Its rack, which differs from the whitetail's in conformation, is generally larger and trophy bucks are more prevalent.

The blacktail deer is a relative of the mule deer, as can be seen by its similar antlers, and bears the same scientific name. It is smaller than the mule deer, however, and inhabits a limited range in the Pacific coastal forests.

Description: The mule deer is a stocky animal with a heavy body and stout legs. A full-grown deer will stand 40 to 42 inches high at the shoulder and measure almost 6 1/2 feet in length. The average weight is 175 to 200 pounds, although large specimens reach 300 to 450 pounds. The blacktail is smaller, standing 38 inches high at the shoulder and measuring 5 feet in length. It weighs up to 150 pounds, but exceptionally large deer have gone as high as 300.

The ears on this deer are large, like those of a mule, measuring 8 to 9 inches long from the opening, or 11 inches overall, and about 6 inches wide. The blacktail's ears are about 6 1/2 inches long and somewhat narrower.

The mule deer's tail is round and has white hairs on top down to the 2-inch black tip, but the hairs wear off on the underside and it is usually bare. The tail of the blacktail deer is, naturally, dark on top, although the underside is white.

Like all deer, in the summer the mule deer's basic color is a reddish-brown. The winter coat is a more somber grayish-brown, and the hairs are air-filled and provide insulation.

A mule deer's face has striking contrasts. The nose and a band around the muzzle are black; the face and an area around the eyes are white. A skull cap of jet black extends down between the eyes. The cheeks are gray and the ears are black-rimmed and lined with white. The throat, which is similar to the pronghorn antelope's, has two white patches divided by a bar of dark color. The belly is whitish as are the insides of the legs; the hooves are jet black. Although there are a few records of albino mule deer, albinism and mutations are not as common among this species as among the whitetail.

The mule deer has four toes on each foot, but the two outside ones are dewclaws situated above and behind the foot.

The antlers on an adult mule-deer buck are large and heavy. Each antler divides into two main beams, and each beam forks into two tines. There is also a brow tine, which westerners disregard in counting the number of points.

The mule deer has conspicuous lachrymal glands in front of the eye. The hair around the outside of these glands flares out when the deer is excited or nervous.

On the outside of the hind leg is situated the metatarsal gland, which is about 5 inches long, the longest of any of our deer family. The blacktailed deer's metatarsals are about 3 inches long.

Both deer also have tarsal glands on their hocks, the inside of the hind legs at the heel. This is the deer's most active gland, and its use is calculated. The deer place their heels together when urinating so that the hairs around this gland become saturated and the gland itself gives off a strong, musky, although not offensive, odor. The secretion of this musk turns the gland a dark auburn-brown. It is the musk from this gland that deer hunters usually get on their hands and on the meat if they are not careful.

The mule deer and the blacktail too have an interdigital gland between the hooves. This gives off a yellow, waxy secretion by means of which the deer track one another.

The mule deer are typical ruminants, having a four-chambered stomach. The rumen, or the first section, is used for storage. The food is cropped and swallowed without any more chewing than is actually needed to get it down. An average of 10 to 12 pounds of browse or forage will completely fill the rumen. Afterward, when the deer is safely concealed, the food mass is regurgitated in small lumps and rechewed as a cud. When reswallowed it then goes into the second section of the stomach and passes on through the digestive system.

These deer have 32 teeth which are classified as 8 incisors, 12 premolars and 12 molars. Actually, the fourth incisor on each side is a modified canine tooth. But these canine teeth appear and are used exactly as the incisors and are usually referred to as such. Deer do not have any teeth in the top jaw at the front of the mouth.

Distribution: Although there is only one species, hunters recognize two kinds of mule deer (*Odocoileus hemionus*). The overall range of the species is from southeastern Alaska to Mexico, east to Hudson Bay, Minnesota,

Distribution of the mule deer.

and western Texas. The deer inhabiting the coastal area from Alaska to central California are generally known as blacktail deer and were formerly considered to be a distinct species (*Odocoileus columbianus*).

Travel: Mule deer travel extensively and usually migrate between winter and summer ranges. Some of these deer merely move down to the more sheltered valleys when the temperature begins to drop and the mountains begin to accumulate snow. In this case, a better term than migration would be seasonal drift. Other mule deer make real migrations. The Interstate deer herd travels about 100 miles from its wintering grounds in California to its summer range in Oregon. The Tehoma herd also travels about 100 miles, but this herd moves only within the State of California. Because of the scarcity of snow along the Pacific coastal regions, the blacktail deer usually inhabits the same range winter and summer or does no more than move lower on the mountainside.

Habits: Like all males of the deer family, mule-deer bucks prefer to keep bachelor habits through most of the year. Although the herds on the wintering grounds are mixed, the deer split up as soon as the winter ends. The pregnant does are usually the first to reach the summer range; the bucks travel more slowly. Summers may be spent at elevations as high as 8,000 feet above sea level.

The deer feed mainly early in the morning and late in the day. As summer progresses the deer feed earlier and later each day to avoid as much of the heat as possible. In midsummer the bucks often quit feeding as soon as the sun climbs over the horizon, the does and fawns feeding for a longer period. On overcast days the deer may feed at any time of the day, and they are particularly active just before a dark, stormy night.

When the deer retire they prefer, if possible, to be on a shady, well-protected ridge where they can have an elevated view of the terrain and receive the rising thermals which carry the odor of any predators up both slopes.

The deer have definite water needs that must be met. A severe drought not only affects the forage plants but can also restrict the fawn's growth by shrinking the mother's milk supply. The deer are aware of every spring and waterhole in their area.

Grasses are an important summer food. Fescue grass, bluegrass, bromegrass, wheat grass, grama grass, rice grass and needlegrass are the most important herbage. In the winter the mule deer abandon their summer range because of deep snow, for they seldom paw through even shallow snow to get at the grasses. Instead they start to feed more heavily upon browse. Snowberry, bearberry, serviceberry, cedar, oak, mountain mahogany, cliffrose, sagebrush, jack pine, sunflower, fir, poplar and bitterbrush are favored mule-deer foods. The blacktail deer, living along the coast, has a few decided food preferences of its own. Filaree oak, bromegrass, fescue grass, wild oats, manzanita, ceanothus, mountain mahogany, chamise, buckthorn and buttercup are all high on its list. Both deer eat fungus, ferns, berries, acorns, nuts, cactus fruit and many of the local wildflowers. Deer do have food preferences, but they can eat almost any vegetation they encounter.

At night the mule deer bed down in the open, usually in the middle of their feeding area, but in the daytime they retire to cover. In some areas the deer have actual spots to which they return day after day. A deer might not use the same bed each day, although it will use the same area. While a group of deer circulates among the beds, ticks and other external parasites are passed from animal to animal. Sometimes the ticks become so plentiful that the deer cooperatively chew them off each others' bodies. Birds often help the deer get rid of these pests. Magpies have been seen walking on the backs of deer, carefully probing for ticks embedded there.

Living in a more inaccessible area, the mule deer has not been subjected to as much hunting pressure and is thus less wary than the whitetail. A whitetail has the good sense to remain hidden if it feels that it is in sufficient cover, but a mule deer usually becomes too nervous to hold still and bounds away. If the whitetail does make a break, it usually doesn't stop until it is again safe in a thick copse. The mule deer habitually stops just before it reaches cover for a last look at whatever disturbed it—often long enough to allow a hunter time to shoot.

Senses: Although both the mule and the blacktail deer have excellent hearing, their sense of smell is more highly developed. The extra length of their ears increases their hearing ability yet they may hear many sounds they cannot identify. The sound will alert the deer, but the noise may be as harmless as a loose piece of rock falling from a cliffside or a dead limb dropping from a tree—or it may be a noise made by a predator. The deer cannot tell. But if the breeze is blowing from the right direction, the deer instantly can identify the scent of a man or a predator.

The deer's eyesight is keen and quick to catch motion, but it often overlooks a stationary object even though that object is in the open.

Communication: When alarmed, a deer stamps its feet, and the vibrations alert all the deer in the area. Also, when alarmed, a deer flares its tarsal glands and discharges musk, alerting nearby deer.

Any hasty action on the part of one deer will be followed by all the rest. A deer can arise leisurely and walk off and the rest of the deer will be unconcerned, but when a deer springs to its feet and bounds off, all the deer will scatter. They may not know what alarmed the first deer, but their survival depends upon their reacting to the possibility that the first deer is reacting to danger.

When alarmed, deer also snort by blasting air through their noses, sometimes producing a whistling sound. The bucks make a coughing-grunting sound. When they call they make a deep, raspy, blatting sound not at all unlike that of an old domestic sheep. The does make a similar sound that is higher pitched. The fawns, if separated from their mothers, bleat like a lamb.

The pale rump patch also serves as a recognition signal.

Locomotion: The mule deer, like most other animals, prefers not to exert itself unless it has to. It prefers to survey its domain from a secluded vantage point. If danger approaches and the deer feels it has not yet been discovered, it attempts to skulk away unseen.

A deer normally walks from place to place. When feeding, it walks a few steps, nips off some vegetation, walks a bit more and then feeds again. If the occasion calls for a little more speed, the deer trots, advancing one front foot and one hind foot on opposite sides of the body simultaneously.

It is when the mule deer goes into a bounding gallop that its gait becomes so different from the whitetail's. The whitetail makes a long, graceful leap, landing on its front feet and pushing off with them before the hind feet contact the ground. The mule deer pushes off from the ground with all four feet at once so that it appears to have a stiff-legged, spring-driven gait—as though it were using a pogo stick. Although the mule deer does not look as graceful as the whitetail, it is as fast. Both deer have been clocked at 35 miles per hour. Mule deer have been known to make horizontal jumps of 25 feet and can jump 8 feet high. This peculiar bounding jump is probably an adaptation to the steep hillsides it prefers to inhabit.

The mule deer is a strong swimmer, and the blacktail deer is frequently seen swimming between the islands off Alaska's panhandle, some of which are 5 miles apart.

Breeding: Man has played a more important role in the lives of deer than he realizes, for his expansion has changed most deer from diurnal to nocturnal creatures; and his illogical "bucks only" law has affected the mule deer's competitive breeding habits. When the fawns are born the crop is usually split 50-50 between the sexes. As the bucks begin to mature, and wear the antlers that signify this maturity, they are shot by hunters, thus upsetting the ratio between the sexes. As there are far more does than there are bucks, this eliminates much of the competition between males, since the bucks are able to service more does without having to fight for them.

Some mule deer bucks may acquire a harem of three or four does, but this is a rather loose relationship and the does may wander off if they care to. A bull elk forcibly tries to keep his group of females intact, but the mule deer buck does not.

Mule-deer bucks do fight for supremacy and breeding privileges, but less often than do whitetail bucks. When the bucks fight, except for the initial impact the contest is usually a pushing, shoving affair with each buck trying to force the other backwards or to his knees. These battles are seldom fatal, although occasionally the bucks' antlers become locked and both perish.

The does begin to come into oestrous in the last part of October and stay in heat for about thirty hours. If a doe is not impregnated during that short time, and most of them are, she will come back into heat in another twenty-eight days. An unbred doe can continue coming into heat for four or five months and, in a few rare cases, does have been bred as late as April.

During September the velvet, which had encased and nourished the bucks' growing antlers, becomes dry, and they remove it by rubbing their antlers against resilient saplings and bushes. Beneath the velvet, the antlers have become hard and strong.

Before the velvet is peeled off, the bucks' testicles drop down and become enlarged and the sperm cells become motile. The bucks' necks become engorged with blood. Their habits change. They now give up their solitary ways or break up their bachelor groups to begin seeking out and consorting with the does.

The breeding season wanes in the last of December and at that time the bucks begin to lose their antlers and their belligerency. By April they generally lose their ability to produce living sperm, although they can still copulate.

Mule deer and whitetail deer occasionally interbreed. The offspring look like blacktail deer, having some of the features of each parent, although most are infertile.

Birth and Young: The gestation period for the mule deer is approximately 210 days, the majority of the fawns being born in late June and July. At birth they weigh about 5 to 7 pounds and have the typical spotted, camouflaged coats. A doe giving birth for the first time usually has a single fawn and twins thereafter.

Even before the mother licks the little ones thoroughly dry, they attempt to gain their feet. Sometimes the young nurse before they can walk, crawling on their knees to the doe's nipples while she is lying down.

As soon as the young can walk, the doe leads them to a spot of safety where she secrets them among the vegetation. The mother does not abandon her young but withdraws from the immediate vicinity so that her body odor does not attract a predator to her babies. At intervals the doe comes back to the fawns to allow them to nurse. The fawns develop rapidly on the doe's rich milk, which has a butterfat content of between 10 and 12 percent as compared to a cow's 3 to 5 percent. Within two weeks the fawns are strong enough to follow the doe and soon start to feed upon some of the available vegetation.

The fawns nurse until fall. Usually by the time they shed their spotted coats in September most of them are weaned. They continue to follow their mother until she gives birth again in the spring. Before birthing again, the doe drives her yearlings away. Sometimes the yearlings are allowed to rejoin the family group after the new fawns are born.

Life Span: A few yearling does may breed in their first fall, but the majority do not breed until they are one and a half years old and are two years old when they give birth to young. Based on that fact, the life span of the mule deer can be reckoned at ten years. Zoos have been successful in raising mule deer to the age of fourteen, but records of wild deer can top that figure. Several

A blacktail doe and her fawn visit a meadow brook to drink their fill. Fawns remain with their mother until she gives birth again in the spring. Sometimes they rejoin her after the new fawns are born.

semi-wild deer on Hardy Island, British Columbia, lived to be sixteen years old. The record is held by a doe on Gambler Island in British Columbia that reached the age of twenty-two.

Sign: The most commonly found sign of the mule deer is its tracks. Because it inhabits dry desert areas or mountainsides, the dewclaws seldom show in the tracks. The buck's tracks are 3 to 3 1/4 inches in length, and the walking stride is about 22 to 24 inches long.

Because of its bounding gait, the tracks of a mule deer make a very different pattern than those of the whitetail. When a whitetail goes all-out for speed, its front feet strike the ground first and the hind feet land ahead. The mule deer bounds with all four feet leaving the ground at once, and the hind-feet tracks are behind the tracks of the forefeet.

In many areas of the West the mule deer are too plentiful for their own good. Overbrowsed bushes have a stunted, scrubby appearance and higher shrubs all bear a browse line. This is referred to as "high-lining," and shows how high a deer can reach for food. It also bears evidence of extremely poor management of the deer in that area.

The brown, hard scat pellets of a mule deer feeding on browse are about 3/4 of an inch long and are usually tapered on one end and squared off on the other like a boattail bullet. Occasionally one end will be concave. When the deer is feeding on grasses, its scat becomes a homogeneous mass.

Enemies: The mountain lion is the main enemy of the mule deer. In areas where the big cat has been eliminated, the deer have multiplied and disease has been rampant. Wherever possible, the lion will kill one or two deer a week.

In the northern portion of the mule deer's range, the wolf also figures prominently among its predators. A wolf is large enough to pull down a deer by itself but, since the wolves usually hunt in family units, the job is made much easier.

Coyotes, too, will attempt to take deer but must be satisfied with young, sick, old or otherwise weakened deer. The coyote is not large enough to be a serious threat to a healthy adult mule deer, except in winter.

Black bear, grizzly bear and, along the Alaskan coast, brown bear will take a mule or blacktail deer if they get the chance. Usually the bears have to content themselves with an occasional fawn. The bears are scavengers and quickly clean up any winter-killed deer they discover.

The bobcat, lynx and wolverine could be called occasional predators. If the opportunity to take a deer should arise, they would avail themselves of that opportunity.

It is also probable that the golden eagle takes an occasional fawn but it cannot be considered a threat to the deer population.

Ticks, mites and even chiggers harass the mule deer. Botflies can make its life miserable. The larvae, which they deposit in the deer's nasal passages, develop in the nasal tracts inside the deer's head. Although these larvae must be extremely annoying, they apparently do no real harm. Internally, lungworms, roundworms and tapeworms of many types are present.

Of the diseases that affect mule deer, hoof and mouth disease has been the most crippling. This disease was transmitted to the mule deer in California by infected cattle. Before the disease had run its course, 22,214 deer were killed. Fortunately the disease has not been found in these deer since 1925.

Human Relations: Proper management of mule deer is necessary to maintain the herds in a healthy balance. When the population outstrips its food supply the deer starve. The most famous case of deer mismanagement is that of the Kaibab deer herd. In 1906 President Theodore Roosevelt set aside the Grand Canyon National Game Preserve in Arizona to protect the mule deer. Through lack of knowledge, the deer were coddled and protected—overprotected. Hunting was banned, predators were eliminated and the deer herd grew. As the deers' numbers increased, so did their food requirements and the forage plants began to suffer. In 1922-23, by unofficial estimate there were over 100,000 deer in the area creating a desert out of what once had been a lush plateau. Conservationists of that time were alarmed and some corrective steps were taken. Commercial grazing of ranch livestock was prohibited and some hunting was allowed, but it was too late. The deer began to starve on the overgrazed range. Even with this evidence, political pressure by the State of Arizona prevented the proper management steps from being taken. From 1929 on, hunting on a large scale relieved some of the pressures and the range began to come back. Again the deer herd multiplied and the state went back to a "bucks only" law. Drought and an excessive deer population combined in 1955 to bring the herd crashing down to about 12,000 animals, an all-time low.

With their newly found knowledge, game managers were finally able to take over the job of managing the game. It is really much easier to manage game than it is to manage people. In order to manage people, the game managers have done a tremendous job of public relations and public education. The hunters and the general public had to be educated to the facts of deer management before they would accept the workings of the game managers. That battle has been long and uphill and is still far from being won. Countless mule deer are still being wasted each year through starvation and ranges are being destroyed due to the policy of not allowing hunters to remove the excess animals. According to latest big-game figures made available in 1978 by the National Rifle Association, and Dr. Sidney Wilcox, a total of 420,329 mule and 130,000 blacktail deer were taken by hunters during 1977. Many states listed no estimates of their current populations, but an average from the states that did shows that one out of every ten to one out of every fourteen deer was taken by hunters. The population of mule deer has declined slightly in recent years, while that of the blacktail has increased slightly.

Trophy Records: The mule deer and the blacktail deer are still treated separately by the Boone and Crockett Club so we shall give the top records of each.

The Number 1 mule deer record was taken by Doug Burris in Dolores County, Colorado, in 1972. It scored 225 6/8 points. The right main beam is 30 1/8 inches long, 5 2/8 inches in circumference, with six points. The left main beam is 28 6/8 inches long, 5 3/8 inches in circumference, with five points. The inside spread is 30 7/8 inches.

The Number 2 mule-deer head came from Hoback Canyon, Wyoming. It is not known when or by whom it was killed, but it is owned by W. C. Lawrence and scored 217 points. The right beam is 24 4/8 inches long, 5 5/8 inches in circumference and has 6 points. The left beam is 28 2/8 inches long, 5 6/8 inches in circumference and has 6 points.

The Number 1 blacktail deer was taken by Clark Griffith in 1962 in Elk City, Oregon. The head scored 170 6/8 points. The right beam is 23 1/8 inches long, is 5 3/8 inches in circumference and has 5 points. The left beam is 24 inches long, is 5 4/8 inches in circumference and has 5 points.

The second-place winner was taken by Dennis King in Jackson County, Oregon, in 1970. The head scored 170 2/8 points. The right beam is 25 6/8 inches long, 4 5/8 inches in circumference and has 5 points. The left beam is 25 5/8 inches long, 4 6/8 inches in circumference and has 5 points.

J. S. Hunter reported weights of two mule-deer bucks in the California Fish and Game bulletin of June, 1924, that are the heaviest records to come to light. These deer, after being dressed out in the field, were weighed on a scale at 380 and 350 pounds. The live weights of these deer would have been about 480 and 450 pounds respectively.

Table Fare: Although venison is a drier meat than beef, it is delicious and enjoyed often by hunters. The type of food that the deer has been eating, the period of the rut and the care of the meat all greatly affect the quality of the venison. Both the mule deer and the black-tail deer are important meat animals in the West. The Sitka blacktail deer is the only antlered game available in its area and because of this is doubly important to the backwoods nimrods.

This huge bull stands about seven feet tall at the shoulder. He's cleaned his antlers of velvet and is in his rutting prime. (Photo by Len Rue Jr.)

Moose

Alces alces

The bull moose is the largest antlered animal in North America, and the largest deer in the world. Its huge body is perched on stiltlike legs, and its long, mulish head is crowned with a pair of tremendous palmated antlers. Yet, appearance to the contrary, the moose is a quick and furtive animal. Hunters often have glassed a moose from a distance and begun a stalk, only to discover on getting within shooting range that their quarry has silently vanished into the timber. During the rutting season, bulls can be located by imitating the call of the cow with a birchbark horn. At that time of the year particularly, a bull is a pugnacious animal and is likely to attack a man.

The early settlers gave the name of the European moose to the elk, and so they borrowed the Indian name for the American counterpart of the enormous deer they knew from the Old World. Although the French Canadian name for the moose, *l'original*, seems well chosen considering the animal's appearance, it is really a corruption of the Basque word for deer, *orenac*, which through usage became *originac* and, finally, *l'original*.

The ancestors of our modern moose crossed the Bering Land Bridge from Siberia at some time during the Pleistocene period, over a million years ago, and spread across the northern portion of North America. Remains have been found in a number of states and as far south as Virginia and Pennsylvania.

Description: The moose is not a graceful-looking animal, but its great strength is immediately apparent.

A large bull may stand 6 1/2 to 7 feet at the shoulder, measure 100 to 125 inches in length and weigh in the vicinity of 1,300 to 1,400 pounds. Weights of up to 1,800 pounds have been noted. The powerful forequarters of the moose taper back to the much smaller hind parts, ending in a stubby 3-inch tail. The moose's long legs keep its belly about 40 inches off the ground. The ears are larger than those of a mule. Its long face ends in a wide, floppy, down-turned muzzle. Beneath its neck hangs a flap of skin, called a bell or pendant, which serves no apparent purpose. The bull moose's gigantic antlers often measure 6 feet across the widest spread and weigh up to 90 pounds. A wet cow moose with her ears hanging

His antlers peeling velvet, this bull puts on fat reserves for a busy rutting season.

down looks like a dejected animal. The bull, however, with its magnificent antlers is a truly impressive specimen.

The moose has four toes on each foot, each encased in the horny sheath of hoof. The two hind toes, or dew-claws, are longer than those of most members of the deer family. The moose frequents swampy, boggy areas, and when the dewclaws are splayed out, the feet can more easily support the moose's weight on soft terrain.

The moose's dominant color is black, although it ranges through all shades of dark brown and russet. The moose's nostrils, eye circles, inner parts of the ear and the lower portions of its legs are grayish-white. Albinos are rare among moose but one was killed by a Canadian trapper and mounted by John Hansen of the American Museum of Natural History. Outdoor writer and photographer Lee Wulff photographed a mutation in Newfoundland that was all white except for a hand-sized patch of brown and brown eyes. As moose are black, melanism, if it occurred, would not be noticed.

The hair of a moose is coarse and brittle because each hair is filled with air cells, providing excellent insulation against the extremes of cold weather that the moose encounters. The moose also has a stiff mane of hair about 10 inches long down the center of its shoulders. When the moose is alarmed or enraged, this mane, or roach, stands on end.

Moose do not have metatarsal glands, but they do have small tarsal glands. They do have the lachrymal gland in front of the eye.

The dentition of a moose is 8 incisors on the bottom jaw, no canines, 6 premolars top and bottom and 6 molars top and bottom, making a total of 32 teeth.

Distribution of the moose.

Distribution: Moose are found from coast to coast in the forested portions of Alaska and Canada, and New-foundland. To the south they range into the United States in the Rocky Mountains of northern Colorado and Utah, and in northern Minnesota, Michigan and Maine. Strag-glers occasionally wander farther south.

Travel: The moose does not migrate in the same sense as do caribou or birds. It is primarily a homebody, content to remain within an area of about a square mile. The size of this home territory varies of course with the availability of food. In the lake country of Quebec the moose stay in the same area year-round. However, in

Alaska moose stray to higher elevations in the summer. On the Kenai Peninsula, which is famous for its moose, a lot of cows and calves are found along the rivers but no bulls. The bulls band together and feed on the mountainside in the summer, coming back to the flats, thickets and swamps with the advent of the breeding season and cold weather. This is also true in Mt. McKinley National Park. During the breeding season a bull may travel miles from his home base in search of a receptive cow.

Habits: Moose are browsing animals and prefer to feed upon brushy twigs. In areas where it is found the dwarf willow seems to be the favored food. In the forested areas balsam fir, white birch and aspen are the main foods. In the summer when the moose are in the lakes to escape the heat and insects, they feed heavily upon water lilies, pondweeds, sedges, and eelgrass. Alder, mountain ash, red osier, striped maple, honeysuckle, chokecherry, snowberry, spiraea, dwarf birch, current, cottonwood, cranberry and elder are all high on the list of preferred food. The moose often eat many other foods, not through preference but because the plants may be plentiful. If all types of food are equally distributed, the moose will feed mainly upon those listed.

The moose's great size is a decided asset in getting food. By merely stretching its neck upwards it has no trouble securing food 10 feet above the ground. In places where the growth is higher the moose will rear upright, straddle the bush or sapling with its legs, force it to the ground with its body and eat the top branches.

When feeding in the water the moose will eat the floating leaves of water lilies, or it will submerge its head to grasp mouthfuls of underwater plants. On occasion I have seen a moose swimming in deep water stop to nibble at a floating water plant. I have also seen moose dive completely beneath the surface of the water to feed on aquatic plants. Because of its long legs and comparatively short neck, the moose must get down on its knees to graze upon grasses or to drink from a shallow spring hole. Moose sometimes make nuisances of themselves by feeding upon farm crops and in the vegetable gardens of people who settle in wilderness areas. Every salt lick in the vicinity will be frequented by moose.

The majority of moose live in areas where there is little disturbance by man except during the hunting season. Although they favor feeding at dawn and again in the later afternoon, because they are not usually disturbed they will feed at any time of the day.

In winter moose tend to band together. It is not that they want to travel together so much as they are forced into the same area by biting cold and wind or the availability of food. It was thought at one time that moose and deer deliberately tramped out networks of trails in their own area, but such trails are made by these animals moving out of their area for food.

Snow does not hamper a moose until it gets over 30 inches deep. At 30 to 34 inches the moose's belly begins to drag and walking becomes difficult when the moose has to push through deeper snow with its chest. If danger threatens when the snow is over 30 inches deep, the moose automatically heads for a stand of young conifers. As these trees always hold part of the snow load on their branches, the snow is always shallower beneath, allowing the moose to run more easily

It has recently been discovered that a snow depth of at least 24 inches is a crucial factor in a moose's survival. When the moose wishes to bed down it will seek out this soft snow. As its body will sink in 14 to 15 inches, the snow acts as a blanket. If the moose were to lie down on bare ground, it would lose a great deal of body heat on nights when the temperature is 50 to 70 degrees below zero. Snug in its soft blanket of snow, the moose's body may be held right around the freezing point. This conservation of heat means a big saving in its food requirements. When a moose has packed down all available bed sites in a small area, it will move to another area, even though food is still available at the first spot. Moose dislike wind and in windy weather seek heavy cover and keep their activities to a minimum.

Senses: The sense of smell is highly developed in the moose, and its hearing also is exceptional. A moose's eyesight is poor and it does not seem to see stationary objects as danger. Often when advancing on a moose, I have frozen in my tracks every time the moose looked in my direction. Generally the animal would stare at me uncomprehendingly and then resume its feeding.

Communication: Moose make a variety of sounds according to the situation. The most common sound is a deep coughing grunt made by both the cows and the bulls, the bulls making the deeper, raspy sound. The calves give a high-pitched bleat. Other words to describe moose sounds are wail, whine, bawl and bellow. The sounds are not too unlike those made by a domestic cow.

Locomotion: Unless disturbed, the moose covers ground with long strides. When in a slight hurry it trots easily. When it is alarmed or angered it steps out in a ground-eating trot. When a moose gallops its feet are grouped together so that the tracks show all four feet in a close group with the hind feet registering ahead of the front feet.

Moose have actually been trained to pull a sulky and have been raced at tracks. They turn in as good a time as trotting horses, being able to do 35 miles per hour and better. Because of their huge lungs they can run at top speeds for a long period without tiring. One observer tells of following a young cow moose on the road of Alaska's Kenai Peninsula for six miles. By checking his car's speedometer he knew she was trotting at 33 miles per hour. When they pushed her a little harder, she broke into a gallop and reached a speed of 45 miles per hour. After 6 miles she evidently tired of the game and took off across a swamp. She did not appear to be breathing hard nor to have been unduly exerted.

Moose do not do much jumping. With their long legs, they usually stride over most obstacles or else walk around them. They have been seen to jump a 6-foot fence. In jumping, the moose raises up on its hind legs, starts its front feet over the hurdle, then follows with its body in a tremendous bound.

Moose are very strong swimmers. Their hollow hair helps to buoy them up, and their large hoofs and great strength enable them to move swiftly through the water.

Breeding: A bull moose has antlers only to fight another bull moose. In fact, it is only during the breeding season that a bull will attack with its head down. At other times it keeps its head up and uses its forefeet to make a slashing, crushing attack.

The antlers are shed in late December or January and start to grow again in late April. By August they have reached their maximum size, and the bulls start to rub the velvet off about the first of September.

Rutting season starts in the middle of September and lasts for about six weeks. By now the bull's antlers are polished to a gleaming hardness and his temper is short. He loses all interest in food and concentrates his energy on finding and breeding a mate. Woe be to the man or creature who comes between a bull and his goal. Many people have been forced to spend hours in trees watching an angry bull paw the earth and batter nearby bushes with his antlers. Bulls during the rut have been known to attack cars, bulldozers and even trains.

Younger, smaller bulls scatter like chaff before the onslaught of the big bulls. Bulls of equal size are only too eager to fight it out. The combatants come together head on with a terrific crash. This impact is so great that many bulls lock antlers and die. Seven pairs of bulls locked in death have been found over an area of 450 miles in Alaska. There are so many records and photographs of this happening that it must be a fairly common occurrence. The fight usually continues until the lesser bull breaks off and dashes away or until one of the bulls is able to kill his rival by goring him. Frequently the victor will grind his victim into the earth by stamping on the prostrate body with his forefeet.

Bull moose often make wallows during the breeding season. These are circular pits about 6 to 10 inches deep that the moose dig and tramp out with their forefeet. They then urinate in these pits frequently and roll in them, caking the urine-soaked mud over their bodies.

Moose usually do not build up harems like elk do, although a bull may be in the company of several cows at one time. A bull usually finds a receptive cow and stays with her for a week or more before breaking off to find another. By the end of October the breeding season is over, the fire goes out of the bull's eye, his fat reserves are depleted and he again tolerates others of his kind.

Birth and Young: The gestation period for moose varies between 240 and 246 days, and the calves are born in May or June. A cow giving birth for the first time will drop one calf. Thereafter, until old age, she will usually produce twins. A moose calf when born weighs between 25 to 35 pounds. It has a light, reddish-brown coat that is not spotted. The calf is helpless for the first few hours but can easily outrun a man when it is four or five days old. At an early age the cow may take the calf swimming. Often a cow seeks out an island to give birth and crosses back to the mainland shortly thereafter. If the calf tires during the swim, it may get help by resting its head across its mother's back and allow her to tow it along.

The cow is very protective of her calves, and most creatures from wolves right up to man had better be cautious. A cow concerned over the safety of her calf is a fury to be reckoned with. The calves stay with the cow throughout the winter and are only driven off by the cow as the time approaches for her to give birth again.

Life Span: Cow moose are mature enough to breed at sixteen months although most of them are not bred

A cow moose and her calf forage for aquatic plants.

for the first time till their third year. The young bulls are probably capable of breeding at sixteen months but are denied the opportunity by the larger adult bulls. Moose reach maturity at the age of six, although they continue to grow in size, weight and antler development beyond this time. Moose have been known to reach the age of twenty years, and some teeth have been found that showed the moose had probably been a few years older than that. Ten to fifteen years could be considered an average life span, with twenty-five years being a possibility.

Sign: The most commonly found sign of moose is their tracks. As moose prefer to frequent areas where the ground is soft, their tremendous weight makes deep-cut, well-defined tracks. Tracks over 10 inches long from toe tip to dewclaws are not unusual.

Almost all the portage trails of the northern canoe country were made by moose. The Indians are usually given credit for these trails but all they did was to follow the network of paths that the moose had tramped out from one lake to another.

Where moose have been feeding on brush, the white scars where the branches and bark have been torn off show vividly. The many broken, splintered saplings show where the moose rode them down to feed on the tops. In the water the lily stalks, deprived of the weight of the eaten leaves, stand up nakedly out of the water while the eelgrasses festoon the branches of the alders along the stream banks.

When the moose are feeding upon winter browse, their pellets are hard, elongated-oval in shape and about 1 1/2 inches long. When more succulent food becomes available the droppings become a segmented mass. In the summer the voiding is one large unsectioned mass.

In the breeding season moose make the conspicuous wallows already described as well as wreaking destruction upon bushes with their antlers. Occasionally shed antlers are found, although these are avidly eaten by rodents for the minerals they contain and seldom last long.

Enemies: The wolf and the bear are undoubtedly the moose's main four-footed enemies. The bears are particularly destructive of the calves. If the bears are early enough in spring they are able, with their huge feet, to walk across the top of deep snow that would bog down a moose and are able to catch and kill it.

The remarkable study of Durward Allen and David

Mech on Isle Royale proved that wolves do kill a large number of moose. But the study also proved that the wolves couldn't kill every moose they wanted to even when they were in a pack of as many as fourteen to sixteen individuals. The study showed that the wolves killed a moose about every third day, yet they would make passing attacks at twelve different moose before they could kill one. Many times the moose eluded the wolves in water, deep snow or by fighting them off. The moose the wolves did kill invariably were old, sick, infirm or were young calves. The study further proved the point that predators improve the breeding stock of the prey animals by culling the unfit.

Wolverine and lynx would also be able to kill a moose weakened by starvation. The whitetail deer may also be considered an enemy of the moose because it passes on the deer brain worm, *tenius*. Harmless to deer, the worm larvae attack the moose's brain, causing blindness, paralysis and death.

Starvation is probably the moose's greatest natural killer. In many areas, such as New Brunswick and Nova Scotia the moose herds were almost wiped out because of overprotection. In both places the moose population crashed shortly after the hunting season closed. The closed season allowed the moose to increase to the point where they destroyed their food supply and starvation was inevitable.

Moose occasionally get bogged down in crossing swamps and may drown or die of exertion. Smooth ice is also a hazard because the moose that falls down may be unable to regain its footing.

Parasites both internally and externally take their toll.

In the summer, life is made miserable for the moose by the clouds of stinging, biting, blood-sucking insects that prey upon them. I have seen moose whose hind legs were a scabrous mess from fly bites. Moose ticks sometimes infest a moose by the hundreds. In the summer, with a plentiful supply of food, the moose can usually withstand the onslaught of the ticks. In the winter the ticks may be such a drain that the moose may be severely weakened. By trying to rub the ticks off, the moose will scrape off a lot of its hair. This in turn causes a loss of body heat, and the moose may suffer.

Moose are also subject to liver flukes, hydatid tapeworms and other intestinal parasites. A moose in a weakened condition may suffer from "moose sickness," an affliction brought on by starvation which affects the brain tissue. A moose in such a condition loses all fear of man and wanders around groggily while its strength lasts. It holds its body in a humpbacked position with its head held low. Pathologists are still studying this disease, which is always fatal.

Human Relations: Man has always been the moose's greatest enemy. The moose can tolerate man but is usually forced out of an area when man comes in, either directly through hunting pressure or through man's destruction of the moose's habitat.

The moose was the staff of life of the northern woodland Indians, and it is still an important food source. One encampment of Tete-De-Boule Indians that I visited several summers ago had killed and eaten thirteen moose in the summer's two-month period. Some Alaskans count on putting a moose or two away each winter because they can't afford to buy beef or live too far out to get it. Moose hide makes exceptionally good leather, which is still used by the natives of the North.

The total population of the moose in North America is difficult to estimate. Alaska and Ontario estimate they have between 80,000 and 90,000 animals each. Other provinces haven't published estimates. In 1964, 10,136 moose were killed in the United States. Alaska's hunters took 8,770, Wyoming's 819, Montana's 480, Idaho's 59 and Utah's 8. In Alaska many moose were taken by homesteaders and natives that do not show up in the records.

The Alaskan Railway has quite a record for killing moose. Even though the snow is deep, the tracks between Anchorage and Fairbanks must be kept open. Many moose follow the tracks because it is easier walking there than floundering through the deep snows.

Sportsmen spend a great deal of money hunting moose. Guides usually get good fees per day per hunter and expect a bonus on a good head. Airplanes are not cheap, but more sportsmen are using them to get back into the roadless areas.

Trophy Records: The trophy moose are divided by the Boon and Crockett Club into three divisions: The Alaska-Yukon moose is the *A. a. gigas.* The Canada moose is both *A. a. americana* and *A. a. andersoni.* The Wyoming moose is *A. a. shirasi.*

The world's-record Alaska-Yukon moose totals 255 points and was killed by Kenneth Best in 1978 in McGrath, Alaska. It has a 77-inch spread. The right palm is 49 5/8 inches long and has 18 points; the left palm is 49 6/8 inches long and has 16 points. The rack weighed

63 1/2 pounds with only a small section of skull attached.

The world's-record Canadian moose with a total of 238 5/8 points, was killed by Silas Witherbee in 1914 near Bear Lake, Quebec. It has a spread of 66 5/8 inches. The right palm is 44 3/4 inches long and has 18 points; the left palm is 43 1/8 inches long with 19 points.

The world's-record Wyoming moose has a total of 205 1/2 points and was killed by John Oakley in 1952 at Green River Lake, Wyoming. It has a spread of 53 inches. The right palm is 38 3/4 inches long and has 15 points, and the left palm is 38 5/8 inches long and has 15 points.

In 1979 Helmut Becker, a German, shot a moose on Alaska's Tasnuna River with an antler spread of 81 1/4 inches. As this second edition went to press, this head had not yet been officially scored. But it should come close to the world's record.

Not all of the records are set by moose from the far North. A set of antlers that hang in the Heller Tavern at Wind Gap, Pennsylvania, was taken from a moose that was run down by Heller's dog around 1780. These antlers measure 78 1/2 inches across.

Table Fare: Moose meat has been favorably compared with beef. The meat is a little drier and darker.

Caribou

Rangifer tarandus

An adult caribou bull in autumn, resplendent in his winter coat and sporting his fully grown antlers, is a strikingly handsome animal. He is also, during this season of the rut, the most eccentric member of the deer family. He may rear up on his hind legs and dash off for no perceptible reason, swap ends in a twinkling and return to his starting place, and then graze quietly for a while. He is so blinded by the mating instinct that he has been known to mistake a pack horse for a female caribou, and when the rutting battles are under way, he fights with a frenzy that allows no time for either food or water.

A relative newcomer among the big-game animals of North America, the caribou crossed the Bering Land Bridge from Asia to Alaska sometime during the mid-Pleistocene period, less than a million years ago. In Europe it is known as the reindeer, and it bears the same scientific name. Caribou is the Indian name for the animal, adopted to differentiate it from its Old World cousin.

Description: The caribou of the woodlands, the largest of the five subspecies, stands about 50 to 60 inches high at the shoulders, is 80 to 90 inches in length, and weighs 400 to 600 pounds. The females are smaller in both size and weight.

The caribou differs from all other American deer in that both the male and the female have antlers. The female's are much smaller and more spindly than the male's. The males usually obtain their antlers earlier and lose them by December and January, while the females carry their head adornment until spring.

These caribou bulls are traveling amicably together, apart from females, calves and yearlings. During the rut, the bulls will become mortal enemies. (Photo by Len Rue Jr.)

The bull's antlers are bifurcated, palmated and many-tined, and may reach 5 feet in length. The main beams sweep backwards and upwards and then bend forward at the tips. The secondary, or bez, tines, branching just above the head, sweep almost straight forward. Usually one or both of the brow tines will be widely palmated vertically in front of the caribou's face and is known as a "shovel."

In the early spring the caribou's coat turns the color of faded canvas due to the bleaching effect of the nearly constant sunshine. In June large patches of this old hair begin to slough off and is replaced by a tidy summer coat that is mostly gray. As the caribou is changing its coat, it is also growing a new set of antlers. By late June the antlers have grown at least 3 feet long, nourished by blood coursing through the velvet.

As fall approaches, the velvet dries up and strips off in long strings. The summer coat is replaced hair by hair by the new winter coat, which has long, air-filled guard hairs lying over thick, curly underfur. When this new coat is completed, the caribou then assumes the appearance and coloration that people have come to associate with this animal.

The muzzle of the caribou is blunt and circled with short white hairs. The face is brown except for a white ring around the eyes and white on the insides of the short ears. The neck or cape of the Barren Ground caribou is a startling white but is darker in the mountain caribou and is further emphasized by a long-haired mane which runs under its neck from the chin to the chest. The main body color is a rich chocolate brown. The underside of the short tail, a small rump patch, a swath across the flanks and a circle above each hoof are white.

The hooves of the caribou, a special adaptation for the boggy tundra in their habitat, are large and almost perfectly round. In the summer the caribou has spongy pads in the center of its hooves. In the winter this pad shrinks and is covered with short hair for insulation. The hoof is then deeply concave and the outer rim becomes very hard to aid the animal in walking on ice. When the toes are spread apart, the tracks of the caribou are actually wider than they are long. The dewclaws are long, almost touching the ground, and are used more than they are by any other member of the deer family. By actual measurements of dried hooves, I have found that the caribou has as many square inches of hoof surface area as does a moose, yet it weighs only one-third to one-fourth as much.

The small ankle bones of the caribou click as the animal walks. The click is quite audible and sounds almost as if the joints were snapping into place. A large herd of caribou can be heard for quite a distance due to the clicking of these joints and tendons.

Caribou do not have the metatarsal gland that is so prominently seen on deer. They do have a conspicuous tarsal gland on the heel, or hock, of the foot. Interdigital glands are also found between the toes and these glands give off a yellow, waxy secretion. The lachrymal or preorbital gland on the caribou is large, close to the eye and covered with hair.

Being a ruminant, the caribou has the four-chambered stomach typical of this group. Mosses, lichens and browse gathered while feeding are stored in the paunch where the mass is softened by digestive juices. Later, as the caribou rests, small portions of this mass are regurgitated, rechewed, reswallowed and passed on for final digestion and assimilation.

The caribou has 34 teeth: 6 incisors, 4 canines, 12 premolars and 12 molars. It has no teeth in the front of the upper jaw. The premolars are sharply cusped while the molars are widely flattened to do the grinding necessary to masticate the cud.

Distribution: Caribou (*Rangifer tarandus*) are found in the coniferous forests and tundra of Canada and Alaska. The woodland caribou, which was formerly considered a distinct species (*R. t. caribou*), inhabits the forested regions from the vicinity of Great Slave Lake to northern Idaho and from the Alaska-Yukon border to Newfoundland. The Barren Ground caribou, also formerly thought to be a separate species (*R. t. granti* and *R. t. groenlandicus*), summers from northern Alaska and Canada as far north as there is land, and in winter mi-

Distribution of the caribou.

grates southward to the shelter of the northern edge of the coniferous forest, south as far as northern Manitoba and Saskatchewan.

Travel: Caribou are among the most migratory of all mammals. They drift along, day in, day out, pausing only long enough to feed and to rest. Caribou may migrate in almost any direction, some even working north in the winter. Many factors influence their direction of travel: weather conditions, wind, predators, food, insects and disturbance of the habitat by man. Of all the factors, food is the most important. Lichens, the caribou's main food, are a very slow-growing plant, sometimes requiring eight to ten years to replace the parts lost to grazing caribou, and when the lichens are exhausted the caribou have to move.

Many members of the Cervidae, such as deer and elk, are selective feeders and move along while eating. They eat a leaf here, a blade there and then move on to the next plant. Caribou do this too, but as they travel in much larger concentrations, they have to move farther to have a constant food supply.

In addition to grazing much of their food, the caribou chop up vegetation with their hooves. This may actually be beneficial because the lichens can stand such abuse while the dwarf birch and willow cannot. Every time shrubs are killed more space is made for lichens.

Usually the females migrate farther than the males. They are the first ones to move out in the spring and the last to return to the general area in the fall.

Habits: The caribou prefers to feed in daylight, and those that are located late in the evening will usually be found in the same spot at dawn unless they have been disturbed. On dark nights they refuse to move any more than they absolutely must.

Caribou feed in a leap-frog manner. When the lead caribou reach a suitable feeding spot, they begin to graze in a counterclockwise direction. The caribou behind them move on ahead and feed in the same fashion. When the leaders have completed their circle, they bypass the second group and start another circle of their own.

When their paunches are filled the caribou lie down to chew their cuds. The resting spots do not seem to be chosen with any particular design. If there is snow in the area, the animals usually rest on it as a deterrent to insects. Open hilltops or gravel ridges are also favored resting spots.

Caribou tend to spread out when traveling or feeding but bunch together when threatened, as if by so doing there is less chance for one animal to be selected by a predator. No record exists, however, of a herd making a concentrated effort for mutual protection, although this stratagem is often used by other animals. Among the caribou, each animal must fend for itself.

Even if the caribou are suspicious of an object or animal, they do not seem to be afraid of it once they have gotten several hundred yards away. Often I have alerted caribou which dashed away but then stopped and either resumed feeding or walked along parallel to me. If caribou are really frightened by something ahead of them, they tend to backtrack to the area that was safe when they passed through it.

In addition to lichens, caribou feed upon dwarf willow, blueberry, bearberry, horsetail, cranberry, Labrador tea and many types of fungus. As the frost begins snuffing out the growing vegetation, the caribou drop to lower levels to feed in boggy places where green growth is still available.

In the winter when snow is deep, caribou use their cloven hooves as snow shovels and scrape through as much as 2 feet of snow to feed. The motions of the caribou's foot are so fast that it appears as a blur to the human eye.

Only on rare occasions does the caribou use its antler shovel to move snow aside to search for food. Caribou cannot feed for long in an area that has been trampled and grazed. The disturbed snow freezes much harder than fresh snow, forcing the animals onward to new spots. Moreover, caribou bulls usually shed their antlers before the deep snow arrives and are then not equipped with shovels. Caribou have been seen chewing on fallen antlers in an effort to get the calcium and phosphorous their systems need.

Senses: The caribou depends on its sense of smell to confirm whatever its eyes have seen or its ears have heard. I spent quite a bit of time among the caribou in Alaska's McKinley Park, and on the relatively flat tundra areas the animals were quick to notice me, but they seldom ran straight away. Instead, they circled around until they could catch my scent before dashing off.

Curiosity is usually a sign of intelligence, but the curiosity of a caribou seems to be a sign of indecision or outright stupidity. When the caribou is alerted to danger it doesn't seem to know what to do. Often it dashes away in alarm, then suddenly turns and dashes back to its original location.

The caribou's ears are short, which is usually an indication that an animal's hearing is not too important to its survival. Caribou sleep so soundly that they have been approached and captured alive. Even the noise of a low-flying plane may not awaken them.

Communication: Caribou do not utter many sounds, though cows and calves sometimes emit a low, coughing grunt to keep in touch with each other. Most communication between these animals seems to be by actions and postures. Dr. William Pruitt did an extensive study of interpreting these actions, and using this knowledge I have often been able to interest caribou enough to hold them still.

Holding both my arms over my head and bobbing forward from the waist duplicated the silhouette of a threatening caribou about to attack. This would interest the bulls and some would respond in like manner. The regular threat attitude is made with the antlers held back and the head extended forward on the same plane as the back. Dr. Pruitt believes that the color pattern of the white cape is broken into different meanings by the raising or lowering of the black face. The white underparts of the tail are also used for signaling. When a caribou is alarmed it holds its head and tail erect, stiffens its body and extends one hind leg far out to the side.

Caribou bulls, when disturbed, often rear up on their hind feet and wheel to one side before dashing off. The pivoting on the hind feet spreads the toes and evidently causes some of the musk from the interdigital gland to be ejected. Even a man can smell this musk if he gets close enough. The scent apparently lingers for quite a while, for it will alarm other caribou which pass the spot afterwards.

Locomotion: The caribou displays a featherlight, floating quality in its movements. Trotting, the most common gait, shows the animal to the best advantage. When walking, the caribou holds its head lowered and seems rather dejected, but when it trots it carries its head horizontally and lays its massive antlers along its back. The head is held rigid to prevent the antlers from swaying, which would throw the animal off balance. Also the caribou lifts its legs higher than any trotting animal; the lower part of the leg comes up parallel to the ground. This is essential so that the caribou can clear low-growing vegetation such as dwarf birch and willow.

When galloping, the caribou attains a speed of well over 30 miles per hour. However, the animal tires quickly at this pace and in a short time its mouth is open wide and its tongue is lolling out. As soon as possible it abandons the gallop and drops into an easy, swinging, ground-eating trot which it can hold for long distances. The woodland caribou can jump higher than the Barren Ground caribou, which have been known to clear a 4 1/2 foot fence, perhaps because they encounter more obstacles in their habitat.

Caribou swim well, their splayed hooves making effective paddles. Their air-filled hair gives them great buoyancy, and they swim with nearly one-third of their body out of the water.

Breeding: Caribou are among the most gregarious of creatures, generally traveling in herds of 200 or less, although some herds have numbered as high as 50,000 individuals. Traveling in single file or in several parallel lines, they may be strung out for a few hundred feet to a mile or more, with the males remaining separate from the females, calves and yearlings.

All of this changes in the early fall. The bulls have been eating well all summer, and by September they are in excellent physical condition. Fat has been larded onto their bodies so that in places it may be 3 inches thick on the rump. There is even a network of fat around the internal organs. Only the bulls become fat; the females and yearlings seldom do. This accumulation of fat is not in preparation for the hard winter months ahead but in anticipation of the coming breeding season.

By September the antlers have reached their maximum growth and the velvet that had covered them has been stripped off. The summer coat has been replaced with the new, heavy winter coat. In the middle of the month the necks of the adult bulls begin to swell and the testicles, which dropped down in August, become greatly enlarged.

October finds the bulls eyeing each other with distrust. Soon each bull begins to gather a harem. In most instances a mature bull "captures" ten to twelve cows, which he considers his own and for which he will fight. At this time migration almost stops, the cows moving just enough to find new food.

Battles between the adult males are frequent. Dominant bulls drive lesser males away merely by making threatening gestures, but well-matched bulls often fight for their harems. When a bull is about to do battle he lowers his head and tucks his chin between his front feet, bringing his huge rack vertical so that all the tines can be brought into play. The bulls come together with a crash. From there on it develops into a mighty shoving contest with each bull trying to break through the other's guard to knife his opponent with his sharp tines. Caribou, like deer, sometimes lock antlers and eventually perish.

The peak of the breeding season occurs in the middle of October. In the four weeks devoted to breeding the bulls seldom get a mouthful of food. They snatch a quick drink of water and then go back to the fray. By the end of the breeding season the bulls are gaunt, weary and battered. Some of their antlers have been broken off, their eyes gouged out and their bodies marked with festering puncture wounds. In December or January their antlers drop off and the bulls return to normal. They feed hungrily, trying to rebuild their wasted bodies before the rigors of winter are upon them.

Birth and Young: The gestation period for the caribou is usually 228 days, with most of the calves being dropped between May 15 and June 15. The females do not breed until they are one and a half years old. Usually the Barren Ground caribou doe has only a single calf; the woodland caribou often has twins. The calf is unspotted, having a soft brown coat, and weighs about 10 to 20 pounds.

The calf is able to follow its mother in just a few hours and can easily outrun a man in a day or two. The calves weigh about 50 pounds by the end of August. Although they are still nursing, most of their nourishment comes from the vegetation that they pick up for themselves. The cows and the calves form a very close attachment, and if one is killed the surviving one will sometimes remain in the area several days searching for the other.

Life Span: The average life span for a caribou is ten to twelve years. Raising caribou in zoos has rarely been successful, but the National Zoological Park in Washington kept a Newfoundland caribou which lived to be nine years and eleven months old, a record for this animal in captivity. In the wild, under normal food conditions, some caribou may live longer, but when a caribou in the wild begins to slow down with age it is soon pulled down by predators.

Sign: No one can travel in caribou country without becoming aware immediately of the deeply worn, rutted paths made by these animals during their migrations. The valleys are laced with these tracks, and the hillsides appear to be splitting apart at the seams with the brown earth spilling out.

The tracks of the caribou are distinctive in that the hooves, when the toes are held together, form an almost perfect circle. On soft ground, when the cloven hooves are spread apart, the curvature of each hoof still shows plainly. The dewclaws, or cloots, of the caribou are longer than those of any other member of the Cervidae and always show on soft ground.

On soft ground the caribou's hoofs spread to give the animal better support. The curvature of each hoof is evident here, as are the marks made by the large dewclaws. Dirt pulled forward by the hoofs indicates direction of travel.

The scat of the caribou is of an elongated bell shape, with one end being tapered and the other end blunt or concave.

In the winter, when the weather is extremely cold, the frozen vapor of the caribous' breath rising above the herd can be seen before the animals themselves come into view.

Enemies: The wolf is the main predator that the caribou faces, but it is also a benefactor. Recent studies have shown that the wolf in feeding on the old, young, sick or crippled caribou actually strengthens the herd by weeding out the misfits, those less well-adapted to their environment. A healthy wolf cannot catch a healthy caribou, only the caribou that falls behind the herd. And for whatever reason those caribou fall behind, the wolves prevent their inferior qualities from being passed on.

Caribou are not afraid of wolves. In Alaska I watched two prime bulls of four to five years of age tease a wolf for about two hours one afternoon. The wolf would lie down in the shade of a bush, and the caribou would walk towards the wolf until they were about 100 feet away. The wolf would attack, but the caribou would outrun it. When the wolf stopped running, the caribou would circle back and tease it again. The wolf could not catch the caribou—and they both knew it.

The bears, both black and grizzly, the lynx and the wolverine all take a caribou when they get the chance, even though most of the time they must content themselves with catching a newborn calf.

Caribou seem to be immune to most diseases and seldom infested with ectoparasites, but they are tyrannized by bloodsucking mosquitoes and flies of various types. In late June and July, during the day the black flies harass the caribou. Mosquitoes are active around the clock, the female sucking the caribou's blood. The nostril fly lays its living larvae in the nostrils of the caribou, which snuff and blow their noses trying to discourage the fly or close their nostrils and hold their noses against the ground. Some paw at their nostrils with their hind feet. The larvae feed upon the mucus of the nasal passages, remaining in the nasal and laryngeal regions until the following spring when they have become over an inch long. Then they drop to the ground and complete their life cycle. The warble fly lays its eggs on the hair along the backs and legs of the caribou. When this is taking place the caribou can be seen dashing about in a vain effort to escape the large, fuzzy adult fly.

The caribou of the woodlands suffer more from these annoying insects than do the caribou of the Barrens. On the Barrens there is often a strong wind that keeps the insects under cover, and there are large areas of snow that are free of these pests. The range of the woodland caribou is farther south, where there is no snow in summer and the forests break the strength of the wind.

Human Relations: The caribou is the staff of life for many northern Indians and Eskimos. Their entire existence depends upon these animals. When the caribou are plentiful and appear when and where they should, these people live well on them. The caribou are killed by the thousands to provide meat for the people and for their dogs. The hides are used for clothing and in some cases are still used for tentage. Almost every part of the animal can be used, even the food in its stomach. Although man cannot eat fresh lichens and mosses, he can eat them after they have been partially digested in the caribou's stomach. The contents of the caribou's paunch are known as "nerrock" and are used as a salad.

When the caribou fail to make their appearance, having shifted their migration routes, starvation is the lot of the natives. Today when such a disaster strikes, help can be brought in from the outside world. In former days it simply meant that many people weakened and died.

Caribou have never been successfully domesticated like European reindeer. In an effort to prevent the recurrence of this periodic starvation among the natives, the United States government imported reindeer. The first shipment of ten reindeer came from Siberia in 1891. Between 1892 and 1902, the government imported 1,270 more reindeer. Lapp herders from Finland were brought in to tend the animals and to instruct the Eskimos in the work. The program met with great success from the start and by the 1930s there were an estimated 600,000 reindeer. By 1949 the herds were in trouble and down to about 28,000 head. The Eskimos resisted changing their way of life, from being hunters to being drovers. Overgrazing ruined much of the area, not only for the reindeer but also for the native caribou.

Reindeer are considerably smaller than caribou and the interbreeding between the species has worked to the detriment of the caribou. Not only are the reindeer themselves detrimental to the caribou, but the herding of reindeer also means that man must make his home nearby. This causes further destruction of the caribou's habitat. The threat of these conditions became so grave that the

American Society of Mammalogists passed a resolution in 1950 to curb the importation of reindeer to areas where caribou were found.

Trophy Records: The Boone and Crockett Club recognizes four different classifications for the caribou.

The world's-record mountain caribou was killed in 1976 by Garry Beaubien on the Turnagain River, British Columbia. It scored 452 points. The right beam is 43 1/8 inches long and has 22 points. The left beam is 42 2/8 inches long and has 19 points. The greatest inside spread is 30 3/8 inches.

The world's-record woodland caribou was killed in Newfoundland prior to 1910. It scored a total of 419 5/8 points. The right beam is 50 1/8 inches long and has 19

This barren ground caribou is possibly of record-book class. (Photo by Tim Lewis Rue.)

points. The left beam is 47 3/8 inches long and has 18 points. The greatest inside spread between the beams is 43 2/8 inches.

The world's-record Quebec-Labrador caribou was taken by Zack Elbow in 1931, at Nain, Labrador. This head scored a total of 474 6/8 points. The right beam is 60 4/8 inches long and has 22 points. The left beam is 61 1/8 inches long and has 30 points. The greatest inside spread between the beams is 58 2/8 inches.

The world's record Barren Ground caribou was taken by Ray Loesche in 1967 at Ugashik Lake, Alaska. This head scored 463 6/8 points. The right beam is 51 2/8 inches long and has 22 points. The left beam is 51 5/8 inches long and has 23 points. The greatest inside spread is 46 7/8 inches.

Table Fare: More people probably depend upon caribou for food than on any other species of our antlered game. It is considered an excellent meat.

PRONGHORN

Family Antilocapridae

PRONGHORN

Pronghorn

Antilocapra americana

The pronghorn is often called an antelope, but it is not related to any members of that group. It is a unique animal, wholly American, and the sole representative of an unusual family. The first antilocaprines, known from fossils, date back some 20 million years on this continent. Some were as small as a jack rabbit, others larger than the modern pronghorn, but they all had one thing in common: they shed their horns each year just as the deer shed their antlers.

One of the fastest animals in the world, the pronghorn offers exciting hunting on the western plains. It lives in a region almost devoid of cover and depends on its keen eyesight and speed to avoid enemies. Stalking a pronghorn is a ticklish business that requires great stealth, and hitting one on the run is a challenge to any marksman.

Description: In body conformation and coloration the pronghorn resembles a small deer. When full grown, a buck stands about 35 to 41 inches high at the shoulder, is 4 to 5 feet in total length, and weighs from 100 to 140 pounds. A doe weighs about 20 pounds less.

Both sexes are marked alike except that the buck has a broad black band extending below the eyes to the nose and a black neck patch. The overall color is a rich reddish-tan on the upper half of the body and the outside of the legs. The underparts, the inside of the legs and a patch on the rump are bright white. Two wide, dark-brown bands cross the white throat. Jet-black horns complete the picture.

Pronghorn does and bucks characteristically graze together.

The difference between a horn and an antler is that a horn is keratin and grows over a bony core that contains the necessary blood vessels needed to foster growth, while an antler is solid bone and is nourished by a network of blood vessels on the outside in a skin covering called velvet. A horn continues to grow steadily throughout the life of the animal; a new antler is grown and shed each year. Horns are never branched; antlers usually are. The pronghorn is the only exception to this rule: it has deciduous forked horns composed of a shell of fused hair which encases the bony core. Every year a new horny sheath begins to develop underneath the old sheath. This starts to grow at the upper tip of the permanent inner bony core, which is bladelike and unbranched. As this sheath-tip grows inside, the old hornsheath loosens and eventually falls off. The new hornsheath then grows rapidly downward towards the top of the skull. In the males and in some females this process is complicated by the production of a small, forward-pointing prong.

This development usually takes four months and is completed early in the year, and by July the horns measure from 12 to 20 inches in length. The female's horns are ordinarily only about 3 to 4 inches in length and do not have the prong. However, does with trophy-sized horns have been noted.

Although the average pronghorn has the prong jutting forward and the tip of the main tine hooking sharply backwards, there are enough variations to warrant mention. On some the main tines branch inward till the tips almost touch. On others the tips hook forward and occasionally the main horn grows forward straight out from the head or even sharply downward past the face. These variations are usually due to injury of some sort whereby the main horn core has been broken or bent.

The hair of a pronghorn is very dense and stiff like the bristles on a scrub brush. It is cellular and filled with air, providing exceptionally good insulation. As the pronghorn favors the open wind-swept ranges it has need for this warm protection. Whereas most mammals have fine underfur beneath their guard hairs, the pronghorn has very little and that is so fine it can hardly be seen.

The hairs on the pronghorn's rump patch are almost double the length of its regular hair, and each hair is controlled by an individual muscle so that the hair may be made to lie flat or erected or flared out. When the

Distribution of the pronghorn.

pronghorn is alarmed, this rosette of white hair almost doubles its visible area and, catching the sun's rays, sends a heliographic warning to every pronghorn in sight.

Unlike members of the deer family which have a set of dewclaws, or an extra first and fourth toe on each foot, the pronghorn lacks them and has only the main middle pair of toes, the dewclaws having been lost through evolution.

Distribution: In prehistoric times pronghorns ranged as far east as Illinois. By the time of the coming of the white man, the pronghorns existed only west of the Mississippi River. They are found today from southern Saskatchewan south along the eastern edge of the high plains to Mexico, and as far west as south-central California, southeastern Oregon, and south-central Washington.

Travel: The pronghorn does not migrate in the true sense of an orderly, predestined trek. Conditions cause the pronghorns to drift from one area to another. Water is probably one of the most important factors. Availability of good food, such as sagebrush, saltbush, rabbitbrush, western juniper and bitterbrush, is very important. Deep snow is another hazard which forces the pronghorn to move to the windswept slopes where forage is uncovered. As long as there is no food shortage, the pronghorn easily bears extreme cold. Thus pronghorns sometimes move north in the winter, and instead of seeking out the valleys and draws, climb to the top of Hart Mountain, Oregon, where the wind has cleared large areas of snow.

Habits: Two characteristics that typify the pronghorn are nervousness and curiosity. Its nervousness stems from the fact that the pronghorn inhabits an area where it can almost always be seen and where only its awareness and speed can save its life. The pronghorn sleeps in short snatches. It dozes, then jerks its head up and takes a quick glance at the surrounding countryside. Then it gathers a few more moments of sleep. The slightest noise or disturbance is enough to send an entire herd galloping over the far horizon. Even when nothing real disturbs them, the pronghorns often bolt from imaginary danger. One skittish pronghorn will keep the herd on the move because they always rely on danger signals from one another. Most wild creatures are curious, but the pronghorn is more so than the rest. In addition to being curious about sightings, the pronghorns also tend to investigate any new sounds.

Pronghorns may be active at any time of the day or night. They do not seem to have any set periods of activity, although they may frequent water holes with some degree of regularity.

Senses: The pronghorn probably has the keenest vision of any American mammal, with the possible exception of the mountain sheep and the mountain goat. All three species live in exposed areas where to survive they must locate danger before it gets close. Their vision is said to be comparable to eight-power binoculars. The pronghorn's eyes protrude from its skull and have such a wide angle of vision that the animal can see backward as well as forward. Its vision is so keen it can notice a small object in motion four miles away. Its sense of smell ranks next in importance. The pronghorn attempts to circle something it cannot define by sight so its nose may verify what its eyes have detected. Its hearing is apparently good, but this sense is not as important as its sense of sight and smell.

Communication: Young pronghorn kids make a high-pitched quivering bleat that carries well, and the adults respond from as far as 500 yards. The adult doe makes a lower-pitched blatting noise. Both sexes, when surprised or angered, snort by blowing forcefully through their nose.

The pronghorn's most conspicuous form of communication is its use of its white rump patch to flash signals. It does not appear to send any set message, but the flashes can be seen for miles and alert other pronghorns.

Locomotion: Pronghorns are designed for speed. Although their legs look as thin as pipestems, the bones are amazingly strong. By actual pressure tests they proved stronger than the bones of a cow's legs, even though the latter has eight to ten times the weight to

With rump patch flared in alarm, this buck is about to bolt away, capable of attaining a speed of 70 mph.

support. It took 45,300 pounds to a square inch to crush the bone of the pronghorn's leg.

The pronghorn may well be the fastest land runner on earth. It is true that the trained hunting cheetah of India and Africa can overtake the pronghorn in a short chase, but even the cheetah falls behind if its first attack fails. The usual speed for a pronghorn is 40 to 50 miles per hour, and there are substantiated records of 60 to 65 and one of 70 miles per hour. The pronghorn can maintain speeds of 40 and 50 miles per hour for an extended period of time.

While the pronghorn has great speed it does not have the ability to jump vertical heights, though records of 27 feet for horizontal jumps are not uncommon. Living on the flat prairie lands, where there is just sufficient moisture to sustain grasses but not trees, the pronghorn seldom encountered vertical obstacles and so this ability was never developed. A pronghorn will jump through a barbed wire fence but seldom over it.

The pronghorn takes great pride in its speed, and it will often race horses, automobiles or trains. Years ago, before our mechanical monsters became so perfected, the pronghorn would run alongside and then, like a porpoise racing a ship, put on a burst of speed and cross over in front of the speeding vehicle.

When the pronghorn runs, it keeps its mouth wide open, its tongue lolling out, and gulps large draughts of air. Its large lungs and oversized heart allow it to run at high speeds without unduly taxing its circulatory system.

Although pronghorns avoid marshy or muddy ground, they do not hesitate to take to the water and swim. There are many records of their swimming such large rivers as the Missouri.

Breeding: With the approach of the breeding season in September and October, the pronghorn buck gets a chance to use his horns. At this time the older males start to gather together a harem of up to fifteen does, and battles between the rival males are often fierce and bloody. The battle is a pushing, shoving, slashing type of fight, with the bucks using the prongs on their horns like knife guards. The victor drives the vanquished from the area, if he does not kill him, and proceeds to service the does.

Birth and Young: The normal gestation period is 258 days (8 2/3 months), and the young are born when the long, warm days of May and June have blanketed the prairies with wild flowers and tasty grasses.

The doe does not seem to select a special place for a nursery. At the moment of birth, she merely separates from the main band and goes off several hundred feet to be by herself. If this is the first birth for a young doe, there will usually be just one kid. Twins will be the rule thereafter, with a rare possibility of triplets. The doe will give birth to one kid, then move several hundred feet away to give birth to the second. This separation is done for protection. The kids are practically odorless at birth, but if a predator should stumble upon one kid there is a good chance that its twin will go undetected.

The newborn kids weigh between 5 and 6 pounds. Unlike the spotted young of the deer family, the baby pronghorns are a pale, solid-dun color. All of the hooved animals' babies appear to be born with oversized legs, ears and eyes, and the pronghorn is no exception.

After the doe has hastened the drying of her young by licking their coats, she moves off some distance where she can watch over them without attracting danger.

The upbringing of the pronghorn is very simple. During the first week the doe visits her kids very discreetly, nurses them and then withdraws. After feeding, the little ones sink back to the ground where their camouflage coloration effectively shields them from sight. By the end of their first week the little ones are fleet enough to follow the mother, and the family then rejoins the main band. Also at this time, the young start to feed upon various types of vegetation.

Enemies: It is only while the young are newborn that the pronghorn has any natural enemies. Bears, coyotes, bobcats and sometimes eagles feed upon the young if they discover them. An adult pronghorn, in good health, can outrun all predators, and many coyotes will forsake a meal of young pronghorns rather than face the slashing hooves of an infuriated mother. On rare occasions, coyotes have been known to team up, but only by running in relays can they bring a pronghorn down. Although a baby pronghorn can walk about on its first day and run awkwardly on the second day, it takes four days before it can outrun a man.

The pronghorn's most deadly enemies cannot be outrun and in many cases they can't even be seen. These are parasites such as lice and ticks, and diseases such as lumpy jaw and pneumonia.

Life Span: According to all available records and experiments, the pronghorn is short-lived. It reaches maturity at four to five years and lives to be about eight years old.

Sign: It is often quite difficult to identify the tracks of the pronghorn. Its front feet measure about 3 1/4 inches long while the hind feet measure about 2 3/4 inches long. When such tracks are encountered on the open prairie, they are usually those of the pronghorn. However, when the pronghorn is found on lightly wooded mountainsides and on the flattops, it shares its range with the mule deer and the mountain sheep, and both of these mammals leave tracks similar to the pronghorn's. Even their droppings are similar. When the pronghorn is feeding upon brush, its droppings are pelletlike and measure about three quarters of an inch long. When it is feeding upon foliage and grasses, the droppings are a segmented mass. The pronghorn frequently scrapes the earth with its hooves and then urinates on the cleared spot.

Human Relations: Owing to terrific hunting pressure, erection of barbed-wire drift fences and the scalping of the prairie by the farmer's plow, the once huge herds of pronghorns were reduced by 1908 to a mere remnant of less than 20,000 individuals. Since then, as a result of closed hunting seasons, and the pronghorn's own adaptability to modern range conditions, their numbers have steadily increased. Today there are an estimated 400,000 pronghorns, and they are found in all the western states except those bordering on the Mississippi River.

The range of the pronghorn is expanding, and new introductions are being made. For the past two years, Kansas has been importing pronghorns from Wyoming in an effort to re-establish the species. Even Florida is attempting to propagate pronghorns. Forty pronghorns from Colorado have been released on Florida's Kissimmee prairie.

In March of 1966 the government ruled that ranchers who graze cattle on public lands could not put up antelope-proof fences. This has been of great help because any species does its best when there is no restriction placed upon its movements. The future does look good for the pronghorn.

Trophy Records: The finest pronghorn head, according to the records, was taken by Edwin Wetzler in Yavapai County, Arizona, in 1975. It scored 93 overall. The right horn is 18 1/8 inches long and has a basal circumference of 7 2/8 inches, and a prong of 7 6/8 inches. The left horn is 18 2/8 inches long and has a basal circumference of 7 inches on the left horn and a prong of 7 2/8 inches.

Table Fare: In the early days the pronghorn was common table fare in the western states. Many commercial hunters kept the markets supplied. At one time the pronghorns sold for as little as 25 cents for three carcasses. Today's hunter not only gets a top-notch trophy but some very good meat when he bags his pronghorn.

CATTLE, SHEEP AND GOATS

Family Bovidae

BISON
BIGHORN SHEEP
DALL SHEEP
MOUNTAIN GOAT

Bison

Bison bison

Hunted almost to extinction for its hide and meat during frontier days, the bison is now found mainly on government preserves and private ranches. This ponderous, slow-witted beast is ranked low as a game animal, but hunters who want to recapture a piece of the Old West can purchase special permits and add it to their trophy collection. Better known as the buffalo, it is unrelated to any of the true buffalo of Asia and Africa but is believed to be descended from wild cattle that crossed the land bridge from Siberia to Alaska during the Pleistocene period.

Description: A large bull bison may stand 6 feet high at the shoulder and measure 11 1/2 feet in length. Many weigh almost a ton, and there are records of some that went nearly 3,000 pounds. The cows are smaller and slimmer, weighing about 800 to 900 pounds.

There is little variation in color among bison; the shadings are from dark brown to black. In the spring the winter hair, which is subsequently shed, may be bleached to a dark tan. Albinism occurs infrequently. The Indians proclaimed such an animal sacred, and the brave who secured the white hide was considered fortunate. In the Harvard Museum of Comparative Zoology is the mounted head of a pied, or white-faced, bison. The animal was black with the exception of a pure white area between its horns and down its face to the nose.

The bison's humped back is further accentuated by the long hair that covers its head, neck, shoulders and

This bison bull is caked with mud from rolling in a wallow. To escape swarming insects, bison dig up earth and roll in the dust or, when it rains, in the more protective mud.

front legs. In the winter this hair attains a length of 8 inches or more. Even in the summer it is about 4 inches long. The bison also has a long beard hanging beneath its chin. The hair on the rear portion of the body is about 4 inches long in the winter and so short in the summer as to appear nonexistent. This exposed flank and rump is a favorite target of flies and other blood-sucking insects, which the bison tries to dispel by constantly switching its short, tufted tail. Because of the long hair protecting its foreparts, the bison will face into a storm instead of away from it as other animals do.

The bison has two thick, short, sharply upturned horns which grow continuously throughout its lifetime.

Being a ruminant, the bison has no teeth in the front of the upper jaw. It pulls out grass with its tongue or snips it off with the lower incisors working against the upper mouth pad. The 32 teeth are classified as 8 incisors, 12 premolars and 12 molars. It stores gathered herbage in the rumen, the first part of the four-chambered stomach. When the bison lies down to rest it also chews its cud, on only one side of the mouth at a time.

There are four toes on each foot. The third and fourth toes are well developed: the first and the fifth toes have regressed into dewclaws which do not come in contact with the earth unless the bison walks along a soft river's edge.

Distribution: When white men arrived in North America the bison's range covered one-third of the entire land mass. It was found in the eastern states from New York south to Florida, west to the Rocky Mountains and north to central Alaska. In several places the bison had

Distribution of the bison.

penetrated the Rockies and was found in northeastern California, eastern Oregon and southeastern Washington. The bison east of the Mississippi River did not usually congregate in the huge herds that were common on the prairies. Still, they were numerous enough to have been an important food item to the woodland Indians as well as to those who dwelt on the plains.

The total number of bison was almost beyond comprehension. It has been reliably stated that at no time in any other place did such a multitude of a single species ever congregate. Herds that covered 50 by 20 miles, containing about 4 million animals, were not uncommon.

Ernest Thompson Seton's calculations placed the total population at better than 60 million animals. Most experts today agree that this estimate is reliable. Today there are no wild, free-roaming bison in the United States. All that remain of these vast hordes are found in our national parks, wildlife refuges or on private ranches.

Bison are found in Yellowstone and Wind Cave National Parks, the National Bison Range in Montana and the Wichita Wildlife Refuge in Oklahoma. Recently bison have been released and are doing well at Big Delta, Alaska. There are some in the Wood Buffalo Park in northern Alberta.

Travel: The bison were gregarious animals that were forced to migrate because of their herding instinct. In some regions they had regular routes, while in other sections they seemed to wander at will. The migrations were not extensive enough for the bison to escape the rigors of winter but were shifts from a summer range to a winter range determined by the availability of food in a particular season. Seton records that the longest migrations were about 400 miles. In traveling from one place to another the bison always sought the easiest grades to circumvent obstacles, and the trails they left formed the basis for the routes of most of our modern highways and railroads.

When the bison were making the seasonal shifts they traveled in huge herds. Once they reached the summer range, the herds broke down into family groups and scattered. Even so, because of their great numbers, the bison continuously, although slowly, moved day by day.

Habits: The herding instinct of the bison undoubtedly gave it the greatest protection from its enemies, especially the wolves which followed the herds in the hope of killing a young or disabled bison, or of being able to feast on one that had been killed accidently or had died a natural death. Against the wolves the bison did well so long as they remained in herds. It was when they scattered that the wolves were able to pull them down.

On the other hand, the herding instinct could be self-destructive. When a herd was frightened and started to stampede, it was hard to stop. Even if the lead bison saw danger and tried to avoid it, they were pressed on by those behind them which blindly followed the leaders. The Indians, before they acquired horses, used to drive the bison over a cliff, killing thousands of the animals at one time. There are also records of numerous bison perishing in boggy ground, the first ones miring down and the rest passing over them in waves. Sometimes the bison crossed rivers or lakes on the ice, and their combined weight caused them to break through and drown. Although the bison was a strong swimmer there were times when herd action forced the leaders into water too swift to be negotiated, again with a heavy loss of life.

Bison were exceptionally hardy and could withstand extremes of heat, cold and drought much better than domesticated stock. Living on the treeless prairies, they seldom were able to escape the sun's rays. Their periods of greatest activity occurred in the early morning and late afternoon. Midday was their time for resting, chewing their cuds and wallowing.

In order to get some relief from the clouds of pestiferous insects, bison created wallows or dust baths. They loosened the earth with their hoofs, and lay down and kicked the dirt over their bodies. Once the sod had been stripped off, such wallows were used by succeeding bison until large saucerlike depressions were formed. Some of these wallows were 50 feet across and 2 feet deep. The dry dust filtering down through the bison's hair choked the insects and reduced their activity. Sometimes rain filled the wallows or the bison urinated there and when they rolled in the mud their bodies became plastered with it, providing the best protection. Cowbirds and magpies often walked on the backs of bison probing for insects among the hair.

The bison is a grazing animal that favors the various grasses—gramagrass, dropseed grass, tumbleweed, buffalo grass, bluestem, hilaria and jointfir. In the winter they paw through the snow with their huge hooves or sweep the snow aside with their heads to expose the vegetation.

Although water was a prime requirement of the bison, they could go three to four days without drinking. In the winter snow would satisfy their thirst.

Senses: None of the senses of the bison is exceptionally well-developed. Owing to its size, the animal was never severely threatened by predators and it always traveled in the safety of large herds. Its sense of smell is the most highly developed, followed by hearing. Its eyesight is considered poor.

Communication: Bison sound like large, deep-voiced cattle, which is precisely what they are. The adults bellow and the young ones bawl. The bulls, particularly during the breeding season, give vent to a deep roar. Bison paw the ground when nervous, and the vibrations undoubtedly alert others of the herd nearby.

Locomotion: The bison attains a speed of about 5 miles per hour while walking and can keep this pace for hours. When pushed, the bison trots or quickly breaks into a lumbering gallop in which all four feet leave the ground together. With its huge heart and lungs, it can run for extended periods of time, at a top speed of between 32 and 35 miles per hour.

When charging, a bison raises its tail, lowers its head slightly and, unlike a domestic bull, keeps its eye on its enemy. Despite its huge size, it is agile enough to swerve and turn in pursuit.

Bison swim well and are buoyant enough to keep their heads, humps and tails above the water.

Breeding: The breeding season occurs in July and August. The bulls, which ordinarily remain separate from the cows within a herd, now begin trying to gather a harem. Bellowing loudly, they paw the ground, throw dust over themselves, raise their tails and challenge their rivals to a fight.

When two bulls fight, they walk to within 20 or 30 feet of each other, lower their heads, raise their tails and charge—colliding with a mighty crash. They bear the brunt of the impact on their foreheads rather than on their horns, but the initial blow does not seem to harm them. They shake their heads, back off and collide again, continuing until one gives up.

Each victorious bull gathers a harem of ten to seventy

cows and their offspring. These cows he considers his private property, and he is ready to fight all comers.

The female comes into heat for about a twenty-four-hour period. During this time the bull serves her as many times as possible. If a female should miss being impregnated during her first oestrous cycle, she will come into heat again twenty-eight days later.

Birth and Young: The gestation period for the bison varies from 270 to 285 days, with most young being born in the month of May. The cows usually give birth to single calves, although occasionally there may be twins.

At the time of birth, the cow may go off a short distance from the herd to be by herself. The newborn calf is a bright russet-red; there are no spots. The calf is able to walk within a matter of hours, and within a day or two the cow and her calf will rejoin the herd.

A bison cow nurses her calf in the herd. Young bison lack the shoulder hump so prominent in older animals. The hump starts to develop when the calf is about two months.

The newborn calf bears no evidence of the hump that later will be so prominent. This starts to develop in about two months. At the same time, the little black knobs of the future horns become noticeable.

It is only during their early youth that bison seem to get any fun out of life. The calves run, jump and butt each other, stopping now and then to rest, nurse or sample the vegetation. Although some of the calves may continue to nurse through the winter, most of them are weaned by late summer.

Bison become mature at about five years of age, although they continue to grow both larger and heavier as they age. The cows usually breed when they are three years old, some as early as two, and every year thereafter.

Life Span: The average life span of the bison is about twenty-five years, and many that have been kept in zoos have reached that age. Bison living on the open range have far surpassed that, one ear-tagged cow living to be over forty years of age. Even at that advanced age the cow was healthy and still bearing young.

Sign: The most commonly seen sign of bison is a large, soft mass of dung which is indistinguishable from that of cattle. Both creatures are about the same size and feed upon the same type of vegetation. In the days of the prairie schooner this dung, known as buffalo chips, was an important source of fuel. Baked by the hot sun, the dung soon dried and when burned gave off a hot, almost smokeless flame.

The trails leading from one part of a buffalo range to another are well-defined and cannot be overlooked, and the large, saucerlike depression of the bison's wallow is another sure sign of the species which cannot be confused with anything else.

Tracks of the bison may be confused with those of range cattle, but the bison's are usually larger and rounder, and the toes are splayed a little wider at the tips.

Enemies: Natural hazards to the bison were prairie fires, boggy ground, flooded rivers, weak ice and deep crusted snows that prevented them from moving.

Of the wild predators, the lobo wolf ranked first. After the bison had been slaughtered, these huge wolves turned their attention to cattle. Their depredations became so heavy that the United States government waged an all-out war of extermination which was successfully completed about 1932. The huge plains grizzly bear, which roamed the bison's range in search of its favorite meat, has also been wiped out. As big and strong as the bison were, they were no match for this bear. Coyotes and mountain lions took an occasional calf, but an adult was more than they could handle. Most of the coyotes scavenged on the remains of bison left by the wolves.

Although plagued by multitudes of flies throughout the summer, the bison do not seem to be affected by the nose flies and warbles that torment so many of the deer family. They also seem to be relatively free of internal parasites and disease.

Human Relations: From an estimated 60 million animals in 1492, the bison were reduced by 1891 to a low of 541 individuals in the United States and 250 wood bison in Canada. Only the unstinting efforts of a handful of dedicated conservationists and outdoorsmen saved the bison. Ranchers such as Michel Pablo of Montana, Colonel Charles Goodnight of Texas and C. J. Jones of Wyoming nursed and protected on their ranches the few bison that became the nucleus of our present herds. Dr. William Hornaday, president of the New York Zoological Society, and Martin Garretson, secretary of the American Bison Society, were in the forefront of those who finally awoke the nation to the fact that the bison were about to pass from the scene.

The bison was the staff of life of the Plains Indians. Its meat provided food; its skin, clothing and covering for their lodges; its horns, ornaments and spoons; its sinews, thread to sew the hides together; its bones, awls, arrow points and other tools and weapons; and its dung, fuel. Whatever the Indians needed, the bison provided. But the Indians did not make a dent in the huge herds. The white man was the bison's nemesis.

At first the bison was shot for food, then for sport and then for business. The railroad provided the hide-hunters with a way to get their product to the eastern markets. Hide-hunting became big business with an annual kill of about 2,500,000 animals a year for the years of 1870 to 1875. By late 1873, most of the southern herd had been wiped out and the hunters concentrated on the northern herd.

The northern herd lasted for a longer period of time because hostile Indians prevented the hide-hunters from slaughtering the animals. The ranchers that were establishing themselves in the prairie regions wanted to get rid of the bison because every bison ate as much grass as three head of cattle, and the ranchers wanted the grass for their cattle.

The United States government at that time favored slaughtering the remaining bison as a means of depriving the Indians of their natural food supply. When the bison were wiped out the Indians could not hold out and were

Old bison bulls like this one sometimes stand 6 feet at the shoulder, measure 11 1/2 feet long, and weigh nearly 3,000 pounds.

finally beaten and forced onto reservations. By 1886 the northern herd had also been wiped out.

After the hide-hunters and the tongue-hunters had completed their carnage, the plains were white with the bleached bones of slaughtered bison. These bones spurred on a new business, and millions of dollars' worth were gathered and shipped East where they were ground into fertilizer. The Santa Fe Railroad shipped 10,793,350 pounds of bones from 1872 to 1874. One bone company, shipping on the Great Northern Railway, figured that they sent 5,950,000 bison skeletons between 1884 and 1891.

Trophy Records: The world's-record bison was killed in 1925 by S. Woodring in Yellowstone National Park. It scored a total of 136 4/8 points. The right horn is 21 2/8 inches long and 16 inches in circumference at the base. The left horn is 23 2/8 inches long and is 15 inches at the base. The greatest spread between the horns is 35 3/8 inches.

The second-place head was killed by Samuel Israel in 1961, in the Northwest Territories. This head has scored 136 2/8 points. The right horn is 19 inches long and 18 4/8 inches in circumference at the base while the left horn is 18 6/8 inches long and 18 4/8 inches at the base. The maximum spread of the horns is 30 1/8 inches.

Table Fare: The many people who used the bison for food could have attested to the good flavor of the meat. The tongue of the bison was supposed to be a gourmet's delight, while the hump meat was also a favored portion. Even today, bison meat from animals killed on private ranches can be obtained in many restaurants.

Bighorn Sheep

Ovis canadensis

The bighorn sheep of North America live in regions so remote and inaccessible that relatively few hunters ever get a chance at them. A sheep hunt means packing into the high country on horseback, then climbing the rugged mountains on foot to locate the game. But those who have done it, and have taken a good ram, call it the best hunting in the world. A bighorn, with its heavy, broomed horns, is a beautiful trophy; and a sheep mountain is a beautiful place.

Descended from the wild sheep of Asia, the bighorns came across the Bering Land Bridge as late as 500,000 years ago. They found good feed and a comfortable climate in Alaska, but the glaciers drove them south and they followed the Rockies as far as Mexico. As the ice receded, some of the sheep returned north, others remained behind, and today two varieties of bighorn are found on the continent: the Rocky Mountain bighorn of the northern regions and the desert bighorn of the Southwest and Mexico.

Description: The bighorn has a chunky, heavily muscled, beautifully proportioned body set on strong, stout legs. A sturdy neck supports the head and the splendid heavy horns.

A bighorn ram stands from 38 to 42 inches at the shoulder, measures between 60 and 70 inches in length and weighs between 200 and 300 pounds or more. The ewes are at least one-fourth smaller in size.

The horns of the bighorn sheep are more massive than those of the Dall. The horns are a dark brown and have

Photos on these two pages show characteristic structural differences between the desert bighorn ram (above) and the Rocky Mountain bighorn (next page). Desert bighorns tend to be of lighter build for equal age. Thus, from a distance their horns sometimes appear to be larger than they are. Note that the right-most ram on the next page has broomed his right horn to promote good peripheral vision. (Photo on next page by Len Rue Jr.)

prominent growth rings. The winter rings are close together, forming definite black bands by which the sheep's
age can be accurately determined. A large ram's horns
will make more than a complete circle, usually passing
close to the face, and have been known to weigh more
than 30 pounds. The thickness of the horns and their
proximity to the face often obscures the ram's side vision.
One of the reasons these horns are so frequently

Three Rocky Mountain bighorn ewes, a ram and a reclining lamb have descended to a 3,000-foot southern slope, warmed by winter's sun.

"broomed," or broken at the tips, is that the rams apparently attempt to wear them away to increase their peripheral vision. The ewes have long, slender horns that curve but do not form more than a quarter circle.

The sheep's eyes are an amber-yellow with black centers. Their vision is remarkable and is comparable to a man's aided by eight-power binoculars. Beneath each eye is a gland that gives off a waxy, odorous secretion which the sheep evidently use in communicating with each other. The bighorn's ears are small but alert.

The bighorn sheep have long, cellular, air-filled hair rather than wool. The domestic sheep's wool is actually an undercoat, developed from some of the Asiatic wild sheep through centuries of selective breeding by man. The hair of the bighorn provides excellent insulation and enables the sheep to withstand the rigors of cold mountain air.

The body color of the bighorns varies from a dark, rich brown in the northern mountain specimens to a pale buff in the desert specimens. This type of coloring is common with most species of mammals that live under similarly diverse conditions. Those living in the open deserts are almost always the lightest in color because their coats reflect more light and heat and keep them cooler. The bighorns have a white muzzle, a white patch around the eye, a light belly, a conspicuous white rump patch, a short black tail and a white edging running down the rear portion of each leg.

The bighorn sheep, like the deer, antelope, goats and other sheep, is a ruminant that fills its paunch, or first stomach, then rechews its food and passes it on to the second, third and fourth stomach compartments. The cud, which is about the size of a large lemon, passes up from the paunch, is chewed for about thirty seconds and is then reswallowed. When the sheep chews its cud, its lower jaw makes a sideways rotary action, giving the animal a most comical appearance. Like the other ruminants, the sheep has no teeth in the front of the upper jaw. Its 32 teeth are classified as 8 incisors, 12 premolars and 12 molars.

Forefoot of bighorn sheep, showing hoof with hard outer edge and spongy pad in the center for gripping rocks.

Of the four toes on each foot only the third and fourth are well developed into hooves; the second and first have degenerated into dewclaws. Actually all ruminants walk upon modified toenails. The outer edge of the hooves is hard and sharp and the center is filled with protruding, spongy tissue which provides the sheep with exceptionally good traction on even the sheerest rock. The sheep's legs are strong and muscular, and the animal is capable of withstanding frequent jolts without breaking or straining them.

Distribution: Bighorn sheep are found in the Rocky Mountains from central British Columbia to Mexico, east to western North and South Dakota, central Colorado and eastern New Mexico, and west to California.

Travel: Weather conditions, food availability and the breeding season are the three main factors governing movement of the bighorns. Most of the sheep have dif-

Distribution of the bighorn sheep.

ferent winter and summer ranges, although a large number remain on the winter range throughout the year. The winter range must be a slope with a southern exposure, have good forage, be swept clean of snow by the winds and have some steep rock areas nearby for safety when the sheep need it. Often the sheep spend the summer at mountain altitudes of 9,000 to 10,000 feet, dropping down to the 2,000 to 3,000-foot lowlands during the winter. Any area receiving more than an average of 60 feet of snow per winter is usually abandoned by the bighorns as winter range. Snow deeper than 18 inches hampers the sheep's movements while snow over 6 to 8 inches usually buries the needed grasses. Many of the sheep will make treks of 25 miles or more in going to and from their winter range. This is likely to be a zig-zag course following the ridges down to the valleys below.

Water and feed, rather than weather, are the crucial factors in the lives of the desert bighorns, causing them to travel further than the mountain bighorns. In the desert areas these two factors limit the range and the movement of the sheep.

Habits: The bighorns are diurnal creatures because they inhabit areas where they are seldom disturbed by man. Their vision is so keen that they can spot a man or a predator two miles away and be out of the area before they are really threatened.

Favored nighttime bedding areas are used repeatedly. This is exceptionally odd because none of the other North American hooved mammals uses its bed more than a single time. A bighorn will return time after time, in some cases year after year, and use the same bed whenever it is in that area. In some cases the beds become hollows that are a foot or more deep and about 4 feet across. The edges of these beds contain mounds of droppings. The beds are also rank with the smell of urine because the rams usually urinate as soon as they get to their feet in the morning before stepping out of bed. Because of the high altitude and the dryness of the air, the beds usually remain dry despite these unsanitary habits. Daytime beds are usually randomly chosen spots.

The sheep are early risers, and by sunup they are already feeding. They feed until about ten in the morning and then lie down to rest and chew their cud. Between one and two in the afternoon the sheep will feed again

Bighorns repeatedly use the same beds in one area, eventually hollowing out forms in the ground. This bed area was easily identified by the abundance of scat.

for a short period after which they take another break. At about five the sheep begin to feed in earnest and stay at it until they are ready to bed down for the night. In the daytime the random beds are usually in the open. Most animals try to avoid the midday sun in the summer but the sheep seem to luxuriate in its warmth. The night-time beds are usually located at the foot of a cliff or on the protected side of a ridge.

Water for the mountain bighorns is generally no problem, since melted snow runoffs are widespread, but the desert bighorns have difficulty finding sufficient water during some of the dry spells. The desert bighorns know the location of every spring and seep in their area, although they often go two or three days without water. If the water is low and the first sheep drain the scanty supply, the others will dig a hole in the soft area with their feet or noses and wait till the depression fills up. Wild burros are keen competitors for available water in the desert. Formerly it was thought that the sheep would avoid water contaminated by burros, but it has since been found that both species frequent the same sources.

The bulk of the bighorns' diet is composed of grasses. Those in the mountainous areas feed upon wheatgrass, fescue, sedges, rushes, horsetail, little ricegrass, pentstemon, June grass, vetch and others. In the winter, when snow covers most of the grasses, they eat browse—mountain mahogany, sagebrush, rabbitbrush, greasebush, bitterbrush, chokeberry, willow and alder. The desert bighorns have been observed feeding heavily upon evening primrose, galleta, desert trumpet, pebble pincushion, rush bebbia, desert holly, parachute plant, wire lettuce and honeysweet. At times this bighorn also feeds upon cactus, occasionally smashing the outer part with its horns and eating the pulpy centers. Bighorns are fond of mineral and salt licks and will frequent every one in their area.

Senses: The bighorn sheep's range is as open as the plains on which the pronghorn antelope spends its time, and both species depend mainly upon their eyesight to warn them of impending danger. Desert bighorn have detected people waving their hands 1 1/2 miles away.

Whether hearing or scent is next in importance is almost impossible to ascertain because bighorns do not react the same way to similar situations. At times they dash off when they catch the scent of an unseen man over 100 yards away. At other times they stare curiously toward the origin of the scent but make no move to retreat. In desert areas scent is dissipated rapidly by thermals lifting it above the animals, so it is unlikely that scent is of great importance. The sense of smell is important to the sheep during the breeding season when the rams use it to locate ewes in heat.

The sheep pay little attention to the sound of falling or sliding rock in the mountainous areas but are alerted by strange sounds when they are in the open.

Communication: Under ordinary circumstances, adult bighorn sheep seldom make any vocal sounds. The lambs bleat when they are hungry, frightened or lost. The ewes blat a gutteral blast if they think they have lost contact with their young. When a ewe blats, its youngster, recognizing the urgency in the call, responds instantly if it is within hearing. When the lambs are weaned they become much more silent because they no longer have the need to call for food. The old rams give an occasional raspy blat when disturbed or when challenging a rival ram during the breeding season.

Locomotion: Bighorn sheep usually walk calmly from place to place. If disturbed they trot. When hard pressed they gallop with all four feet striking the earth at about the same instant. So seldom do bighorns gallop that the sight or sound of one of the sheep galloping instantly galvanizes the entire flock into similar flight. Bighorns have been clocked at better than 35 miles per hour for short distances. They can cover 17 feet at a bound.

The fame of the bighorn, however, rests on its jumping and climbing abilities. These sheep have been known to run down talus slopes at full speed and never stumble, the wide-spread toes and dewclaws acting as brakes when needed. They have been seen jumping off ledges 25 to 30 feet in height without any apparent damage to themselves. The sheep sometimes ascend rock chimneys where they have to leap from one cliff face to a ledge 4 inches square, turn and jump higher on the opposite face and so on up to the top. Cats do not have a monopoly on the ability to turn their bodies in midair in order to alight on their feet. Bighorns possess this same ability and must often put it to good use when a rock or ledge breaks off under their weight.

Bighorns are strong swimmers and have often been seen swimming with ease across fairly wide rivers.

Breeding: Except during the breeding season, bighorn adults separate according to sex. The males form bachelor clubs and the ewes and the lambs form nursery groups. Some of the older males are solitary. The females always travel in larger groups because the young males stay with the females their first year. The female groups always travel farther than the ram groups, for they have more mouths to feed.

In October the rams begin to show a growing interest in the ewes and a growing antagonism towards one another. At first they engage in mock battles but by November the battles have become real. The older rams try to dominate all the lesser rams to keep them at a distance. No ram has a natural right to any of the ewes; it is strictly a case of might making right. Smaller rams scatter like chaff before the onslaught of a large adult in his prime. Although they scatter, they continue to hang around the fringes and hope for the best.

Large, evenly matched rams seem to glory in bone-crushing battles. Sometimes the rams will appear to "Indian wrestle" by hooking the curls of their horns together in a pushing-pulling contest. At other times the two rams slug it out. These battles are ritualistic and the proper procedure must be carried out. The rams appear to be ignoring each other, but they are watching each other constantly. When they are 30 or 40 feet apart they suddenly rear up on their hind legs. Because this maneuver is performed simultaneously, almost resembling a ballet movement, it shows how closely attuned the rams are to each other's actions. When they drop back to the ground, they lunge at each other with all the force their bodies can deliver. Either both rams turn their heads to the same side or make an exact counter turn, so that when they meet the force is evenly distributed on their heavy horns. Two rams, weighing as much as 300 pounds each, charging faster than 20 miles per hour, produce an impact of well over a ton and make a noise that can be heard for a great distance. On impact the rams' bodies recoil and shock waves run from their necks down to their tails. The rams recover, shake their heads groggily as if to clear them, walk apart and then repeat the charge. This continues until one ram gives in to the other and withdraws.

In spite of the care the rams take to hit each other squarely, they do miscalculate on occasion, causing accidents in which a ram may lose an eye, break off part of the horn or break a nose or jaw. In rare cases, when the horn and brain case are torn loose, the injuries are fatal.

While the ewe is in oestrous the ram may mount her many times, with breeding reaching its peak in the last of November and the first part of December. As soon as the breeding season is over, the rams forget why they bothered with the ewes in the first place and go back to their bachelor social groups.

Birth and Young: Gestation is about 180 days, most of the lambs being dropped in the latter part of May and the first part of June. Occasionally a few lambs will be born as late as July. Prior to giving birth, the ewe separates herself from the rest of the flock and seeks out a steep cliffside in the most inaccessible area she can find. Bighorn sheep seldom give birth to more than one lamb, although twins have been known.

The young at birth are covered with a dark-gray fuzz, stand about 14 to 15 inches high at the shoulders and weigh approximately 8 to 9 pounds. The ewe gives the lamb a thorough licking, which serves the dual purpose of cleaning the little one off and drying its coat.

Within a few hours the lamb can stand well enough to reach up and nurse, although its legs are so wobbly it can hardly walk. In a few days the lamb can gallop, but the female keeps it near the cliffside where an enemy can approach from only one side. Thus the female is able to offer the lamb the greatest possible protection. At the end of the week the lamb has started to feed upon bits of grass and the tips of plants, and the female then leads it back to the main flock.

The young lambs gambol about under the watchful eye of the ewes. Occasionally a yearling wants to join in the play and is permitted so long as it doesn't play too roughly. This play toughens the muscles and develops the coordination that will be needed by the sheep for survival throughout their lives.

Life Span: The horns of the bighorn sheep provide the information which establishes their potential life span at about fifteen years. Many of the finest rams are taken in their thirteenth and fourteenth years, so some must reach their potential. It is unlikely that many of the ewes will breed beyond their twelfth year.

Enemies: Research into the predators of the bighorn sheep has proved that, although the coyote, mountain lion, bobcat, black and grizzly bears and the golden eagle all can and occasionally do kill and eat sheep, they are not a controlling factor. In nearly every case, a combination of factors allowed a predator to kill a bighorn and not just the predator's ability. Deep snow, which either hampers the sheep's activities or covers their food so they are weakened by hunger, is probably the most important single factor working against the bighorns. Accumulations of snow in the form of avalanches also kill some sheep. In many cases the study of the sheep-predator relationship is based on an examination of the scat of a predator. There has been scarce evidence of sheep in the scat of predators, and that which has been found does not prove whether the sheep was killed by the predator or eaten as carrion. Coyotes probably are the bighorns' primary predator, although there is one record of a mountain lion in Idaho that had six fresh bighorn carcasses cached.

Ticks, mites and, in former days, scabies all attack and in some cases may weaken the bighorn sheep. Necrotic stomatitis, pneumonia and coccidiosis occasionally prove fatal. Tapeworms, pinworms, whipworms and lung-worms are important controlling parasites. The lungworm is found fairly commonly in the sheep and is a decimating factor.

Competition with other large animals, particularly elk and domestic sheep and cattle, also limits the bighorns. When available food is eaten by other species, it is denied to the bighorns and they suffer because of it.

Sign: Tracks are the most commonly seen sign of the bighorn, for they inhabit areas where tracks can be found in dust, dirt or mud. One difficulty in reading sheep tracks is that they are so often confused with mule deer tracks. However, sheep have shorter legs and bigger feet than the average deer and their tracks are larger and closer together. Then, too, their hoof marks are squarer and the tip of the hoof more open. In the mud around springs and seeps, the protruding spongy center of the sheep's hoof will leave a concave track while the sunken center of the deer's hoof will leave a convex track.

The scat of the bighorn is usually bell-shaped, pointed at one end and flattened on the other. Deer scat is rounded on both ends. Also, the hair of the bighorn is much longer than that of the deer, in addition to being much darker in color.

Human Relations: Man has reduced the range of the bighorn to such an extent that the species now inhabits about 4 percent of its former region. Besides actual hunting, disturbance of the area by man's presence and competition with man's domesticated stock for food, the bighorns have had one reversal after another. The picture is brighter now than it used to be. Better protection is afforded the species; studies were undertaken that allowed many of the sheep's hitherto unknown problems to be understood; and transplants have encouraged the re-establishment of the sheep on some of their former ranges. Wise management policies have opened land and hunting seasons where it was thought hunting for sheep was a thing of the past.

Before the white man, the mountain Indians hunted the sheep as an important food item. The Shoshonis and Gros Ventre made bows of sheep horn and wood or of laminated horn. Such bows were short and stiff, but very powerful.

Trophy Records: The world's-record bighorn sheep was killed by Fred Weiller in Blind Canyon, Alberta, in 1911. The right horn is 44 7/8 inches long and 16 5/8 inches in basal circumference. The left horn is 45 inches long and 16 5/8 inches at the base. The greatest spread is 22 6/8 inches. The head scored 208 1/8 points.

The Number 2 bighorn sheep was killed by Martin Bovey in 1924 at Oyster Creek, Alberta. It scored a total of 207 2/8 points. The right horn is 45 inches long and 15 6/8 inches in circumference at the base. The left horn is 45 2/8 inches long and is 16 inches at the base. The greatest spread is 23 1/8 inches.

The world's-record desert sheep was killed by an unknown Indian in Lower California in Mexico in 1940. It scored 205 1/8 points. The right horn is 43 5/8 inches long and 16 6/8 inches in basal circumference. The left horn is 43 6/8 inches long and 17 inches at the base. The greatest spread is 25 5/8 inches.

Table Fare: Many big game hunters believe that bighorn sheep is the finest of all wild game meat.

Dall's and Stone's Sheep

Ovis dalli dalli and *Ovis dalli stonei*

The Dall's sheep, with its subspecies the Stone's and intermediate-phase Fannin sheep, differs from the bighorn in coloration and in the shape of its horns. The Dall's has thinner horns that flare outward at the tips and do not obstruct its vision when grown into a full curl. These sheep live farther north than the bighorns, in the high, snowy mountains of Alaska, the Yukon and British Columbia. Some of this country is too high and remote even for horses, and hunters use airplanes to take them into base camps from where they climb into sheep habitat. Along with the bighorn and the desert bighorn, the Dall's and Stone's sheep make up the Grand Slam in trophy hunting.

Description: Various color phases may be found where ranges of the Dall's and the Stone's sheep overlap. Generally, though, there is a gradual shading, from the pure-white Dall's of Alaska southward to the bluish-black Stone's of British Columbia. The sheep in the upper Yukon have a few black hairs in their tails; those farther south have all black tails; still farther south the sheep have black saddles, until finally the coat becomes a rich blue-black. Even the black Stone's have a white rump patch, a light belly and a white edging running down the rear of all four legs. There is usually some white on the face, an area that becomes larger as the sheep grows older. The hooves are dark. The horns on the Stone's rams are slightly heavier than those of the Dall's and the specimen with the longest horns in North America is a Stone's. This head, taken by L. S. Chadwick on the

The Dall's ram above and the Stone's ram below are of the same species. The Stone's occupies the southern portion of the overall range. (Top photo by Tim Lewis Rue.)

Prophet River in 1936, has horns that measure 50 1/8 inches and 51 5/8 inches. Any ram that has horns measuring over 40 inches in length is sporting a trophy head. Because the pronounced flare keeps the horns away from the ram's head so they do not obstruct its sight, the Dall's brooms off the tips less than the bighorns do.

An average ram will weigh approximately 180 pounds with about 220 being a top weight. It stands about 38 inches high at the shoulders and is about 6 feet or more in length. The horns are a light yellow in color and usually flare out from the head. The horns show well-defined annual growth marks so that an animal's age can be determined simply and accurately. The ewes also have horns, but these are slender spikes and seldom, if ever, reach 15 inches in length. The pupil of the eyes appears to be three bands, the top and bottom band being yellow while the center is black. The hooves are a yellowish-brown in color. There are four toes on each foot, but only the second and third are developed into hooves; the first and fourth toes are designated as dewclaws.

These sheep are ruminants, having a four-chambered stomach, and rechew their cud before it can be passed on for further digestion. They do not have any teeth in the top of their mouths at the front. They have a total of 32 teeth: 8 incisors, 12 premolars and 12 molars.

Their hair is cellular and filled with air, and it is waxy with natural lanolin. In the winter the hair over most of the body is about 3 inches in length. This coat is shed in June and replaced with a shorter coat for the summer. When the hair is sloughing off in big patches, the sheep have a bedraggled, moth-eaten appearance, and they

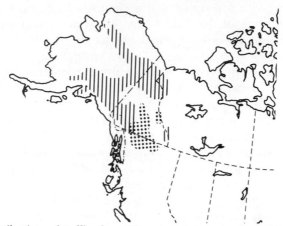

Distribution of Dall's sheep (lines) and Stone's sheep (dots).

leave pieces of hair on bushes they brush against. Mountain sheep have hair, not wool like domestic sheep.

Distribution: The sheep live on mountain slopes from northern British Columbia to northern Alaska, east as far as western Mackenzie.

Travel: Mountain sheep do not travel or migrate unless forced to by food and weather conditions. In many sections they feed high on the mountains during the summer and drop down into the more protected valleys during the winter.

In McKinley National Park, many of the sheep winter on the north side of the park road because the snowfall is light there and the wind keeps the ridges swept free of snow. In the summer the sheep like to feed on the headwaters of the Toklat and Thoroughfare rivers. To cross from the one ridge to the other side means crossing the valley, which is about 3 miles wide. In June of 1966, the sheep came right down to the road near the Eilson Visitor Center. Everyday they would feed low and then work back up the northern slope. It seemed as if they were either trying to get up their courage or wanting to make sure that the coast was clear before they crossed over. About the 25th of June conditions looked right to them and a big herd of rams started across. Without actually running they hurried across and reached the other side safely. Bones and pieces of hide with the white hair attached showed that other herds had not been so fortunate in previous crossings when predators had taken advantage of the situation.

Habits: Since the sheep are grazing animals, the bulk of their diet is the grasses and forbes of the alpine meadows. They will eat some browse, particularly the dwarf willow. In areas where wolves are scarce these sheep feed quite low; as the pressures of wolf predation increase, the sheep work their way higher into the mountains because only there can they find their needed margin of safety. The entire herd feeds together in the winter, not so much from choice as from the restriction of their feeding areas to windswept ridges.

As spring comes the sheep split up, the rams going their own way while the ewes, their lambs and most of the yearlings stay together. In both cases, each of the segregated flocks has a leader, usually the oldest individual. This is sometimes hard to ascertain with the ewes, but when the rams are alarmed, the rest of the herd usually falls in behind the ram with the biggest horns, which is usually the oldest.

Occasionally some of these older sheep prefer to lead a solitary existence and do not mingle with the others. Such solitary males are always exceedingly wary because they have had to depend on only themselves for safety. Although the mountain sheep do not appear to post sentinels as the mountain goats do, they are all very alert and even while resting usually lie down facing in different directions to observe all points of the compass.

The sheep feed from early dawn until mid-morning. Although they may feed in a basin, they usually retire to a ridge or hillside before resting to chew their cud. The sheep feed again briefly about noon, take another rest, and then feed heavily in late afternoon. Apparently the sheep are relatively inactive at night, because at dawn the flock can usually be found in the proximity of the previous night's feeding grounds.

Water is seldom a problem for the sheep because most of them frequent mountains that retain some snow on the peaks all year long, and the melting snow and the underground seeps provide them with a surplus of water. The sheep visit salt or mineral springs in their areas once or twice a week to drink the water and eat the soil. In some areas where the wild sheep have eaten mineral clays, they pass scat that is formed almost like marbles.

Senses: The eyesight of these sheep is comparable to that of a man using eight-power binoculars. It is capable of spotting the slightest movement at great distances but often overlooks nearby stationary objects.

When stalking rams, you should keep out of sight if at all possible, but once seen it is better to stay in sight and try to approach slowly at an oblique angle. If the rams spot you, and you try to take cover, the whole flock will take to its heels as soon as you disappear. Try to approach from above because sheep expect danger from below.

If the wind is blowing steadily in one direction, a hunter had better be downwind of the sheep because their sense of smell is good. On most mountaintops, though, the wind is usually gusty and capricious and blows so wildly in so many directions that scent seldom helps the sheep.

The sheep's ears are good but sheep are accustomed to the sound of falling and sliding rock. The sound of any rock movement will alert them but not alarm them so that a careless hunter will often have another chance if he takes the time to wait till they relax. An unfamiliar sound, such as metal banging on rock or a loud voice, will frighten the sheep away.

Communication: Sheep do not utter many sounds. The young lambs bleat much as do their domestic counterparts, and if they are separated from their mother, they will bleat almost continuously. At such times the female will also be calling out to the young. The old rams emit a deep, raspy, blatting sound during the breeding season.

Locomotion: When sheep travel from one place to another they walk. At an all-out gallop, they have a peculiar rocking gait. As the sheep seldom have to run for any distance, they are not accustomed to such exertion, and even climbing 1,000 feet in a hurry will leave them panting.

Breeding: Dominance within a resident bachelor group is decided and maintained throughout the year, though rams from rival groups, and sometimes within the group, will fight. In October the rams, which have kept themselves apart from the ewes, now begin to look upon them more favorably, and regard other rams with some hostility. By November, the necks of the rams have swollen and they can no longer tolerate each other's presence.

Sheep are polygamous. Each ram breeds with as many ewes as possible. In this case, a ewe may accept the services of a number of rams, which travel from one ewe flock to another seeking ewes in oestrus.

When two rams battle they usually walk apart for about 15 to 20 yards. Turning, they suddenly rise up on their hind feet, then drop swiftly to all fours and with straining muscles fly at each other. The resounding shock as they meet head-on can be heard for over a mile. The force of the impact has been calculated to be well over a ton. The rams will sometimes stand and shake their heads as if the impact had gotten through to them, but it seldom changes anything. Again they walk apart and again they crash head-on. Sometimes the contest, after the initial impact, becomes one of pushing and shoving and it is here that the better ram soon shows up. Pure strength and body weight win out and the weaker ram finally turns and runs off, leaving the victor to breed the ewe.

The rut continues for about a month, and then the

rams and ewes return to a tranquil existence. The rams again form bachelor groups or some may stay with the ewes. In any case, both sexes will be found in the same general area because of restricted winter range.

Birth and Young: The gestation period is about 171 days with most of the young being born in the latter part of May. Single lambs are the rule, although occasionally there may be twins.

As her time for giving birth draws near, the ewe leaves the flock and seeks out a ledge or cliffside. The most inaccessible spots are chosen so that the mother can offer the greatest protection to her young.

At birth a Dall's lamb is pure white, stands about 14 inches high at the shoulder and weighs about 8 pounds. Within an hour or two it is dried off and tries to stand. By the time it is three or four hours old, it is able to walk, although its legs are very wobbly. It will have nursed before this time and gets additional feedings about once an hour. When the lamb is three or four days old, the ewe attempts to lead it back to the main flock. The young can now dash about, but they attempt to climb over obstacles instead of walking around them.

The lambs grow very rapidly, and by the time they are a week old they have begun to sample some of the grasses that their mothers eat. Feeding is the most important activity in the lamb's life. At birth it had to stretch its neck to reach its mother's nipples. Within three weeks it has grown so large that it must kneel down to reach the nipples. While it feeds, the lamb butts and punches with its mouth at the ewe's udder, keeping its tail jerking back and forth in contentment as its belly swells with the thick warm milk.

Play ranks next in importance to the lambs, and they spend hours each day this way. Tag and follow-the-leader appear to be as popular with lambs as with human young. Every rock and boulder is an Everest that must be conquered, and the lambs promptly dash up to the top, often bumping one of their companions off in the process. This play quickly strengthens their muscles, and when they are threatened with danger the young can usually keep up as the adults dash for the broken rock areas.

Most of the lambs are weaned by the time they are three months old, although many of them will still try to nurse. Usually the mothers refuse to stand still for nursing. Some, however, may nurse until winter.

The horns on the baby rams start to sprout in their second and third months. By their third month the lambs are about one-half the body size of the adults and the horns are 1 to 1 1/2 inches long. At five months of age the horns are about 3 inches long. By winter, the lambs are nearly three-fourths full size and have acquired coats similar to those of the adults.

Life Span: Dall's sheep have a potential life span of about fifteen years. It is exceedingly unlikely that many live to be that old, although most of the record heads are from animals twelve, thirteen and fourteen years old.

Sign: The tracks of Dall's and Stone's sheep, mountain goat and blacktail deer are similar. But the blacktail range does not overlap with that of sheep and goats. The mountain goat's hooves are much squarer than those of the sheep. The dark pellet-like scat is another commonly found sign. In fact, on hard ground scat is more often seen than tracks. Gobs of the long white hair shed from the winter coat are another eye-catching sign.

Enemies: The timber wolf easily ranks as the Dall's sheep's principal enemy. When the wolf is scarce in an area the sheep become more plentiful and feed upon the lower hills. When wolves are present the sheep are driven back to high ridges and escarpments and their numbers are curtailed. Wolves enjoy eating mutton and waylay the sheep whenever possible. Yet, one observer tells of seeing two Dall's sheep kill five wolves foolish enough to follow them out on a mountain ledge. The wolves were promptly butted over the edge.

Mountain lions, lynx, bears and coyotes also take occasional sheep but not in numbers great enough to really be a controlling factor. The golden eagle is ever alert to the possibility of snatching an unguarded lamb, a fact that the ewes are quick to realize. When an eagle is in the area most ewes will stand directly over their lambs to protect them with their own bodies. If the eagle persists in trying for the lamb, the ewe lashes out at the bird with her sharp horns.

Dall's sheep live in such high, open, windy country that they are seldom molested by flies and mosquitos, but they are pestered by ticks and mites. The sheep are often seen rubbing against projecting rocks to get relief from these parasites. Internally, lungworms are the gravest threat, although sheep also suffer from flatworms and tapeworms. Necrotic stomatitis is sometimes found in sheep. And, of course, accidents on the high ledges cause occasional deaths, and even the agile sheep can be caught in avalanches.

Human Relations: These northern sheep were one of the last of the big-game animals to be discovered and exploited. Their inaccessibility gave them a tremendous margin of safety. Now aircraft take sportsmen into some of the best hunting regions; helicopters can put them on the tops of mountains. To protect the sheep, the use of aircraft has been restricted and the use of helicopters forbidden. Most sportsmen feel that high-powered rifles have given man enough of an advantage.

The Dall's sheep have rarely been transported from one area to another. The fluctuations in their numbers can usually be attributed to extremely deep snow or excessive predation.

Trophy Records: The Number 1 Dall's sheep head was taken by Harry L. Swank, Jr. in 1961, in the Wrangell Mountains of Alaska. It scored 189 6/8 points. The right horn is 48 5/8 inches long and has a circumference at the base of 14 5/8 inches. The left horn is 47 7/8 inches long and is 14 6/8 inches at the base. The greatest spread is 34 3/8 inches. The record book treats the Dall's and the Stone's sheep separately.

The world's-record Stone sheep, mentioned previously, was killed by L. S. Chadwick in 1936, on the Muskwa River of British Columbia. It scored 196 6/8 points. The right horn is 50 1/8 inches long and is 14 6/8 inches in circumference at the base. The left horn is 51 5/8 inches long and is 14 6/8 inches at the base. It has a maximum spread of 31 inches. This head is often cited as the finest North American trophy.

Table Fare: The meat of the mountain sheep is highly esteemed and is rated far superior to domestic sheep. It is one of the best-tasting meats I have eaten.

This goat's coat is filling out for winter's onslaught. (Photo by Irene Vandermolen.)

Mountain Goat

Oreamnos americanus

A unique animal with no near relatives on this continent, the mountain goat is not really a goat but is distantly related to the Old World antelopes. Its closest relatives are the goral and serow of Asia and the chamois of Europe. It is believed that the animal originated in Asia and crossed to this continent via the Bering Land Bridge about 600,000 years ago.

Like the wild sheep, the goat is a creature of the high places, the bleak cliffs and pinnacles of the western mountains. Hunters have taken them to round out a trophy collection, but their meat is inferior to the sheep's and their horns far less striking. It can be safely said that the mountain goat is one of the few animals in North America that may never be on the endangered list.

Description: The mountain goat stands 36 to 40 inches high at the shoulder, measures 5 to 6 feet in length from nose to tail and weighs up to 300 pounds. Its long hair is almost pure white tinged slightly with yellow. Its hooves, eyes, horns and nose are jet black.

Both sexes wear horns that grow continually over bony cores. The horns on a big billy may reach 12 inches in length while the nanny's seldom exceed 9 inches. The males use their horns for fighting, the females for defense of their young. The horns are dagger-like, hooking slightly backward, and although the goats give them rough usage, they are brittle. A goat's age can be accurately determined by the annual growth rings on its horns.

At birth, the kid has two tiny black buttons which soon develop into miniature horns. By the first winter of its

Two goat kids and their nanny make their summer's trek to high terrain. The kids are sure-footed from birth.

life the kid's horns will be about 3 inches long. There is no growth ring the first year. By the time the goat is sixteen months of age, the horns have grown to 5 or 6 inches in length. In the period between winter and spring, when the goat is on reduced feed, the horn growth is compacted, leaving a well-defined ring. Each succeeding year adds another ring, so that by counting the rings and adding a year and a half, one can determine the goat's age.

Both the nanny and the billy sport beards, which do not start directly beneath the chin but are long hairs coming from below the jaw. Even when the goats shed their long winter hair, which they do throughout early

During the summer, the mountain goat sheds its thick winter coat (above), leaving traces of its passage on trees and bushes throughout its range (right).

summer, they retain the beards. A goat's hair is rich in lanolin and feels waxy to the touch. The guard hair often reaches a length of 7 inches. The lower 8 inches of each leg is the only place that does not have this luxuriant growth.

The hooves of the mountain goat are a special adaptation to allow this animal to safely make its way over all but sheer perpendicular rock. The hoof on the front foot of an adult male goat is almost square and measures about 2.7 inches by 2.4 inches wide. The hind foot is slightly smaller, with the female's slightly smaller yet. The pad of the foot, instead of being concave like the hooves of most animals, is convex. The cushions give the bottom of the foot a slightly rounded appearance and their spongy composition gives excellent traction.

The goat is a ruminant and has the four-chambered stomach typical of this group. It must chew its cud in order to reduce its food mass to a usable condition. Like other ruminants, the goat has no teeth on the top jawbone in the front of its mouth. It has a total of 32 teeth: 8 incisors, no canines, 12 premolars and 12 molars.

There are no records of either albino or melanistic mountain goats. Albinism would scarcely be noted in an animal that is all white. There are records of young goats having dark-brown hairs running along the center of their backs, but these usually disappear before the goats are a year old.

The mountain goats have a very conspicuous crescent-shaped gland encircling the back half of each horn. These glands are associated with the breeding season, at which time they become greatly enlarged. Although both sexes have these glands, the male's are much larger and during

Distribution of the mountain goat.

the breeding season give off a waxy, odorous substance. It is believed that this odor is important in exciting the female in preparation for copulation. Seton claims to have seen male goats depositing this waxy substance on the bushes and branches of trees by rubbing against them, for much the same purpose that other animals mark with scent.

Distribution: The mountain goat lives along the steep slopes of the western mountains, generally above timberline, from Idaho and Washington to southern Alaska and central Yukon. They also occur in the Black

Hills of South Dakota where they were introduced.

Travel: The mountain goat is one of the few large animals which has remained diurnal in habits. This can only be attributed to the fact that the mountain goat has always inhabited areas where it seldom encounters man. Any movements made by the goats are governed by the breeding season, weather conditions and food availability.

If food is plentiful the goats may feed for several weeks in an area of 100 to 200 acres. In the winter the goats may concentrate in areas that the wind has swept clear of snow. There is a general shift in range between winter and summer, but this is usually too short a trip to be considered a migration. As the early winter storms begin to pile the snow up on the peaks, the goats move down the mountainside, seeking slopes that have a southern exposure and less snow. Sometimes snow depths drive the goats back up to the higher peaks where the wind has swept off the snow, exposing the vegetation beneath. Late spring finds the goats at their lowest elevations, where they seek out the new green growth that starts earliest in the lowlands.

The trip back to the peaks is a gradual one, the males making the trip first while the females and their kids follow along behind at a more leisurely pace. The advance of the green growth up the side of the mountain usually determines the goat's rate of travel. In any event, the goats seldom travel more than 15 to 20 miles in their year-round movement.

Habits: The goat's period of peak activity is usually from before sunrise to mid-morning. They arise early and feed slowly. In fact, the goats seldom do anything in a hurry. By eleven o'clock in the morning, the goats are bedding down to chew their cud. In the middle of the afternoon they again start out to feed and are ready to retire by sunset.

In the summer the goats seek out shady spots in which to rest to escape from the heat. They will lie up against the northern side of the cliff faces or lie in the shade of whatever bushes are available. If neither situation is convenient, they will often go out and lie down on whatever snow or ice is left in the gullies and pockets. High in the mountains most of the gullies will retain some snow all summer long.

During the summer some males do not associate with the females but keep to themselves in small bands. The males are usually found on the very highest peaks at this time. The females and their young band together and must find areas with sufficient food.

In the summer about two-thirds of the goat's food is composed of grasses while the balance is made up of browse and forbes. Purple milk vetch, alpine sorrel, blue-grasses, wheatgrass, alpine equisetum, green lily and strawberry are some of the most important foods. They also eat snowbush, huckleberry, aspen and horsetail. In the winter snow covers most of the low-growing plants, and the goats change to more brushy material. Balsam fir, aspen, dwarf birch, red osier, bearberry juniper and willow are important winter foods. At all times of the year the goats feed upon mosses and lichens. Water is never a problem because their range is usually covered with snow or melted snow.

Goats frequent natural salt and mineral springs. In some areas where ranchers run cattle high in the mountain meadows, the goats descend to partake of the commercial salt blocks that the ranchers have placed out for their cattle.

Mountain goats dislike rain. If at all possible they get under a ledge or enter caves to escape the downpour. If the rain is light, they may stay out and continue to feed, vigorously shaking themselves to disperse the water before it accumulates. In the winter the goats take shelter in caves during the worst of the storms, venturing forth only when driven to it by hunger.

Senses: The eyesight of the mountain goat is exceptionally keen and is the sense it most frequently depends on. The hearing ability of the goat is good but is not of great importance to the animal. A mountain is a very noisy place. Constant wear and exposure to the elements causes erosion, and little chunks of rock are always breaking off and tumbling down. One small piece of rock can start a much larger slide area moving. The clattering of rock may alert the goat, but it does not necessarily interpret the noise as danger.

Air currents in the mountains seldom blow in one direction but swirl and eddy, particularly about the peaks. In the daytime the thermals rise and at night they go down the mountainsides. As the goats prefer to frequent the highest peak, they are usually secure in the knowledge that nothing is above them. This is often their undoing, because hunters take advantage of this weakness, and of the uprising thermals, and climb above the goats. The goats don't bother to look up but concentrate on the area below them. Some hunters will deliberately have an accomplice show himself in the open below. The goats easily spot the decoy hunter and concentrate their attention on him while the other hunter keeps out of sight and tries to get in a position above the goats for a shot.

Although their eyes are exceptionally keen at long distances, the goats do not seem to notice stationary objects. They have been known to approach a man sitting in the open whom they had not detected previously by scent or sound.

Communication: Mountain goats are comparatively quiet animals. The kids bleat frequently, particularly if they become separated from their mothers. Even yearlings occasionally bleat. The bleating is similar to the sound made by domestic sheep. The adults sometimes make a soft grunting sound.

Locomotion: The mountain goat almost never hurries; every move is made with great deliberation. The goats move with a rather stiff-legged walk. No animal of prey can follow the goat over the almost perpendicular cliffs that it seeks out in time of danger—and the goats know this. They also know that speed could be disastrous. If threatened by danger, the goats stride off at a strong, purposeful gait, choosing each step with great care. The goat's sense of balance is exceptional. When climbing, it appears to defy gravity and seems akin to a fly, often ascending rock faces that have no visible ledges. If the goat runs out of footholds it does not panic; it calmly surveys the situation before it takes further action. If there is no possible way to advance, it will raise up on its hind feet, pivot around and go back the way it came.

In climbing an almost shear rock wall, a goat often pulls itself up to a higher ledge using its forefeet like a man.

The goats are not good at broad jumping; a distance of 6 feet is about their maximum. They can jump much farther when jumping down. They sometimes work their way down a mountain by jumping from one rock face to another and then back. Sometimes when the goats drop down into wooded areas, they walk along fallen timber and windfalls high above the ground.

Goats sometimes wade across streams, but no records are available of their swimming ability, though most animals can swim.

Breeding: Breeding activity among the goats becomes evident in November and December. At that time the males, many of which had been solitary, now begin to associate with the females. The male does not gather a harem but will often consort with one or perhaps two females that he considers his own. When other males attempt to approach the females, the first male drives them away. There is actually very little combat between the males; most of it is just threatening bluff and posture. When on the rare occasions the males do fight, they use their horns like daggers.

To woo the female, the male often rubs his head and neck against her body. To satisfy his own urgings, he often forces a reluctant female to get to her feet and then follows her until she finally stands for him.

Birth and Young: The gestation period for the mountain goat is about 178 days, with most of the young being born between the middle of May and the Middle of June. Most females give birth to a single kid, although twins are not uncommon.

At birth a kid weighs between 7 and 8 pounds and stands about 13 inches high at the shoulder. The young are precocious and within three or four hours can follow the mother over rough country. The female usually chooses one of the roughest and most remote areas in her range in which to give birth because of the added protection such spots afford. The mother and the new-born kid usually remain by themselves for three or four days and then join similar family groups.

Within a week or two the kids start to nibble at the various food plants they see their mother eating. Much of their time is taken up with play, and the young dash helter-skelter over rocks and cliff sides. They seem to delight in dashing up to the lip of a chasm and stopping abruptly at the edge to solemnly survey the depths below. The kids *do not* imitate some of the older goats, which often stand immobile in one spot for hours.

By the time the kids are six to eight weeks old they are weaned, and although independent of the mother so far as food is concerned, they still need her for leadership and protection. A group of female goats and their kids do not appear to have a leader, each goat being too in-dividualistic. The herd moves according to each goat's advance as it seeks food. When danger threatens, each goat selects its own escape route, although it may follow another goat if it likes the route. The herd stays together until the following spring when the females go off to give birth to their new young. Some of the yearlings may stay with the main group or become solitary.

Life Span: One mountain goat kept in the National Zoological Park lived to be eleven years, three months and nine days old. As the goats do not fare too well in captivity, it is likely that their life span in the wild could be about fifteen years. This is borne out by the fact that most of the females do not breed until they are two and a half years old.

Sign: The most commonly found sign of the mountain goat is its droppings. However, if mule deer or bighorn sheep are also frequenting the area, it may be difficult to tell the droppings apart. The composition of the droppings depends upon the time of the year. When the goats are eating grasses, the droppings are loose. When the goats are feeding upon brush and browse, the scat is much more compacted and usually bell shaped— pointed on one end and flat or even slightly concave on the other. In areas frequently used by goats the ground is covered with scat.

The tracks of the goats are hard to confuse with those of any other animals because of their almost square shape. But as the goats spend so much time walking on rocks, their tracks are usually found only around the salt licks and in the dust of some of their trails.

Big patches of white hair are also a sign of goats. This hair cannot be confused with anything else except the hair of the Alaskan Dall sheep. The Indians of British Columbia have long gathered these clumps of white hair and have spun them into strands for knitting and weaving garments that are very warm.

Enemies: Avalanches are the goat's prime enemy.

These may be avalanches of either snow or slides of rock. Each year the remains of goats are found which have been swept off ledges or crushed by these slides.

The golden eagle is credited with taking a toll of young goats. The eagle will attempt to kill a kid by driving it over a cliff. Only a bird is capable of getting near a goat; no other animal in North America can challenge it in its own environment.

When snow and bitter weather drive the goats off the peaks, or when they cross the wooded valleys between two ranges, they are then subject to predation. Wolves, coyotes, mountain lions, bobcats and bears are all capable of overtaking and killing a goat under such circumstances. The task is never easy because the goat is strong and a plucky fighter and its sharp horns are dangerous weapons.

Wood ticks are a common parasite of mountain goats. To rid themselves of these and other noxious, blood-sucking pests, the goats take frequent dust baths in warm weather. They sometimes use pits that are 4 to 5 feet across and a foot deep which have been used by successive generations of mountain goats for just this purpose. The goats paw the dirt and dust loose and then lay down in the hollow, flicking dust over their bodies with their forefeet.

Tapeworms, liver flukes and pinworms infest the mountain goats internally. Disease is comparatively rare in the goats although coccidiosis and pasteurellosis have both been found in specimens.

Human Relations: As previously mentioned, man has done less to disrupt the life pattern of the mountain goat than any of the other big-game animals mainly because of the difficulty of getting into the goat's habitat. The goat is fortunate not to inhabit an area that man covets. Some transplants of goats have been made that have turned out to be very successful. Six mountain goats that were transplanted from Alberta to the Black Hills of South Dakota in 1924 had developed into a herd of more than 200 individuals by 1942.

Trophy Records: The world's-record mountain goat was shot by E. C. Haase in 1949 in the Babine Mountains of British Columbia. It scored a total of 56 6/8 points. Both horns are 12 inches long, 6 4/8 inches circumference at the base and have a maximum spread of 9 2/8 inches.

The second-place head was taken by W. H. Jackson in 1933 at Helm Bay, Alaska. This head totaled 56 2/8 points with each horn being 11 5/8 inches long. The right horn has a base circumference of 5 6/8 inches while the left is 5 5/8 inches. Maximum spread is 7 2/8 inches.

One female currently listed in the record books as Number 80 had a horn length of 12 inches and was at one time the world's-record head. Now more than horn length is considered.

The heaviest goat on record is one killed in Alaska in 1913 that is reported to have weighed 502 pounds.

Table Fare: Trophy billies do not make the most desirable meat for the table, for by the time the goat has grown an impressive set of horns he is old and tough. Younger animals, however, are often used for food.

Musk-Ox

Ovibos moschatus

Hunted to extinction in North America by explorers and natives, musk-oxen have been successfully reintroduced in Alaska and Canada. Worldwide there are over 26,000 wild musk-oxen—with about 15,000 in Greenland, about 10,000 in the Canadian Arctic and about 1,000 in various parts of Alaska. There are also transplanted herds in Norway and Siberia.

The Latin name derives from the animal's appearance and features. The *ovibos* means sheep-ox and *moschatus* refers to the bull's musky odor during the rutting season.

In 1780 a man named Zimmerman assigned a wild ox-like animal with the Latin *bos* (meaning a cow and because the animal is a member of the cattle family) and *moschatus* because of its scent glands. In 1822 Desmarest changed the name to *ovibos moschatus.* The *ovi* means sheep and was added because of the exceedingly long hair and dense undercoat of the musk-ox.

Description: Musk-oxen are sturdy, chunky-bodied members of the cattle family. Both male and female have humps on their shoulders, and both sport horns. Both body size and horns of the male are much larger than the female. The horns of an old bull form a casque across the top frontal portion of the skull, while the horns of a female are always separated by a hair line. The horns cover the top of the skull, swoop down along the side of the head and flare out and up.

The weights of the musk-oxen depend upon the area in which they are taken. Adult bulls from Nunivak Island off Alaska's western coast average 500 to 600 pounds, the cows 300 to 400 pounds. Adult bulls from the Canadian mainland weigh 700 to 750 pounds, the cows up to 500 pounds. John Teal of Huntington Center, Vermont, had two captive bulls that weighed 1,135 and 1,450 pounds. Two of his cow musk-oxen weighed 620 and 655 pounds. Such weights are possible only with captive animals that are fed a constant, highly nutritious diet and that are not subject to the vagaries of the weather and periodic starvation.

A really large bull will stand 4 1/2 to 5 feet at the shoulders and be up to 8 feet in total length. The tail doesn't add to that total, it being only about 4 inches long. Cows again are much smaller.

The weight of any musk-ox can be deceptive because of the exceedingly long guard hair that may be 24 inches in length and hangs like a sheet draped over the animal. This long hair nearly obscures the legs; only the feet stick out. The climate at Nunivak Island is slightly warmer than the true Arctic homeland of the musk-ox, and is subject to frequent thawing and freezing conditions. Musk-oxen have been found frozen to death because their long hair has frozen to the wet snow, pinning them down and keeping them from reaching heat-generating foods.

Beneath the long, outer guard hair is a dense under-coat that Eskimos call *qiviut*. This hair is one of the softest animal fibers in the world. It allows the musk-ox to brave the most bitter cold and howling winds. As this *qiviut* is shed each spring, the ragged patches make the musk-ox look as though moths had gotten to it. Bushes are festooned with it and small sheets of it are blown about by the wind. The Eskimos gather it and use it to knit fan-

When threatened, musk-oxen often seek high ground and form a defensive circle. Here they retreated to water's edge to guard their backsides and then formed a defensive line. If you approach too close at this time an old cow or bull will likely attempt to gore you.

Distribution of the musk-ox.

tastically warm socks, mittens and scarves. The musk-ox also has short hair on most of its nose pad.

The musk-ox is basically dark brown to almost black, although in summer the hair tips on its back become bleached almost blonde. The lower part of the foot, above the hooves, is white.

The musk-ox has four toes on each foot, two of them dewclaws which do not touch the ground but they show up in musk-oxen tracks. The two main hooves make a track that is almost perfectly round, about five inches in diameter.

The musk-ox has 32 teeth classified as eight incisors, 12 premolars and 12 molars. Not having any teeth in the front of its upper jaw, the musk-ox pulls off swatches of long grass with its tongue or tears it off by holding it with its incisors against the upper jaw pad. When the musk-ox browses on twigs, it will bite onto them and then shake its head up and down, tearing them loose.

Distribution: During the Pleistocene Era, the musk-ox was found circumpolar and its range extended southward to Ohio in North America and to Poland in Eurasia. Within historic times, the musk-ox has been found in Greenland and in Canada, south to lower Hudson's Bay and in Alaska. Intensive hunting all but exterminated the musk-ox. Recent introductions have started a number of successful transplants in Alaska, Norway and Siberia. Greenland and the Canadian Arctic islands still contain descendants of the original wild herds.

Travel: Musk-oxen do not migrate but tend to wander almost continuously over an area. This is a common habit with all grazing, herd animals, and this helps prevent the depletion of their food base. Musk-oxen usually travel 6 to 10 miles per day, circling so that they come back to their starting point in a week or so. Solitary bulls wander farther than the herd animals do.

Habits: Musk-oxen are herd animals. In the past, when the animals were more plentiful, herds of 60 to 100 animals were reported. However, today herds usually number from 8 to 16 animals. These herds are actually harems headed by a dominant bull, and include the bull's cows and their young. During times of great hardship, when musk-oxen tend to concentrate in the best food areas, the harems join with others. Although harems may also congregate at choice food areas in summer, in winter congregations are usually larger. The larger winter concentrations also afford better protection against the wolves when the wolves are a greater threat.

Young males are allowed to stay with the herd until the end of their second year, but when the breeding season commences, they are driven away by the dominant bull. Young males may rejoin the herd after the breeding season. These young males will usually seek out the company of other males that are not yet big enough and strong enough to have harems of their own. Older bulls that have been defeated and chased away from their old harem usually remain solitary. This is a common phenomenon for hoofed animals.

During the rutting season, the dominant male is in command. However, at all other times of the year, an old cow assumes leadership. She determines where they feed, where they stop, when they stop, when they run and why. She will often lead the herd away from danger to the top of the nearest high ground. If the old cow senses imminent danger, her distressed movements will signal the others to form the defensive circle.

The defensive circle evolved to meet the threat from wolves and occasional bears. The herd gathers into a tight-packed circle with the calves in the center or sandwiched into the line between adults. When the wolves or other enemies move close, the old cow or the dominant bull charges out of the line trying to gore the enemy. The chase is short and the animal then returns to the circle until the enemy moves in again. Against a single enemy, the musk-oxen may form a straight line with all animals facing the enemy.

Musk-oxen inhabit regions that are almost continuously light in the summer and continuously dark in the winter. Because of this their feeding activity is governed more by hunger than by conditions of light. Being ruminants, musk-oxen fill their paunches over about a 2 1/2 hour period and then lie down or stand to rest and chew their cuds for a comparable period.

Favored foods are dwarf willow and birch, Labrador tea, crowberry, mountain avens, sedges, fireweed, cottongrass, horsetail, foxtail, blueberry, wheatgrass, wild parsley, lovage and beach rye grass.

The water requirements are usually satisfied by the vegetation eaten, augmented by the pools of melted snow in summer and the snow itself in the winter.

Except during the breeding season, musk-oxen usually have a placid temperament and are very tolerant of one another.

Senses: The musk-ox probably depends more upon

its sight than other senses for protection. Since musk-oxen generally live in flat terrain, they usually ascend to the highest elevation in their area for better vantage when threatened. They can see well in the darkness, as befits an animal that spends months in almost total darkness. Their eyes have adapted so that the sun's glare on ice or snow does not bother them.

The olfactory glands of the musk-ox undoubtedly help it to smell food under the snow. Explorers give conflicting reports about the musk-ox using its sense of smell to detect danger.

Consistent with Allen's rule, which correlates the size of an animal's extremities (ears and tail) with the latitude and temperature of the region that it inhabits, the musk-ox has short ears, less liable to freezing than long ears would be. Hearing is important to the musk-ox but it is not a primary sense. Yet the musk-ox's food preferences show that it has a well-developed sense of taste.

Communication: The only sound I have heard musk-oxen make was a deep lowing, much like that of cattle, not quite a mooing, but a deep *MMMMMMMMMM*. It was made when the musk-oxen formed a defensive circle. I could not differentiate between the sounds made by the cows and the bulls.

Locomotion: Musk-oxen appear stocky, and part of this impression results from their short legs in comparison with their bodies. Because of this, when they walk they take a shorter stride. I have seen musk-oxen walk slow and fast. And I have seen them gallop, but I have not seen them trot.

Musk-oxen usually walk slowly as they feed. There is seldom need for hurry. When I first encountered the herd, they just stood and stared at me, then turned and started to walk off. They then broke into a gallop at what I estimated to be about 25 miles per hour. When they reached a beach, they stopped and formed a defensive circle and then stood fast. They showed me no aggressive signs.

The Eskimos told us of one old solitary bull that had charged several photographers. That must have been quite an experience because on the musk-ox's turf there are no trees to climb or anything to hide behind. Musk-oxen run at least twice as fast as a man.

Breeding: During the rutting season from late July through September, dominant bulls drive off lesser bulls and are extremely antagonistic. Battles between the big bulls are awesome because the rivals crash head-on. Each attempts to push the other off his feet and to hook his rival. Death occasionally results from these clashes. Some of the fights are sheeplike, with repeated head-on crashes.

The cows come into oestrus in the latter part of August. Throughout August the bulls are constantly fighting, chasing off lesser bulls or chasing after cows that are neither ready nor able to receive services.

The cows come into oestrus for 24 to 30 hours, and most of the cows are bred a number of times during that period. If any cow does not conceive, she will come back into oestrus three or four weeks later. The females do not usually breed till their third year.

Birth and Young: The gestation period is 8 to 8 1/2 months, with most of the young being born in May. Some cows don't bear calves every year. Cows rarely give birth to more than one calf each year.

The newborn calf is chunky and black and weighs 30 to 33 pounds. The calf is able to walk within an hour and able to follow its mother in a few hours. Unless the herd is frightened and runs off, a two-day-old calf can keep up with the herd as it feeds.

Within a week, the calf is able to feed upon the same vegetation that its mother is eating. From that time on forage becomes increasingly important, but most calves continue to suckle for up to a year, even though they can do without milk before then.

The relationship between the cow and the calf is a close one. The calf follows its mother closely or runs to her the instant anything disturbs the herd. At times the calf will crowd underneath its mother and be almost obscured by her long hair.

Some musk-oxen cows breed only every second year, while others breed every year.

Life Span: The musk-ox can live for about 25 years. One cow was 23 years old when she was killed.

Sign: Tracks and dung are the most commonly seen sign. These are almost identical to that of domestic cattle, but can't be mistaken for that of cattle because cattle could not survive in musk-oxen ranges. Another sign is pieces and patches of *qiviut* (soft under layer of hair) draped on bushes or blowing about.

Enemies: The wolf is the most important natural enemy. Occasionally a bear may take a young musk-ox. The defensive circle that the musk-oxen use against wolves and bears is successful. But the defensive circle proved to be the musk-ox's undoing when native hunters approached using dogs and modern rifles.

Mosquitos make life miserable for every being in the Arctic in late spring and summer. Yet the musk-ox's dense hair protects all but the musk-ox's eyes and nose.

Musk-oxen have also been known to have various intestinal parasites that apparently do the host animal little, if any, harm.

Human Relations: The musk-ox has long been a staple of diet for some Eskimos. And musk-oxen meat has kept many Arctic explorers and fur traders from starving to death. Domestication of the musk-ox for the production of qiviut has proved possible, but there is still a question as to the economic feasibility. For a number of years, a large captive herd was held at the University of Alaska at Fairbanks. The herd was then removed to Unalakleet.

Trophy Records: Musk-oxen can be hunted today on a limited basis. The permits are issued as culling tools to prevent overbrowsing and range destruction.

The world's-record musk-ox was taken on a controlled hunt on the Perry River in the Northwest Territories in 1979. It is owned by Robert Decker. Length of the right horn is 29 inches, with a 10-inch boss (casque). Length of the left is 28 1/8 inches, with a 9 7/8-inch boss. Greatest spread is 30 5/8 inches. Total score is 122.

The second ranking head was taken by I. S. Wombath,

on Ellesmere Land, Canada, in 1900. It scored 115 2/8 points. The right horn is 26 inches long and the left is 27 inches. The boss or casque is 10 6/8 inches and 10 2/8 inches in width. The tip to tip spread is 27 inches.

Table Fare: Musk-oxen is reported to taste good, although the meat is a little darker and quite a bit drier than beef.

This musk-oxen bull shows a casque of horns over his skull, characteristic of bulls. Female horns are separated by hair. Also note the tufts of shedding qiviut (soft undercoat) clinging to the long guard hairs.

Selected Bibliography

General Reading

Anthony, H. E. *Field Book of North American Mammals*. New York: G. P. Putnam's Sons, 1928.

Banfield, A. W. F. *The Mammals of Canada*. Toronto, Ontario: University of Toronto Press, 1974.

Burt, William H. *The Mammals of Michigan*. Ann Arbor, Michigan: The University of Michigan Press, 1946.

———— and R. P. GrossenHeider. *A Field Guide to the Mammals*. Boston, Massachusetts: Houghton-Mifflin Co., 1952.

Cahalane, Victor. *Mammals of North America*. New York: The Macmillan Co., 1947.

Doutt, J. Kenneth, Caroline A. Heppenstall and John E. Guilday. *Mammals of Pennsylvania*. Harrisburg, Pennsylvania: Pennsylvania Game Commission, 1966.

Gray, James. *Animal Locomotion*. New York: Norton, 1968.

Grzimek, Bernhard. *Grzimek's Animal Life Encyclopedia*. New York: Van Nostrand Reinhold Co., 1972.

Hamilton, W. J., Jr. *American Mammals*. New York: McGraw-Hill Book Company, Inc., 1939.

———— and John Whitaker, Jr. *Mammals of the Eastern United States*. 2nd ed. Ithaca, New York and London: Cornell University Press, 1979.

Ingles, Lloyd G. *Mammals of the Pacific States*. Stanford, California: Stanford University Press, 1947.

Jackson, Hartley H. T. *Mammals of Wisconsin*. Madison, Wisconsin: University of Wisconsin Press, 1961.

Long, Charles A. *The Mammals of Wyoming*. Lawrence, Kansas: University of Kansas, 1965.

Lowery, George H., Jr. *The Mammals of Louisiana*. Baton Rouge, Louisiana: Louisiana State University Press, 1974.

Milne, Lorus J. and Margery. *The Senses of Animals and Men.* New York: Atheneum, 1962.

Murie, Olaus. *A Field Guide to Animal Tracks.* Boston, Massachusetts: Houghton Mifflin Co., 1954.

O'Connor, Jack. *The Big Game Animals of North America.* 2nd ed. New York: Outdoor Life Books and Scribners, 1977.

Palmer, Ralph S. *The Mammal Guide.* Garden City, New York: Doubleday and Company, Inc., 1954.

Paradiso, John L. "Mammals of Maryland," *North American Fauna No. 66.* Washington: Bureau of Sport Fisheries and Wildlife, U. S. Government Printing Office, 1969.

Rue, Leonard Lee, III. *Pictorial Guide to the Mammals of North America.* New York: Thomas Y. Crowell Co., 1967.

Schmidt, John L. and Douglas L. Gilbert, eds. *Big Game of North America—A Wildlife Management Book.* Harrisburg, Pennsylvania: Stackpole Books, 1978.

Schwartz, Charles W. and Elizabeth R. *The Wild Mammals of Missouri.* Kansas City, Missouri: University of Missouri Press, 1959.

Seton, Ernest Thompson. *Lives of Game Animals.* Boston, Massachusetts: Charles T. Branford Co., 1953.

Silver, Helenette. *A History of New Hampshire Game and Furbearers.* Concord, New Hampshire: New Hampshire Fish and Game Department, 1957.

Soper, J. Dewey. *The Mammals of Alberta.* Edmonton, Alberta: The Hamly Press Ltd., 1964.

Walker, Ernest P. and John L. Paradiso. *Mammals of the World.* 3rd ed. Baltimore, Maryland, and London: the Johns Hopkins University Press, 1975.

Pouched Mammals

Fitch, Henry S. and Lewis L. Sandidge. *Ecology of the Opossum on a Natural Area in Northeastern Kansas.* Lawrence, Kansas: University of Kansas, 1953.

Hamilton, William J., Jr. *Life History and Economic Relations of the Opossum in N. Y. State.* Ithaca, New York: Cornell University, March 1958.

Hartman, Carl G. *Possums.* Austin, Texas: University of Texas Press, 1952.

Keefe, James F. and Don Wooldridge. *The World of the Opossum.* Philadelphia and New York: J. B. Lippincott Co., 1967.

Carnivores

Allen, Durwood.*Wolves of Minong.* Boston, Massachusetts: Houghton Mifflin Co., 1979.

Arnold, David A. *Red Foxes of Michigan.* Lansing, Michigan: Michigan Dept. of Conservation, 1956.

Barnes, Claude T. *The Cougar or Mountain Lion.* Salt Lake City, Utah: The Ralton Co., 1960.

Beebe, B. F. *American Wolves, Coyotes and Foxes.* New York: David McKay Company, Inc., 1964.

Bekoff, Marc, ed. *Coyotes: Biology, Behavior and Management.* New York: Academic Press, 1978.

Bueler, Lois E. *Wild Dogs of the World.* New York: Stein and Day, 1973.

Burk, Dale, ed. *The Black Bear in Modern North America.* New York: Boone and Crockett Club, 1979.

Colby, C. B. *Wild Cats.* New York: Duell, Sloan and Pearce, 1964.

Craighead, Frank C., Jr. *Track of the Grizzly.* San Francisco, California: Sierra Club Books, 1979.

East, Ben. *Bears.* New York: Outdoor Life Books and Crown Publishers, 1977.

Fiennes, Richard. *The Order of Wolves.* Indianapolis, Indiana: Bobbs-Merrill, 1976.

Fox, Michael. *Behavior of Wolves, Dogs and Related Canids.* New York: Harper & Row, 1971.

Goldman, Edward A. "Raccoons of North and Middle America," *North America Fauna No. 60.* Washington: U. S. Department of Interior, 1950.

Guggisberg, C. A. W. *Wild Cats of the World.* New York: Taplinger Publishing Co., 1975.

Hall, Roberta L. and Henry S. Sharp, eds. *Wolf and Man.* New York: Academic Press, 1978.

Harrington, C. Richard. "Denning Habits of the Polar Bear," *Report Series No. 5,* Canadian Wildlife Service, Ottawa, Ontario, 1968.

Haynes, Bessie Doak and Edgar Haynes, eds. *The Grizzly Bear.* Norman, Oklahoma: University of Oklahoma Press, 1966.

Holzworth, John M. *The Wild Grizzlies of Alaska.* New York and London: G. P. Putnam's Sons, 1930.

Hopf, Alice L. *Wild Cousins of the Dog.* New York: G. P. Putnam's Sons, 1973.

Johnson, Sydney A. "Biology of the Raccoon," *Bulletin 402.* Auburn, Alabama: Alabama Department of Conservation and Agricultural Experiment Station, June 1970.

Klinghammer, Erich, ed. *The Behavior and Ecology of Wolves.* New York: Garland STPM Press, 1979.

Koch, Thomas J. *The Year of the Polar Bear.* Indianapolis, Indiana: Bobbs-Merrill, 1975.

Lopez, Barry Holstun. *Of Wolves and Men.* New York: Charles Scribner's Sons, 1978.

Matson, J. R. *The Adaptable Black Bear.* Philadelphia, Pennsylvania: Dorrance and Co., 1967.

McCracken, Harold. *The Beast That Walks Like a Man.* London: Oldbourne Press, 1957.

Mech, L. David. *The Wolf.* New York: American Museum of Natural History, 1970.

Mills, Enos A. *The Grizzly.* New York: Ballantine Books, 1973.

Murie, Adolph. "Ecology of the Coyote in the Yellowstone," *Fauna Series No. 4.* Washington: U. S. Government Printing Office, 1940.
———. *Following Fox Trails.* Ann Arbor, Michigan: University of Michigan Press, 1936.
———. *The Wolves of Mount McKinley.* Washington: U. S. Government Printing Office, 1944.

Perry, Richard. *The World of the Polar Bear.* Seattle, Washington: University of Washington Press, 1966.
———. *The World of the Jaguar.* New York: Taplinger Publishing Co., 1970.

Ricciuti, Edward R. *The Wild Cats.* New York: Ridge Press, 1979.

Rue, Leonard Lee, III. *The World of the Raccoon.* Philadelphia and New York: J. B. Lippincott Co., 1964.
———. *The World of the Red Fox.* Philadelphia and New York: J. B. Lippincott Co., 1969.

Rutter, Russell J. and Douglas H. Pimlot. *The World of the Wolf.* Philadelphia and New York: J. B. Lippincott Co., 1967.

Ryden, Hope. *God's Dog.* New York: Coward, McCann and Geohegan Inc., 1975.

Schoonmaker, W. J. *The World of the Grizzly Bear*. Philadelphia and New York: J. B. Lippincott Co., 1968.

U.S. Fish and Wildlife Service. *Predator Damage in the West: A Study of Coyote Management Alternatives*. Washington: Department of Interior, December 1978.

Van Wormer, Joe. *The World of the Bobcat*. Philadelphia and New York: J. B. Lippincott Co., 1963.

―――. *The World of the Coyote*. Philadelphia and New York: J. B. Lippincott Co., 1964.

―――. *The World of the Black Bear*. Philadelphia and New York: J. B. Lippincott Co., 1966.

Whitney, Leon F. and Acil B. Underwood. *The Raccoon*. Orange, Connecticut: Practical Science Publishing Co., 1952.

Woodworth, Jim. *The Kodiak Bear*. Harrisburg, Pennsylvania: The Stackpole Co., 1958.

Wright, Bruce S. *The Ghost of North America*. New York: Vantage Press, 1959.

―――. *The Eastern Panther*. Toronto, Canada: Clarke, Irwin and Company, Ltd., 1972.

Wright, William H. *The Grizzly Bear*. New York: Charles Scribner's Sons, 1909.

―――. *The Black Bear*. New York: Charles Scribner's Sons, 1910.

Young, Stanley P. and Edward A. Goldman. *The Wolves of North America*. Washington: The American Wildlife Institute, 1944.

―――. *The Puma: Mysterious American Cat*. Washington: The American Wildlife Institute, 1946.

――― and Hartley H. T. Jackson. *The Clever Coyote*. Harrisburg, Pennsylvania: The Stackpole Co., 1951.

―――. *The Bobcat of North America*. Harrisburg, Pennsylvania: The Stackpole Co., 1958.

Seals and Walrus

Haley, Delphine. *Marine Mammals*. Seattle, Washington: Pacific Search Press, 1978.

King, Judith E. *Seals of the World*. London, England: Trustees of the British Museum, 1964.

Loughrey, Alan G. "Preliminary Investigation of the Atlantic Walrus," *Wildlife Management Bulletin*, Series 1, No. 14, Ottawa, Ontario, Queens Printer, 1959.

Maxwell, Gavin. *Seals of the World*. Boston, Massachusetts: Houghton Mifflin Co., 1967.

Perry, Richard. *The World of the Walrus*. New York: Taplinger Publishing Co., 1967.

Scammon, Charles M. *The Marine Mammals of the Northwestern Coast of North America*. New York: Dover Publications, 1968.

Scheffer, Victor B. *A Natural History of Marine Mammals*. New York: Charles Scribner's Sons, 1976.

Rodents

Allen, D. L. *Michigan Fox Squirrel Management*. Lansing, Michigan: Dept. of Conservation, 1943.

Barkalow, Frederick, Jr. and Monica Shorten. *The World of the Gray Squirrel*. Philadelphia and New York: J. B. Lippincott Co., 1973.

Barnett, S. A. *The Rat*. Chicago, Illinois: Aldine Publishing Co., 1963.

Brown, Louis G. and Lee E. Yeager. *Fox Squirrels and Gray Squirrels in Illinois*. Urbana, Illinois: Illinois Natural History Survey, 1945.

Calhoun, John B. *The Ecology and Sociology of the Norway Rat*. Washington: U. S. Dept. of Health and Welfare, 1962.

Costello, David F. *The World of the Porcupine*. Philadelphia and New York: J. B. Lippincott Co., 1966.

————. *The World of the Prairie Dog*. Philadelphia and New York: J. B. Lippincott Co., 1970.

Dugmore, A. Radclyffe. *The Romance of the Beaver*. Philadelphia, Pennsylvania: J. B. Lippincott Co., 1919.

Hamilton, W. J., Jr. *The Life History of the Rufescent Woodchuck*. Pittsburg, Pennsylvania: Carnegie Museum, 1934.

Howell, Arthur H. "Revision of the American Marmots," *North American Fauna No. 28*. Washington: U. S. Government Printing Office, 1915.

Johnson, Charles Eugene. "The Beaver in the Adirondacks," *Roosevelt Wild Life Bulletin*, vol. 4, no. 4. Syracuse, New York: Syracuse University, 1927.

King, John A. *Social Behavior, Social Organization and Population Dynamics in a Black-tailed Prairie Dog Town.* Ann Arbor, Michigan: University of Michigan, 1955.

MacClintock, Dorcas. *Squirrels of North America.* New York: Van Nostrand Reinhold Co., 1970.

Madson, John. *Gray and Fox Squirrels.* East Alton, Illinois: Olin Mathieson Chemical Corp., 1964.

Mills, Enos A. *In Beaver World.* Boston, Massachusetts: Houghton Mifflin Co., 1913.

Packard, Robert L. *The Tree Squirrels of Kansas.* Topeka, Kansas: University of Kansas, 1956.

Rue, Leonard Lee, III. *The World of the Beaver.* Philadelphia and New York: J. B. Lippincott Co., 1964.

Schoonmaker, W. J. *The World of the Woodchuck.* Philadelphia and New York: J. B. Lippincott Co., 1966.

Taylor, Walter P. *Ecology and Life History of the Porcupine.* Tucson, Arizona: University of Arizona, 1935.

Wilson, Lars. *My Beaver Colony.* Garden City, New York: Doubleday and Company, Inc., 1968.

Zinsser, Hans. *Rats, Lice and History.* New York: Bantam Books, 1935.

Hares and Rabbits

Haygood, John Lewis. *Cottontail Rabbit Populations.* Baton Rouge, Louisiana: Louisiana Wildlife and Fisheries Commission, 1963.

Kirkpatrick, Ralph D. *San Juan Rabbit Investigation.* Indianapolis: Indiana Dept. of Conservation, 1959.

Lord, Rexford D., Jr. *The Cottontail Rabbit in Illinois.* Springfield, Illinois: Illinois Dept. of Conservation, 1963.

Orr, Robert T. *The Rabbits of California.* San Francisco: California Academy of Sciences, 1940.

Rue, Leonard Lee, III. *Cottontail.* New York: T. Y. Crowell Co., 1965.

Sevaraid, Joye Harold. *The Snowshoe Hare.* Augusta, Maine: Maine Dept. of Inland Fisheries and Game, 1942.

Vorhies, Charles T. *The Life Histories and Ecology of Jack Rabbits.* Tucson, Arizona: University of Arizona, 1933.

Hoofed Mammals

Anderson, Chester C. *The Elk of Jackson Hole.* Cheyenne, Wyoming: Wyoming Game and Fish Commission, 1958.

Boyce, Mark S. and Larry D. Hayden-Wing, eds. *North American Elk: Ecology, Behavior and Management.* Laramie, Wyoming: The University of Wyoming, 1979.

Brandborg, Stewart M. *Mountain Goat in Idaho.* Boise, Idaho: Idaho Dept. of Fish and Game, 1955.

Brown, Ellsworth Reade. *The Black-tailed Deer in Western Washington.* Olympia, Washington: Washington State Game Dept., 1961.

Buechner, Helmut K. *The Bighorn Sheep in the United States: Its Past, Present and Future.* Washington: The Wildlife Society, 1960.

Casebeer, Robert L., Merle J. Rognrud and Stewart Brandborg. *The Rocky Mountain Goat in Montana.* Helena, Montana: Montana Fish and Game Commission, 1950.

Clark, James L. *The Greak Ark of the Wild Sheep.* Norman, Oklahoma: University of Oklahoma Press, 1964.

Dahlberg, Burton L. and Ralph C. Guettinger. "The White-tailed Deer in Wisconsin," *Technical Wildlife Bulletin No. 14.* Madison, Wisconsin: Wisconsin Conservation Dept., 1956.

Dary, David A. *The Buffalo Book.* Chicago: The Swallow Press, Inc., 1974.

Dugmore, A. Radclyffe. *The Romance of the Newfoundland Caribou.* Philadelphia and New York: J. B. Lippincott Co., 1913.

Einarsen, Arthur S. *The Pronghorn Antelope.* Washington: The Wildlife Management Institute, 1948.

Forbes, Stanley E., Lincoln M. Lang, Stephen A. Liscinsky and Harvey A. Roberts. *The White-tailed Deer in Pennsylvania.* Harrisburg, Pennsylvania: Pennsylvania Game Commission, 1971.

Garretson, Martin S. *The American Bison.* New York: New York Zoological Society, 1938.

Geist, Valerius. *Mountain Sheep.* Chicago: University of Chicago Press, 1971.

———. *Mountain Sheep and Man.* Ithaca, New York: Cornell University Press, 1975.

Graf, William. *The Roosevelt Elk.* Port Angeles, Washington: Port Angeles Evening News, 1955.

Harper, Francis. *The Barren Ground Caribou of Keewatin.* Lawrence, Kansas: University of Kansas, 1955.

Hoover, Robert L., C. E. Till and Stanley Ogilvie. *The Antelope of Colorado.* Denver, Colorado: Colorado Department of Fish and Game, 1959.

Houston, Douglas B. *The Shiras Moose in Jackson Hole, Wyoming.* Grand Teton, Wyoming: Grand Teton Natural History Association, 1968.

Kitchen, David W. *Social Behavior and Ecology of the Pronghorn.* Washington: The Wildlife Society, 1974.

Knight, Richard R. *The Sun River Elk Herd.* Washington: The Wildlife Society, 1970.

Knipe, Theodore. *The Javelina in Arizona.* Phoenix: Arizona Game and Fish Department, 1955.

Linsdale, Jean M., and P. Quentin Tomich. *A Herd of Mule Deer.* Berkeley, California: University of California Press, 1953.

Madson, John. *The White-tailed Deer.* East Alton, Illinois: Olin Mathieson Chemical Corporation, 1961.

———. *The Elk.* East Alton, Illinois: Olin Mathieson Chemical Corp., 1966.

McHugh, Tom. *The Time of the Buffalo.* New York: Alfred A. Knopf, 1972.

Meagher, Margaret Mary. *The Bison of Yellowstone National Park.* Washington: National Park Service, 1973.

Merrill, Samuel. *The Moose Book.* New York: E. P. Dutton and Co., 1916.

Miller, Frank L. *Biology of the Kaminuriak Population of Barren-ground Caribou. Part 2.* Ottawa, Canada: Canadian Wildlife Services, 1974.

Murie, Adolph. *The Moose of Isle Royale.* Ann Arbor, Michigan: University of Michigan Press, 1934.

Murie, Olaus J. *Alaska-Yukon Caribou.* Washington: Bureau of Biological Survey, 1935.

———. *The Elk of North America.* Harrisburg, Pennsylvania: The Stackpole Co., 1951.

O'Conner, Jack. *Sheep and Sheep Hunting.* New York: Winchester Press, 1974.

Park, Ed. *The World of the Bison.* Philadelphia and New York: J. B. Lippincott Co., 1969.

Peterson, Randolph L. *North American Moose*. Toronto, Canada: University of Toronto Press, 1955.

Pratt, Jerome J. *White Flags of Apacheland*. New York: Vantage Press, 1966.

Pruitt, William O., Jr. "Behavior of the Barren-Ground Caribou," *Biological Papers of the University of Alaska*, No. 3. Fairbanks, Alaska: University of Alaska, 1960.

Roe, Frank Gilbert. *The North American Buffalo*. Toronto, Canada: University of Toronto Press, 1951.

Rue, Leonard Lee, III. *The World of the White-tailed Deer*. Philadelphia and New York: J. B. Lippincott Co., 1962.

———. *The Deer of North America*. New York: Outdoor Life Books and Crown, 1978.

Russo, John P. *The Desert Bighorn Sheep in Arizona*. Phoenix: Arizona Game and Fish Dept., 1956.

Smith, Dwight R. *The Bighorn Sheep in Idaho*. Boise, Idaho: Idaho Dept. of Fish and Game, 1954.

Stadtfeld, Curtis K. *Whitetail Deer: A Year's Cycle*. New York: Dial Press, 1975.

Swank, Wendell G. *The Mule Deer in Arizona Chaparral*. Phoenix: Arizona Game and Fish Dept., 1958.

Taber, Richard D., and Raymond F. Dasmann. "The Black-tailed Deer of the Chaparral," *Game Bulletin*, No. 8. Sacramento: California Department of Fish and Game, 1958.

Taylor, Walter P. *The Deer of North America*. Harrisburg, Pennsylvania: The Stackpole Co., 1956.

Tener, J. S. *Muskoxen of Canada*. Ottawa, Canada: Dept. of Northern Affairs and National Resources, 1965.

Van Wormer, Joseph. *The World of the American Elk*. Philadelphia and New York: J. B. Lippincott Co., 1969.

———. *The World of the Pronghorn*. Philadelphia and New York: J. B. Lippincott Co., 1969.

———. *The World of the Moose*. Philadelphia and New York: J. B. Lippincott Co., 1972.

Wells, Ralph E. and Florence B. Welles. *The Bighorn of Death Valley*. Washington: National Park Service, 1961.

Yoakum, James D. and Donald E. Spalinger, compilers. *American Pronghorn Antelope*. Washington: The Wildlife Society, 1979.

TROPHY SCORING CHARTS The following pages contain facsimiles of some of the Boone and Crockett Club scoring charts used to determine world-record standings for North American big game. The Club established this scoring system in 1950, jointly sponsored records keeping with the National Rifle Association (NRA) from 1973 through 1980, and resumed full responsibility for records in 1981.

To promote fair chase and sportsmanlike hunting methods, the Club disqualifies trophies taken as follows: (1) by spotting or herding from the air, followed by landing in its vicinity for pursuit, (2) by herding or pursuing game with motor-powered vehicles, (3) by using electronic communications for attracting, locating or observing game, or guiding the hunter to that game.

To obtain official scoring charts, instructions for chart preparation, a list of official scorers, or a copy of the latest record book, write the Club at the address shown on the upper right corner of the forms.

OFFICIAL SCORING SYSTEM FOR NORTH AMERICAN BIG GAME TROPHIES

RECORDS OF NORTH AMERICAN
BIG GAME COMMITTEE

BOONE AND CROCKETT CLUB

RETURN TO:

Boone and Crockett Club
424 N. Washington St.
Alexandria, Virginia 22314

Minimum Score:	Bear
Alaskan Brown	— 28
Black	— 21
Grizzly	— 24
Polar	— 27

BEAR

KIND OF BEAR
_____

SEX _____

SEE OTHER SIDE FOR INSTRUCTIONS	Measurements
A. Greatest Length Without Lower Jaw	
B. Greatest Width	
TOTAL and FINAL SCORE	

Exact locality where killed
Date killed _____ By whom killed _____
Present owner _____
Address _____
Guide's Name and Address _____
Remarks: (Mention any abnormalities) _____

I certify that I have measured the above trophy on _____ 19___
at (address) _____ City _____ State _____
and that these measurements and data are, to the best of my knowledge and belief, made in accordance with the instructions given.

Witness: _____ Signature: _____

Official Measurer

621

Whitetail and Coues Deer

OFFICIAL SCORING SYSTEM FOR NORTH AMERICAN BIG GAME TROPHIES

RECORDS OF NORTH AMERICAN
BIG GAME COMMITTEE

BOONE AND CROCKETT CLUB

RETURN TO:
Boone and Crockett Club
424 N. Washington St.
Alexandria, Virginia 22314

Minimum Score: **Deer**
Whitetail: **Typical 170**
Coues: **Typical 110**

WHITETAIL and COUES DEER

KIND OF DEER _____

Detail of Point Measurement

SEE OTHER SIDE FOR INSTRUCTIONS	Supplementary Data		Column 1	Column 2	Column 3	Column 4
	R.	L.	Spread Credit	Right Antler	Left Antler	Difference
A. Number of Points on Each Antler			/////	/////	/////	/////
B. Tip to Tip Spread			/////			
C. Greatest Spread						
D. Inside Spread of MAIN BEAMS — Spread credit may equal but not exceed length of longer antler						
IF Inside Spread of Main Beams exceeds longer antler length, enter difference			/////	/////	/////	
E. Total of Lengths of all Abnormal Points			/////			
F. Length of Main Beam			/////			
G-1. Length of First Point, if present			/////			
G-2. Length of Second Point			/////			
G-3. Length of Third Point			/////			
G-4. Length of Fourth Point, if present			/////			
G-5. Length of Fifth Point, if present			/////			
G-6. Length of Sixth Point, if present			/////			
G-7. Length of Seventh Point, if present			/////			
H-1. Circumference at Smallest Place Between Burr and First Point			/////			
H-2. Circumference at Smallest Place Between First and Second Points			/////			
H-3. Circumference at Smallest Place Between Second and Third Points			/////			
H-4. Circumference at Smallest Place between Third and Fourth Points or half way between Third Point and Beam Tip if Fourth Point is missing			/////			
TOTALS						

ADD	Column 1		Exact locality where killed	
	Column 2		Date killed	By whom killed
	Column 3		Present owner	
	Total		Address	
SUBTRACT Column 4			Guide's Name and Address	
FINAL SCORE			Remarks: (Mention any abnormalities)	

MEASURING INSTRUCTIONS

All measurements must be made with a flexible steel tape to the nearest one-eighth of an inch. Wherever it is necessary to change direction of measurement, mark a control point and swing tape at this point. To simplify addition, please enter fractional figures in eighths. Official measurements cannot be taken for at least sixty days after the animal was killed. Please submit photographs of trophy front and sides.

Supplementary Data measurements indicate conformation of the trophy, and none of the figures in Lines A, B and C are to be included in the score. Evaluation of conformation is a matter of personal preference. Excellent, but nontypical Whitetail Deer heads with many points shall be placed and judged in a separate class.

A. Number of points of each Antler. To be counted a point, a projection must be at least one inch long AND its length must exceed the length of its base. All points are measured from tip of point to nearest edge of beam as illustrated. Beam tip is counted as a point but not measured as a point.

B. Tip to Tip Spread measured between tips of Main Beams.

C. Greatest Spread measured between perpendiculars at right angles to the center line of the skull at widest part whether across main beams or points.

D. Inside Spread of Main Beams measured at right angles to the center line of the skull at widest point between main beams. Enter this measurement again in "Spread Credit" column if it is less than or equal to the length of longer antler.

E. Total of lengths of all Abnormal Points. Abnormal points are generally considered to be those nontypical in shape or location.

F. Length of Main Beam measured from lowest outside edge of burr over outer curve to the most distant point of what is, or appears to be, the main beam. The point of beginning is that point on the burr where the center line along the outer curve of the beam intersects the burr.

G-1-2-3-4-5-6-7. Length of Normal Points. Normal points project from main beam. They are measured from nearest edge of main beam over outer curve to tip. To determine nearest edge (top edge) of beam, lay the tape along the outer curve of the beam so that the top edge of the tape coincides with the top edge of the beam on both sides of the point. Draw line along top edge of tape. This line will be base line from which point is measured.

H-1-2-3-4. Circumferences - If first point is missing, Take H-1 and H-2 at smallest place between burr and second point.

Editor's Note: Score chart and instructions are reprinted with permission.

RECORDS OF NORTH AMERICAN BIG GAME COMMITTEE

BOONE AND CROCKETT CLUB

RETURN TO:
Boone and Crockett Club
424 N. Washington St.
Alexandria, Virginia 22314

Minimum Score: Deer
Col. Blacktail: Typical – 130
Mule: Typical – 195

MULE and BLACKTAIL DEER

KIND OF DEER: _____

Detail of Point Measurement

SEE OTHER SIDE FOR INSTRUCTIONS		Supplementary Data		Column 1	Column 2	Column 3	Column 4
		R.	L.	Spread Credit	Right Antler	Left Antler	Difference
A. Number of Points on Each Antler							
B. Tip to Tip Spread							
C. Greatest Spread							
D. Inside Spread of MAIN BEAMS	Spread credit may equal but not exceed length of longer antler						
IF Inside Spread of Main Beams exceeds longer antler length, enter difference							
E. Total of Lengths of all Abnormal Points							
F. Length of Main Beam							
G-1 Length of First Point, if present							
G-2 Length of Second Point							
G-3 Length of Third Point, if present							
G-4 Length of Fourth Point, if present							
H-1 Circumference at Smallest Place Between Burr and First Point							
H-2 Circumference at Smallest Place Between First and Second Points							
H-3 Circumference at Smallest Place Between Main Beam and Third Point							
H-4 Circumference at Smallest Place Between Second and Fourth Points							
TOTALS							

ADD	Column 1		Exact locality where killed	
	Column 2		Date killed	By whom killed
	Column 3		Present owner	
	TOTAL		Address	Zip
SUBTRACT Column 4			Guide's Name and Address	
FINAL SCORE			Remarks: (Mention any abnormalities)	

624

RECORDS OF NORTH AMERICAN
BIG GAME COMMITTEE
Wapiti Minimum Score: 375

BOONE AND CROCKETT CLUB

RETURN TO:
Boone and Crockett Club
424 N. Washington St.
Alexandria, Virginia 22314

WAPITI

Detail of point Measurement

SEE OTHER SIDE FOR INSTRUCTIONS		Supplementary Data		Column 1	Column 2	Column 3	Column 4
		R.	L.	Spread Credit	Right Antler	Left Antler	Difference
A. Number of Points on Each Antler							
B. Tip to Tip Spread							
C. Greatest Spread							
D. Inside Spread of MAIN BEAMS	Spread credit may equal but not exceed length of longer antler						
	IF Inside Spread of Main Beams exceeds longer antler length, enter difference						
E. Total of Lengths of all Abnormal Points							
F. Length of Main Beam							
G-1. Length of First Point							
G-2. Length of Second Point							
G-3. Length of Third Point							
G-4. Length of Fourth (Royal) Point							
G-5. Length of Fifth Point							
G-6. Length of Sixth Point, if present							
G-7. Length of Seventh Point, if present							
H-1. Circumference at Smallest Place Between First and Second Points							
H-2. Circumference at Smallest Place Between Second and Third Points							
H-3. Circumference at Smallest Place Between Third and Fourth Points							
H-4. Circumference at Smallest Place Between Fourth and Fifth Points							
TOTALS							

ADD	Column 1		Exact locality where killed	
	Column 2		Date killed	By whom killed
	Column 3		Present owner	
	TOTAL		Address	
SUBTRACT Column 4			Guide's Name and Address	
FINAL SCORE			Remarks: (Mention any abnormalities)	

RETURN TO:

RECORDS OF NORTH AMERICAN
BIG GAME COMMITTEE

BOONE AND CROCKETT CLUB

Boone and Crockett Club
424 N. Washington St.
Alexandria, Virginia 22314

MINIMUM SCORE: Barren Ground - 400
Mountain - 390
Quebec-Labrador - 375
Woodland - 295

CARIBOU

KIND OF CARIBOU

Rack			Code
Wt.			

Detail of point measurement

SEE OTHER SIDE FOR INSTRUCTIONS	Supplementary Data	Column 1	Column 2	Column 3	Column 4
		Spread Credit	Right Antler	Left Antler	Difference
A. Tip to Tip Spread					
B. Greatest Spread					
C. Inside Spread of MAIN BEAMS — Spread credit may equal but not exceed length of longer antler					
IF Inside Spread of Main Beams exceeds longer antler length, enter difference					
D. Number of Points on Each Antler excluding brows					
Number of Points on Each Brow					
E. Length of Main Beam					
F-1. Length of Brow Palm or First Point					
F-2. Length of Bez or Second Point					
F-3. Length of Rear Point, if present					
F-4. Length of Second Longest Top Point					
F-5. Length of Longest Top Point					
G-1. Width of Brow Palm					
G-2. Width of Top Palm					
H-1. Circumference at Smallest Place Between Brow and Bez Points					
H-2. Circumference at Smallest Place Between Bez and Rear Point, if present					
H-3. Circumference at Smallest Place Before First Top Point					
H-4. Circumference at Smallest Place Between Two Longest Top Palm Points					
TOTALS					

ADD	Column 1		Exact locality where killed	
	Column 2		Date killed	By whom killed
	Column 3		Present owner	
TOTAL			Address	
SUBTRACT Column 4			Guide's Name and Address	
FINAL SCORE			Remarks: (Mention any abnormalities)	

**RECORDS OF NORTH AMERICAN
BIG GAME COMMITTEE**

BOONE AND CROCKETT CLUB

RETURN TO:
Boone and Crockett Club
424 N. Washington St.
Alexandria, Virginia 22314

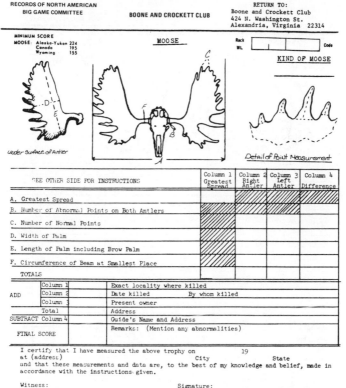

MINIMUM SCORE
MOOSE: Alaska-Yukon 224
Canada 195
Wyoming 155

MOOSE

Rack
WL

Code

KIND OF MOOSE

under surface of Antler

Detail of Point Measurement

SEE OTHER SIDE FOR INSTRUCTIONS	Column 1 Greatest Spread	Column 2 Right Antler	Column 3 Left Antler	Column 4 Difference
A. Greatest Spread				
B. Number of Abnormal Points on Both Antlers				
C. Number of Normal Points				
D. Width of Palm				
E. Length of Palm including Brow Palm				
F. Circumference of Beam at Smallest Place				
TOTALS				

ADD	Column 1		Exact locality where killed
	Column 2		Date killed By whom killed
	Column 3		Present owner
Total			Address
SUBTRACT Column 4			Guide's Name and Address
FINAL SCORE			Remarks: (Mention any abnormalities)

I certify that I have measured the above trophy on   19
at (address)   City   State
and that these measurements and data are, to the best of my knowledge and belief, made in
accordance with the instructions given.

Witness: _____   Signature: _____

Official Measurer

OFFICIAL SCORING SYSTEM FOR NORTH AMERICAN BIG GAME TROPHIES

RECORDS OF NORTH AMERICAN
BIG GAME COMMITTEE

BOONE AND CROCKETT CLUB

RETURN TO:
Boone and Crockett Club
424 N. Washington St.
Alexandria, Virginia 22314

Minimum Score: Sheep
Bighorn   — 180
Desert   — 168
Stone   — 170
White or Dall — 170

SHEEP

KIND OF SHEEP _____

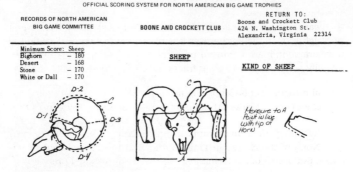

Measure to A
Point in line
with tip of
Horn

SEE OTHER SIDE FOR INSTRUCTIONS	Supplementary Data	Column 1	Column 2	Column 3
A. Greatest Spread (Is often Tip to Tip Spread)		Right Horn	Left Horn	Difference
B. Tip to Tip Spread (Enter again here) *(If Greatest Spread,*				
C. Length of Horn				/////////
D-1. Circumference of Base				
D-2. Circumference at First Quarter				
D-3. Circumference at Second Quarter				
D-4. Circumference at Third Quarter				
TOTALS				

ADD	Column 1	Exact locality where killed	
	Column 2	Date killed	By whom killed
	TOTAL	Present owner	
SUBTRACT Column 3		Address	
FINAL SCORE		Guide's Name and Address	
		Remarks: (Mention any abnormalities)	

I certify that I have measured the above trophy on _____ 19___
at (address) _____ City _____ State _____
and that these measurements and data are, to the best of my knowledge and belief, made in
accordance with the instructions given.

Witness: _____   Signature: _____

Official Measurer

628

MEASURING INSTRUCTIONS

All measurements must be made with a flexible steel tape to the nearest one-eighth of an inch. Wherever it is necessary to change direction of measurement, mark a control point and swing tape at this point. To simplify addition, please enter fractional figures in eighths.

Official measurements cannot be taken for at least sixty days after the animal was killed. Please submit photographs of trophy front and sides.

Supplementary Data measurements indicate conformation of the trophy. None of the figures in Lines A and B are to be included in the score. Evaluation of conformation is a matter of personal preference.

A.   Greatest Spread measured between perpendiculars at right angles to the center line of the skull.

B.   Tip to Tip Spread measured from outer edge of tips of horns.

C.   Length of Horn measured from lowest point in front on outer curve to a point in line with tip. DO NOT press tape into depressions. The low point of the outer curve of the horn is considered to be the low point of the frontal portion of the horn, situated above and slightly medial to the eye socket (not on the outside edge of the horn).

D-1. Circumference of Base measured at right angles to axis of horn. DO NOT follow irregular edge of horn.

D-2-3-4. Divide measurement C of LONGER horn by four, mark BOTH horns at these quarters even though other horn is shorter, and measure circumferences at these marks.

Editor's Note: Score chart and instructions are reprinted with permission.

OFFICIAL SCORING SYSTEM FOR NORTH AMERICAN BIG GAME TROPHIES

RECORDS OF NORTH AMERICAN BIG GAME COMMITTEE   **BOONE AND CROCKETT CLUB**

Boone and Crockett Club
424 N. Washington St.
Alexandria, Virginia 22314

Minimum Score
Pronghorn: 82

PRONGHORN

SEE OTHER SIDE FOR INSTRUCTIONS	Supplementary Data	Column 1	Column 2	Column 3
		Right Horn	Left Horn	Difference
A. Tip to Tip Spread				
B. Inside Spread of Main Beams		/////	/////	/////
IF Inside Spread of Main Beams exceeds longer horn length, enter difference.		/////	/////	
C. Length of Horn				
D-1. Circumference of Base				
D-2. Circumference at First Quarter				
D-3. Circumference at Second Quarter				
D-4. Circumference at Third Quarter				
E. Length of Prong				
TOTALS				

ADD	Column 1		Exact locality where killed	
	Column 2		Date killed	By whom killed
	Total		Present owner	
SUBTRACT Column 3			Address	
			Guide's Name and Address	
			Remarks: (Mention any abnormalities)	
FINAL SCORE				

I certify that I have measured the above trophy on   19
at (address)   City   State
and that these measurements and data are, to the best of my knowledge and belief, made in
accordance with the instructions given.

Witness:_____   Signature:_____

A IM TOP   Official Measurer

MEASURING INSTRUCTIONS

All measurements must be made with a flexible steel tape to the nearest one-eighth of an inch. Wherever it is necessary to change direction of measurement, mark a control point and swing tape at this point. To simplify addition, please enter fractional figures in eighths.

Official measurements cannot be taken for at least sixty days after the animal was killed. Please submit photographs.

Supplementary Data measurements indicate conformation of the trophy. None of the figures in Lines A and B are to be included in the score. Evaluation of conformation is a matter of personal preference.

A. Tip to Tip Spread measured between tips of horns.

B. Inside Spread of Main Beams measured at right angles to the center line of the skull at widest point between main beams.

C. Length of horn is measured on the outside curve, so the line taken will vary with different heads, depending on the direction of their curvature. Measure along the center of the outer curve from tip of horn to a point in line with the lowest edge of the base.

D-1. Measure around base of horn at right angles to long axis. Tape must be in contact with the lowest circumference of the horn in which there are no sierrations.

D-2-3-4. Divide measurement of LONGER horn by four, mark BOTH horns at these quarters even though one horn is shorter, and measure circumferences at these marks. If the prong occurs at approximately D-3, take this measurement immediately above the swelling of the prong.

E. Length of Prong—Measure from the tip of the prong along the upper edge of the outer curve to the horn; thence, around the horn to a point at the rear of the horn where a straight edge across the back of both horns touches the horn. This measurement around the horn from the base of the prong should be taken at right angles to the long axis of the horn.

Editor's Note: Score chart and instructions are reprinted with permission.

RECORDS OF NORTH AMERICAN
BIG GAME COMMITTEE

Goat Minimum Score: 50

BOONE AND CROCKETT CLUB

RETURN TO:
Boone and Crockett Club
424 N. Washington St.
Alexandria, Virginia 22314

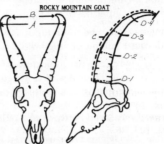

ROCKY MOUNTAIN GOAT

SEX _____

SEE OTHER SIDE FOR INSTRUCTIONS	Supplementary Data	Column 1	Column 2	Column 3
		Right Horn	Left Horn	Difference
A. Greatest Spread				
B. Tip to Tip Spread				
C. Length of Horn				
D-1. Circumference of Base				
D-2. Circumference at First Quarter				
D-3. Circumference at Second Quarter				
D-4. Circumference at Third Quarter				
TOTALS				

ADD	Column 1		Exact locality where killed
	Column 2		Date killed By whom killed
	TOTAL		Present owner
SUBTRACT Column 3			Address
			Guide's Name and Address
FINAL SCORE			Remarks: (Mention any abnormalities)

I certify that I have measured the above trophy on   19
at (address)   City   State
and that these measurements and data are, to the best of my knowledge and belief, made in
accordance with the instructions given.

Witness:_____ Signature:_____
                                                     Official Measurer

Index

Alaska-Yukon moose, 507
Alaskan brown bear, 39-53
Alaskan hare, 376
  See also Arctic hare
Alces alces, 493-508
Alces alces americana, 507,
  508
Alces alces andersoni, 507, 508
Alces alces gigas, 507
Alces alces shirasi, 507, 508
Allen, Durwood, 104, 289,
  504-505
Alopex lagopus, 137-149
American lion, *see* Mountain
  lion
Anderson, Robert, 178
Antilocapra americana,
  528-539
Antilocapridae, 527-539
Apache fox squirrel, 285
Arctic fox, 137-149
Arctic ground squirrel,
  297-303
Arctic hare, 375-382
Arizona gray squirrel, 271
Artiodactyla, *see* Hoofed
  animals

Bachman, John, 271
Bailey, Vernon, 282
Ball, Sam, 37
Barnes, Claude, 187
Barren Ground caribou,
  512-513, 518, 520, 525
Bartram, William, 101
Bastard fox, 125
Bay lynx, *see* Bobcat
Bears, 19-81
  Alaskan brown, 39-53

  black, 21-37
  grizzly, 55-69
  polar, 71-81
Beaubien, Garry, 525
Becker, Helmut, 508
Bering, Vitus, 148
Best, Kenneth, 507
Bighorn sheep, 555-571
Bison, 541-554
Bison bison, 541-554
Black bear, 21-37
Blacktail deer, 475, 478, 490
Blacktailed jackrabbit,
  383-386, 390, 393
Blacktailed prairie dog,
  305-313
Bobcat, 201-212
Bovey, Martin, 571
Bovidae, *see* Cattle; Mountain
  goat; Musk-ox; Sheep
Bridger, Jim, 68
Brown, Tolla, 97-98
Brown rat, 327-335
Brush rabbit, 346
Buffalo, 541-554
Burris, Doug, 490
Burroughs, John, 194-195

Cahalane, Victor H., 58
Canadian moose, 507, 508
Canidae, *see* Foxes; Wolves
Canis latrans, 151-160
Canis lupus, 101-112
Canis niger, 101-112
Caribou, 509-526
Carnivora, *see* Carnivores;
  Pinnipedia
Carnivores, 17-212
  bears, *see* Bears

cats, *see* Cats
coyote, 151-160
foxes, *see* Foxes
raccoons, 82-98
wolves, 101-112
See also Seals; Walrus
Carson, Kit, 68
Cartier, Jacques, 78
Catamount, *see* Mountain lion
Cats, 161-212
bobcat, 201-212
jaguar, 163-171
lynx, 188-199
mountain lion, 172-187
Cattle, *see* Bison; Musk-ox
Cervidae, *see* Deer
Cervus elaphus, 426-443
Cervus elaphus manitobensis,
431
Cervus elaphus merriami, 431
Cervus elaphus nannodes, 431
Cervus elaphus nelsoni, 430,
431
Cervus elaphus roosevelti,
430-431
Chadwick, L. S., 572-573, 583
Collared peccary, 403-412
Corbin, Austin, 415
Cottontail rabbit, 341-360
Cougar, *see* Mountain lion
Coyote, 151-160
Craighead, Frank, 60
Craighead, John, 60
Crokyndall, Herman, 37
Cynomys gunnisoni, 306, 309
Cynomys leucurus, 306
Cynomys ludovicianus,
305-313
Cynomys parvidens, 306

Dall's sheep, 572-583
Daniels, Merrill, 36

De Jong, Jim, 179-180
Decker, Robert, 608
Deer, 423-526
blacktail, 475, 478, 490
caribou, 509-526
elk, 426-443
moose, 493-508
mule, 475-491
whitetail, 444-473
Desert bighorn sheep, 555, 564,
571
Desert cottontail, 345
Desmarest, 599
Dicotyles tajacu, 405-412
Didelphiidae, 3-16
Didelphis virginiana, 5-16

Eastern cottontail, 344
Eastern fox squirrel, 283-295
Eastern gray squirrel, 267-282
Edman, Doug, 69
El tigre, *see* Jaguar
Elbow, Zack, 525
Elk, 426-443
Erethezontidae, 314-326
Erethizon dorsatum, 315-326
Esplin, Homer, 179
European rabbit, 394-400
European wild hog, 413-422

Fannin sheep, 572
Felidae, *see* Cats
Felis concolor, 172-187
Felis onca, 163-171
Florida Key deer, 446
Fox squirrel, 283-295
Foxes, 113-149
Arctic, 137-149
gray, 113-122
red, 123-135
Funk, Jack, 171

Garretson, Martin, 552
George III, King of England, 329
Gibson, Larry, 472
Glass, Hugh, 68
Goat, mountain, 585-598
Goodnight, Charles, 552
Gray fox, 113-122
Gray squirrel, 267-282
Gray wolf, 101-112
Green, Dwight, 472
Griffith, Clark, 490
Grizzly bear, 55-69
Ground squirrels, 297-303
Groundhog, *see* Woodchuck

Haase, E. C., 598
Hair seal, 215-223
Hamilton, William, 9
Hansen, Erling, 53
Hansen, John, 495
Harbor seal, 215-223
Hardy, Richard, 37
Hares, 361-393
    Arctic, 375-382
    jackrabbit, 383-393
    varying, 361-374
    See also Rabbits
Hartman, Carl, 8-9
Hedbany, Otto, 37
Heller, Walter, 187
Hicks, Homer, 198
Hoary marmot, 259-265
Hogs, 413-422
Hollister, N., 180
Hoofed animals, 401-609
    bison, 541-554
    deer, *see* Deer
    hogs, 413-422
    mountain goat, 585-598
    musk-ox, 599-609
    peccaries, 403-412

pronghorn, 527-539
    sheep, *see* Sheep
Hornaday, William, 552
Horschwael, *see* Walrus
Hrossvalr, *see* Walrus
Hunter, J. S., 491
Hvalross, *see* Walrus

Israel, Samuel, 553

Jackrabbit, 383-393
Jackson, W. H., 598
Jaguar, 163-171
Jarvis, John, 335
Javelina, *see* Peccaries
Jonas Bros., 232
Jones, C. J., 552
Jordan, James, 472

Kelsey, Henry, 67-68
King, Dennis, 491
King, Glen, 97-98

Lagomorpha, *see* Hares;
    Rabbits
Larson, Albert, 97
Lawrence, W. C., 490
Leporidae, *see* Hares; Rabbits
Lepus, 383-393
Lepus americanus, 361-374
Lepus arcticus, 375-382
Lepus californicus, 385
Lepus othus, 375, 376
        See also Lepus arcticus
Lepus townsendii, 386
Lindsley, Roy, 53
Linnaeus, Carolus, 11, 101, 217, 283
Lives of Game Animals (Seton), 139
Lobo wolf, 101-112
Loesche, Ray, 525

Longoria, Shelly, 81
L'original, see Moose
Louis XV, King of France, 111
Loup cervier, *see* Lynx
Lund, Alma, 36
Lynx, 188-199
Lynx lynx, 188-199
Lynx rufus, 201-212
Lynx subsolanus, 191

McElroy, C. J., 171
Madson, John, 272, 435
Manitoba elk, 431
Marmota broweri, 261
Marmota caligata, 259-265
Marmota flaviventris, 251-257
Marmota monax, 237-250
Marmots, 237-265
 hoary, 259-265
 woodchuck, 237-250
 yellow-bellied, 251-257
Marsh rabbit, 346
Marsupialia, 1-16
Mech, David, 104, 504-505
Meek, Joe, 68
Merriam's elk, 431, 442
Moore, George, 415
Moose, 493-508
Mountain caribou, 525
Mountain cottontail, 344
Mountain goat, 585-598
Mountain lion, 172-187
Mule deer, 475-491
Muridae, 327-335
Murie, Adolph, 302
Murie, Olaus, 142
Musgrave, E., 178
Musgrave, M. E., 179-181
Musk-ox, 599-609
Mussato, Louis, 81

Nemeth, Ken, 249-250
New England cottontail, 342, 345

New World opossums, 3-16
Norwegian rat, 329-335

Oakley, John, 508
Odobenidae, 224-232
Odobenus rosmarus, 225-232
Odocoileus columbianus, 478
Odocoileus hemionus, 475-491
Odocoileus virginianus, 444-473
Opossum, 3-16
Ord, 55
Oreamnos americanus, 585-598
Oryctolagus cuniculus, 394-400
Osgood, N. H., 307
Ott, Fred, 171
Oves, C. M., 374
Ovibos moschatus, 599-609
Ovis canadensis, 555-571
Ovis dalli dalli, 572-583
Ovis dalli stonei, 572-583

Pablo, Michel, 552
Painter, *see* Mountain lion
Panther, *see* Mountain lion
Peccaries, 403-412
Peterson, Rex, 37
Phoca vitulina, 217-232
Phocidae, 215-223
Pigmy rabbit, 345
Pinnipedia, *see* Seals; Walrus
Plute, John, 443
Polar bear, 71-81
Porcupine, 314-326
Pouched mammals, 1-16
Prairie dog, 305-313
Procyon lotor, 84-98
Procyonidae, 82-98
Pronghorn, 527-539
Pruitt, William, 517
Puma, *see* Mountain lion

Rabbits:
  cottontail, 341-360
  European, 394-400
  See also Hares
Raccoons, 82-98
Rafinesque, C. S., 201, 444
Rangifer tarandus, 509-526
Rangifer tarandus caribou, 512
Rangifer tarandus granti, 512
*Rangifer tarandus groenlandi-
    cus*, 512
Rats, 327-335
Rats, Lice and History (Zins-
    ser), 335
Rattus norvegicus, 329-335
Red fox, 123-135
Red wolf, 101-112
Reindeer, *see* Caribou
Roberts, Garth, 187
Rockchuck, *see* Yellow-bellied
    marmot
Rocky Mountain bighorn
    sheep, 555
Rodents, 233-335
  marmots, *see* Marmots
  porcupine, 314-326
  prairie dog, 305-313
  rat, 327-335
  squirrels, *see* Squirrels
Roosevelt, Theodore, 488
Roosevelt elk, 430

Samson fox, 125
San Juan rabbit, *see* European
    rabbit
Sciuridae, *see* Marmots; Prai-
    rie dog; Squirrels
Sciurus apache, 285
Sciurus arizonensis, 271
Sciurus carolinensis, 267-282
Sciurus griseus, 271
Sciurus niger, 283-295
Seals, 215-223

Seton, Ernest Thompson, 139,
    270, 366-367, 545
Sheep, 555-583
  bighorn, 555-571
  Dall's, 572-583
  Stone's, 572-583
Shelton, James, 69
Siblette, Milton, 68
Siemel, Sasha, 170, 171
Siffleur, le, see Hoary marmot
Snowshoe rabbit, *see* Varying
    hare
Spermophilus undulatus,
    297-303
Squirrels, 267-303
  Arctic ground, 297-303
  fox, 283-295
  gray, 267-282
Stone's sheep, 572-583
Suidae, 413-422
Sus scrofa, 415-422
Swamp rabbit, 346
Swank, Harry L., Jr., 583
Sylvilagus, 341-360
Sylvilagus aquaticus, 346
Sylvilagus auduboni, 345
Sylvilagus bachmani, 346
Sylvilagus floridanus, 344
Sylvilagus idahoensis, 345
Sylvilagus nuttalli, 344
Sylvilagus palustris, 346
Sylvilagus transitionalis, 345

Tayassuidae, 403-412
Teal, John, 600
Timber wolf, 101-112
Tree squirrels, 267-295
  fox, 283-295
  gray, 267-282
Tule elk, 431

Urocyon cinereoargenteus,
    113-122
Urocyon littoralis, 115

Ursidae, *see* Bears
Ursus americanus, 21-37
Ursus arctos horribilis, 55-69
Ursus arctos middendorffi,
    39-53
*Ursus horribilis, see Ursus
    arctos horribilis*
Ursus maritimus, 71-81

Vail, Roy, 232
Valley, Oliver J., 98
Varying hare, 361-374
Vulpes vulpes, 123-135

Wade, Jack, 250
Walrus, 224-232
Wapiti, *see* Elk
Webb, Frank, 211-212
Weiller, Fred, 571
Western gray squirrel, 271
Wetzler, Edwin, 539
Whistle pig, *see* Woodchuck
Whitetail deer, 444-473

Whitetailed jackrabbit, 383,
    385-386, 390, 393
Whitetailed prairie dog, 306,
    309
Whitney, Leon F., 84
Wilcox, Sidney, 489
Wild hog, European, 413-422
Wildcat, *see* Bobcat
Witherbee, Silas, 508
Wolves, 101-112
Wombath, I. S., 609
Woodchuck, 237-250
Woodland caribou, 509, 512,
    518, 523, 525
Woodring, S., 553
Wulff, Lee, 495
Wyoming moose, 507, 508

Yellow-bellied marmot,
    251-257
Young, Stanley P., 212

Zimmerman, 599
Zinsser, Hans, 335